SINCLAIR COMMUNITY COLLEGE
444 WEST THIRD STREET
DAYTON, OHIO 45402

THE PHILOSOPHY
OF HEGEL

A SYSTEMATIC EXPOSITION

BY

W. T. STACE, B.A.

DOVER PUBLICATIONS, INC.

Published in Canada by General Publishing Company, Ltd.,
30 Lesmill Road, Don Mills, Toronto, Ontario.

Published in the United Kingdom by Constable and Company, Ltd.,
10 Orange Street, London WC 2.

This Dover edition, first published in 1955, is an unabridged and unaltered republication of the work originally published in 1924 by Macmillan & Co., Inc. This edition is published by special arrangement with the author.

Standard Book Number: 486-20254-2

Library of Congress Catalog Card Number: 55-13745

Manufactured in the United States of America

DOVER PUBLICATIONS, INC.
180 Varick Street
New York, N. Y. 10014

PREFACE

THE primary object of this book is to place in the hands of the philosophical student a complete exposition of the system of Hegel in a single volume. No book with a similar purpose, so far as I know, exists in our language. There are several books which expound, in more or less detail, the *Logic*. There are several books dealing with special aspects of Hegel, his ethics, his aesthetics, and so on. There are a number of books which set forth the general principles of his philosophy without entering upon the detailed deductions. And there are many books of criticism. The English reader, even by studying all these expository or critical books, cannot get a complete and connected view of the system. And if, eschewing expositors and commentators, he turns to the writings of Hegel himself, he is faced with the task of mastering at least ten or twelve appallingly difficult volumes before he can gain any adequate idea of the whole doctrine. (And even then, of course, he has read nothing like the whole of Hegel's works.) The present volume contains, in Part I., an explanation of general principles, and in the subsequent parts it sets forth the detailed deductions of the entire system with the exception of the philosophy of nature, of which only a short general account is given. This exception is justified by special reasons which are stated in their appropriate place.[1] What they amount to is that no ordinary student requires a knowledge of the details of the philosophy of nature, which are out of date and valueless.

The position of Hegelian studies at our universities seems to me very unsatisfactory. The student who has taken an

[1] § 435.

honours degree in philosophy usually has a very considerable knowledge of Kant based upon actual study of Kant's writings. But he has little knowledge of Hegel beyond general ideas picked up in lectures. This is not to be wondered at. For the undergraduate's time is insufficient to carry him through any considerable portion of Hegel's works. And there exists no book giving a satisfactory exposition of the whole system in a reasonable compass. If the present book can remedy this state of affairs, its existence will at least have been justified.

The book is, therefore, primarily an exposition. But it is also critical. Exposition involves interpretation, and interpretation merges into criticism. In addition to this, I have included in many places criticisms upon the details of Hegel's deductions. I have not carried out such criticism systematically, as has been done, for example (for the Logic only), in Dr. McTaggart's *Commentary on Hegel's Logic*. Such a procedure would make a book which has to take in the *whole* system far too long, and would also entirely alter its general character. My guiding principle has been to include only such criticisms as seemed necessary to give the student an *intelligent* understanding of Hegel. Consequently, where I have merely stated Hegel's argument and left it without comment, it does not follow that I regard the argument as above criticism. Part III., which deals with the philosophy of nature, is no doubt more critical and less expository than the other parts. This was unavoidable. The character of Hegel's passage from Logic to nature has always been profoundly obscure, and is the point against which the most determined attacks upon Hegel have been directed. I could not rest satisfied with the views expressed by a host of critics from Schelling to Professor Pringle-Pattison, which have now become common. And I had, therefore, to work out my own solution.

The difficulty of Hegel's writings is notorious. And, therefore, I have aimed especially at lucidity. The student who cannot read Hegel's own works will find here, I hope, all Hegel's essential thoughts stated as easily and simply as is possible. And if the student who is prepared to labour at the actual text of Hegel will read this book side by side with

PREFACE

Hegel's own deductions, he will, I trust, find that many of his difficulties are cleared up. But there are two ways in which the simplification of difficult thought may be attempted. The first is to think it out clearly and to the bottom, and then set it down in lucid language. The second is to avoid and leave out difficult conceptions, or to slur them over, or to rob them of their profundity, making them shallow on the pretext of making them easy. I have set before me as my ideal the former of these two methods, and have eschewed the latter. Whether I have succeeded in this or not is, of course, not for me to judge.

Modern writers have dwelt more especially upon the epistemological aspect of the Logic, and have tended to relegate its ontological aspect to the background. If, in the present book, I have re-emphasised the ontology of the Logic, it is for two reasons. Firstly, it seems to me that the ontological side was very prominent in Hegel's own mind, and I have conceived it to be my duty to try and present his philosophy as he himself thought it. This is mere historical truthfulness. Secondly, even if ontological enquiries are somewhat at a discount in the general esteem at the moment, yet this cannot remain so for long. The desire to penetrate beyond appearance to the inner reality of things is a permanent trait and an ineradicable demand of the human spirit.

My treatment of pre-Hegelian philosophers, especially the Greeks, demands a word of explanation. I have everywhere been intent, not on these earlier philosophers themselves, but on the way in which they affected Hegel, and on what Hegel found in them as material for his own system. Consequently, it is the Hegelian view of them which has necessarily been presented. Whether this view is always historically correct is another question. Modern Greek scholarship has made some inroads upon the older views. And even as regards Kant and the famous thing-in-itself, it may be that other interpretations and estimates, with which I am not here concerned, are possible.

The compression of a great teacher's thought into a small compass necessarily involves some measure of injustice to him.

I am especially conscious of this, in the present case, in the spheres of the philosophy of art and the philosophy of religion. Here Hegel has left behind him such an immense body of matter that the brief chapters in which I have had perforce to summarise it, while they do, I think, embody all the essential principles, can give little idea of the vast fields which Hegel covered, the profuse wealth of his concrete illustrations, the enormous learning which he brought to bear upon these studies, the profundity and breadth of his vision.

The arrangement of the categories in the larger *Science of Logic* differs very considerably from that given in the first part of the *Encyclopaedia of the Philosophical Sciences*. I have followed the *Encyclopaedia*.

Numbers in brackets appearing in the text thus (247), refer the reader to the numbered paragraphs of the book.

Thick black type has been used for the names of categories in the Logic and for the names of 'notions' in the philosophy of spirit at that point where they first definitely emerge in the course of the logical deduction as fully completed categories or notions—that is to say, at the point where the *deduction* of them is finished. Elsewhere the names appear in ordinary print. This should assist the reader to distinguish clearly between the actual deduction and such further explanations, subsidiary remarks, comments, etc., as it has been found desirable to make.

I am indebted, directly or indirectly, to the majority of commentators on Hegel. But in especial am I indebted to my own teacher, Professor H. S. Macran of Trinity College, Dublin, whose lectures were to me, in my student days, nothing less than an inspiration.

W. T. S.

LONDON,
19th September, 1923.

CONTENTS

	PAGE
PREFACE	v
LIST OF ABBREVIATIONS	xi

PART I

FUNDAMENTAL PRINCIPLES

CHAPTER

I. GREEK IDEALISM AND HEGEL — 3-31
   A. Eleaticism and Hegel — 4
   B. Plato and Hegel — 7
   C. Aristotle and Hegel — 18
   D. Results — 30

II. MODERN PHILOSOPHY AND HEGEL — 32-49
   A. Spinoza and Hegel — 32
   B. Hume and Kant — 34
   C. The Onward March from Kant — 43
   D. Criticism of the Conception of the Unknowable — 45

III. HEGEL — 50-119
   A. Explanation: Cause: Reason — 50
   B. Reason as the Universal — 55
   C. Reason as self-determined — 57
   D. Pure Thought — 60
   E. Being and Knowing — 69
   F. Monism and the Deduction of the Categories — 78
   G. Which is the First Category? — 84
   H. The Dialectic Method — 88
   I. The Dialectic Method (*continued*) — 98
   J. Divisions of the System — 115

PART II

THE LOGIC

Introduction — 123

FIRST DIVISION. THE DOCTRINE OF BEING — 134-174
   Introduction — 134
   Chapter I. Quality — 135
   Chapter II. Quantity — 154
   Chapter III. Measure — 167

CONTENTS

	PAGE
SECOND DIVISION. THE DOCTRINE OF ESSENCE	175-220
Introduction	175
Chapter I. Essence as Ground of Existence	182
Chapter II. Appearance	198
Chapter III. Actuality	211
THIRD DIVISION. THE DOCTRINE OF THE NOTION	221-294
Introduction	221
Chapter I. The Subjective Notion	226
Chapter II. The Object, or the Objective Notion	262
☆ — Chapter III. The Idea	277

PART III

THE PHILOSOPHY OF NATURE

THE PHILOSOPHY OF NATURE	297-317

PART IV

THE PHILOSOPHY OF SPIRIT

INTRODUCTION	321
FIRST DIVISION. SUBJECTIVE SPIRIT	325-373
Introduction	325
Chapter I. Anthropology. The Soul	328
Chapter II. Phenomenology. Consciousness	339
Chapter III. Psychology. Mind	361
SECOND DIVISION. OBJECTIVE SPIRIT	374-438
Introduction	374
Chapter I. Abstract Right	381
Chapter II. Morality	393
Chapter III. Social Ethics	404
THIRD DIVISION. ABSOLUTE SPIRIT	439-518
Introduction	439
Chapter I. Art	443
Chapter II. Religion	484
Chapter III. Philosophy	515
INDEX	519
DIAGRAM OF THE HEGELIAN SYSTEM	

☆ See p. 288 – 296

LIST OF ABBREVIATIONS

Phil. of Mind = Hegel's *Philosophy of Mind*, tr. William Wallace, Clarendon Press, Oxford, 1894.
Phil. of Right = Hegel's *Philosophy of Right*, tr. Dyde, London, 1896.
Encyclopaedia = *The Encyclopaedia of the Philosophical Sciences*.
Wal., *Log.* = *The Logic of Hegel*, tr. William Wallace, Clarendon Press, Oxford, 1892.
Phen. = Hegel's *Phenomenology of Mind*, tr. Baillie, London, 1910.
Osm. = *The Philosophy of Fine Art*, by Hegel, tr. Osmaston, London, 1920.
Macran = Hegel's *Doctrine of Formal Logic*, by H. S. Macran, Clarendon Press, Oxford, 1912.
Croce = *What is Living and What is Dead of the Philosophy of Hegel*, by Benedetto Croce, tr. Ainslie, London, 1915.
Dial. = *Studies in Hegelian Dialectic*, McTaggart, Cambridge, 1896.
Com. = *A Commentary on Hegel's Logic*, McTaggart, Cambridge, 1910.
Secret = *The Secret of Hegel*, Stirling, London, 1865.
Schw. *Handbook of the H. of Ph.* = Schwegler's *Handbook of the History of Philosophy*.
Z. = Zusätze, *i.e.* Hegel's lecture notes and addenda annexed to Hegel's text by his editors. In Wal., *Log.*, those are given in smaller print, and the references in the present book should be read thus: Wal., *Log.* § 163, Z. = the smaller print at end of § 163.

The names of books, other than the above, given in the text or references, appear in full unabbreviated.

PART I

FUNDAMENTAL PRINCIPLES

CHAPTER I

GREEK IDEALISM AND HEGEL

1. Hegel claims that the substance of all previous philosophies is contained, preserved, and absorbed, in his own system. But there are two influences upon him which far outweigh in importance all the others. These are the idealism of the Greeks and the critical philosophy of Kant. The fundamental principles of Hegel are the fundamental principles of the Greeks and of Kant. And our object in this and the next chapter will be to extricate these principles from the earlier thinkers. It is not our intention to expound Plato, Aristotle, or Kant. We assume that the main outlines of their teachings are already known. Not what is stated by them expressly, but what is implicit in them, what Hegel discovered as the underlying substratum of them beneath the surface,—this it is our aim to set forth. We do not wish—so far as it can be avoided—to state over again what can be found in any competent history of philosophy. We have no academic penchant for treating things historically. But it will be found that the fundamental philosophical basis of Hegel is the same as the historical basis. We shall try to inflict upon the reader as little as possible of the lumber of historical learning or the familiar gossip of the professorial class-room.

"What Hegel proposes to give," says Wallace," is no novel or special doctrine, but the universal philosophy which has passed on from age to age, here narrowed and there widened, but still essentially the same. It is conscious of its continuity and proud of its identity with the teachings of Plato and

Aristotle."[1] What, then, is this one universal philosophy? Evidently it is not simply the philosophy of Plato, nor yet simply the philosophy of Aristotle. The systems of these men are but special presentations of the one universal philosophy, special forms which it assumed in their hands, in the particular age and circumstances in which they lived. It is to be found in them as the inner essence of their thought. It is what they held in common, to which each added special points of view of his own. This underlying substance will be the substance of Hegel also.

2. We shall begin, however, not with Plato and Aristotle, but with the Eleatics. For even here, important determinations of the one universal philosophy are to be found,—embedded beneath the dim gropings of Parmenides and Zeno.

A. *Eleaticism and Hegel.*

As everyone knows, the Eleatics denied the reality of becoming, or change, and of multiplicity. The sole reality, they said, is Being. Being alone veritably *is*. Becoming is not at all. It is illusion. And Being is One. Only the One is. The many is not. It also is illusion. The illusory world of becoming and multiplicity is the world of sense. It is this ordinary world that is known to us through our eyes and ears and hands,—through sensation generally. True Being is apprehended only by the eye of reason. It is not known to the senses. It cannot be seen, touched, felt. It is neither here nor there, neither then nor now. Only by thought, reason, can we reach it. It is true that Parmenides incongruously said that Being is globe-shaped and occupies space. And this implies that it is material and so ought to be perceptible by the senses. But this is merely one of the crudities natural to primitive thinking. Parmenides could not help trying to frame a pictorial *image* of Being, and all such images must necessarily be thought of as having some shape. And so Parmenides fell into this inconsistency. But the opposite thought, that Being is

[1] *Phil. of Mind*, p. 9.

nowhere and nowhen, that it is not an object of sense, is the real inner teaching of the Eleatics.[1]

Now this clearly marked distinction between sensation and reason, and this assertion that reality is apprehended by the latter and not by the former, is a characteristic of all idealism of the Greek type. It is part of the one universal philosophy. It is just as much Hegelian as Eleatic. It is true that this *absolute* separation between the true and the false, between reason and sense, would be repudiated by Hegel. For him even the sense-world has a truth of its own. But this is an Hegelian modification of the one universal philosophy with which we are not yet ready to deal.

3. What meaning are we to attribute to the Eleatic assertion that the world of sensuous objects is unreal? Our question is not what meaning the Eleatics themselves understood it to have, but what meaning *we* can attribute to it. It may well be that the Eleatics themselves, in these their primitive gropings, understood very little of what was implied in their own dim ideas. But the implications, the thoughts which lay wrapped up, implicit, hidden away,—unseen perhaps by the Eleatics themselves,—these are what are valuable to us.

Multiplicity and motion, then, and the sense-world of which they are the main characteristics, are unreal. What does this mean? Does it mean that the sense-world, multiplicity and motion, are not *there*, do not exist? If motion is illusory, does this mean that an express train from London to Bristol does not move, that at the end of its journey it is still in London? If multiplicity is unreal, if Being is an absolute unity, does this mean that, when we suppose ourselves to have twenty sovereigns, the truth is that we have only one? Manifestly this is nonsense. To say, in this sense, that the world of sense does not exist, has no meaning. No sane person ever denied that things, this table, that hat, exist. Berkeley is popularly supposed to have propounded the

---

[1] In my *Critical History of Greek Philosophy*, pp. 46-52, I have given in full my reasons for disagreeing with the opinion of Professor Burnet that Parmenides was essentially a materialist. I need not repeat them here.

absurd opinion that matter does not exist. Doctor Johnson, hearing this, proceeded to refute it by kicking a stone with his foot. Doctor Johnson generally gets the credit of being a stupid Philistine who did not understand philosophy. But the fact is that, if Berkeley had really propounded the insane opinion attributed to him, Doctor Johnson's refutation would have been conclusive and final. The views which Berkeley actually did express—and which no amount of mere kicking can refute—were these, that matter exists only in and for our minds and the mind of God, that its essence consists in its being perceived, and that there is beneath its visible and tangible appearance no unknown and unknowable substratum. That the material world does not exist at all, that is to say, is not there, no sane human being has ever, so far as I know, had the hardihood to affirm.[1] Obviously, the material world is there,—as Doctor Johnson proved. You may, if you like, call it a dream, or an illusion, or an appearance. But still the dream, the illusion, the appearance, is there. It quite certainly exists.

But if the Eleatic philosophy does not mean that the external world does not exist, it does mean that the external world is not the true being, is not *real*. Clearly, therefore, there is implied in this philosophy a distinction between reality and existence. Whatever exists, elephants, comets, multiplicity, motion, is mere appearance. Only Being is real. But Being does not exist. For it is nowhere and nowhen. And whatever exists must at least exist at some time, if not at some place. And we may sum up these results in two propositions. *Firstly, existence is not real. Secondly, what is real does not exist.* These propositions, we say, are implied in Eleaticism. It is not, of course, to be supposed that the Eleatics themselves would or could have used such language.

This result sounds paradoxical. That existence is not real,—this is just supportable. Anyone who knows that, according to the Hindus, the existing world is Maya, illusion, is familiar with this thought. But that what is real does not exist,—that seems intolerable. We suspect that we are being

---

[1] Unless it were Gorgias! And Gorgias was perhaps partly a jester.

made the dupes of words, that this is one of those everlasting quibbles which metaphysicians—etc. Yet we must leave the matter here for the moment. These difficulties will be cleared up shortly. What we have now to note is that the result we have reached, however it is to be explained, is of vital moment for the understanding of Plato, Aristotle, and Hegel.[1] It is part of the one universal philosophy. Three-quarters of the failures to understand Hegel are due to the fact that this is not understood.

B. *Plato and Hegel.*

4. There is much dispute nowadays as to what is the true interpretation of Plato's philosophy, and even as to whether what has always been known as Plato's philosophy was not really the work of Socrates. With none of these disputes are we in any wise concerned. The view of Plato which we shall take as the basis of our discussion is the traditional view. It may or may not be historically correct. That question does not concern us because we are attempting to understand, not Plato, but Hegel. And it was this traditional interpretation of Plato which influenced Hegel. Even if what we shall here put forward as the philosophy of Plato were to be regarded as a wholly imaginary philosophy, it would still be, just the same, one of the foundation stones of Hegelian thought.

5. The Eleatics had distinguished between appearance and reality, between sense and reason. These distinctions held their ground till the time of Protagoras, whose teaching amounted to a denial of them. Protagoras said that whatever seems to me true is true for me, and whatever seems to you true is true for you. This implies that whatever seems or appears, is the reality, or at least that there is no other reality than this seeming or appearance. Thus reality and appearance are the same thing. Moreover, what the senses present to us is what appears. What the senses give us is, therefore,

---

[1] But in Hegel it undergoes modification. The *actual*, for Hegel, is the synthesis of what we have here called the *real* and the *existent*. This will be explained in its due place.

the truth, the reality. Since whatever seems is true, one seeming is as good as another. What seems to my senses to be true is quite as much the truth as what may seem to me true after I have applied my reason to these sense-data. Hence reason adds nothing to our knowledge of reality. Reality is given through sensation. Knowledge is sense-perception. The distinction between sense and reason, or at any rate the value of the distinction, disappears with the disappearance of the distinction between appearance and reality.

6. In order to refute this doctrine, which practically involves the denial of all values, Plato undertook the analysis of sensation. He showed that mere sensation is so far from giving us knowledge that it can barely give us consciousness of any sort, that even the knowledge of my own sensations, as when I say " I am warm," implies organs of knowledge which have nothing in common with the physical senses.

Suppose I know that my body feels warm. I can only express this in the form " my body is warm," *i.e.*, in the form of a proposition. Even if I do not *say* it, but only *think* it, it must still take that form. But how do I know that what feels warm is a body? And how do I know that what it feels is warmth? I can only know that my body is a body because I have seen other bodies before, and can compare it with them, and find it is like them; and because I see that it is unlike other objects, such as houses, trees, or triangles. And I only know that what I feel is warmth because I compare it with previous similar sensations, and contrast it with other sensations such as those of redness, hardness, sweetness, or coldness.

Now this implies classification. The word " body " stands for a class of objects, and the word " warmth " stands for a class of sensations. Thus ideas of classes, that is to say, concepts, are involved even in the most sensuous knowledge. Every word in every language,—except perhaps proper names, which are said to have no connotation,—connotes a concept. For there are not only concepts of substantive things, but also concepts of qualities, actions, relations. " To give " is a concept, for it describes a whole class of actions. " This " is a concept, since it applies, not only to one individual thing, but to all things. Everything is a " this." " Is " is a concept, since all things " are." " In " is a concept, for it expresses an entire class of relations. There are no words in any language which do not stand for concepts. Thus not merely some knowledge, but all knowledge, is conceptual. Hence from bare sensation, as such, no knowledge can arise. Concepts are not perceived by the senses, but are the work of the mind which compares, contrasts, and classifies what the senses give it.

We can know nothing whatever of any object except the concepts which apply to it. No matter what we say of an object, what we say consists in asserting that such and such a concept applies to it. For whatever we say is a word, and every word stands for a concept. I say that this object before me is a white, oblong, soft, material, solid, useful thing called paper. All these predicates are concepts. But if such is the nature of my knowledge of the paper, what is the paper itself? A concept is not a particular thing; it is a general class; it is a " universal." All I can know of the paper is that such and such universals, or concepts, apply to it, or, in other words, that it belongs to such and such general classes. It is oblong, soft, white, *i.e.* it belongs to those classes. Then what is " it " ? It belongs to various classes, but there must, one would think, be a " something " which belongs to these classes, just as, in order to have motion, one supposes there must be something to move. What is this " it," *apart from* the classes to which it belongs? Obviously, if there is any " it," we cannot know it. It must remain for ever unknowable to us. For all our knowledge is conceptual, *i.e.* is a knowledge of classes. Therefore anything apart from classes, such as this " it," cannot be known. But it is perfectly gratuitous to assume the existence of that of which we have, and can have, no knowledge. For if it did exist we could not know it. And therefore to affirm its existence is to affirm something of which we have no knowledge, something which, accordingly, we can have no possible grounds for affirming.

It would seem, therefore, that there is no " it," even that such an " it " is an inconceivable and self-contradictory thought; for every thought is conceptual, is the thought of a class, and the " it " in itself *cannot* be thought, and is therefore strictly *unthinkable*. There is no " it." The entire nature of this piece of paper lies in the fact that it belongs to various classes. The classes alone are real. The paper is simply a congeries of concepts or universals. There is nothing else in it. Hence if we admit that the paper is not a mere figment of my imagination, that it exists outside my mind, it will follow that concepts or universals likewise exist on their own account, objectively, independent of my, or any other, mind. These objective universals are called by Plato Ideas.

It would seem that nothing is real except universals. It is true that Plato spoilt the consistency of this theory by admitting the existence of what he called " matter," a formless, indefinite, substrate of things. This matter is simply the unknowable " it." He failed to see that " matter " is itself a universal. He admitted the existence of the " it." But with this side of his theory we are not here concerned.

7. At the present time there is a school of philosophers, the New Realists, who admit the reality, or the " subsistence," of universals, but insist that they are not " mental." According to this view it would be wrong to speak of them as objective *concepts*. And even the traditional Platonic " Ideas " are now, by these philosophers, designated " forms." It is doubtful whether there is anything here but a dispute about terminology. By saying that universals are not " mental " they appear to mean that they are not the thoughts of any individual mind, mine or yours or God's, but that they " subsist " independently of minds. This is, of course, just what Plato, Aristotle, Hegel, and all idealists, mean. Whether we say, in the language of idealism, that universals are objective, not subjective, thoughts, or in the phraseology of new realism, that they are not " mental," *i.e.* not subjective, does not seem to matter.[1]

8. According to Plato, at any rate, universals are real, are

[1] But on this question see also §§ 33, 34 below.

objective. It is not merely *I* who classify objects. The classes themselves have a being independent of my mind. What is real in the sense-object is the universals. But the source through which we receive knowledge of universals is not sensation, but reason. For sensation cannot give us concepts. Concepts are formed by abstracting, by reasoning. Therefore reason is the source of truth, sensation the source of error. Sensation gives us the world of sense, the world of particular objects, and this is the false world. What is alone genuinely real is universals, and we know of these through reason. Sensation gives us appearance; reason gives us reality.

9. Thus not only are the distinctions between sense and reason, appearance and reality,—which are part of the one universal philosophy—reasserted. But we have now arrived at a further point. And this is *the* essential determination of the universal philosophy, namely, that *the real is the universal*. This is the central and distinctive doctrine of all idealism,[1] whether it be that of Plato, of Aristotle, or of Hegel.

10. This conclusion throws a great deal of light upon the seeming paradox to which Eleaticism led us,—that the real does not exist. For the real is now the universal. And the universal cannot be said to exist. White things exist, but not " whiteness " itself. There are in existence chestnut horses, white horses, black horses, race horses, cart horses. But where is the universal " horse," the horse in general? To exist means to exist at some specific space or time. But not by searching all space shall we find " whiteness " quartered in any part of it. And not by ransacking all time shall we find the universal horse that is neither chesnut nor white nor black, neither a racehorse nor a cart horse, but simply " horse." The universal, then, is neither in place nor in time. It is nowhere and nowhen. And to say that something is nowhere and nowhen is the same as saying that it does not exist. We may put the same thing in another form by saying that to exist means to be an *individual* existence. Whatever exists is an

---

[1] Of course, I do not include here the subjective idealism of Berkeley. The sense of the word idealism is there quite different.

individual. But the universal is just that which is *not* individual. The universal, therefore, does not exist. It is, of course, no answer to say that the universal exists in time in the form of a concept in the stream of human consciousness. We are not speaking of concepts, subjective universals, but of objective universals which we have found to be the essence of reality and to have a being independent of minds.

11. We can now see a little deeper into the Eleatic position. Being is real, but it is nowhere and nowhen. It does not exist. This is possible because Being is a universal. It is what all things have in common. For all things "are." Being is the "isness" which is common to all things. "Whiteness" is not here or there, then or now, is not anything individual, and so does not exist. The same is true of Being. It is not any *particular* being, such as this horse or that tree. It is Being in general,—a universal. It is not to be supposed that the Eleatics themselves understood this. Yet they were groping for it. Even Plato himself did not get so far as definitely saying that universals, the Ideas, do not exist. But he said that the Ideas are not in space or time. And that amounts to the same thing.

12. The one universal philosophy holds then that the universal is the real, and that the real does not exist. This is now, to some extent, intelligible. But not fully so. What is still wanting is that we should have clear definitions of the words reality and existence. We will begin by getting a clear idea of the distinction between reality and appearance. It may occur to someone to say that this distinction is on the face of it an absurd one. For an appearance also is real. Even a dream is real. It exists in the mind just as certainly as elephants exist in the world. It is a real thing. Now this is true. But it will at once be seen, from this very example, that we do, even in common speech,—apart from metaphysics altogether—make a distinction between reality and appearance, and this must surely have some meaning, some foundation. A dream, a delusion, we say, is unreal. Now it is quite easy to see what is meant by this. A real mountain is one which exists independently of us. A dream-mountain

is called unreal because it does not exist independently of the dreamer. It is produced in some way by him, by his brain. And in the same way we say that a shadow is unreal. The shadow really exists. But popular thought conceives that the object which throws the shadow exists on its own account, independently, whereas the existence of the shadow is dependent on the object which throws it. And so we say that the object is real, the shadow unreal.

These popular distinctions are vaguely conceived. But they contain the germ of the philosophic distinction between appearance and reality. The philosophic thought is only the clear and consistent development of the popular thought. Reality, in the philosophic sense, is that which has a wholly independent being, a being of its own, on its own account, which does not owe its being to anything else. Appearance is that which has only a dependent being.[1] Its being flows into it from something else which is itself an independent being, a reality. It will be noticed that we do not speak of dependent and independent *existence* here. We do not use the word existence, but the word *being*. This is merely because we have already assigned another meaning to the word "existence." We have seen that the real has no existence. We cannot therefore define it as that which has independent existence. This raises a fresh problem, namely, the nature of the distinction between "existence" and "being." The question is, what sort of being have universals, if they have not existence? We shall solve this question shortly.

13. Meanwhile we come to another point. Appearance is that which depends on the reality. Its being arises out of, is in some way produced by, the reality. Hence if we say that the universal is the real, and that the world of sense is appearance, it then becomes incumbent upon us to show that the universal produces the world of sense. This is precisely why Plato tried to show that the Ideas are the beings which actually produce the world, that they are the primordial

---

[1] These views are common to most idealistic philosophies. The special Hegelian doctrine of appearance involves these views, but advances beyond them and more completely analyses the notion of appearance. Hegel's definitions will be found in §§ 271 to 273 below.

foundation and cause of all things. The conception of reality necessarily involves this. If something in the universe is real, and all else is appearance, then this means that that reality produces this appearance. For the one universal philosophy the real is the universal. Hence we now get a further determination of the universal philosophy, namely, that *the universal is that absolute and ultimate being which is the foundation of all things, which produces the world out of itself*. For it must be remembered that, according to this philosophy, not only does the real not exist, but, further, what exists is not real. Hence whatever exists, *i.e.* the whole universe, is appearance, and arises out of the universal.

14. We have now got clear conceptions of reality and appearance, and it only remains to gain a similarly clear conception of " existence." Such a conception is implicit in what has already been said. Only that exists which is a particular thing, an individual. " Whiteness " does not exist because it is not an individual object. But my white hat exists because it is an individual object. This also implies that existence appertains solely to time or space or both. For an individual thing must exist at least at some definite time, and if it is a material thing it must also exist at some definite place. Another way of expressing the same thought is to say that only that exists which is, or might be, an *immediate* presentation to consciousness. For what exists at a specific place or time is *there*, is present. These remarks apply, of course, just as much to psychic as to material entities. A dream, a feeling, or a thought, is there. It exists at a definite time in the stream of conscious states. And it is an individual thing. It is *this* particular feeling, *this* thought, *this* dream.

15. According to the universal philosophy all existence is appearance. The definitions, *i.e.* connotations, of the two terms existence and appearance, are different. Appearance is that which has only a dependent being. Existence is that which is individual and not universal, is or may be an immediate presentation to consciousness, and is present at some particular place or time or both. But the denotations of the

two terms are identical. This means that whatever is an immediately present individual is a merely dependent being. And this follows from the position that the sole reality (independent being) is the universal.

16. It is undoubtedly implied in this, not only that material beings are appearances, but also that psychic entities, such as particular thoughts, feelings, volitions, are appearances. For all these are individual existences. This is perhaps not always realised, and whether Plato himself would have admitted it outright may be a matter of doubt. If we are asked whether such entities as the " soul " are denied reality under these determinations we can only reply that, according to most idealists, the soul, as distinguished from its particular states, feelings, ideas, etc., is not an individual thing, but is a universal, and is therefore real. But to discuss the point at this stage would take us beyond the immediate purpose of this chapter.

17. That the entire existent world is appearance may seem at first sight to be a conclusion repugnant to the common sense of humanity. It may be well, therefore, to show here that philosophy is not divorced from the common beliefs of mankind. For this very doctrine makes its appearance popularly in the religious consciousness. From Christianity we understand that God created the world, but that God Himself is uncreated and primordial. This means that God owes His being to nothing other than Himself, and is therefore real, but that the world owes its existence to God, who is the source of its being, and is accordingly an appearance. But popular thought seems generally to be affected by a vague notion that God, having once created the world and flung it spinning into space, left it to assume thereafter a sort of independent existence. It goes on by itself without further support. This is probably contrary to Christian theology, but it seems vaguely to underlie popular consciousness. This would explain the repugnance of common sense to the doctrine that the world is an appearance. As it is thought to possess this kind of half-independent being, it is taken for a reality. But the oriental mind thinks otherwise. The Hindu does not

think that God created the world once and for all, and then left it to itself. For him the world is not the creation, but the *manifestation*, of God. This conveys the idea that the world is, at every moment of its existence, so utterly dependent on God that without Him it would collapse. Consequently, it appears perfectly natural to the Hindu mind to regard the world as appearance, Maya. And lastly, one may reiterate that philosophers do not mean by this doctrine anything so absurd as the teaching commonly credited to them. They do not mean that the world is not *there*; or that it does not exist. That it exists is an immediate indisputable fact which, as we observed before, no sane man could deny. The statement that the world is an appearance means only that its existence is dependent on an ulterior being.

18. Since philosophy recognises that the universal, as the real, is the absolute ground of the world, it thereby imposes upon itself the task of showing how and why the world arises out of this absolute being. Plato clearly recognised this obligation and attempted to discharge it. Here, however, his philosophy tends to become vague and incoherent. He cannot give a rational explanation, and so takes refuge in poetical myths and metaphors. With the details of his attempt to solve the problem we need not concern ourselves, because they are peculiar to himself and form no part of the universal philosophy. But the outlines of it are as follows: Things in the world are "copies" of universals or Ideas. Individual horses are copies of the Idea of the horse. These copies are made by the images of the Ideas being stamped upon matter by God. This matter is not what we understand by the term. It is not iron, hydrogen, brass, etc. Such things have definite form. They are already "things," and as such are fully completed copies of Ideas. Plato's matter is formless, featureless, indeterminate. It is emptiness. It is the formless substrate of things. It is, in fact, the "something," the "it," which belongs to various classes but is not itself any class, and which we saw (6) to be a self-contradictory and unthinkable thought. We saw that an object, such as this paper, is a collection of universals. These

universals are the classes to which it belongs. But when we ask what " it," apart from the universals, is, we find that " it " is nothing. Plato, however, regarded this " it," this substrate of the universals as something really existing, and called it matter. Yet he so far recognises the non-existence of the " it " that he declared that matter is " not-being." This landed him in contradictions. Matter is not-being, nothing. Yet, he thinks, it must have been there from eternity in order to have the images of the Ideas stamped upon it. It is something which has not arisen out of the Ideas, which is equally primordial with them, underived, independent, and, therefore, from this point of view, not an absolute not-being, but rather an absolute being, a reality. For what is independent and is not derived from anything else is a reality. Plato did not recognise this latter point of view. If he had he would have seen how impossible and self-contradictory his conception of matter was.

19. Another point which it is important for us to notice is that Plato apparently believed that the Ideas, the universals, had a separate existence of their own in another world beyond space and time. The souls of the righteous may visit these abodes after death, and actually *see* the Ideas there. Thus the universals of which this paper is composed are not merely *in* the paper, composing it, but exist on their own account outside the paper in a world of their own. It is a very doubtful point how far this is to be taken literally or how far it is mere poetry. But Aristotle, at any rate, thought that Plato meant it literally. And it is important for us to notice that, if it is taken literally, it involves a departure from, even a contradiction of, the universal philosophy. For it implies that the Ideas *exist*; they exist, that is, in a world of their own. But it is essential to the universal philosophy that universals, though they are real, do not *exist*. The universal is that which is not *individual*. But Plato in this part of his philosophy seems to think of the Ideas as individual existences in some extra-spatial world. This, of course, is self-contradictory. And what it shows is that Plato did not keep clearly before him the distinction between reality and

existence. He began by making that distinction clear—though not of course in those words. For he said that the sense-world, *i.e.* existence, is not real; and that what is real is universals which are not in space or time, *i.e.* do not exist. But it seems that he was unable to withstand the inferior thought that what is real must somehow exist, and consequently invented this supramundane world for the Ideas to exist in. Perhaps this latter idea is merely poetical. But if so, it is very misleading.

C. *Aristotle and Hegel.*

20. According to Aristotle, " things " are composed of matter and form. Aristotle's matter is the same as Plato's, the " it," the indefinite substrate of things. His form corresponds to Plato's Idea. It is the universal. But Aristotle denied that forms, Ideas, or universals, have a special existence of their own in a separate world. They only exist—if we are to use the word exist—*in* things. What, asked Aristotle, can be regarded as having separate existence on its own account? Not forms, universals, for these are only predicates. The Idea of man is the same as the predicate " humanness." A universal is simply a predicate which is common to all the members of a class. The universal, " whiteness," is the predicate which is common to all white objects. And predicates have no existence apart from the subjects of which they are predicated. Gold is yellow. But the yellowness does not exist apart from the gold. We say that something is shiny. But we do not conceive that shinyness can exist by itself. There must be a something which is shiny. Universals, therefore, cannot have a separate existence, as Plato thought. But neither does matter exist separately. Gold is yellow, heavy, soft, etc. The yellowness, heaviness, softness do not exist apart from the gold. But neither can the gold exist apart from its qualities. Strip off in thought the yellowness, the softness, and *all* other predicates, and what is left? Nothing at all. The gold, then, apart from its predicates, is nothing, does not exist. The substrate, the

"it," has no being apart from the universals or predicates which apply to it. Thus neither matter nor form has a separate existence. What alone exists is the gold with all its predicates, that is to say, the combination of matter and form, the formed " thing "—this piece of gold, that bed, this tree, that man. Thus Aristotle comes back to the doctrine of the universal philosophy that existence means *individual* existence. The universal is still, for Aristotle just as much as for Plato, the real. But the universal, the real, does not *exist*. Only individual things exist, and these are not universals.

21. Now this doctrine of Aristotle's, that matter and form are inseparable, that neither exists separately from the other, throws light upon a problem which we raised in the section on Plato but were compelled to leave unsolved. If reality is that which has independent " being," but which does not " exist," what do we mean by such " being " ? What sort of being can be attributed to universals if they do not exist ? We cannot completely solve this problem at the present point. But we can partly solve it. What we now see is that universals do not exist but that all existence depends upon them. A " thing " is a combination of matter and form. Without the form, which is the universal, it would be simply matter by itself. But matter by itself is nothing, does not exist. Therefore without the form or universal the thing would not exist. Therefore the existence of the thing depends on the universal. It is true that, according to Aristotle, it also depends on the matter, but that fact does not affect our present argument. The existence of things, then, depends on universals. Without them things would not exist. Now we cannot suppose that universals, on which the very existence of things depends, are nothing, have no being of any sort. We must admit, then, that universals have being. But when we deny their existence we mean that they cannot stand by themselves, that they have no *separate* existence. If we wish to use the word existence of them, we can say, if we like, that they exist *in* things. But they cannot stand alone. This hat exists. It is a complete thing. It has an independent existence of its own. But a universal, *e.g.* the whiteness of the hat, has

no existence independent of the hat. It is only a factor, or element, of the existence of the hat. Considered by itself it is an abstraction. We are justified in saying that the universal *is*, because without it nothing could be. It has being. But it has not existence, because it cannot stand by itself, as a stone, or any other existent thing can.

22. But this seems to involve us in a contradiction. The universal *is*, but it has not an independent being on its own account. The individual " thing," on the other hand, exists, and by existence, it seems, we mean just that independent being which the universal lacks. But we previously came to the conclusion that the universal, because it is real, is precisely that which has independent being; whereas every existence, because it is merely appearance, has only a dependent being. Now we shall find that this contradiction is only apparent. But in order to explain it we must seek help again from Aristotle.

According to Aristotle the form, the universal, of a thing, is also its end or purpose. The final cause (end) is identical with the formal cause (form). The purpose of a thing may be defined as the reason why the thing exists. Thus in saying that the form is the same as the end, Aristotle meant that the universal is the reason of the thing, the reason why it exists. Now the reason of a thing is obviously prior to the thing. The thing only comes into existence because of the reason, and therefore, *after* the reason. Thus the end of the thing is prior to its beginning.

23. Now the universal philosophy holds that all individual existences are dependent beings; that only the universal has independent being; and that individual things owe their existence to the universal, *i.e.* that their being is dependent upon the universal. But we have not yet asked ourselves what *kind* of dependence and independence is here involved. The Aristotelian doctrine just stated gives us the clue to the solution of this question. The end of a thing is prior to its beginning. This seeming paradox is only rendered intelligible in one way. The priority spoken of is not time-priority but logical priority. In time one event happens after another.

That which happens first has time-priority over that which happens second. In logic, the premises come first, the conclusion second. The premises have logical priority over the conclusion. But they have not time-priority. In the relation of reason and consequent, the former is logically first, but no one would contend that the order in which they occur means that the reason is an event which happens in time before the consequent. Just in this way, Aristotle means, the end of a thing is prior to the thing; or in general the end of the world-process is prior to the world. The end is the purpose. And a purpose is logically prior to its execution. As far as human purposes are concerned, of course, the purpose has also time-priority over its execution, for we must form our purpose before we can carry it out. But the world-purpose is not to be thought of in this anthropomorphic way. There is, according to Aristotle, no mind which consciously designs and executes. The world-purpose is immanent in the world itself. It is not a psychic event which happens in a mind. It is a logical reason. What happens happens for a reason. This reason is the purpose of what happens. The events are the consequents of the reason, of the purpose. The purpose or end, then, is prior to the world, not as its cause in time, but as its reason. The principle of form, the universal, is the reason, and the world is the consequent. The universal is therefore logically prior to things, not prior to them in time.

24. The universal is the source of all things, the first principle from which the world arises. It is "before all the worlds." But now we see that this does not mean that the universal existed at some time in the past before the world began. This is in every way impossible. For in the first place the universal does not exist at all. And in the second place, being timeless, it certainly does not exist in time, either now or in the past. We have here a new determination of the one universal philosophy, a determination of incalculable importance. The germ of it is found here in Aristotle's conception of the logical priority of the universal. But it is only in Hegel that it becomes explicit in the form in which we

shall now state it, a form in which it goes far beyond Aristotle. The universal is the source of all existence. But the dependence of the world upon the universal is not a causal, but a logical, dependence. In other words, *the world flows from the universal, not as an effect flows from its cause in time, but as a conclusion flows from its premises.*

25. These considerations enable us to resolve the apparent contradiction noted above and to explain what sort of " being " universals have. The universal, we said, must, as real, have an independent being of its own. On the other hand it is a mere abstraction. It has no existence apart from the individual things in which it is realised, and from that point of view its being seems to be dependent on the things. Now, however, we see that the universal is the absolute first of all things, not in the sense of having existed before them, but only in the sense of being logically first. This means that it is logically dependent on nothing before it. Its independence is a logical independence. It is not a conclusion from any prior reason. It is the first reason. " Things " are its logical consequences. The universal is not *in fact* separable from things. But it is separable *in thought*. It is logically separate, logically independent. The answer to the question what sort of being universals have, apart from things, is that they have *logical being*. But things have *factual* being, existent being. And the supposed contradiction is thus resolved. For the universal has independent being in the sense that its being is logically independent of things, *i.e.* is separable from things in thought, and is logically prior to them. It has a dependent being in the sense that, if it is to cease to be an abstraction, if it is to enter as a component part into actual existence, it can only do so, it can only become a *fact*, in combination with the particular. Its logical being is independent. Its factual being is dependent.

26. If this still seems strange, the following consideration may assist the reader. The universal is the source of the world, not in the sense of being a thing which existed before the world, but in the sense of being the *reason* of the world. Now even in every-day matters everyone would admit that

the reason of a thing is a reality, yet no one would attribute existence to it. The reason why an artist paints a picture is for the sake of its beauty. This beauty is the reason why the picture comes into being. The beauty is surely something very real. Yet no one would say that, apart from the picture, the beauty exists, or that it existed in time before the picture. It is not an existent " thing."

27. There are in the philosophy of Aristotle a number of other doctrines which profoundly influenced Hegel. One of these is the distinction between potentiality and actuality. These reappear in Hegel under the names of the " implicit " and the " explicit," or that which is " in itself " and that which is " in and for itself." According to Aristotle matter is potentiality, form is actuality. Matter in itself is absolutely formless. It is the entirely indeterminate substrate of things. It is what is left if we remove from anything all its determinations. Gold is soft, yellow, heavy, opaque, etc. If we remove all these determinations in order to come to the substance itself in which the determinations inhere, we shall find that, in point of fact, we have left only a total blank, an absolute nothingness and emptiness. For we have removed all the universals. And since whatever we can say or think of the thing is necessarily a universal (6), it follows that we can neither say nor think anything whatever of what is left. There is in fact nothing left. The natural conclusion is that the supposed substrate is non-existent. But neither Plato nor Aristotle could rid themselves of the idea that there is such a substrate. Both saw clearly, however, that this substrate is a complete emptiness, a not-being. Therefore they said that " matter," as they called the substrate, is a not-being which yet is.

Aristotle's " matter," being in itself nothing, is capable of becoming anything whatever. What it becomes depends upon what universal, what form, is impressed upon it. Endow matter with the universals, white, ovoid, hard, eatable, etc., and, behold, it is an egg. Impose upon it the universals yellow, malleable, heavy, metallic, etc., and, lo, it is a lump of gold. Thus matter itself is actually nothing, but it is potentially everything. It is the potentiality of all things. But it only gains actuality, becomes a "thing," by the acquisition of form. Form, therefore, is actuality.

28. But Aristotle believed that, in the combination of form and matter which constitutes a thing, either the form or the matter may predominate. In some things matter preponderates over form; in other things the reverse is true. Consequently, there is a scale of beings which passes by continuous gradations from formless matter at the bottom to matterless form at the top. Neither the one extreme nor the other *exists*, for form and matter cannot exist apart from each other. But the intermediate terms exist and constitute the universe. Such low things as inorganic matter come at the bottom of the scale of existence. In them matter predominates. Next come plants. Above plants are animals. And the highest existence in the sublunary sphere is man, in whom form vastly preponderates over matter. All things are continually striving to become higher forms. Their attempt to do so is the cause of becoming in the world, the *process* of the world in general. The motive power of the world-process is the end, the form, the universal. Things strive towards their ends. Hence the form is the impelling force, the energy which makes things move. Form compels and moulds matter into higher and higher states of existence. Thus the end operates throughout the whole process from the beginning. The end therefore was present in the beginning, for if not it could exert no force. But it was present in the beginning only potentially. It only becomes actual when the end is realised. Thus if the acorn is the beginning, and the oak is the end, the oak is already in the acorn potentially. Man is already potentially in the ape, though he is only actual in man himself. If this is not so, the phenomena of growth are inexplicable. How can the oak come out of the acorn, if it is not already in it? For it to do so would involve something coming out of nothing, and if this were so, all becoming, all change, would be, as Parmenides saw, inconceivable and impossible. Change involves the arising of something new. But if this new element is wholly new, then we have the impossibility of some-

thing being created out of nothing. The new element, therefore, cannot be wholly new. It was already present as a potentiality in the old.

Development is thus conceived as the coming to light of what was latent and hidden. What a thing already is inwardly, that it becomes outwardly also. The acorn is the oak, but in a state of *in*wardness. " In itself " it is the oak. But it is only to the searching eye of philosophic thought that it is the oak. Thought sees the oak " in it." It is only the oak *for us*, for us whose thought can penetrate down to what is latent in it. It is thus the oak *for us*, but not yet *for itself*. It only becomes the oak for itself when it has actually grown into the oak. Hence what is potential or latent Hegel calls " in itself." What is actual he calls " for itself." And these terms are usually rendered by translators as " implicit " and " explicit " respectively. The acorn is the oak implicitly, but not yet explicitly. This term " in itself," which we find on almost every page of Hegel, is apt to be very puzzling to the beginner. And hence it is very important to grasp the conception of it. The systems of Aristotle and of Hegel are both theories of evolution, and both are based upon the same conception of the nature of development. Development does not involve the arising of something totally new. For Aristotle it is the transition from potential being to actual being. For Hegel it is the transition from the implicit to the explicit.

29. We are not to understand from these remarks that the whole paraphernalia of Aristotle's matter and form are bodily appropriated by Hegel. Both Plato and Aristotle regarded matter as something real, although they called it not-being. And from this arose the fundamental dualism of their philosophies. Matter is not something which is produced by the universal. It existed there from the beginning; the universal moulds it into shape and makes " things " of it. Matter and the universal, therefore, are primordial beings neither of which can be reduced to the other. This is dualism. Hegel saw that the substrate of things is a mere abstraction, an empty nothing. And he therefore abolished

it from his system.[1] Hegel's "implicit" is not Aristotle's "matter." Nor is his "explicit" the same as Aristotle's "form." According to Aristotle's application of the terms, pure matter is potentiality, while pure form is actuality. Hegel's words implicit and explicit mean the same as Aristotle's potential and actual. But he did not apply them to the same things or in the same way. We are at present concerned only with the meaning (connotation) of the words, not with their application (denotation).

30. The last Aristotelian doctrine which we need mention as directly influencing Hegel is the doctrine of the Absolute, or God. We have seen that to say that anything is, in the philosophic sense, reality, is to say that it is that primordial being which is the source of all things in the world. In other words it is the Absolute. Philosophers also frequently use the word God for the Absolute, because, in religion, God is looked upon as the primordial being from which all things flow.

31. Now at the top of the scale of being in Aristotle's philosophy comes absolutely matterless form. This absolute form is what Aristotle calls God,—because form is the source of all existence. This pure form contains no matter. Its only content is itself. Thus it is not the form of matter, but the form of form. And this becomes transformed into the famous Aristotelian definition of God as the "thought of thought." God does not think matter. He thinks only thought. He is thought, and the object of this thought is thought itself. He thinks, therefore, only Himself. God is self-consciousness. Hegel's Absolute is also self-consciousness, the thought of thought.

32. Now it is evident that in this transformation the phrase "thought of thought" is taken as equivalent to the phrase "form of form." This is only justifiable if form is thought. And so we reach here a new determination of the universal philosophy. Form is the universal. The universal is the real, the Absolute. Hence *the real, the Absolute, is thought.* And since thought is the essence of mind, we may also express

---

[1] Hegel, however, practically introduces it again in his conception of the "contingent," that which cannot be deduced. See below (423-5).

GREEK IDEALISM AND HEGEL

this by saying that *the Absolute is mind*. It remains for us to justify these determinations.

33. The question resolves itself into this: is a form or universal a thought? That it is, was clearly the opinion of both Aristotle and Hegel. And the same opinion is suggested by the historical origin of the theory of universals. Plato was led to the fundamental tenets of his philosophy by discovering that knowledge consists wholly of concepts. The universal, as it first came under his consideration, was the subjective concept, the thought which we have in our minds when we use a class-name. The core of his philosophy is reached at that point where it is seen that a universal is not merely something subjective, but that there are objective universals which have being outside of, independent of, minds. These are to be regarded as objective thoughts, because universality is a quality of thoughts and not of things. Things are individual.

Still, as has already been indicated (7), there is a school of philosophy now much in fashion according to which universals are not thoughts, although it is admitted that they "subsist," *i.e.* possess being. Universals, it is said, are "not mental."[1] This may be, as already suggested, partly a mere matter of words. If it means merely that universals are not *subjective* thoughts, *i.e.* not thoughts existing in a particular mind, such as yours or mine or God's, then idealism will not only admit this but will insist emphatically upon it. But if it means further that universals are not of the nature of thought, apart from the question of their existence in minds, it must be disputed.

34. The ground of the idealist contention is that universals are abstractions. It is only by abstracting from the differences and concentrating on the common elements of a class that we obtain a universal. But abstraction is clearly a thought-process. And a universal is a thought because it is an abstraction. An objection will doubtless be raised to this. True, it will be said, that it is only by abstraction that *we*

---

[1] See, for example, Mr. Bertrand Russell's admirable little book, *The Problems of Philosophy*, pp. 152-5.

obtain a universal. But this universal which *we* obtain is only a subjective concept. So that this argument proves only what we know already, viz. that subjective concepts are thoughts. It proves nothing as to the nature of objective universals. But this is to misconceive the argument. The point is, not that concepts are abstractions, but that objective universals are abstractions. For if not they have no being, no objectivity. We have seen that they do not exist. They have no existence separate from individual things. It is only *in thought*, and *as* thoughts, that they have separate and independent being. Therefore, so far as they have being they are abstractions, *i.e.* thoughts. We have seen, too, that the only being which can be attributed to universals is a *logical* being. And what is only a logical entity is a thought. Or again, we have seen that they are "reasons." And a reason is surely a thought.

35. But, of course, it is of fundamental importance to understand that when idealism says that the ultimate reality is thought, it does not mean thought in the common sense of subjective thought, psychic processes going on in an individual mind. It does not assert that the universe is dependent on the operations of human minds, or even on the operations of a divine mind in the popular theistic sense. Idealism is perfectly consistent with the view that there was a time when no minds, human or divine, existed, when there was nothing but masses of incandescent vapour with no trace of life anywhere. For such a world was still dependent on thought, was the product of thought, *was* thought—not subjective, but objective thought.

36. But against this it is urged that "thought implies a thinker," that thought without a thinker is inconceivable. This difficulty is only a recrudescence of the difficulty which the common mind experiences in understanding how anything can be real and yet not exist. What this assertion means is that thoughts cannot *exist* except in the mind of a thinker. And this is perfectly true. Every existence is an individual entity which is *there*, at some place or time. An existent thought must be such an individual

entity, which is there, which is present as this particular thought in the stream of some particular consciousness. But universals do not exist and are therefore not present in a stream of consciousness, in a mind. Thoughts cannot *exist* without a thinker. But universals do not exist. They are *real*. And since all existence is appearance, since no existence is reality, and because every thought in the mind of a thinker is an entity which exists, it follows that universals are not in the mind of a thinker. If they were, they could not be real. For they would exist.

37. It should be noticed that when idealists use such expressions as that the Absolute is thought, they are using the word thought in a restricted sense as meaning only universal thought. The popular usage, according to which I may have, for example, a thought of my mother's face, is different. In such popular language thought includes particular mental images, and sometimes even sensations. In our sense only universals are called thoughts.

38. The expression that the Absolute is mind means no more than that it is thought. Thought is the essence of mind; and if one expression is legitimate, the other is also. But here again it is not a subjective existent mind that is meant, but an objective real mind. The mind spoken of is that system of universal thought of which reality is composed. It is not *a* mind, this mind as opposed to that, my mind or even God's mind—if by God is meant a particular existent intelligence. This primordial mind from which the universe flows is no psychic entity. It is real. But it does not exist. It is universal mind, abstract mind. It is indeed the mind at work in the world, and that such mind is at work in the world is the truth of the theological doctrine of divine governance. But it is the mind at work *in* the world, not outside it. It is the reason *in* things, or *of* things, but not a reason which is external to them, stands apart from them, as a human mind stands apart from the objects it observes or controls. It is reason which does not imply a reasoner in the sense of a person who reasons. Of course, too, it does not exist; it did not exist before the beginning of the world, did not " create " the world

as an act in time. Its relation to the world is a logical relation, and its being a logical being.

D. Results

39. In tracing the development of Greek idealism we have attempted to extract from the historical facts their essential significance. We have thereby expounded part of the fundamentals of the universal philosophy, and since Hegel is but the last great teacher of this philosophy, we have expounded at the same time some of the fundamental principles of Hegel. It may be well now to gather up in a brief statement the results we have obtained. The essentials of the universal philosophy, or those essentials which have so far emerged, are the following:

I. The real is what has a wholly independent being, a being dependent only on itself.

II. Appearance is what depends for its being upon another being. This other being is the real.

III. Existence is what can be immediately presented to consciousness. It may be either a material or a psychic entity.

IV. The real is the universal.

V. The real is not an existence. Its being is logical being.

VI. Existence is appearance.

VII. The real, that is, the universal, is also thought, mind, or intelligence; but this thought, mind, or intelligence is not an existent, individual, subjective mind, but an abstract, universal, objective mind. It has a logical and not a factual being.

VIII. The real, that is, objective thought, is the first principle or ultimate being, the Absolute, which is the source of all things, and from which the universe must be explained.

IX. This first principle is first only in the sense that it holds logical priority over all things. It is not first in order of time.

These propositions constitute the idealist creed only so far as it has developed up to the time of Aristotle. We have yet to consider the modifications and additions which modern thought has effected in it.

40. The philosophy of Hegel, it will be seen, is not something simply invented out of nothing by himself and flung at random into an astonished world. It is no crazy fancy of an individual's brain, no gimcrack novelty. It is not the pet theory of some erratic genius, nor is it merely one theory among many rivals. The true author of it is, not so much Hegel, as the toiling and thinking human spirit, the universal spirit of humanity getting itself uttered through this individual. It is the work of the ages. It has its roots deep in the past. It is the accumulated wisdom of the years, the last phase of the one " universal philosophy." For the truth is, to use a phrase of Hegel's, neither new nor old, but permanent. Yet Hegel, too, is profoundly original. But his originality is not mere novelty. It is new, but it is old too. It recognises all past truth, absorbs it into itself, *and advances*. Hence its attitude to other philosophies is neither envious, nor hostile, nor destructive. It sees in every one of them some phase or aspect of truth which has to be recognised and absorbed into itself. It is for this reason a genuinely universal philosophy.

CHAPTER II

MODERN PHILOSOPHY AND HEGEL

41. After the death of Aristotle idealism of the classic type disappeared until comparatively modern times. The Stoics, Epicureans, and Sceptics neglected it. Neo-Platonism was, at the best, a mystical distortion of it. Scholasticism caricatured it. Thinkers from Descartes to Leibniz did not revive it. Among these early modern philosophers there are, of course, affinities with Greek idealism. But they are slight. The revival of idealism comes with Kant, and is his work. Not that Kant is a direct offshoot of Greek idealism. His work shows but little the influence of the Greeks. Nor would it be true to say of him, without many provisos, that he is an exponent of the universal philosophy. He would have completely repudiated some of the most important of the propositions formulated at the end of the last chapter. Yet he became the parent, even against his own will, of an idealism of a fundamentally similar type to that described in the last chapter.

But before coming to Kant we must briefly refer to the one pre-Kantian thinker who influenced Hegel more profoundly than any other. This was Spinoza.

A. *Spinoza and Hegel.*

42. Spinoza formulated the profoundly important principle that *all determination is negation*. To determine a thing is to cut it off from some sphere of being and so to limit it. To define is to set boundaries. To say that a thing is green

limits it by cutting it from the sphere of pink, blue, or other-coloured things. To say that it is good cuts it off from the sphere of evil. This limitation is the same as negation. To *affirm* that a thing is within certain limits is to *deny* that it is outside those limits. To say that it is green is to say that it is not pink. Affirmation involves negation. Whatever is said of a thing denies something else of it. All determination is negation.

43. This principle is fundamental for Hegel also, but with him it takes rather the converse form that *all negation is determination*. Formal logicians will remind us that we cannot simply convert Spinoza's proposition. But it is sufficient to point out in reply that not only does affirmation involve negation; negation likewise involves affirmation. To deny that a thing belongs to one class is to affirm that it belongs to some other class,—though we may not know what that class is. Positive and negative are correlatives which mutually involve each other. To posit is to negate : this is Spinoza's principle. To negate is to posit : this is Hegel's.

When, therefore, we meet Hegel talking about " the portentous power of the negative," we have to consider that for him negation is the very process of creation. For the *positive* nature of an object consists in its determinations. The nature of a stone is to be white, heavy, hard, etc. And since all determinations are negations, it follows that the positive nature of a thing consists in its negations. Negation, therefore, is of the very essence of positive being. And for the world to come into being what is above all necessary is the force of negation, " the portentous power of the negative." The genus only becomes the species by means of the differentia, and the differentia is precisely that which carves out a particular class from the general class by excluding, *i.e.* negating, the other species. And the species again only becomes the individual in the same way, by negating other individuals. These thoughts are no casual reflections of Hegel. They underlie his entire system. We must get to understand that these three ideas, determination, limitation, and negation, all involve each other.

44. The Hegelian doctrine of the infinite also owes much to Spinoza. To be infinite means to be unlimited. Now to be determined is to be limited. For determination is limitation. This would lead to the conclusion that the infinite is the undetermined. And since what has no determinations has no character of any kind, since nothing can be predicated of it, the undetermined is, therefore, the completely empty. It is, in fact, nothing, mere vacancy. And the substance of Spinoza is really this undetermined vacancy. But there is another thought which lies, inconsistently perhaps, at the root of the philosophy of Spinoza. He says that substance is *causa sui*, the cause of itself. It is, therefore, not the undetermined but the self-determined. Its determinations do not arise from any outside source but only from itself. And that the infinite is not merely the endless, the unlimited, the undetermined, as in popular conception, but is the self-determined,—this is the fundamental Hegelian conception of infinity. Not, of course, that this exhausts the Hegelian doctrine of the infinite. On the contrary it leaves out its most characteristic element. But the roots of Hegel's teaching on the subject lie here in Spinoza.

B. *Hume and Kant.*

45. Greek idealism naïvely assumed that the human mind is capable of cognizing reality. To suppose that only appearance is knowable to minds constituted as ours are was an idea which never occurred to Plato or Aristotle. Yet the problem was bound to force itself at some time into philosophic consciousness. It was Kant who formally raised the question. What is knowledge? How is it possible? What can be known, and what cannot be known? Has knowledge any necessary limits? These were the questions which Kant set himself to answer, questions which, he tells us, were forced upon him by the philosophising of Hume.

46. Hume attempted to show that some of the most fundamental conceptions, such as cause, identity, substance, upon which our knowledge of things depends, are illusory. First

of all, causality. This idea involves the two elements of *necessity* and *universality*. Suppose that A is the cause of B. This means, firstly, that B *must* follow A. It is not a mere fact that it does so. It *must*. This is necessity. It means, secondly, that B *always* follows A, provided there is no counteracting cause, provided, that is, that no third phenomenon, C, interferes with the operation of A. A properly constructed bell, A, will, when shaken, *always* produce sound, B—unless, of course, it is shaken in a vacuum, C. This is universality. Such is the conception of causality.

But is this conception justified? Is it a true description of reality? Is there in the objective world any reality which corresponds to this our mental conception? Or is it merely a chimera of the mind? Hume took it for granted that we have no source of knowledge except experience. And experience means, for him as for Locke, the experience which comes to us either through the physical senses, or through reflection upon our own mental processes. Knowledge of anything external to our minds, such as this house, this tree, this star, comes through the senses. Knowledge of anything within the mind, such as the fact that I feel angry, comes through reflection or introspection. *But experience thus defined can never give us either necessity or universality.* I can only see, hear, or feel that a thing *is*, never that it *must* be. My eye tells me that this paper *is* here. But no amount of gazing at it will give me the information that it *must* be here. Nor is there any kind of logical necessity to be found in causation. Cold solidifies water. But there is no logical connection between cold and solidification. By analysing the idea of a triangle I can see that its three angles must equal two right angles. But no analysis of the idea of cold will yield the idea of solidification. The one cannot be deduced, as a logical necessity, from the other. So far as one can see, cold might just as well turn water into steam. We have to wait on experience to see which, if either, will happen. And experience merely gives us the fact, not the necessity. Likewise experience can only tell us that B follows A in those particular cases to which experience extends. It cannot possibly give us any grounds for believing that B always does, and always will, follow A. This is specially obvious with regard to the future. We have no experience of the future. How then can experience inform us that fire will produce heat to-morrow? But this difficulty, though more obvious in regard to the future, really arises with equal force in the cases of the past and the present. Water freezes at 0° Centigrade. But what is the evidence of this? Experience merely shows that this has been true in all the cases which we happen to have investigated. But there are millions of cases of the freezing of water which no one has ever observed, and of which, therefore, we have no experience. And how can experience warrant us in making statements about that of which we have no experience? Therefore knowledge of universality can never be given us by experience. And since experience is, according to Hume, the only source of true knowledge, and since the essential elements of causality, namely universality and necessity, cannot be found in experience, it follows that causality is an illusion. And Hume proceeds to explain how the illusion arises through the laws of the association of ideas. Having invariably seen A followed by B, we associate the two together, and imagine that the sequence is necessarily and universally true.

47. Hume, following Berkeley, criticises the idea of substance in much the same way. A stone has whiteness, hardness, etc. And we are accustomed to say that there is a substance in which these qualities inhere. But experience gives us knowledge *only* of the qualities, not of the substance. We cannot form any idea of the substance or substratum apart from its qualities. But we are accustomed to associate the hardness, the whiteness, etc., with each other, and so our imagination produces the idea of some underlying substance which is supposed to support these qualities and link them together. We have no warrant in experience for the idea of substance which is, accordingly, an illusion like that of causality.

48. Kant was seriously perturbed by these considerations and cast about to find an answer to them. Such an idea as that of causation is absolutely necessary to knowledge. All science rests upon the assumption of causation. And if the

foundations of knowledge are thus cut away the entire fabric will collapse. The possibility of any knowledge whatever depends upon an answer to Hume being found.

49. There are, according to Kant, two elements in knowledge, sensation and thought. In sensation we are passive. We receive the raw material of knowledge in the form of sensations which are *given* to us from an outside source. In thought we are active. Thought is a spontaneous operation of the mind which works up the raw material of sensation into knowledge. All this, says Kant, has been universally admitted ever since the time of Plato. Kant proceeds to study these two elements of knowledge separately.

50. First, as to sensation. Every object of external sense is in space and time. Every object of internal sense, *i.e.* introspection,—such objects as feelings and ideas—are in time. But these latter are not in space. Thus time is the universal form of internal sense; space and time are the universal forms of external sense. Now do we possess any cognitions about space and time which possess those characters of universality and necessity which were found so puzzling in the case of causality? The answer is that we do. All geometrical knowledge consists of universal and necessary propositions about space. And we have also universal and necessary cognitions regarding time, *e.g.* that two moments cannot be simultaneous. Arithmetical propositions are also universal and necessary. But Hume has proved conclusively that experience cannot yield us universality and necessity. Hence this knowledge *does not arise from experience*.

51. Perhaps, however, this universality and necessity of mathematical propositions may be due to the fact that they are merely analytic. That a horse is an animal must be universally and necessarily true so long as we continue to use the words " horse " and " animal " in the same sense. The idea of a horse includes the fact that it is an animal, so that the proposition merely gives a partial analysis of the meaning of the word horse. In the same way, it might be urged, the proposition $2+2=4$ is universal and necessary because it is merely a definition of 4. And that two straight lines cannot

enclose a space is universal and necessary because it merely expresses what we mean by straight lines.

This is a plausible, but unsound, objection. The propositions in question are not analytic but synthetic. Two plus two is not a definition of four. No one can know that $2+2=4$ merely by analysing the idea of 4. No one can know it until it has been *pointed out in experience* that two beads and two beads taken together, or any similar objects, make four. Similarly no amount of analysis of the idea of a straight line will give us the knowledge that two straight lines cannot enclose a space. This also has to be *pointed out*, either in a real space or in an imaginary space. Ordinarily, no doubt, in order to understand this we try to imagine two straight lines enclosing a space, and we find that we cannot. This experiment in imagination is of the same character as an actual experiment in real space. It consists in a process of *pointing out* to ourselves, and is not an analysis of a concept.

52. Yet the universality and necessity of these propositions cannot arise from experience. We no doubt require experience before we can come to know them, for, as we have just seen, they have to be pointed out *in* experience. But all that experience can ever give us is that *this* two and *this* two make *this* four, or that *this* pair of straight lines does not enclose a space. Yet, immediately these particular facts are pointed out in experience, we leap beyond their particularity and add universality and necessity to them. We see that what is true of *this* case is, and *must* always be, true of *all* cases. Experience cannot yield this universality and necessity. So that these propositions are, on the one hand synthetic, while on the other they are independent of experience or, to use Kant's phrase, *a priori*. And the question is, *how are a priori synthetic propositions possible?* They do not arise from experience, nor do they arise from mere analysis of our ideas.

53. The key to the mystery is to be found in certain considerations regarding space and time. Space is the condition of the appearance to us of external objects. We cannot conceive this table existing except on the condition that it exists in space. On the other hand, we can easily picture the

space without the table, or empty space without any objects at all. We can, in imagination, destroy all objects in space, and conceive of totally empty space remaining. But we cannot reverse the process. We cannot destroy the space in imagination and yet retain the objects. Therefore the cognition of space is the prior condition of the cognition of objects. But the cognition of objects is precisely what we call experience. Hence the cognition of space is prior to all experience; for it is the condition of all experience, and a condition must be prior to what depends upon it. Therefore the cognition of space does not come to us from experience, from the outside, and space is not something external to us which we passively receive through the senses. It is not a form of things which exists outside us; it is a form of our own perceptive faculty. It is the creation of our own minds. It is we who impose space upon things, not things which impose space upon our minds. Space does not exist apart from us. It is *our* way of perceiving things. And Kant applies similar arguments to prove the same thing of time.

54. Now if this is true, we can understand the necessity and universality of propositions regarding space and time, and in no other way can we understand them. For if space and time are subjective forms of our perceptive faculty, then the laws of space and time,—and propositions of geometry and mathematics are such laws—are the laws of our own minds, and a law of our own perceptive faculty is naturally true universally and necessarily of whatever we perceive. If we wore coloured spectacles we should see everything coloured. And so, since space and time are our ways of perceiving things, the laws of our perception impose themselves on everything we perceive.

55. A word of warning is desirable here. When Kant says that the cognitions of space and time are prior to all experience, he does not, of course, mean that we come into the world with a ready-made knowledge of space and time. Psychologists have laboriously investigated the ways in which the knowledge of space and time grows up in children and young animals. Of course such knowledge is acquired gradually in experience. But psychological conclusions of this sort in

no way conflict with Kant's theory,—and have, indeed, no bearing upon it. Nobody, least of all Kant, supposes that the cognitions of time and space are prior to experience in order of time; they are prior to it in logical order only, because they are its logical condition. And Kant's theory is that, though we doubtless come to gain a knowledge of space and time by degrees in the manner described by psychologists, yet what we are thus coming to know is not anything external to us, but something of which we ourselves are the authors. We are gaining knowledge, not of an alien outer something, but of the contents of our own minds. Failure to understand this distinction is the source of some of the crudest misunderstandings both of Kant and of Hegel.

56. Space and time are the only elements of sensation which possess universality and necessity. They are the necessary *forms* of sensation. The filling of these forms, *e.g.* such sense-data as those of colour, taste, etc., are not universal or necessary. For example, this poppy *is* red. But we cannot see that it *must* be red. It might as well be blue. Neither can we extend our conception of redness to all things, or even to all poppies. Hence there is no reason to assume that any element of sensation, except space and time, is the work of our minds. With the exception of these two, all else comes from outside, from an external thing. Hence sensation may be said to have two sources. The *forms* of sensation, *i.e.* space and time, are the spontaneous products of the perceiving mind. Its *matter* is *given* us from outside by the object itself. It follows that the object itself, the thing-in-itself, as it is apart from the work of our minds upon it, is not in space or time at all. Hence the objects perceived by us in space and time are not the real objects. They are appearances.

57. This concludes the consideration of the first source of knowledge, sensation. The next question is, whether there are any universal and necessary elements in the second source of knowledge, viz. thought. Thought is conceptual. Hence the question may also be framed thus: are there any universal and necessary concepts? Now we have already seen that the concepts of cause and substance possess universality and

necessity. Are there any others? If so, they too, like space and time, must be prior to experience, must be *a priori*, must be contributed to knowledge, not by things-in-themselves, but by the cognising mind. And if so, they too will be pure forms having nothing of the matter of sensation in them. For the matter is given by the thing-in-itself; it is the form that mind contributes. The concept "red" is no more *a priori* than the percept "red." Neither have any universality or necessity. Both belong to the matter, not to the form, of knowledge. Now the faculty of concepts is also the faculty of judgment. The mind judges when it applies its concepts to objects. Hence the pure non-sensuous forms of thought, *i.e.* the pure non-sensuous concepts, will be given to us in the formal judgments of logic. " Some poppies are red " is a material judgment, and gives us the sensuous concepts "poppy" and "red." But "Some S is P" is purely formal, and gives us none of the matter of sensation. But does it involve any concepts at all? It does. First of all, it is a particular and not a universal proposition. It refers to more than one but not to all. This is the concept of plurality. Secondly, it states that something " is." This involves the concept of reality. These then must be pure non-sensuous concepts, which are not derived from experience, but which the construction of our minds contributes to knowledge. To find the complete list we have only to see what concepts are involved in the different kinds of logical judgment. The full list of such judgments divides them as follows :—

Quantity.	*Quality.*	*Relation.*	*Modality.*
Universal	Affirmative	Categorical	Problematic
Particular	Negative	Hypothetical	Assertoric
Singular	Infinite	Disjunctive	Apodeictic

and from this list Kant derives the corresponding concepts as follows :—

Quantity.	*Quality.*	*Relation.*	*Modality.*
Totality	Reality	Substance and Accident	Possibility and Impossibility
Plurality	Negation	Cause and Effect	Existence and non-existence
Unity	Limitation	Reciprocity	Necessity and Contingency.

58. These twelve pure concepts are called by Kant *categories*. They are, like space and time, (1) pure forms without content or matter, (2) prior to all experience, and (3) not given from any external source but contributed to cognition by the mind itself. These categories are also universal and necessary. A thing may or may not be red. But it must be the effect of some cause. It must be a substance having accidents. It must be one or many. We can conceive a universe without whiteness, or without weight, but not one without unity, plurality, reality, negation, and so on. And this universality and necessity are to be explained in the same way as the universality and necessity of time and space. The categories are the work of our minds. Our minds are so made that things *must* appear to us through these forms. Hence these forms apply to everything, and are, for us, universal and necessary. And just as the thing-in-itself is not in space or time, so now the categories cannot apply to the thing-in-itself. The thing-in-itself is not a cause, or a substance; it is neither one nor many; it has neither quantity, quality, nor relation. These concepts apply only to what appears to us, not to the thing as it is in itself.

59. Now to say all this amounts to saying that reality is unknowable. The thing-in-itself is the reality; it is what really exists apart from the subjective conceptions of our minds. The thing as we know it is an appearance. The thing as it is in reality is not in space or time, has neither quantity, nor quality, nor relation, and is, in a word, entirely inconceivable to us. What, then, is to be said of our so-called knowledge? What must be said is this, that our knowledge is sound and good, within the limits of appearance, within the limits of our experience. No doubt the entire world as we know it is appearance, but it is not mere illusion, because the forms of this appearance are universal and necessary. They apply to all minds constructed as ours are. They are not merely the groundless fancies of an *individual's* mind; which is what is meant by illusion. So we may say that this world of appearance is a reality *for us*. But if we imagine that it is possible for us to know reality as it is in itself, then we are

MODERN PHILOSOPHY AND HEGEL

deluding ourselves. Hence knowledge must stick to the world of experience. Beyond this it cannot go. It cannot penetrate to the secret inner reality of the world. That reality is for ever unknowable to us by reason of the very way our minds are constructed. And since experience means only the universe as surveyed by our external and internal senses, the last word of Kant must needs be that only knowledge of phenomena is possible, the phenomena of the sense-world on the one hand, and the phenomena of the inner psychic world of mind on the other.

C. *The onward march from Kant.*

60. Philosophy, then, according to Kant, is to abate its claims. It is warned off the premises of everything except immediate existence in space and time. It must give up all attempts to know reality, to penetrate behind appearances. But the effect of this solemn warning upon the philosophic world was truly astonishing. No sooner had Kant thus cried " Halt ! " to philosophy than philosophy, forming its adherents into a sort of triumphal procession, proceeding, so to speak, with bands playing and flags waving, marched victoriously onward to the final assault, confident of its power to attain omniscience at a stroke, to occupy the very citadel of reality itself. And, strangest of all, this was to be done with the very weapons which Kant himself had forged. It was under the Kantian banner that philosophy moved forward. It was Kant's own philosophy, hailed as the greatest discovery of all time, which was to accomplish this final and triumphant victory. Philosophy, instead of being sobered by the warnings of the master, rose at once to an exuberant ferment of enthusiasm. It set no bounds to itself. It was to accomplish the impossible, know the unknowable. Such is the confident enthusiasm of the philosophies of that time.

61. The reason for this astonishing change was that while philosophy fastened upon the ideas of universality, necessity, and pure thought as an *a priori* construction of mind, it rejected the Kantian thing-in-itself. Everyone saw at once that the

conception of the thing-in-itself is a self-contradictory and impossible abstraction. It is a flat self-contradiction. Its existence is assumed because Kant thought there must be an external *cause* of our sensations. On the one hand, therefore, the thing-in-itself is alleged to be the cause of appearances. On the other hand, however, it cannot be a cause, because cause is a category of our minds, and the categories do not apply to the thing-in-itself. Nor can this contradiction be resolved by calling the thing-in-itself the ground of appearances instead of their cause. This, it is evident, is a subterfuge, a mere change of words without any real change of meaning. Moreover, even if we say that the thing-in-itself is not a cause, but that it nevertheless exists, this position is, firstly, still self-contradictory, and secondly, quite gratuitous. It is self-contradictory because, though it drops the category of cause, it still applies to the thing-in-itself the category of existence, and this contradicts the fundamental Kantian position that none of the categories apply to it. It is gratuitous because, if the thing-in-itself is not the cause of our sensations there is no ground for assuming its existence. Why assume that there is a thing-in-itself at all? Why not suppose that things as they appear to us, appearances, are all that exist? Only because, according to Kant, our sensations must have an external cause. This is the only ground for assuming the existence of the thing-in-itself. Hence, since it now appears that the thing-in-itself cannot be such a cause, there is, consequently, no ground for assuming its existence. Lastly, this whole conception of an unknowable existence is self-contradictory. Knowledge is nothing but the application of concepts. If we know that a thing exists and is a cause, we know that the concepts of existence and causation apply to it. We have, therefore, some knowledge of it, and it is not unknowable or even unknown.

62. Thus the whole conception of the thing-in-itself collapses. And we must carefully note the effect of this collapse on the Kantian philosophy. The forms of knowledge, space, time, and the categories, are the product of our minds and issue from nothing external. Kant assumed that

the *given* factor of knowledge, sensation, the matter or filling of the forms of space, time, and category, are due to an external source. This leads to the self-contradictory thing-in-itself. Therefore, the only conclusion is that this given factor does not arise from any external source. And in that case it must be, just as the *a priori* forms are, the product of mind. But if both matter and form are the product of mind, this means that the whole object of knowledge, and every object, and so the entire universe, is a product of mind. This leads to an absolute idealism.

Lastly, the belief that there can be anything unknowable in the universe is exploded with the thing-in-itself. To say that anything is unknowable is self-contradictory. Hence everything must be knowable. There is no limit to the aspirations of human knowledge. The infinite, the Absolute itself, lie open to us. And these are the thoughts which inspired the victorious march of philosophy after Kant. Fichte, Schelling, Schopenhauer, and Hegel,—these were the offspring of the Kantian philosophy shorn of its unnecessary appendage, the thing-in-itself.

D. Criticism of the Conception of the Unknowable.

63. It may be supposed that, though the particular theory of the unknowable which Kant espoused proved untenable, yet some other theory of an unknowable may work better. The collapse of Kant's thing-in-itself may have been due to the special doctrines of Kant's philosophy. And though Kant may have failed here, yet an unknowable of some kind there must surely be. These are natural reflections. And yet they are erroneous. And we have, therefore, to generalise the results reached, to show that they are not peculiar to the Kantian way of putting the problem, and that not merely his but *any* theory of an unknowable will give rise to the same contradictions. We have to prove that the unknowable is, in itself and apart altogether from its setting in this or that particular philosophy, a self-contradictory and impossible conception.

64. We must distinguish clearly between the unknown and the unknowable. There are, of course, millions of things which are, and will probably always remain, unknown. And many of these are probably unknowable in the sense that, through lack of opportunity or of suitable instruments, they must remain for ever hidden from us. If there is a lump of gold at the bottom of an ocean on a planet which revolves round a star which is invisible to the greatest telescopes, this, we might say, is unknowable in the sense indicated. But this is not what is meant in philosophy by the unknowable. It is merely unknown, and will remain so, not because it is in itself unknowable, but merely through the accidental fact that we are too far away to acquire a knowledge of it. Were it not for this accidental circumstance the fact itself would be quite as easily knowable as the gold sovereign in my pocket. What is meant in philosophy by the unknowable is something which, apart from all accidental circumstances, is such that the constitution of our minds is radically incapable of knowing it, something which is totally outside any conceivable human knowledge, something from which we are completely cut off, not by distance, lack of intruments and the like, but by the nature of our mental processes. This is the conception which, we say, is impossible and self-contradictory, whether it appears in the form taught by Kant or by Spencer, by sceptic, empiricist, or idealist.

65. For it is indisputable that all knowledge is conceptual. And the ability to apply suitable concepts to a thing constitutes knowledge of that thing. Now existence is a concept. Therefore to say that an unknowable exists is to apply a concept to the unknowable. But to apply a concept to it is to have knowledge of it. Therefore the theory that an unknowable exists involves the contradiction that we have knowledge of the unknowable.

It is no reply to these arguments to say that we may know the bare existence of the thing but that we can know nothing of its nature. The distinction between the existence and the nature of the thing has no foundation, for its existence is part of its nature. The nature of the thing consists in the concepts which apply to it, and existence is one of these. Nor again is it relevant to point out that mere knowledge of the existence of the thing, without any further knowledge of it, amounts to such a trifling quantity of knowledge that we may legitimately say that, for the rest, the thing is practically unknowable. The *quantity* of our knowledge is not in question. If anything is unknowable, this means that it is absolutely unknowable. And if we have any knowledge of it, however slight, it is not unknowable. To be able to apply a hundred concepts to a thing may constitute a great deal of knowledge. To be able to apply only one concept may constitute the minimum amount of knowledge. But still it is knowledge. Or if we go on to say, as Kant does, that the unknowable is the cause of appearances, thus applying the concept of cause, or if we say, as Spencer does, that it is a power which causes the universe, thus applying the concepts of power and cause, then we are claiming a quite considerable quantity of knowledge about the unknowable, and our theory becomes correspondingly more self-contradictory.

66. Another consideration, which is peculiarly Hegelian, is applicable here. It is only possible to be aware of a limit to anything by knowing what is beyond the limit. No one could be aware of the end of a straight line unless he were aware of the empty space beyond the end. Hence if knowledge itself has any absolute limit we could not be aware of the fact; for we could only know the limit by being aware of what is beyond the limit; and that would mean that knowledge has already passed beyond its supposed limit, or in other words that the limit is no limit. Total ignorance of a thing involves total unawareness of it, and therefore it involves unawareness of our ignorance. To be aware of our ignorance of a thing is only possible if we know something of the thing and realise that this knowledge is very slight. But complete ignorance of the thing would be complete unconsciousness of it and would involve that we could not even be aware of our ignorance of it. Now the theory of the unknowable ignores these considerations. It implies, in the first place, that there is an absolute limit to our knowledge and that we know the

limit and know nothing of what lies beyond the limit,—an impossibility. And it implies in the second place an absolute ignorance of something combined with an awareness of this ignorance,—also an impossibility.

67. People imagine that it is inconsistent with due humility to suppose that there are no limits to the possibility of our knowledge. But we may fully admit the depth of our ignorance, our pitiable liability to error, our puny resources. These admissions have no bearing upon the question of an unknowable. They would be relevant to prove that many things are unknown, but not that anything is unknowable. The mind of an Aristotle or a Hegel may well appear like the mind of a baby to the superman of to-morrow. But what the superman knows is knowable, though possibly unknown, to a Hegel, and what Hegel knows is knowable, though doubtless unknown, to the baby. The differential calculus is not understood by the baby. But it is not unknowable to the baby, as is proved by the fact that the baby comes to understand it when it grows up. If it were unknowable in the philosophical sense, that would mean that the baby could never come to know it because the fundamental construction of its mind renders such knowledge a radical impossibility. A particular person may be stupid or uneducated and for that reason may find it impossible to understand the calculus. But no one would say that the calculus is unknowable. For the unknowable means not something which this or that mind cannot understand, but something which mind as such cannot understand, however highly it may be developed. Our actual ignorance of the universe, then, is no argument for the existence of an unknowable.

68. But there is still one last stronghold out of which the partisans of the unknowable must be thrust. Our arguments, it may be said, prove that it is self-contradictory to assert the existence of an unknowable. But they do not prove that we can deny its existence. It is self-contradictory to say that we know that the unknowable exists. But it is not self-contradictory to say that it may exist even though we do not know it. For here we do not apply the concept of existence,

we only say that we do not know whether it applies or not. We may have no good grounds for asserting the existence of the unknowable; but we equally have no good grounds for denying its existence. The answer is that we have perfect grounds for denying its existence, and that this position is as self-contradictory as the last. For suppose that an unknowable exists. Then the category of existence is applicable to it. It is quite irrelevant whether we actually apply it or not. It is applicable. And that one of our mental categories applies to the unknowable means that it is, to the extent of that category, knowable. So that we have the same contradiction as before.

69. We can, therefore, positively deny the existence of an unknowable. And it follows that *there is nothing in the universe which the human mind cannot know*, neither the infinite, nor the Absolute, nor the thing-in-itself. Popular phrases about the finite mind of man being unable to comprehend the infinite are, therefore, mere superstition. And the principle which lies at the root of these results is the following. The word existence has no meaning except the possibility of being known, the possibility of being an object to consciousness. To say that anything exists means that it is a possible object for consciousness. Existence, therefore, is relative to, and depends upon, consciousness. And the theory of the unknowable is self-contradictory because it assumes that existence is possible independently of mind and consciousness. It may perhaps be asked whether this result is as true of *reality* as of existence. Reality, as we said, has independent being, but it has not existence. Perhaps all existence may be relative to mind, so that an unknowable cannot *exist*. But may not an unknowable have independent being and reality? The answer is in the negative. For we saw that this independent being which we ascribed to reality is only a logical being, a being *for thought*. It cannot, therefore, have being apart from thought. It cannot be unknowable.

CHAPTER III

HEGEL

A. Explanation : Cause : Reason.

70. Stated in the most general terms possible the problem of philosophy is to explain the universe. No doubt the problems of philosophy are, in one sense, numerous. There are the questions of ethics, metaphysics, aesthetics, epistemology. But to explain the universe would be to solve all these. It may be urged that to undertake to explain the universe with our limited knowledge and faculties is like undertaking to lift the world with a feather. But if this means that the ultimate explanation of things is unknowable to us, we have already seen that such a position is untenable. If it only means that we can never hope for a perfect and complete explanation, we may admit it. But that our knowledge can never be complete is no reason for abandoning the attempt to gain as much knowledge as we can. We are, therefore, justified in seeking for an explanation of the universe.

71. Philosophers have disputed whether the explanation of the universe is to be found in matter or mind, in an inscrutable first cause, or in an intelligent Creator. But the first question which ought to be settled is, what is explanation ? When we demand that the universe shall be explained, what is it that we wish to know about the universe ?

Now an isolated fact is usually said to be explained when its cause has been discovered. And if its cause cannot be ascertained, it is said to be an unexplained fact. My cold feet are explained by the existence of a draught. But we cannot explain the universe in this way. If the universe could be said to have a cause, then either that cause is the effect of a prior cause, or it is not. Either the chain of causes extends back in an infinite series, or there is somewhere a " first cause " which is not the effect of any prior cause. If the series is infinite, then no final and ultimate explanation is to be found. If there is a first cause, then this first cause is itself an unexplained fact. If by explaining a thing we mean assigning a cause for it, then a first cause is by hypothesis unexplained and inexplicable, since we cannot assign any prior cause to it. To explain the universe by something which is itself an ultimate mystery is surely no explanation.

72. It would seem, then, that causation is a principle capable of explaining particular facts but incapable of explaining the universe as a whole. But when we look a little deeper, we find that causation is not really capable of explaining even particular facts. Cold solidifies water. Cold is the cause (or part of the cause); ice is the effect. But it is impossible to see why cold should cause solidification. The cause and the effect do not resemble each other in any way, nor can one see any connection between them. That cold solidifies water is an unexplained and mysterious fact which nobody could possibly foresee. For anything one could predict to the contrary, cold might just as well turn water into steam.

This difficulty is not due to our ignorance of intermediate causes. The cause A is followed by the effect B. No doubt between A, cold, and B, ice, there may be innumerable minute molecular or other changes, which occupy so infinitesimal a time that human faculties cannot apprehend them. But even if we knew all these intermediate causes and effects, the whole process would still be a mystery. Suppose the series then becomes A, A^1, A^2, A^3 ... B. Then the sequence A A^1 is just as inexplicable as the sequence A B. For A^1 is something different from A ; and the point is that it is impossible to see how one particular fact can produce an entirely different fact. Our difficulty is that we can see no reason why A should be followed by B. This is not solved by discovering intermediate causes, because it is just as difficult to see why A should be followed by A^1. It is not our insufficient knowledge of causes that is at fault. It is the principle of causation itself. Causation explains nothing.[1]

Popular thought invariably supposes that any philosophy which attempts to explain the universe must do so by means of the principle of causation, and in particular by the idea of a first cause. Thus idealism is popularly supposed to be the philosophy which asserts that the ultimate cause of all things is mind. Materialism is supposed to mean that the cause of everything is matter. Popular theology looks upon God as the cause of the universe. But what we have now shown is that this entire mode of explanation is futile. No matter whether we say that the first cause is matter, or is a personal God, or is mind, or is a vortex-atom, or an electrical force,— all such assertions must leave the universe an inexplicable mystery. If we became omniscient, if we knew not only the first cause but the entire subsequent series of causes and effects, we should still be no nearer understanding the universe. For in the first place our first cause would be an ultimate mystery, an inexplicable fact, and in the second place every subsequent sequence of cause and effect would be a fresh mystery. We must abandon this entire line of thought. We must look for some principle of explanation other than causation.

73. We return to our original question, what is explanation? And we may now frame it in the following way: what kind of knowledge about a thing would enable us no longer to regard it as a mystery? Let us speak of one of the greatest mysteries in the world, the mystery of evil. When we ask for an explanation of evil what is it that we want to know? We do not, it is evident, want to know the origin or cause of evil,— though it is true that the problem is often called the problem of the origin of evil. Suppose someone discovered that the existence of evil is caused by the presence of an unknown gas in the atmosphere. (That the supposition is an absurd one

---

[1] It may perhaps be objected that change is here treated as a series of discrete phenomena, whereas it is in reality a continuous flow. But even if we could formulate our conception of causation in terms of continuity, the argument of this section would not be affected. It would still be a mystery why one state of things should be followed by a different state of things.

does not affect our argument.) Suppose science isolated this gas, discovered its properties, and gained a full knowledge of the laws of its operation. Should we be in any way satisfied about the problem of evil? Would this be what we wanted to know? Evidently not. We should reply that, despite the discovery of its cause, evil still appears to us something incomprehensible and irrational. Evidently it is the apparent *irrationality* of evil that constitutes it a mystery. What we really want to know is how it is *reasonable* that evil should exist in the world. And this suggests to us that a genuine explanation of the universe would consist in showing that the universe is *rational*, in finding for the universe, not a *cause*, but a *reason*. It suggests that the first principle of the world is not a cause of which the world is the effect, but that it is a reason of which the world is the consequent. This is in accordance with the results which we reached through the consideration of Greek idealism, as will be seen by turning back to the ninth proposition there explicated (39).

74. If we compare the sequence of reason and consequent with the sequence of cause and effect we shall find that it does not possess the disadvantages which attach to the latter. We could not see why any particular cause should be followed by any particular effect. We could not see why cold should be followed by solidification. But this is just what is not true of a reason and consequent. We can see why the consequent follows the reason. The reason itself gives us the reason. In any train of valid reasoning the conclusion *must* follow from the premises, and we see why. Solidification follows cold. We cannot see why this *must* be so. There does not seem to be any *necessity* in it. Cold might just as well be followed by anything else. But a reason *must* be followed by its consequent. It is a logical necessity, and we understand this necessity. We could not *deduce* solidification from cold. The idea of cold does not involve the idea of solidification. But we do deduce the consequent from its reason. The idea of the reason does involve the idea of the consequent. That is what is meant by saying that *this* consequent follows from *that* reason.

If we could logically deduce the world from our first principle we should have explained the world. We know that the world is a fact, and we know that it is just this particular sort of world. What we want is to see why this *must* be so. If we could discover a first principle, and could prove that it follows by logical necessity from that first principle that there must be a world, and that it must be just the sort of world it is, then we should have an explanation. But this can only mean that our first principle must be a reason and that the world and all it contains must be its logical consequent. It means that we must be able to deduce the world logically from the first principle.[1]

75. It is of vital importance to understand that explanation involves the idea of logical necessity. It is just the apparent absence of necessity in the world which makes us complain that it is incomprehensible. Cold produces ice. This is a fact which simply *is*. We cannot see why it *must* be. It dogmatically asserts itself in the world, without giving any reason for itself. It *is* so, and that is an end of the matter. It is just because of this that we cannot understand it and call it a mystery. If, instead of being a mere fact, we could see that it is a logical necessity; if we could see the *reason* of it, and that it follows from that reason as necessarily as a logical consequent from its antecedent, then we should understand it. It would be explained. Thus a philosophy which would genuinely explain the world will take as its first principle, not a cause, but a reason. From this first reason it will proceed to deduce the world, not as an effect, but as a logical consequent. We shall then see not merely that things are as they are, but we shall see why they are as they are. This is the fundamental Hegelian idea of explanation. This is what Hegel's philosophy attempts to do. And it was for this that the Greeks, especially Aristotle, were groping, when they said that the first principle of the world is not prior to the world

---

[1] In this section and those which follow it is assumed that Hegel's transition from the Logic to nature is an attempted logical deduction—an assumption which is not undisputed. My reasons for taking this view will be given in the proper place; see below (419-22). For an expression of the opposite view see Macran, p. 84.

in time, *i.e.* as a cause is prior to its effect, but is *logically* prior to the world, *i.e.* as a logical antecedent is prior to its consequent.

B. *Reason as the Universal.*

76. The last section leaves us a legacy of two immediate and pressing problems. The first is to ascertain further what is meant by reason; for we have so far formulated only a vague conception of it. The second is to clear up the following difficulty. Assuming that we can find a first reason of the world, will it not involve the same disadvantage as the idea of a first cause? A first cause is an ultimate mystery because it is not the effect of a prior cause. Will not a first reason be an ultimate mystery because it is not the consequent of any prior reason, because, although it is the reason of the world, it is itself not accounted for by an earlier reason? The first of these problems will be dealt with in the present section, the second in the section which follows.

77. The universe consists of a multitude of individual things. These things may be material entities or they may be psychic entities, such as minds, ideas, feelings. But in either case they are individual things. Now the first principle of which we are in search cannot be itself an individual thing; for it is the reason of individual things. A first cause would itself be a thing. But a reason is not a thing. Suppose we were to say, as Plato did, that the reason of everything is the Good, that everything is as it is because it is good that it should be so. The Good, on such a view, is not a thing. Individual things are no doubt good. But goodness itself is not this or that individual good thing. In the same way the reason why a triangle is equiangular may be because it is equilateral. But equilateralness is not a thing which exists on its own account independently of triangles. Every individual thing exists in time or space. But reasons are not things floating about in space. They cannot be found by telescopes or microscopes. Nor do they exist in time as psychic entities in minds. If there were no minds in existence, equilateral triangles would still be

equiangular, and the *reason* of this would be just what it is now.

A reason is thus not a thing having a separate existence of its own. It is an abstraction. We speak of a thing and its reason as if they were separate. It is, however, only in thought that they are separate. The reason of a thing, apart from the thing itself, is an abstraction. Goodness is an abstraction from good things, equilateralness an abstraction from equilateral figures. And the first principle, or first reason, of the world, is not a thing that exists apart from the world. If we must in thought separate it from the world, then it is an abstraction. But an abstraction is a universal. Therefore reasons are universals. And the reason of the world is, in general, the universal. We have reached this result simply by considering what is involved in the process of explanation. And we see now that it is the same result as we reached by a different route in Greek philosophy. The first principle of the world, the Absolute, the source from which all things flow, is the universal. And the universal is to be regarded as the reason of the world, from which the world flows as a logical consequent, so that it ought to be possible actually to deduce the world from it.

78. Reason, it may be objected, is the process of arguing, not a mere collection of concepts or universals. But if we consider any actual argument, such as:

>All poppies are beautiful.
>Some poppies are red.
>Therefore, some red things are beautiful,

we see that it is nothing but a process of universals. "Poppy" is a concept; so is "red"; so is "beautiful." "All" and "some" are the categories of totality and plurality. "Are" is the concept of being, or perhaps of inclusion. And if, like the formal logician, we proceed to isolate the reasoning process from the subject matter to which it is applied and write the argument thus:

>All M is P.
>Some M is S.
>Therefore some S is P,

then the symbols M, S, and P, still represent concepts, but far more abstract concepts than before. Thus even from this point of view reason is a process of universals. This statement is not dependent upon what is known in logic as the doctrine of conceptualism. It is not denied that we are arguing about real things, poppies, red things, etc. It is not affirmed that we are merely reasoning about ideas. The reasoning process applies to things. But the reasoning process *itself*, which thus applies to things, is a process of ideas or universals. That reason, as thus regarded, is not merely a collection of motionless universals, but is a *process*, a movement of universals, by means of which we pass from one universal to another,—this is a very pregnant hint as regards Hegel. But it is a hint which we must leave undeveloped at the moment. For the present the only point is that the first reason of the world consists of universals, or is the universal. This is still, of course, exceedingly vague. But this vague principle will specify and define itself as we proceed.

C. *Reason as self-determined.*

79. Assuming that we could find the first reason of the world, would not this be, like a first cause, an ultimate mystery, a mere unexplained fact? That is the second problem with which we had to deal. Any first principle by means of which we seek to explain the universe must of necessity fulfil two conditions. Firstly, it must be capable of explaining the world. We must be able to see how of necessity the world arises out of it. This condition is fulfilled by the principle of a first reason, but not by the principle of a first cause. Granted a first cause, it could not explain the world, because it is impossible to see any necessary connection between a cause and its effect. But if the first principle be a reason, and if we can show that the world is its necessary consequence, then the explanation is so far good, because we do see a logically necessary connection between reason and consequent. The second condition which any first principle must fulfil is that it must explain itself. It must be a self-explanatory

principle. If it is unexplained, then it is an ultimate mystery. If it is explained by something other than itself, then it is not the first principle. For in that case the other something which explains it would itself be a prior and more ultimate principle of explanation. Therefore the first principle must be such that it is its own explanation. This is not the case with a first cause. A first cause would be an existent thing of which we should insistently demand a higher cause. But *reason is a self-explanatory principle*.

80. That the first principle must be self-explained was realised by Spinoza. Spinoza's first principle is substance, and he defines substance as " that which is in itself and is conceived through itself : that, the conception of which does not depend on the conception of another thing from which it must be formed." [1] He also describes substance as being *causa sui*, its own cause. The word cause is no doubt used in a wider sense than that in which we have used it here. For we have seen that the first principle cannot be regarded as a cause of any sort. But this is merely a matter of terminology. What Spinoza means is that substance is self-determined and self-explained. That which is determined by something other than itself cannot be understood, and so cannot be explained, except by reference to that other thing.

81. Now reason is the only possible self-explanatory principle. To understand this accurately is impossible until we have mastered the contents of the Hegelian Logic ; or, at least, until we are familiar with its main determinations. But meanwhile the following considerations, necessarily at this stage very general in character, will afford a preliminary insight into the matter. If anything else, other than reason, be given as the first principle of things, it is always possible for the mind to demand a higher principle. If we say that matter is the reason of the world, the question at once arises, what is the reason of matter ? But this is so simply because matter is not and cannot be a *reason*, though it may be a cause. Such a difficulty does not arise in the case of a genuine reason. For though it is quite sensible to ask the reason of

[1] Spinoza, *Ethics*, Definition 3.

matter, of evil, of this book, of that house, it is absurd to ask the reason of reason. The demand for an explanation of the world means, as has been shown, that we wish it proved to us, that the world is not a mere fact which *is* so, but that it is a logical necessity. We wish it shown that it does not merely assert itself dogmatically to consciousness as a fact, but that it is rational, that it flows from, and is the embodiment of, reason. We question the rationality of the world. If our question is answered, if the world is demonstrated to be rational, we cannot go on to question the rationality of reason. To ask that reason itself should be proved rational is to make a demand which has no meaning. If we could gain a conception of what pure reason in itself is, such a pure reason would necessarily be wholly rational. And nothing further can be asked. Reason is its own reason. It is, by its very conception, self-explanatory and self-determined.

82. It may be answered that though these remarks may be true of reason in general, they are not true of this or that particular reason. The distinction between reason and *a* reason is similar to that between causation and *a* cause. Cold is a cause; but cold is not causation. Equilateralness is a reason—a reason of various properties of a triangle—but it is not reason in general. And just as we may demand the cause of a cause, so we may ask to know the reason of a reason. A train of reasoning may consist of a series of propositions which we may call A, B, C, D, etc. C is the reason of which D is the consequent. But this reason C is itself the consequent of the prior reason B. So that we may ask to know the reason even of a reason which is set down as the first reason of the world,—just as we should demand the cause of a first cause.

These considerations show—and this is the answer to the objection—that the first reason of the world is not *a* reason, not this or that particular reason, but is reason itself, reason in general, the principle of reason. For it is only of rationality as such that we cannot demand a further reason. And we shall find in the Hegelian Logic that it is reason as a whole, the entire principle of rationality, which is given as the source and foundation of the world. But the detailed explanation of this must be postponed for the present.

D. Pure Thought.

83. If the first principle is reason, and reason consists of universals, the next question will be: does this reason comprise all universals, or only some? And if only some universals are included, on what principle are the others excluded? How are we to know which universals are the reason of the world and which are not?

Hegel found the answer to these questions implied in the philosophy of Kant, and it was at this point that Kant made possible an advance upon Plato. The first principle by means of which Plato sought to explain the universe was what he called the world of Ideas, or as we should call it, the system of universals. But he made no discrimination among universals. Any and every universal was included in his first principle. There was the Idea of the horse, the Idea of the table, the Idea of the chair, the Idea of the good, the Idea of redness, the Idea of dirt, and so *ad infinitum*. Every conceivable class of objects or relations had its Idea. And these Ideas were supposed to explain the existence of actual things. Thus chairs exist in the mundane world because there is the Idea of the chair in the world of Ideas. But how and why the Idea of the chair should give rise to the actual existence of chairs Plato was entirely unable to explain. Even if there is such an Idea we cannot see any necessity why it should produce actual chairs. And the same is true of the relations between the other Ideas and the individual things over which they preside.

84. Now Kant also had a theory of universals. His categories are universals. He did not, of course, regard these universals as objective in the way Plato conceived the Ideas to be objective. On the contrary, Kant insists that the categories are simply subjective concepts of the human mind. They are in no sense objectively real entities. Consequently, Kant did not attempt to use his categories as a first principle for the explanation of the world. They were not ontological

principles of being, but only epistemological principles of knowing. But his doctrine contained the pregnant hint that the categories form a special class of universals distinct from all other universals. They are non-sensuous and *a priori*, whereas all other universals, such as " red," " chair," " horse," are sensuous and *a posteriori*. These sensuous universals are obtained from experience. But the categories are prior to all experience because they are the conditions on which experience depends.

Hegel, in searching for a principle of explanation, adopted, like Plato, the belief that the first principle consists of objective universals. But he took from Kant the thought of a distinction between sensuous and non-sensuous universals. The latter are the categories or " pure " concepts—pure in the sense that they contain no sensuous admixture. The first principle of the world, the first reason of things, is for Hegel, not all universals as with Plato, but a system of pure non-sensuous universals.

85. It is not at first sight obvious how such a discrimination could help Hegel. But we can get a hint as regards this from the separation between things and thought which is effected by formal logic. In such an argument as

>All poppies are beautiful.
>Some poppies are red.
>Therefore, some red things are beautiful,

the entire reasoning involved here is preserved intact in the form :

>All M is P.
>Some M is S.
>Therefore, some S is P.

What is dropped out in this latter form is not any part of the reasoning process, every particle of which is retained, but only the element of sense. Now we are in search of a principle which shall be the reason of things. But the principle that reason is the explanation of things obviously involves the separation of the things from the reason. If reason is to explain things we must not have in the reason any of the things which are to be explained. For it is useless to adduce as explanation of a thing that very thing itself. We must therefore have reason as it is in itself, pure reason. We must get wholly rid of the sensuous element, for the sensuous element is just the element of " things," the things which we have to explain.

Formal logic does to some extent bring about such a separation. It abstracts altogether from the things about which we reason. It excludes the sensuous element—redness, poppies, and the like—and retains only the pure process of the reason itself. Hence if we find that any concepts are involved in the use of the formal syllogism, such concepts will be pure concepts, and are more likely to form part of the pure reason of which we are in search than concepts involved in the material syllogism. But the concepts involved in the formal syllogism are just the Kantian categories, " all," " some," " are," or totality, plurality, existence, and so on.

86. But this yields us only a glimmering of the truth which Hegel saw. That which explains the world must be before the world. It must be prior to the world. For it is a *first* principle. But is this firstness a time-priority or a logical priority? That it is not a time-priority became evident in our discussion of Greek idealism. The ninth proposition (39) in which we summed up the results there attained stated: " This first principle is first only in the sense that it holds logical priority over all things. It is not first in order of time." What is first in order of time would be a cause. It is the causal sequence which is a time-sequence. A first principle which was before the world in time would have to be regarded as the cause of the world. But our principle is not a first cause. It is a reason. It is the reason of which the world is the consequent. And a reason is not before its consequent in order of time. Its priority is a logical priority.

Now the Kantian categories are prior to the world in just this sense. It is true that Kant would not have used such a phrase as that the categories are " prior to the world." What he said was that the categories are prior to *experience*. But experience *is* the world. Experience was the term Kant used because he looked at everything from a subjective and epistemological point of view. But what is, subjectively, our experience, is, objectively considered, the world. For the Kantian term " experience " means all possible experience, whether it be experience of outward objects in space or experience of inward objects such as feelings and thoughts. It thus includes all possible objects in space, and all possible psychic entities. Experience, therefore, is coterminous with the universe.

87. The Kantian categories, then, are prior to the world. Moreover, they include only pure universals. Sensuous universals, such as " chair," " horse," " white," are not prior to the world. For non-sensuous universals are universal and necessary and are, therefore, the conditions of experience, but sensuous universals are not so. It would be impossible to have experience, *i.e.* to have a world, without these pure universals. That is what is meant by saying that they are necessary. But it would be quite possible to have a world without these sensuous universals. Take, for example, the concept " white." It is quite easy to imagine a world in which there should be no white things. Or again, it is quite easy to picture a universe in which such concepts as " chair," " horse," have no application. But this is not the case with such concepts as " unity," " plurality," " existence," " non-existence," " substance." A world without unity is inconceivable. Any conceivable world must itself be one world. And it must contain objects each of which is one object. " Many," again, is just as much a necessary attribute of any conceivable world as " one." The same applies to totality, affirmation, negation, existence. It is impossible to think of a world of which nothing could be affirmed or denied, in which we could not say " is " and " is not " about things.

88. Categories, then, constitute just the kind of first principle of explanation of which we are in search. The categories must be the reason of which the world is the consequent, and if we can show this in detail we shall have therein an explanation of the universe. But it will be seen that this imposes upon the categories a duty which we have not as yet

seen any reason to suppose them capable of performing. We have proved that the categories are the logical condition of the world. But though we can argue back from a fact to its logical conditions, we cannot always reverse the process and argue forward from the conditions to the fact. In this respect logical conditions resemble causal conditions. If it rains we can argue that there must be clouds in the sky, because clouds are a necessary causal condition of rain. But we cannot argue that because there are clouds there must be rain, for clouds often appear when there is no rain. In just the same way, it would seem, though we have proved that the categories are a necessary condition of the world, it does not follow that the world is a necessary consequent of the categories. But to prove this is essential if we are genuinely to explain the world. A real explanation must show that, granted our first principle, the world necessarily follows. And since the first principle is related to the world, not as cause to effect, but as reason to consequent, this means that the world must be logically *deduced* from the categories just as a conclusion is deduced from its premises. We cannot at present see how this is to be done. Suppose we grant that the categories are ontological realities which are prior to the world. Why, it may be asked, should they produce a world? How does the world *follow* from the categories? Why should they not remain in themselves what they are for all eternity without any world arising? We were unable to see that, even if we granted the reality of Plato's Idea of the chair, this in any way explains the actual existence of particular chairs. And we are now unable to see that, even granted the reality and priority of categories, this explains the existence of things. To answer these questions we must demonstrate that the categories necessarily give rise to a world, that they are a reason from which the world follows as consequent; and we can only do this by deducing the world logically from the categories.

Now in carrying out this task Hegel found that he could get no help at all from Kant. Explanation here involves two conditions. Kant gave him one. He had to discover the other for himself. The first condition is that the categories must be the logical conditions of the world. Kant showed that they are so. The second condition is that the world must be deducible from the categories as their logical consequent. To show how this is possible was the special discovery of Hegel, the secret of his dialectic method. We cannot at this stage give any indications of how Hegel solved this problem. We shall take up that point at a later stage, turning our attention meanwhile to other considerations.

89. There are several ways in which a beginner's mind is liable to serious confusion and mistake as regards the reality of an alleged sphere of pure thought, or pure non-sensuous universals. The chief difficulty is that the unsophisticated mind always insists upon regarding the assertion of their ontological reality as equivalent to an assertion of their *existence*. When it is said that the first principle of the world, the Absolute, is a system of categories,—a whole train of popular but erroneous ideas is apt to spring up in the mind. This system of categories is the first principle; it is that which was "before all the worlds," and the world is its creation. Hence, it is thought, the categories must have been in existence billions of years ago, before the universe was made. But how is this possible? *Where* were the categories? Where are they now? Are they hidden in the remote spaces beyond the stars? No, for this would involve that they are material things. Does this mean, then, that they are non-material things, psychic entities, souls or spirits? Do they constitute a sort of soul of the world? And then, if they existed before the world was made, how can we conceive this? How, for example, could the category of "cause" exist all alone by itself without any actual causes and effects? How can "unity" exist without being a unity of something? What do we mean by "one" existing before the world, before there was one horse, or one man, or one planet, or one anything else?

Now if Hegelianism is thus interpreted it naturally gets regarded as mere learned gibberish, which is not the less gibberish because it is learned. But Hegel does not teach any of these absurdities. No one, indeed, can say where the categories are for the simple reason that they are nowhere. They are not " things " which existed before the world began. They are neither material nor psychic things. They do not exist, never have existed, and never will exist. They are pure abstractions. Nevertheless they are *real*. This means that their being is independent, whereas the being of " things " is dependent upon them. Things are dependent upon them because, as Kant showed, they are the necessary conditions of the world. The world could have no existence without them. Its being is dependent upon theirs. But they depend for their being only upon themselves. This last statement can only be proved in detail by the whole argument of the Hegelian Logic. But in a general way we have already seen that the system of categories constitutes reason, and that reason is its own reason, is self-explained and self-determined. And this means that it is dependent only upon itself. And this in turn means that it is real.

90. As for the other difficulty, that it is impossible to conceive of unity which is not the unity of something, of " one " by itself apart from one man, one horse, or one object of some kind,—this difficulty is based upon the same misapprehension as the last. What it means is that it is impossible to conceive of " one " *existing* apart from one thing. And this is perfectly true. But Hegel never supposed that the unity can *exist* apart from that of which it is the unity. The separation between them is only a *logical* separation, a separation in thought. The category of quantity cannot exist by itself. There must be a quantity of butter, of manure, of iron, or of something else. The quantity and the butter cannot be separated *in fact*. We cannot put the quantity in one pocket and the butter in another. But they can be separated *in thought*. We can abstract from the butter, the iron, or the manure. The thought of butter is logically separable from the thought of quantity, simply because it is a different thought. The thought of quantity is not the same as the thought of butter. That is all that is meant.

91. It is only another form of the same confusion when it is objected to Hegel, on psychological grounds, that concepts

as mental processes are subsequent to perceptions, and come after the consciousness of individual objects. This, it is supposed, constitutes a fatal objection to the Hegelian doctrine that universals, the categories, are prior to experience and to the world. Now, no one, least of all Hegel, would ever dream of denying the psychological fact that the consciousness of particular things comes earlier than the consciousness of universals. Hegel is quite aware of this fact, although, as a rule, he considers it too obvious even to be worth stating. But it is quite irrelevant to our point, which is that the categories are prior to sense-perceptions, not in time but in logical order of thought. No doubt we, as individual subjects, get to know about causation by studying the world around us, and in this sense the concept of causation, or any other concept, is posterior to perception and is derived from experience. But what we come to know last is logically first, just as we often learn a fact before we know the reasons for it. Animals and infants may not have the idea of unity. Children learn it only by coming into contact with things, only from experience. Not till we have seen one horse, one cow, one tree, do we form the idea of one. But although we only became conscious of this idea late in our mental experience, yet it was implicitly present in our crude sensations and perceptions from the first. Those perceptions would have been impossible without it, and it is, therefore, the condition of the perceptions, and has logical priority over them. It is just the same with Hegel's categories as it was with Kant's space and time. We saw that Kant's assertion that space and time are forms of our intuition which are prior to all experience was not invalidated by, and has nothing to do with, the psychologist's analysis of the way in which we become aware of space and time through experience. Space and time are logically prior to experience, because they are the conditions of it. This does not mean that we become aware of space and time before we have any experience. It is the same with the categories.

This psychological confusion is the brother of the popular confusion previously discussed. The questions how we are to conceive of the categories existing before the world and apart from actual things arose from supposing that Hegel believed the categories to be objective existences. The present confusion arises from supposing that he regards them as subjective existences, *i.e.* as subjective concepts existing in minds. Subjective concepts come to exist in the mind late in its development. But categories, as objective *realities*, are prior to all subjective minds and to the world.

92. Another psychological misunderstanding consists in saying that pure non-sensuous thought is an impossibility. There is, it is said, no such thing. We cannot completely separate the non-sensuous form from its sensuous filling. Every thought is accompanied by images and we cannot have the thought without the sensuous images. Now, even regarded as psychology, this statement is very doubtful. Psychologists now, apparently, believe that concepts entirely without images are possible.[1] But whether this is so or not the whole matter is entirely irrelevant to our present enquiry. When we say that pure thought is the first principle and foundation of the world, there is no question of what *we* can or cannot think, but only of what objectively *is*. It may be a fact that, by reason of association, I cannot think of an east wind without at the same time thinking of a cold in the head. It may be a fact that I cannot think of quantity, cause, unity, and the like, without some vague image floating before my mind. But the east wind *is*, quite independently of the cold in the head. And the category is, quite independently of my images. The thought of quantity is *logically* separate and distinct from the thought of any sensuous object. It is quite irrelevant whether the two thoughts are *psychologically* separate or not. The present psychological objection is based, like the others, on the confusion in the popular mind between reality and existence. For this objection merely asserts that subjective concepts cannot *exist* in minds without some kind of sensuous attachment. But what we have contended is, not that pure universals can exist apart from a sensuous

[1] See, for example, Aveling's *Consciousness of the Universal and the Individual*.

filling, either objectively in the external world, or subjectively in minds, but only that the categories are *logically* separable from any such sensuous matter.

93. It must be admitted, however, that the inability to think purely, to think without an accompaniment of pictorial images, is a grave impediment to the understanding of philosophy, especially the philosophy of Hegel. It is this pictorial thinking which is the cause of most of the confusions we are trying to clear up. If Hegel makes a statement about a category, the reader is apt to think of it as, or in close association with, an image. Then the image gets mistaken for the category. And since every image is sensuous in character, since every image is an image of something as existing in time or space, the result is that the category too is taken for an existence. It must have been just such a mental confusion which led Parmenides to picture Being as globe-shaped. He must have substituted an image for the pure thought, and as every image must have some shape or outline, he began to ask himself what shape Being has. In just the same way it must have been the habit of pictorial thought which led Plato into supposing that the Ideas exist as things in some other world beyond this. And it is pictorial thinking again which prevents people from understanding such assertions of Hegel as that " being " is identical with " nothing." Hegel is here speaking of the pure categories, being and nothing. And so long as this is kept in mind the statement is perfectly intelligible. But immediately images obtrude themselves, being is mistaken for the particular being of some individual object such as this house. Then people ask incredulously whether it is the same thing for this house to be and not to be. And so the statement is turned into an absurdity. If we are to understand Hegel we must learn to think in the abstract, to move freely among pure thoughts, and to keep sensuous images out of our minds, or at least not to mistake them for pure thoughts.

E. Knowing and Being.

94. The categories began their history, so far as modern philosophy is concerned, in the system of Kant, where they

appeared as subjective mental processes, concepts. In Hegel they get transformed into objective ontological entities, having a being independent of any particular mind. How has this come about? What grounds are there for regarding them in this new way? Now we have seen that Kant's own assertion that the categories are prior to all experience really implies this, since what is prior to experience is prior to the world, and prior, therefore, to any particular mind. But we shall have to look more profoundly into this transformation of subjective concept into ontological reality. For it is the crux of all idealism.

95. In the first place, Hegel had exactly the same grounds for asserting the objectivity of categories as Plato had for asserting the same of universals in general. Any existing object, say a stone, turns out on analysis to be nothing but a congeries of universals. There is nothing there except the whiteness, roundness, hardness, etc. All these elements of the stone are universals. Therefore to deny the objectivity of the universals is to deny the objectivity of the stone. It may be objected that this proves too much. It proves, if anything, not merely that categories, *i.e.* non-sensuous universals, are objective, but that all universals including such purely sensuous universals as "chair," "house," etc., are objective. This, it seems, would contradict Hegel in favour of Plato. Moreover, the stone is objective in the sense of existing. And the argument that universals are objective because the stone is objective would seem to mean that, because the stone exists, the universals must exist; whereas our whole point is that categories have reality but not existence.

The reply to the latter objection is that it is the stone which exists, not the universals of which it is composed. The congeries of universals exist, because, taken together, the universals constitute an individual. But each universal, taken separately, is a mere abstraction, not an individual, and therefore does not exist. Turning to the former objection, namely, that our argument would prove the objectivity of all universals and not merely of categories, we see that the difficulty lies in the following point. We have asserted that the categories are real but do not exist. Now our argument tends to show that even sensuous universals are objective. But sensuous universals do not exist. Hence, apparently, the only kind of objectivity which we can attribute to them is reality. And in that case what difference is there between categories and sensuous universals? And if sensuous universals are real, this implies that they constitute part of the first principle of the world, and that Hegel was wrong and Plato right as regards the nature of the ultimate reality. Now this problem, it must be confessed, is never directly faced in the writings of Hegel. And we shall see in a later chapter that it is connected with the greatest difficulty of the Hegelian philosophy, the transition from Logic to Nature. We may, however, even at this point, develop our own solution. All universals, we would say, have objective being, but categories have an *independent* objective being while sensuous universals have only a *dependent* objective being. For the categories are the logical conditions of all experience, of all consciousness, and therefore of that part of consciousness which consists in sensuous universals. This means that in logical order the categories come first, and that it ought to be possible to deduce sensuous universals from the categories as their logical consequents. And we shall, in the right place, argue that this is what Hegel was actually trying to do in his philosophy of nature, though he himself perhaps imperfectly realized the fact. Meanwhile we may note that, if this be the true view, it involves the recognition of three distinct kinds of being. The categories have independent being and absolute logical priority. This is *reality*. Sensuous universals have dependent being which is yet not existence since they are universal and not individual. This may be called *subsistence*. Lastly, individual objects have *existence*.

96. But the ultimate foundation of the belief in the objectivity of universals consists in what is sometimes called the identity of knowing and being. The word being is used somewhat loosely here to mean external being—the object of consciousness in general as opposed to the subject. The

phrase means that the subject (the side of knowing), and the object (the side of being), are identical. Subject and object are not two independent realities external to one another. They do not face each other as two absolutely different entities. They are identical because they are but two different aspects of one reality. And the ground for this assertion is that, if we do not accept it, the problem of how knowledge is possible appears to be insoluble.

All knowledge is conceptual. We know nothing of any object except through the concepts which we apply to it. Every word in language stands for a concept, and any kind of thought without concepts is an impossibility. Now from this we have inferred that the object itself *is* no more than a congeries of universals, and therefore that universals are objective. But at this point common sense supposes that it scents a fallacy. Doubtless, says common sense, *we* can only think an object by means of concepts. But that is merely due to the construction of our minds. It does not imply anything as to the nature of the object as it exists in itself outside our minds. We think of the thing in concepts. But the thing itself may be something quite different.

97. Now it will be seen at once that this rests upon the supposition that there exists a thing in itself, outside our minds, a thing which may be totally different from the thing as it appears to us. This objection is, in fact, nothing but the old Kantian theory of the unknowable thing-in-itself, championed now by common sense. If the thing itself is something quite different from the thing as it appears to us, if it is something different from what our thought and the construction of our minds makes of it, then it is unknowable. And we have seen that this theory is self-contradictory. So we are driven back to our conclusion that the object is relative to the subject, and this implies the objectivity of universals. If the object is something quite different from that which thought makes of it, then subject and object, knowing and being, are two incommensurable opposite realities, facing each other, cut off from each other by an impassable chasm. The object is unknowable. Knowledge is impossible. We hold, there-

fore, that the object itself *is* precisely what thought makes of it. This is the identity of knowing and being.

98. To repudiate the superstition of the unknowable thing-in-itself is to establish the principle of the identity of knowing and being. Being *means* being *for* consciousness. And there is no being other than being for consciousness. An object is not an object unless it stands in relation to a subject. The universe is nothing but the content of consciousness. If we deny these truths we land ourselves in the quagmire of contradictions connected with the theory of the unknowable. But if we admit them we are bound to admit also the objectivity of concepts or universals. For then the object *is* wholly and solely the object as we know it. And we know it only as a congeries of universals. And if we accept this view we are committed to an objective idealism.

The identity of knowing and being is, in fact, the basic principle of all idealism. The philosophies of Plato and Aristotle depend absolutely upon it. But whereas the Greeks naïvely assumed it as a matter of course, for Hegel it has become a consciously formulated part of philosophy.

99. But if subject and object are identical, they are also distinct. It is certain that, in some sense or other, the object stands over against me. It is the not-self. That knowing and being are identical and yet distinct is, in fact, an example of the famous Hegelian principle of the identity of opposites. We have not yet explained that principle. Consequently, the exact relations between knowing and being cannot as yet be fully expounded.[1] But we may say at once that their identity is compatible with their difference. That the *thing* is identical with the *thought*,—this means that there is no absolute separation between subject and object, for the object is *within* the subject. That the thing is *different* from the thought,—this means that the subject expels part of itself, viz. the object, from itself, and opposes itself to it. This stone is certainly external to me. It is not-me. This is the separation of knowing and being. But the stone is still *within* the unity of

[1] The complete solution will be found in the *Logic*. See below (§§ 382 to 387).

thought. It is not external to me in the sense that it is something utterly *outside* thought, unknowable. This is the identity of knowing and being. And the same thing is sometimes expressed by Hegel by saying that thought over-reaches the gulf between itself and its object,—or that the separation between thought and thing is a separation *within* thought itself. If the thing could break away completely from the unity of thought, it would become an unknowable thing-in-itself. And that is impossible.

100. To keep the identity of knowing and being firmly before our minds will often assist us to understand passages in Hegel which would otherwise appear very puzzling. For example, the reader who comes to Hegel with the fixed idea that materialism and idealism are irreconcileable opposites will be astonished to find that Hegel regards materialism as itself a crude kind of idealism and seeks to show that it is possible to develop his own idealistic views out of it. Here, for example, is such a passage: " All philosophy is essentially idealism, or at least possesses it as its principle, and the question is only how far it has carried out the principle. . . . The principles of the ancient or modern philosophies, water,[1] or matter, or atoms, are *thoughts*, universals, . . . not things."[2] To say that the atom is really a thought, and therefore that the materialism of Democritus is a form of idealism, appears strange to our ordinary modes of thought. The key to the difficulty is the identity of knowing and being. Hegel quite recognizes the distinction between materialism and idealism, but what he contends is that if Democritus had understood the identity of knowing and being he would have been forced beyond materialism into some kind of idealism. For *materialism really depends upon the complete separation of knowledge and its object*, and this is its fundamental fallacy. It supposes that the object, matter, is something absolute, which *is* on its own account, quite independent of mind. It believes that the object can have being apart from the knowing subject. Atomism alleges that this *thing*, the atom, is the ultimate

---

[1] The reference, of course, is to Thales.
[2] *Greater Logic*, first section, chapter ii., final ' remark.'

reality. Let it be so. But what is this thing? It is nothing but a congeries of universals, such perhaps as " indestructible," " indivisible," " small," " round," etc. All these are universals, or thoughts. " Atom " itself is a concept. Hence even out of this materialism proceeds idealism.

101. Another source of perplexity in Hegel is the fact that he claims to have incorporated all previous philosophies into his system by merely including in his list of categories the names of the most important conceptions of earlier philosophers. Thus being and substance appear among the Hegelian categories. Now being was the most important conception in the philosophy of Parmenides. By merely inserting the category of being in the *Logic* Hegel claims to have embodied in his system the philosophy of the Eleatics. And by including substance among his categories he claims to have appropriated the central truth of Spinoza. Now to this procedure the tyro in Hegel will almost certainly raise some such objection as the following. The Hegelian Absolute is a system of categories, or thoughts. But the Absolute of Spinoza is not of the nature of thought at all. Spinoza did not say that the Absolute is the *thought* of substance, the category of substance. He said that the Absolute is substance itself. He was not an idealist but a pantheist. He did not believe that the Absolute is a system of categories, nor that it is a single category, such as that of substance. Hegel regards the Absolute as thought. Spinoza regards it as something quite different from thought, namely substance. And Spinoza expressly declared that substance is not thought, for he said that thought is merely one of the attributes of substance. Thus Hegel's assertion that the category of substance is one of the categories which constitute the Absolute is a position totally different from Spinoza's position, and therefore Hegel had no right to identify the two positions or to maintain that he had incorporated Spinoza.

The key to the difficulty is the principle of the identity of knowing and being. Spinoza no doubt supposed that substance itself is something quite different from the thought, or category, of substance. But, understanding the principle of the identity of knowing and being, we see that this *thing*, substance, is nothing else than the universal, the category. Spinoza did not realize this because he was affected by the modern idea that there is an absolute separation between things and thoughts. This idea was originated by Descartes and dominates modern philosophy until it culminates in Kant, whose philosophy is nothing else than the *reductio ad absurdum* of it. The truth is that substance is a universal, as should be obvious from the fact that it is an abstraction. It abstracts from all attributes. Substance itself and the thought of substance are one and the same thing.

102. Exactly the same difficulty may be illustrated by the following passage from Hegel : " Being itself," he says, " and the special sub-categories of it, as well as those of Logic in general, may be looked upon as definitions of the Absolute." [1] The categories, then, are *definitions* of the Absolute. Does this mean that the categories themselves *are* the Absolute, or does it mean that they are descriptions or definitions of something else which is the Absolute? This is the kind of question which puzzles a reader who has not yet grasped the central Hegelian idea. The answer is that it makes no difference whether we say that the categories are the Absolute, or whether we say that they are definitions of the Absolute. The two statements mean exactly the same thing. This difficulty, as well as that about Spinoza's substance, arises from an erroneous view of the nature of knowledge. It is supposed that we have concepts in our mind, and that outside our mind there is some sort of a "thing," and that the concept in some way fits on to the thing, and that this fitting of the concept to the thing is knowledge. There is the category of substance on the one hand, and there is the substance itself on the other. And the category " applies to " this external thing, the substance. Or there are the categories on the one side, and there is a thing called the Absolute on the other, and if these categories correctly fit on to that thing, then they are good definitions of the Absolute. Now this whole point of view has to

[1] Wal., *Log.*, § 85.

be scrapped. It depends upon the theory that there is a
"thing" outside the mind, something quite different from the
concepts of the mind itself. It depends upon the theory of
the thing-in-itself, which is perpetually cropping up, in new
forms, even after it has been exploded in the form which
Kant gave to it. It depends, again, upon the theory of the
absolute separation of subject and object, upon the denial
of the principle of the identity of knowing and being.
The categories are definitions, concepts, or thoughts, of the
Absolute. But the definition and that which it defines, the
category and the Absolute itself, are one and the same thing.
The stone is not an external thing-in-itself to which the
universals "white," "round," "hard," etc., are applied. The
stone *is* the universals. And the Absolute is not a mysterious
something to which the categories, being, substance, cause,
etc., apply. The Absolute *is* the categories. Yet there is
also distinction at the same time as identity. "Whiteness,"
"roundness," "hardness," looked at from the subjective
point of view are *our* concepts, part of our consciousness,
part of the subject. Looked at objectively, they are
objective universals, part of the object. And the categories,
too, are, on the one hand, *our* mental forms, while on the
other hand they are objective entities, and as such are the
Absolute.

103. Failure to understand these principles is almost universal, not only among students and beginners, but even among philosophical writers of the highest repute. It explains, for example, the common complaint against Hegel that his Absolute is nothing but a collection of empty abstractions. Mr. Bradley criticises the Hegelian Absolute as no more than an "unearthly ballet of bloodless categories." If Hegel, instead of saying that the Absolute *is* the categories, had said that the Absolute is some kind of solid *thing*, and that the categories *apply* to it, these critics, it seems, would have raised no clamour. Hegel said that the Absolute is the categories, cause, substance, being, quality, etc. At this the critics are furious. But had he said that the Absolute is something which is a cause, is a substance, has being, has

quality, etc., they would have been silent. They would have imagined that this was to conceive the Absolute, not as a mere abstraction or collection of abstractions, but as something solid, real, and substantial. Yet the first statement, to which the critics object, and the second to which they agree, are identical in meaning. The Hegelian may be asked whether, in his view, the Absolute is the category of substance or substance itself, whether it is the category of quality, or something which has quality, whether it is the category of being, or something which *is*. His reply must be that these distinctions are illegitimate. Substance itself *is* the category of substance, just as the stone *is* the universals " white," " round," " hard," etc. If the critic so desires, the Hegelian will quite admit that the Absolute is substance itself, etc., but he will add the proviso that though this formula, properly understood, is unobjectionable, it is highly objectionable and must be repudiated if it is a cloak under which lurks the thought that there is a mysterious thing-in-itself, outside thought, to which the categories of substance, cause, etc., merely apply in an external fashion.

F. *Monism and the Deduction of the Categories.*

104. Explanation necessarily means monism. A tendency towards monism has always been evident in philosophy. But the philosophical basis of monism was first definitely enunciated by Spinoza. Spinoza saw that the first principle of the universe must be a single principle, and that this principle must be a unity. For the ultimate reality is only real in virtue of the fact that it is dependent on nothing outside itself. To be thus self-dependent is to be self-determined. And what is self-determined must be a unity. For if there be two ultimate realities, the one is limited, and therefore determined, by the other. And in that case neither is self-determined.

105. This is the philosophical basis of monism. But even in popular attempts at explanation the monistic principle is always a guiding idea. It appears in religion in the form of

monotheism, and it appears even in empirical science. Facts are explained by causes; this means that a multitude of particulars are subsumed under a single law. And the laws are in turn explained by being subsumed under more general laws. Such a process of explanation would find its goal only in the reduction of everything in the universe to a single principle.

106. But if monism is a necessity of thought, the history of philosophy has shown that an absolute or abstract monism defeats its own end. The Absolute must be one; but it must also be many. To exclude the many altogether from our conception of it is to cut off all possibility of deriving the manifoldness of the actual world from it. The many can only issue from the one if, in some sense or other, the many is already present in the one. From the Eleatic abstract one there is no passage to the actual world. Nor is there from the one of the Neo-Platonists. And the philosophy of Spinoza is itself an example of a system ending in absolute dualism because it attempts to establish an absolute and abstract monism. The substance of Spinoza is a unity utterly excludent of all multiplicity. Hence it is quite impossible to see how substance can give rise to its many attributes, namely, thought, extension, and the rest.

107. That the Absolute must be a many in one was dimly seen by Plato. In the *Parmenides* he showed that the notion of the one and the notion of the many involve each other so that the one without the many is unthinkable. And his own Absolute, the world of Ideas, is a many in one. It is many because it contains many Ideas. It is one because these Ideas constitute a single organized system of Ideas under the final unity of the Idea of the Good. Just as all white things are subsumed under the Idea of whiteness, so a number of Ideas, such as whiteness, redness, blueness, are subsumed under a higher Idea, that of colour. Colour, again, taste, and so on, would presumably be subsumed under the Idea of quality. Ultimately we should in this way reach one supreme Idea, under which all other Ideas whatever are subsumed. And, according to Plato this supreme Idea is the Idea of the Good.

108. Now suppose we represent a fragment of Plato's system by some such diagram as this:—

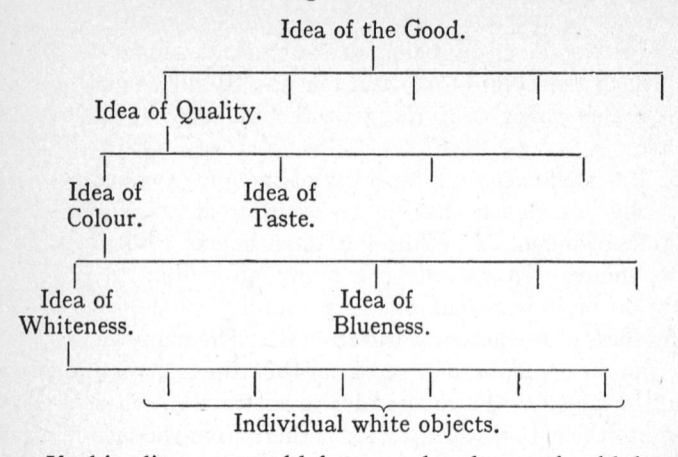

```
                    Idea of the Good.
        ┌──────┬─────────┼─────────┬──────┐
        Idea of Quality.
    ┌─────┬──────┼──────┬──────┐
    Idea of      Idea of
    Colour.      Taste.
    ┌────────────┼──────┬──────┐
    Idea of              Idea of
    Whiteness.           Blueness.
    ┌────┬────┬────┬────┬────┐
         Individual white objects.
```

If this diagram could be completed, we should have all individual objects, *i.e.* the entire universe, at the bottom, and all the Ideas would appear in their proper places above. And the question we have now to ask ourselves is, how would such a system, even if satisfactorily completed, explain the universe? Why, for example, do white objects exist? They exist, according to Plato, because there is an Idea of whiteness in the world of Ideas. The Idea of whiteness produces white things. Now, assuming for a moment that the Idea of whiteness does thus satisfactorily explain the existence of white things, still the Idea of whiteness is itself unexplained. Why is there an Idea of whiteness? Because, apparently, there is an Idea of colour. Then why is there an Idea of colour? Because there is an Idea of quality. Why an Idea of quality? Because there is an Idea of the Good. Why an Idea of the Good? Here we come to a stop. There is no higher Idea to explain the Idea of the Good, and it is, therefore, unexplained. It is a dogmatic fact, an ultimate mystery.

109. But apart from the fact that the supreme Idea is a mere unexplained fact, it is clear that the Idea of whiteness does not really explain the existence of white objects, the Idea of colour does not explain the Idea of whiteness, nor is any

other step in the explanation genuinely satisfactory. Even granting that there is an Idea of whiteness we cannot see how it explains the existence of white objects. Their existence does not follow as a logical necessity from the Idea of whiteness. If we could see that, granted the Idea of whiteness, there *must* be white things, if we could *deduce* the white things from their Idea, then only should we have an explanation. In just the same way we ought to be able to deduce the Idea of whiteness from the Idea of colour, that from the Idea of quality, and that again from the Idea of the Good. Finally, it ought to be possible to deduce all the lower Ideas from the supreme Idea of the Good.

Even this would leave the Idea of the Good an ultimate mystery. To complete the explanation we must show that the Idea of the Good, since it cannot be explained by anything higher than itself, is self-explanatory, *i.e.* self-determined. Or, in the alternative, we might show, not that the Idea of the Good is self-determined, but that the entire world of Ideas, considered as a totality, is such a self-determined whole that it constitutes a satisfactory first principle, or first reason, of the world. In this case, what we require to prove is, that every separate Idea logically involves every other separate Idea, and that the world of Ideas as a whole is an organic, self-explained, self-determined, unity, and finally that the actual world of objects follows by logical deduction from this self-determined unity. Such a system would meet the requirement of a concrete monism. Its Absolute, its first principle, would be a many in one. As a self-contained, self-determined, totality, it would be one. As a multiplicity of Ideas it would be many.

110. Hegel's *Logic* contains just such an attempt. Instead of Plato's Ideas, which included even sensuous universals, we now have categories. But these Hegelian categories constitute no mere aggregate or miscellaneous heap of universals like Plato's world of Ideas. Hegel *deduces* the categories from one another. Just as Plato should have shown that the Idea of colour can be logically deduced from the Idea of quality, so now Hegel proves that the category of cause can be deduced

from the category of substance. He shows that every single category necessarily and logically involves every other single category. Kant had named twelve categories. But he made no effectual attempt to deduce them from one another. There was no reason why he should do so, because the categories were for him not an ontological principle of explanation of the universe, but merely subjective epistemological forms of our minds. But the fact remains that he did not deduce them. He merely threw down the twelve categories as so many unexplained facts. A man has twelve categories in his mind just as he has ten toes on his feet. That is fact; and that is the end of the matter,—as far as Kant is concerned.

Such dogmatism was quite sufficient for Kant because he only aimed at analyzing the human mind. If he could state the facts correctly, his object was attained. But as soon as the categories are converted from subjective concepts into objective realities which are to constitute the first principle of the world, the case is entirely altered. It will not do to name twelve categories and to say that they constitute the first principle. For in that case we have not one first principle, but twelve first principles. And monism forbids this. Our first principle is to be many in one. It will be many, because it contains many categories. And it can only be shown to be also one by fusing these many categories into a single rationally articulated organic whole, each part of which runs on continuously into, *i.e.* logically leads to, every other part. If the categories are, as with Kant, simply isolated units, then they are a mere multiplicity without unity. But if each category logically involves every other, then they cannot be regarded as separate units, but they cling together and form a single indivisible organic system of categories, a genuine unity.

111. It is but saying the same thing when we add that, if the categories are to be the first *reason* of the world, they must themselves be shown to be *rational*. Charity begins at home. And reason must begin by setting its own house in order. If we say that reason is the first principle of the world, and if we hope to deduce the world from it, we must surely begin by

giving a rational account of reason itself. And to say that reason is constituted by twelve categories, by twelve undeduced and unexplained facts, is to give a very irrational account of it. We may say, like Kant, that there *is* a category of causation, that this is a fact, and that there is no more to be said about it. But in such case the category is merely an ultimate mystery. It dogmatically asserts itself without giving any reason for itself. It is irrational. But we propose to deduce the category of cause from that of substance, that of substance from some prior category, and so on. Our categories will then be no longer irrational facts. We shall in that way show the logical necessity of them. We shall show, not merely that there *is* the category of cause, but that there *must* be such a category. And to show its logical necessity is to explain it, to show its rationality.

112. The task which Hegel undertakes in the *Logic* is, therefore, this: to give an account of the first reason of the world; to show of what categories it is composed; to complete the list of these categories, for Hegel believed that there are many more besides the twelve of Kant; not to leave them isolated, standing by themselves, but logically to deduce one from another; and finally to show that all the categories, regarded as a single whole, constitute a self-explained, self-determined, unity, such that it is capable of constituting the absolutely *first* principle of the world, of which, because it is self-explained, we do not need to seek a yet earlier and prior principle of explanation. The *Logic* is necessarily the first part of the system because it gives an account of the first principle of the world. When we have reached a complete account of this first reason of the universe, the next step will be to deduce the existence of the actual universe from it, to show that it is the reason of which the universe is the consequent. The attempt to do this constitutes the second and third parts of the system of Hegel.

113. Plato, of course, had no idea of deducing the lower Ideas from the Idea of the Good. He did not perceive the necessity of this. But it will be of inestimable value to us to

note that, even if Plato had wished to deduce his Ideas, he could not have done so ; and that for this there was a specific reason. For Plato's higher Ideas do not contain the lower in themselves, and therefore the lower cannot be extricated from them, logically or otherwise. On the contrary, the higher Ideas expressly exclude the lower. They contain only what is common to the lower Ideas. For example, the Idea of colour is what the Ideas of white, blue, green, etc., have in common. It expressly excludes their specific differences. The specific quality of green colour, *i.e.* its greenness, is excluded from the Idea of colour, which contains only what green has in common with blue and the other colours. It is clear that the greenness of green is not possessed by blue, and is therefore not a quality common to both colours. Hence it is not contained in the Idea of colour. Hence the Ideas of blue, green, etc., cannot be deduced from the Idea of colour. They cannot be got out of it, because they are not in it.

Plato's Ideas, in fact, are *abstract* universals, and it is for this reason that no deduction of them was possible for him. An abstract universal is a genus which does not contain its species within itself. A wholly new conception of the nature of universals has to be evolved if deduction is to be possible, a conception according to which the universal, the genus, contains its differentiae and its species within itself, so that they can be extricated from it by a logical deduction. Such universals are called by Hegel *concrete* universals, and the discovery of their nature was the great advance which Hegel claimed to have made upon previous philosophers. We are not yet in a position to expound this discovery. And all that we have at present to note is that Plato's universals were abstract, so that the lower Ideas could not be deduced from the higher.

G. *Which is the first Category?*

114. If we are to deduce the categories from one another, two questions at once present themselves. Firstly, where are we to begin ? What is to be our first category ? Secondly, by what method are we to deduce the others. The first question

will form the subject of the present section, the second will be dealt with thereafter.

115. Which is the first category? We cannot begin with any category taken at random. For the deduction of the categories is no mere piece of subjective ingenuity. It is an objective process of reality itself. The categories are the system of reason, the objective reason which is in the world. It is of the essence of reason that its entire process is necessary. Nothing in it can be arbitrary or accidental. It does not begin and end anywhere. Its progress is fixed by its own rational principles and cannot be altered by our individual whims. Even in formal logic we cannot begin with the conclusion and end with the premises. The necessity of reason itself compels us to put the premises first. There is no room for our subjective vagaries. The essential character of reason is necessity. To make our beginning by chance would accordingly be to make an irrational beginning. The first category must be necessarily first.

116. The same remarks apply, not only to what comes first, but also to all that comes after. The whole order in which the categories are deduced must be necessary. It must be determined, not by us, but by the nature of reason itself. It is, in fact, not *we* who deduce the categories at all. They deduce themselves. We are engaged, not in creating a network of categories in our imaginations, but in *discovering* the nature, order, and connection of that system of reason which objectively *is*, whether we think it or not. Even in formal logic it is not we whose brains create the fact that because Socrates is a man, and because all men are mortal, therefore Socrates is mortal. This process of reason is no doing of ours. We can neither create nor alter it. We can only discover it. And the chain of categories which the Logic discloses is likewise no doing of ours or of Hegel's. It is the world-reason, the Absolute, which is there, in the world, from all eternity. Our deduction of the categories is but the discovery of how the categories deduce themselves.

117. How, then, are we to discover the first category? It will be that category which comes first in reason, first in order

of thought, that one which is logically first, logically prior to all others. And we can ascertain which this is by simply consulting our own reason and seeing which of all our universal and necessary concepts is presupposed by, and logically prior to, all others. For though we are engaged upon the discovery of an objective reality, this is not opposed to our subjective *reason*, but only to our subjective unprincipled and arbitrary *fancies*. Discovery here differs from the ordinary process of physical discovery. We cannot find out which was the first planet to be formed merely by consulting our own minds. But we can discover the first category in this way. For though it is the objective reason that we seek, yet this objective reason is identical with our subjective reason. There is but one reason in us and in the world. This follows from the principle of the identity of being and knowing. Our reason is no mere subjective phantasy. To think that it is so is to adopt the subjective position of Kant, according to which the categories are true *for us* but do not apply to things in themselves. If our subjective categories are not objective also, then things as they are in themselves must be unknowable, and we have already rejected this supposition as untenable.

118. Thus the world-reason is also our reason, and the first category of the Absolute will be the one which is, for us, logically prior to all others, and which is involved in all others as their logical presupposition. Now with regard to concepts in general, the principle is that the more universal is prior to the less universal, the genus to the species. For example, the concept "horse" presupposes the concept "animal." You cannot have the idea (concept) of horses without first having the idea (concept) of animals. You cannot know what a horse is if you do not know what an animal is. The more universal, the genus, "animal," is presupposed by, and logically prior to, the less universal, the species, "horse." But the opposite is not true. "Animal" does not presuppose "horse." You might fully understand what an animal is without having any idea of horses. This principle applies to all concepts, and therefore to the categories. The more abstract and general a category, the

earlier will be its place in the *Logic*. The more specialized it is, the later will be its place. Therefore, the first category will be the most general of all, the *summum genus*.

A more general universal differs from a less general one by being more abstract. Given the species we find the genus by abstracting from the differentia. Man may be regarded as a species of the genus animal, and defined as a rational animal. Rationality is the differentia. Obliterate rationality from the concept of man and we are left with the generic concept of animal. By further abstraction we pass to still more general concepts. By abstracting from the differentia "life," which is inherent in the concept of animal, we should reach the concept "material object," and so on. Hence the first category will be the most abstract category, and will be reached by carrying the process of abstraction to its extreme limit.

119. The highest possible abstraction, that which is common to every conceivable object in the universe, is the concept of being. Not all things are material. But all have being. All objects *are*. There are many objects of which it would not be true to say that they are green, or that they are material, or that they are heavy. But whatever object in the universe we choose, it must always be true to say of it that it *is*. Being, therefore, must be the first category. Being, the quality of "isness," is clearly the highest possible abstraction. Suppose we take any object in the world and proceed to abstract from all its attributes. This table, for example, is square, hard, brown, shiny. Abstract from the shininess, and we are left with the proposition, "This table is square, hard, brown." Abstract from the brownness and we are left with "This table is square, hard." Abstract lastly from the hardness, and then from the squareness, and we are left with "This table *is*." "Is" is the last possible abstraction. Being is the first category.

120. We can see that being is presupposed by, and logically prior to, all other categories. For example, quantity, quality, cause, substance, all presuppose being. A cause is a special kind of being. Nobody could have the idea of a cause unless

he first had the idea of being. But the opposite is not true. One can frame the simple idea of being without knowing what is meant by the complicated idea of cause, just as one can have the idea of animal without the idea of horse. So too one cannot know what quantity is without the idea of being. And the same is true of the other categories.

H. *The Dialectic Method.*

121. The next question is, how are we to deduce the other categories from being? What method are we to adopt? Now just as we could not decide upon the first category by chance or caprice, in the same way our method of deduction must not be merely any random method that happens to hit our fancy. Here again it is not *we* who deduce the categories. It is not *we* who create connections between them by our ingenuity. The logical connections are there, and we have to discover them. The deduction is an objective process of reason which takes place independently of us—not of course a process in time, but a logical process. Our task is, not to invent a method by which we can deduce categories, but to discover the method by which the categories deduce themselves.

Now it appeared above (118) that the more general and abstract concept is always prior to the less general and abstract. And this principle not only decides for us that the first category is being, but also determines the order of the subsequent categories. The more abstract concept will always be prior in thought, in the objective reason, to the less abstract. Therefore, the Logic will proceed from the *summum genus*, being, through further and further specifications, to the least abstract category of all, whatever that may be. Our method will be to proceed from the genus to the species, and then, treating the species as a new genus, to pass from it to a further and lower species, and so on. But we can only proceed from genus to species by adding a differentia to the genus. Therefore the order of progress will be through genus, differentia, species. Then treating the species as a genus we must find a new differentia to convert it into a new species. And with this triple rhythm of genus, differentia, species, our method will proceed throughout.[1]

122. But if we start with an abstraction such as being, how are we to ever deduce differentia and species from it? It is an essential of all logical deduction that the consequent should be contained in the reason or antecedent. The breach of this principle in formal logic is what is called the fallacy of illicit process. There cannot be anything present in the conclusion which was not present in the premises. This is really the old principle *ex nihilo nihil fit*. You cannot get something out of nothing, and you cannot get out of a thing what is not in it. It will be found that this is just as true of the Hegelian Logic as of the humble formal logic. If from one category, A, we are to deduce another category, B, this can only be done if A, in some sense or other, contains B. But if we can show that category A does contain category B, then this is equivalent to deducing B from A. That is what deduction means in formal logic, and that is what it means here.

Now how can we deduce the species from the genus? How can the genus be shown to contain the species? To get from genus to species we have to add differentia. We have, therefore, to show that the genus contains the differentia. But the genus is expressly defined as excluding the differentia. To deduce the differentia from it would seem to be an illicit process. We have already seen this when we pointed out that Plato's Ideas are abstract universals. The Ideas of red, green, blue, cannot be deduced from the Idea of colour, because the latter does not contain the former. It contains only what is common to red, green and blue. The redness of red is not a property of green and blue, and therefore is not contained in the Idea of colour. What is specific to the lower Ideas, their differentiae, are expressly excluded from the higher Idea. In the same way the category being contains what is common to all things, but excludes all specific differences and determinations, and therefore it would seem impossible that any

---

[1] There is, however, only *one* species under each genus in the Hegelian Logic. This follows from the fact (169) that everything in the universe is an example of each and every category.

differences and determinations could be deduced from being. For example, cause, effect, substance, quantity, are specific kinds of being, and the ideas of them are excluded from the concept of being, and cannot, therefore, it would seem, be deduced from it. How, then, is any deduction possible?

123. The solution of this problem constitutes the central principle of the Hegelian philosophy, the famous dialectic method. It rests upon the discovery that it is not true, as hitherto supposed, that a universal absolutely excludes the differentia. Hegel found that a concept may contain its own opposite hidden away within itself, and that this opposite may be extricated or deduced from it and made to do the work of the differentia, thus converting genus into species. The simplest way of explaining the dialectic method will be to give a concrete example of it, and thereafter to state the general logical principles which it involves. We take as our example the first triad of categories of the Hegelian Logic,—being, nothing, becoming.

We begin with the category of being. It is the pure category that we have to think, not any particular sort of being, such as this pen, that book, this table, that chair. It is the entirely abstract idea of being, being in general, pure being. We have to abstract from all specific determinations whatever. We can form this abstract idea, if we wish, from a concrete object, say, this table. We have to abstract from all its qualities whatever, its squareness, brownness, hardness, even its very tablehood. We have to think its mere " isness," its being, what it has in common with every other object in the universe. Such being has in it no determinations whatever, for we have abstracted from all determinations. It is therefore absolutely indeterminate and featureless, completely empty and vacant, a pure vacuum. It has no content, for content of any kind would be a specific determination. This vacuum, this utter emptiness, is not anything; it is the absence of everything, of all determinations, quality, character. But such absence of everything is simply nothing. Emptiness, vacancy, is the same as nothing. Being, therefore, is the same as nothing. And the pure concept of being is thus seen to *contain* the idea of nothing.

But to show that one category contains another is to deduce that other from it. Hence we have deduced the category nothing from the category being.

124. The statement that being is nothing, or that being and nothing are identical, must not be understood in the absurd sense that a particular sort of being, *e.g.* this table, is the same as nothing, or that dinner is the same as no-dinner. The category being is an abstraction, whereas the table and the dinner are concrete objects with all kinds of specific determinations besides mere being. We are speaking of the pure abstract idea of being after all specific determinations, such as the squareness, brownness, hardness, of the table, have been abstracted from. It is only this utterly empty thought of being which is the same as the thought of nothing.

We may put the same thing in another way. To say that a thing " is," but that beyond its mere " isness," it has no qualities or characteristics of any kind,—this is equivalent to saying that the thing is nothing at all. The table is square, brown, hard, etc. Suppose that we could destroy its shape, its hardness, its colour, and *all* its qualities, it would then be nothing at all. To say that it " is," but that apart from the " isness " it has no qualities or character, is the same as to say that it " is not." Pure " is," therefore, mere " is " without any further determination, is the same as " is not." Being is identical with not-being or nothing.

125. Since they are identical the one passes into the other. Being passes into nothing. And conversely, nothing passes back into being; for the thought of nothing is the thought of emptiness, and this emptiness is pure being. In consequence of this disappearance of each category into the other we have a third thought involved here, namely, the idea of the *passage* of being and nothing into each other. This is the category of becoming. Becoming was long since analyzed by Parmenides and shown to contain only two forms, the passage of nothing into being, and the passage of being into nothing.[1] The first form is beginning, arising, coming into being; the second is

---

[1] For elaboration and proof of this point, see my *Critical History of Greek Philosophy*, p. 75.

ending, ceasing, passing away. Thus we have already three categories. We began with being. From that we deduced nothing. And from the relations between these two we deduce becoming. These are the first three categories of the Hegelian Logic.

126. We may now consider the general principles of method involved here. Firstly, these three categories are respectively genus, differentia, species. Being is the genus. Becoming is a special kind of being and is therefore a species of it. This special kind of being is being which has its negative in it, which is infected with not-being. Combine the idea of not-being with that of being, and we get the idea of becoming. Not-being or nothing, the second category, is therefore the differentia.

Being, nothing, becoming, is the first Hegelian " triad." Throughout the entire system there is this triple rhythm. The first category in each triad is always, as here, an affirmative category. It lays itself down as a positive assertion, *e.g.* being, is, etc. The second category is always the negative, or opposite, of the first. It denies what the first affirmed, *e.g.* not-being, is not, etc. This second category is not brought in by Hegel from any external source. It is deduced from the first category, and this means that the first contains the second, and is shown to produce it out of itself. This is what is meant by saying that it is not we, it is not Hegel, who deduce the categories; they deduce themselves. Thus the first category contains its own opposite and is identical with it. At this point the two categories stand confronting and contradicting each other. But it is impossible to rest in this contradiction, for it means that opposite categories are applicable to the same thing at the same time. It means, in the case of the present triad, that if we affirm that anything " is," we must at the same time admit that it " is not." For being necessarily involves not-being, and therefore if a thing has being, *i.e. is*, it also necessarily has not-being, *i.e.* is *not*. How can the thing both be and not be? The answer is that it both is and is not when it *becomes*. The category of becoming therefore resolves the contradiction. In other words the contradiction between the first and second categories is always reconciled in a third category which is the unity of the two preceding. The third category contains within itself the opposition of the other two, but it also contains their underlying harmony and unity. Thus becoming is a being which is not-being, or a not-being which is being. It is a single thought which yet combines in a harmonious unity the contradictory ideas of being and nothing. The three members of a triad are sometimes called the thesis, antithesis, and synthesis, respectively. The synthesis being reached now posits itself as a new assertion, as an affirmative category which thereby becomes the thesis of a new triad. For as soon as it lays itself down as a positive assertion its opposite is seen to issue out of it and to involve it in self-contradiction. This new contradiction has again to be resolved in the higher unity of a new synthesis. This in turn becomes the thesis of a new triad, and so on throughout the whole series. It will be seen that this entire process of categories is a compulsory process forced onwards by the compelling necessity of reason. By rational necessity the thesis gives rise to its opposite and so to a contradiction. Reason *cannot* rest in what is self-contradictory, and is therefore forced onwards to the synthesis. And so throughout. This process cannot stop. It *must* go on until a category is reached which does not give rise to any contradiction. This will be the final category of the Logic. It will then be possible to pass from the first reason of the world to the world itself, the spheres of nature and spirit. And we shall see that, in developing the details of nature and spirit, Hegel uses the same dialectic method of triads as he has used in the Logic.

127. The dialectic method apparently performs the miracle of getting out of each category what is not in it. The problem was how to pass from genus to species in view of the fact that the genus expressly excludes the differentia. Now Hegel's discovery consists in this, that the required differentia is always the negative, and that, when this is understood, it is seen that the old view that the genus excludes the differentia is not the complete truth. This latter point will be discussed more fully later (135-9), when we shall see that the older view

of the genus is the view of what Hegel calls the "understanding," as opposed to the true view which is the view of "reason." The understanding believes that two opposites, such as being and nothing, absolutely exclude each other. Reason admits that they exclude each other inasmuch as they are opposites. But this exclusion is not absolute and is not incompatible with the identity of the two opposites. Thus the old view of the genus as totally excluding the differentia is not the full truth. And it is this discovery which enables Hegel to perform what at first sight seems an impossible miracle. As regards the point that the required differentia is the negative, this is based upon the principle that negation is determination. To advance from genus to species what is required is some specific determination. The genus is indeterminate, the species determinate. Add a determination to the genus and we get a species. Spinoza had laid it down that determination is negation, and Hegel now uses this principle in the converse form that negation is determination (43). By adding its negative, its opposite, to the genus, we limit it, and therefore determine it, and to determine it is to turn it into a species.

128. The principle that each category contains, and in fact *is*, its own opposite, is what has sometimes been described as Hegel's denial of the law of contradiction. That being and not-being are identical seems to infringe that law. But that it is not true to say that Hegel denied the law of contradiction is evident from the fact that it is this very law which compels us to pass from the second to the third category of each triad. It is just because reason cannot rest in a contradiction that the contradiction between thesis and antithesis has to be resolved in the synthesis. Nevertheless it must be allowed that the Hegelian principle of the identity of opposites is one of the most striking pieces of speculative audacity in the history of thought. But this audacity is justified and was necessary if philosophy was ever to solve its ancient problems. And it will be found on examination that this principle of Hegel's was not, as is usually supposed, anything absolutely new. Apart from explicit anticipations of it in earlier writers, it is in reality implied in all previous philosophy. All that is new in Hegel

is that he was the first person explicitly to state and formulate it as a logical principle, previous thinkers having, while actually relying on it, been frightened to state it in so many words. For whatever philosophy reduces the variety of the world to a unity, *e.g.* the doctrines of the Eleatics, the Vedantists, Plotinus, Spinoza, must believe in the identity of opposites. In every one of these philosophies we are told that reality is the one, and yet that the many proceeds out of the one, or in other words that the many *is* the one, that these two opposites, many and one, are identical. Vedantism proceeds explicitly upon the principle that "All is one." "All," however, is clearly the many, the multiplicity of the world. And this principle means, therefore, that the many is identical with its opposite, the one. And the age-old assertion that the many proceeds out of the one, characteristic of all pantheistic systems, is precisely parallel to Hegel's assertion that not-being proceeds out of being (which does not mean, however, that Hegel was a pantheist). In all these philosophies, again, the one is the infinite, while the many is the finite. The infinite produces the finite out of itself, becomes finite, and therefore *is* finite. The infinite is identical with its opposite the finite.

Yet all these philosophies have been unable to state this principle openly, to realize it, and it was just for this reason that they all failed to solve the ancient dualism of philosophy. The many, they said, proceeds out of the one, *is* the one. Yet how can this be, since the many and the one are opposites, since the many is *not* the one? The many, therefore, does *not* and cannot proceed out of the one. And beyond this see-saw of contradictions the old philosophies never got. Some thinkers emphasized multiplicity, and could find no bridge from it to unity. These were the pluralists and materialists. Other thinkers emphasized unity, and could find no bridge from it to multiplicity. These were the pantheists, mystics, and abstract idealists. The history of philosophy was a continual oscillation between these two tendencies. And both necessarily ended in dualism. Hegel's audacity and originality consists simply in this, that he explained and showed in detail how it is logically possible for two opposites to be identical while yet retaining their opposition. The thought that the many and the one are identical frightened the older philosophers so much that they never even examined it to see how it could be possible. Yet we shall find in the Logic that this very problem is solved. We shall find that Hegel explains with perfect precision and clearness how and in what sense the thought (category) of unity is identical with that of multiplicity, and how and in what sense they are different (208). We have already seen that he explains, perfectly logically and rationally, without any mystery, how being can be identical with its opposite, nothing.

129. What is new in Hegel, then, is that he formulates, as an explicit logical principle, what was tacitly implied in previous systems. Hitherto it had always been assumed that, logically speaking, a positive and its negative simply excluded each other, were cut off from each other by an impassable gulf. It had always been assumed that we can only say A is A, and that we can never under any circumstances say A is not-A. For example, Spinoza regarded the infinite and finite as mutually exclusive opposites. Spinoza, therefore, found it impossible to solve the problem how the finite could ever issue out of the infinite. If we can only say A is A, the infinite is the infinite, then A must remain A for ever, the infinite must remain infinite, and therefore sterile within itself, for ever, and the finite world can never arise out of it. We can only solve this problem if the infinite contains the finite, just as being contains not-being, if the infinite *is* the finite, if A is not-A.

130. It is of paramount importance to observe that the identity of opposites does not exclude the opposition of those opposites. A and not-A are identical. But they are also distinct. It is not only an *identity* of opposites; it is also an identity of *opposites*. The opposition is just as real as the identity. If we forget this and imagine that the identity means that the opposition is illusory, then this destroys our principle, for what we then have is not an identity of opposites, but merely an identity of identicals, of which the logical formula would be the old A=A. Thus being and nothing are

identical because they are both the same complete emptiness and vacancy. Yet they are also distinct and opposite; for being is being, and nothing is nothing. But this position is self-contradictory. First we say that the two terms are distinct. And then we assert that they are identical. It is this contradiction which forces us to advance to the third category, becoming, in which we see that the identity is not the whole truth, and that the difference is not the whole truth, but that the whole truth is the identity *in* difference. For becoming combines both the identity and the difference.

131. We have now described the dialectic method and some of the more important logical principles upon which it is based. This method and these principles are supposed to be accurately followed throughout the whole of Hegel's system. A word of warning is, however, necessary. It must not be supposed that Hegel has actually succeeded in rigorously applying these principles throughout his system. The description of the dialectic method given above is an *ideal* description, a description of what the method aims at being or ought to be. In practice it is sometimes difficult to see how this description applies to some of Hegel's actual triads. For example, in the philosophy of spirit Hegel puts forward as one of his triads the notions of art, religion, and philosophy. Here art is supposed to be the thesis, religion the antithesis, philosophy the synthesis. It is very difficult to see in what sense religion is the opposite of art; and it is quite impossible to see that art and philosophy are related as genus and species, or that religion can be regarded as the differentia. Numerous similar examples might be given.[1] There are even cases of "triads" which contain four terms! These irregularities do not indicate, however, that our description of the dialectic method is wrong. What they do show is that Hegel has not himself been able to carry out his own dialectic method with absolute consistency in all cases. This is of course an imperfection in his system. Yet the fact that he has made mistakes in the application of his principles does not necessarily invalidate the principles themselves. No one would dream of supposing

[1] See Croce, p. 97.

that the biological principle of evolution is invalidated by the fact that science may be wrong in the pedigree it gives of some particular organic species. And the principles of Hegel are entitled to as much consideration as those of Darwin, in spite of occasional errors and inconsistencies.

I. *The Dialectic Method (continued).*

132. The dialectic method stands in contrast, on the one hand, to what Hegel calls *raisonnement*, and, on the other, to the mathematical method of Spinoza. By *raisonnement* Hegel means the ordinary modes of argument adopted in books and discussions on all subjects. Such discussions begin by stating facts or reflections arbitrarily selected by the author to suit his purpose, and then building conclusions thereupon. They weigh pros and cons and balance probabilities. It is hopeless, Hegel thinks, to expect certainty, to expect knowledge, from such haphazard and meandering methods. In philosophy we must have system, and we must have necessity. Nothing must be assumed; everything must be deduced. But *raisonnement* begins anywhere, goes on as it pleases, and stops when it likes. Instead of this procedure, governed as it is by chance and random thought, philosophical method will be governed by rigorous necessity. Its beginning will be fixed by necessity, and every step thereafter will be a necessity of reason, and no mere series of random reflections. For *raisonnement*, with its perpetual to and fro of arguments, its endless see-saw of pros and cons, may obviously go on for ever without any certain conclusion being reached. In place of this we must have method, system, necessity, certainty. And Hegel claims that the dialectic method ensures these.

133. Hegel's objections to *raisonnement* and his attempts to found a more scientific method are parallel in every way to the similar efforts of Descartes. When Descartes pointed out that, by reason of their unsystematic ways of arguing, men hold different opinions on nearly all important subjects, so that it is impossible to know which opinion is true, he was really raising the Hegelian objection to *raisonnement*. And

just as Hegel proposed to substitute a rigorous logical method for this *raisonnement*, so Descartes and Spinoza proposed that philosophy should adopt the rigorous methods of geometry. Geometry begins with axioms, which are not mere opinions, but necessary truths, and proceeds by rigorous deductions to draw only those conclusions which follow by absolute logical necessity. If philosophy adopts this method, it was thought, it will attain the same certainty as attaches to mathematics. At present everyone holds whatever philosophical opinions he pleases. But in mathematics there is no choice of opinions. There can be no two opinions on the question whether the three angles of a triangle equal two right angles. This is because geometry starts from necessary truths (axioms), and admits nothing that does not follow of necessity from these. Philosophy by adopting the same procedure should be able to abolish opinions and attain certainty. Hence Descartes hunts about for an axiom to be the foundation of philosophy, as the geometrical axioms are of geometry, and produces as such axiom the proposition " I am." And Spinoza, more formally, begins his *Ethica* with a series of definitions and axioms, and proceeds, in imitation of Euclid, to develop philosophical " theorems."

134. Hegel agrees with Descartes and Spinoza to the extent that he, like them, wishes to abolish mere opinions, and to attain certainty by a rigorously logical method. But he considers the geometrical method unsuitable. " That these methods," he says, " however indispensable and brilliantly successful in their own province "—*i.e.* mathematics—" are unserviceable for philosophical cognition, is self-evident. They have presuppositions ; and their style of cognition is that of understanding, proceeding under the canon of formal identity." [1] This passage states two objections to the geometrical method, first, that it has presuppositions, and second, that it is the method of the understanding. We will consider these objections in that order.

The presuppositions or assumptions to which Hegel refers are the axioms, the definitions, or indeed any other propositions

[1] Wal., *Log.*, § 231.

with which the science may begin. The point is that the mere fact that we make a beginning means that we make an assumption. The *first* proposition is necessarily an assumption simply because it is the first, because it is not deduced from, or proved by, any prior proposition. Axioms may no doubt be regarded as "self-evident," but that what is self-evident is also true is itself an assumption. And in any case, even if it be admitted that the axioms are true, they are yet unexplained, because undeduced. No reason is given for them, and therefore they are mere dogmatic *facts* and ultimate mysteries. And we have already seen that philosophy cannot begin with such unexplained facts. It may be an axiom, an indisputable fact, that "I am"—as Descartes thought. But the question still remains, "Why am I?" If philosophy begins here, it begins with a mystery, and even if it succeeds in explaining the entire universe *from this point*, yet the whole will remain a mystery because it begins with one.

It would seem that whatever beginning we make must be an assumption, an ultimate fact, because every beginning, as a *first*, is undeduced from anything prior to it. And in that case it would seem that the problem of philosophy is hopeless, and that it is just as useless for Hegel to begin with being as it was for Descartes to begin with "I am." But Hegel shows, as we shall see presently, that the dialectical method, unlike the geometrical method, is not subject to this infirmity.

135. The second objection to the geometrical method is that it is the work of the understanding and proceeds according to the canon of identity. This means that it has not reached the principle of the identity of opposites, but proceeds upon the pre-Hegelian assumption that opposites absolutely exclude each other, that we can only say A=A (the canon of identity), and never that A=not-A. It is obvious that mathematics proceeds upon this principle, which is suitable to it; but Spinoza, in supposing that it would be suitable to philosophy, made a mistake. It is just for this reason that Spinoza, having posited an infinite substance, finds it utterly impossible to deduce the finite from the infinite, because to do so would

infringe the canon of identity, according to which not-A can never issue out of A, nor the finite out of the infinite.

136. By the understanding (*Verstand*) Hegel means that stage of the development of mind at which it regards opposites as mutually exclusive and absolutely cut off from each other. The Aristotelian laws of identity, contradiction, and excluded middle, are the canons of its procedure. Distinguished from understanding is reason (*Vernunft*), which is that stage of the development of mind which rises to the principle of the identity of opposites. For understanding each category remains an insulated self-existent being, completely cut off from the others. The categories thus regarded are static, fixed, and lifeless. To the eye of reason, however, the categories are seen to be alive with movement, to be fluid, to break up and flow into each other, as we have seen that being flows into nothing. For the understanding any deduction of category from category is impossible, for there is no passage from one to the other. Only reason can deduce the categories. Understanding meets every question with an inflexible " either . . . or." The truth is either A or not-A, either being or not-being. A thing either is, or is not. Reason breaks up this hard and fast schematism of the understanding, sees that A and not-A are identical in their very difference, that the truth does not lie, as understanding supposes, *either* wholly in A, *or* wholly in not-A, but rather in the synthesis of the two.

137. Understanding is the mode of mind which seeks precision above all things, and insists upon clear distinctions. As such it is a necessary factor of every philosophical method. For without precision of thought, without clear distinctions, we become lost in hazy and vague ideas, in the cloudlands of mysticism. We must be clear as to the distinctions between the finite and the infinite, being and not-being, many and one. Thus understanding performs in philosophy a just work. But its truth is not the whole truth. Beneath these distinctions there is identity, and to see this is the work of reason. When Hegel inveighs against the fallacies of " mere " understanding, he does not mean to deny that distinctions are real, nor that understanding has its proper place in philosophy. But

understanding has a tendency to imagine that its truth is the only truth, that distinctions and oppositions are real and that identity in opposition is unreal. And this is the error for which Hegel blames the understanding.

138. It is not to be supposed that understanding emphasises only distinction, difference, while reason emphasises only identity. In that case reason would be just as one-sided as understanding. The truth rather is that understanding insists upon both identity and difference, but takes each separately. Reason also insists upon both, but takes them together. For understanding A and B are *either* identical *or* different. For reason they are *both* identical and different. The principle of reason is identity *in* difference. Understanding has a two-fold canon: (1) the identical is the identical, A=A; this is the law of identity: and (2) the different is the different, A is not not-A; this is the law of contradiction. The canon of reason is rather that what is different is also identical, that A is not-A. Understanding will insist that, either two categories are the same, in which case there is no difference between them, or they are different, in which case they are not identical. Reason asserts that they are at the same time both identical and distinct. Being is different from nothing; for it is its opposite. But being is also identical with nothing, for both are the same vacancy. Thus it is quite wrong to think of reason as being opposed to understanding, or to imagine that understanding is one point of view and reason merely *another*, so that one must be wrong and the other right. Reason includes and transcends understanding, for it fully admits the differences and the identities on which understanding insists, but it sees further that difference and identity are not, as understanding supposes, incompatible with each other.

139. Western thinkers have as a rule exhibited a tendency to emphasize distinctions and ignore identities. Hence their thought has been clear and precise. Indian thinkers, such as the founders of the Vedanta, on the other hand, have exhibited a tendency to emphasize identity and ignore even essential distinctions. Hence their thought is hazy, vague, and mystical. Both these tendencies are one-sided, half-true, and

both are the work of the mere understanding. The West is apt to believe that only difference is real, and that identity is illusory. Its formula is, A is not not-A. The East is apt to believe that only identity is real, and that differences are illusory—which is in fact explicitly stated in the doctrine that only the one is and that the world of difference and multiplicity is Maya, illusion. Its formula is A is A. Both formulas are the work of understanding. The Hegelian principle combines both these half-truths in the whole truth that difference and identity are both equally real, and that what is different is also identical, A=not-A. This is the principle of reason, the principle of the identity of opposites. And it will be seen that it does not oppose, but includes, the principles of the understanding. It only opposes the one-sidedness of understanding.

140. Reason, as we have seen, is the Absolute, is objective, and is independent of us. But the beginner may be puzzled by the fact that the same word "reason" is also used by Hegel to describe the subjective mental processes which we have just distinguished from understanding. Is not the fact that one word is used for two such totally different things an example of looseness of thought? But it is the "understanding" of the reader which is raising this difficulty and insisting that the two things here described by one word are "totally different," thus ignoring their identity! Reason, the subjective mental process, is certainly distinct from reason, the objective Absolute. The first is reason as subject, seen from the side of knowing. The second is reason as object, seen from the side of being. But being and knowing are identical in their difference. Subjective reason is identical with the objective world-reason. Our reason *is* the absolute reason. There is no confusion either of terms or of thought.

141. Certain other Hegelian terms may here be explained. "Logical doctrine," says Hegel, "has three sides, (α) the Abstract side, or that of understanding: (β) the Dialectical, or that of negative reason: (γ) the Speculative, or that of positive reason."[1] In this way the three terms of each triad are

[1] Wal., *Log.*, § 79.

described. The first term is the work of understanding. For it simply asserts itself as the sole category in existence. Thus being lays itself down, asserts that being is being, and that is all. This involves nothing but the canon of identity, A=A, the principle of the understanding. The second term is that of negative reason. For example, nothing is negative; and it involves reason because to reach it we have had to produce it out of its opposite, being, and to see its identity with being. The last term, becoming, is that of positive reason. It is positive because it is not a mere negation, like the second term, but is a return to a positive affirmation which is capable of becoming the thesis of a new triad. The term " dialectical," ordinarily used to express the entire deductive process of the Logic, is, in this passage and elsewhere, used to signify specially the passage of a thing into its opposite, the breaking down of the absolute distinctions set up by the understanding. The word "speculative," when used by Hegal, does not imply hazardous, but on the contrary imports certainty. That is " speculative," according to Hegel, in which the principle of reason, the reconciliation of opposites, is involved. Hence the word is, in the above passage, applied to the third term in the triad. And "speculative" philosophy is a term used by Hegel to describe his own system, because the identity of opposites is its leading principle. He also occasionally speaks of previous philosophies, *e.g.* those of Plato and Aristotle, as " speculative," by which he means that the principle of reason, the identity of opposites, is implicit in their teachings although they did not explicitly recognize it. To call a philosophy " speculative " imports, for Hegel, a high measure of praise.

142. The terms "abstract" and "concrete" are perhaps the commonest of all terms in the Hegelian technical vocabulary. Whether he has always consistently used them in the same sense may well be doubted. But according to his most characteristic usage the first two terms of each triad are relatively abstract, while the third is relatively concrete. Thus the first category of the Logic, being, is the most abstract of all, since it abstracts from all determinations. It contains no differences. But becoming encloses within itself the dis-

tinction of being and nothing. Being and nothing, taken apart from each other, are both abstractions. Each is a false abstraction, a one-sided half-truth, which cannot stand alone. Only when they are taken together do we get the concrete truth of becoming. This usage of the terms is based upon the common usage. We say that each quality of a thing, say this table, if taken by itself, is an abstraction. There is no such thing as brownness by itself. Brownness, considered apart from the brown thing, is an abstraction. It is only when the brownness, the squareness, the hardness, etc., are all taken together, that we get the concrete thing, the table. In the same way being and nothing, taken separately are abstractions, but together they constitute the relatively concrete category of becoming. But though becoming is concrete as compared with being and nothing, it is itself abstract as compared with later categories. For becoming will, in a new form, become the thesis of a new triad, and will be opposed by an antithesis. This thesis and antithesis will, taken apart, each be one-sided abstractions as against their concrete unity, the synthesis. Thus, as the Logic advances, the categories become more and more concrete, and the final category is the most concrete of all.

143. The thesis is always regarded by Hegel as " immediate," or as characterized by " immediacy." The second term is " mediate," or characterized by mediation. The third term is the merging of mediation in a new immediacy. The immediate is the simple and undifferentiated ; it stands directly and immediately confronting us, and purports to be in itself the sole truth without reference to anything else. Being, as it first comes before us, is of this character. It is simple and undifferentiated, for it has not yet split up into being and nothing. It asserts itself as the complete truth, and does not refer to nothing or to any other category. When we pass to nothing, however, we have mediation. At that stage being and nothing refer to each other, stand in a relation to each other. They mediate each other. Immediacy is the same as simple identity, that within which no differences have yet disclosed themselves. Being is simple and self-identical, and

has as yet no distinctions within itself. Mediation is the same as difference, division, distinction. With the second member of the triad, nothing, being has sundered itself, has developed within itself the distinction between being and nothing; and this differentiation is mediation. With the third term, becoming, the differences are again absorbed in an identity; the mediation and difference are merged in a new unity. We have again a new immediacy, a fresh self-identical category. When this in turn gives birth to its opposite we have a fresh field of mediation, which is again merged in a further synthesis; and so on. The final category of the Logic will be immediate in the sense that all previous mediation, all distinctions and differences of all lower categories, are absorbed and merged in its unity. Yet inasmuch as it still retains and preserves all distinctions within this its unity it is, in that way, the highest mediation.

144. The synthesis of a triad both abolishes and preserves the differences of the thesis and antithesis. This two-fold activity of the synthesis is expressed by Hegel by the word *aufheben*, which is sometimes translated " to sublate." The German word has two meanings. It means both to abolish and to preserve. The English phrase " to put aside " has a similar double meaning. To put a thing aside may mean to put it out of the way, to have done with it, abolish it. Or it may mean to put it aside for future use, to keep and preserve it. The differences between the first and the second members of each triad are " sublated " by the third. Firstly, the difference is abolished. The mediation and distinction are merged in a unity. Being and nothing and the opposition between them are merged in the unity of becoming. But at the same time the difference is preserved within the new category. It is not simply wiped out. The new category is an identity of differences, not a simple identity. The fact that it is an *identity* of differences means that the differences are merged. The fact that it is an identity of *differences* means that they are preserved. We have not a mere identity, *i.e.* simple abolition of differences. Nor have we a mere opposition, *i.e.* simple preservation of differences. What we have

is an identity of opposites. Simple abolition would mean that we have an identity, but no opposites. Simple preservation would mean that we have opposites, but no identity. Becoming is the unity of being and nothing and in it their difference is absorbed. Yet being and nothing are still there, present in becoming, and may be got out of it by analysis. They have ceased to exist *as separate entities*, as opposite abstractions. In this sense they are abolished. But they now exist in combination, as factors of a concrete unity. They exist in absorption, in solution. Thus being and nothing are preserved in becoming, and not lost. And when the synthesis becomes the thesis of a new triad it will in its turn be merged but yet preserved, along with its opposite, in a further synthesis. Thus the synthesis of the second triad has, preserved within it, the antithesis and thesis of that triad. And since the thesis of this second triad has, as synthesis of the first triad, preserved within it the thesis and antithesis of the first triad, this means that the synthesis of the second triad preserves everything that went before it including the thesis and antithesis of the first triad. In this way, as the dialectic proceeds, *nothing is ever lost.* Each step in the process takes up into itself what went before it and is in turn taken up by the step that follows. The final category of the Logic retains and preserves within itself all previous categories whatever. They are all merged in it, gathered up into its unity, their differences and contradictions resolved. They are all fused into one. Yet they retain their existence in this unity, as the factors of its being. It is for this reason alone that it is concrete. Were all previous categories not contained within it, it would be merely an abstraction, just as Plato's Ideas are, for the same reason, abstract universals. The Idea of colour excludes, wipes out, the specific Ideas of white, green, red, and the differences between them. It is a simple unity, not a unity of differences. It does not contain the lower Ideas and is therefore abstract. The higher categories of Hegel contain the lower, and are therefore concrete.

145. The higher categories contain the lower. But it is also true, in another sense, that the lower categories contain

the higher. Becoming contains being. But being also contains becoming. This is evident from the fact that becoming is deduced from being, and we have seen that it is only possible to deduce from a category what that category contains. We may formulate the truth here by saying that higher categories contain lower categories *explicitly*, but that lower categories contain the higher categories *implicitly*. The first term in a triad is called by Hegel " in itself " (*an sich*), that is to say, implicit. The third term is " in and for itself " (*für sich*) that is to say, explicit. The first term is implicitly or potentially the same as the third, just as the acorn is implicitly the oak. For the third term grows out of the first in the course of the dialectic. Being implicitly contains becoming. For in passing from the one to the other nothing has been added from the outside. The new material has been put forth from the womb of being itself. Being first gave birth to nothing. The category nothing was therefore within it. Becoming arises from being and nothing, both of which were within being. Becoming, therefore, was within being. Being, therefore, is implicitly or potentially becoming. It contains becoming implicitly within it, and it is only for this reason that becoming can be deduced from it. Becoming on the other hand contains being and nothing explicitly. Becoming is hidden in being, implicit. But being is obviously, openly, explicitly, contained in becoming. It is patent that becoming is a kind of being.

What is true of the first triad is true of the entire series. Just as being is implicitly becoming, so becoming is implicitly the next synthesis, and so on. And since of all these syntheses each issues out of the last, and since there is never at any point any new material brought in from outside, it follows that being is not only implicitly becoming, but is also implicitly all the subsequent categories. There are several dozen categories in the Logic. All these are implicitly contained in being. If they were not, then the deduction of them would be impossible. If there were, in any of these categories, any thought-content which was not contained in the first category, being, then, in passing to those categories from being, we should have somewhere in the chain of deductions an illicit process, an introduction into the consequent of something not contained in the antecedent. Being is implicitly all the categories which follow it. The final category is explicitly or actually all the categories which precede it. In the forefront of the smaller Logic Hegel places the words, "Being is the Notion implicit only."[1] The Notion is the name of the final sphere of categories.

146. Since being is implicitly becoming, it follows that in thinking of it simply as being we have not as yet seen the full truth about it, for we have not seen all that it contains. The truth of being is becoming, and, in general, it is a characteristic phrase of Hegel's that the synthesis is "the truth of" the thesis and antithesis. Even becoming, of course, does not give us the full truth. For not only becoming, but all the categories, including the final category, are implicitly wrapped up in being. Only the final category gives us the complete truth. But becoming is a step towards the truth; it is the proximate truth of being. Another characteristic phrase of Hegel's is the word "moment." The first and second terms of a triad are the "moments" of the third, *i.e.* the factors which go to compose it.

147. We are now in a position to solve completely the problem of how a beginning is possible. We have seen that to begin with being means that being is itself undeduced. Just because it is the first, it seems, for that reason, to be a mere unexplained fact, an ultimate mystery. And it would seem that any other beginning must, as a beginning, suffer the same disability. Descartes began with the axiom, "I am." It may be a fact that I am, a fact which it is impossible to doubt. But it still remains an unexplained, because undeduced, fact, and to explain the universe from it is therefore merely to reduce the universe to an ultimate mystery, *i.e.* to explain nothing. Doctor McTaggart thinks that Hegel's beginning with being is justified by the fact that it is impossible to doubt that something "is," since the existence of the doubt at least implies that the doubt itself "is."[2] But it will be seen that

[1] Wal., *Log.*, § 84.   [2] *Dial.*, §§ 17-18.

this account of the matter is open to the same objections as Descartes' own axiom. It may be indisputable that there is being. But this is a mere blind irrational undeduced fact. And philosophy cannot begin with such a fact. This then is not the solution. We must look elsewhere for it. Hegel has himself stated it in many passages.

148. Now becoming is implicitly present in being. The deduction proves that being implies becoming. Therefore you cannot have being without becoming. Becoming is, therefore, a condition on which being depends. The condition is necessarily prior to that of which it is the condition. Hence becoming is prior to being. Being in reality *presupposes* becoming, and becoming is the *foundation* of it. For if there were no becoming there could be no being. And although becoming is the end, the later term in the deduction, it is also in truth the beginning, the foundation, the logical first. The subsequent course of the deduction proves that being necessarily involves, not only becoming, but all the categories including the final category, which Hegel calls the Absolute Idea. Being presupposes becoming, which presupposes the next synthesis, and so on throughout till we reach the final presupposition of all the categories, the Absolute Idea. Becoming is the foundation of being, is logically prior to being. The next synthesis is logically prior to becoming, is the foundation of becoming. Hence the last category, the Absolute Idea, is the absolute first, the absolute foundation and presupposition of being and of all the other categories.

149. This conception, that the last is also the first, that the end is the true beginning, is found already in a highly developed form in the philosophy of Aristotle. The first and lowest term in Aristotle's scale of being is formless matter. Because this is wholly indeterminate, completely vacant of all character or quality, it corresponds in all respects to Hegel's pure being. And since it is thus empty of any determination Aristotle declares that it is nothing, an absolute not-being. This is precisely the same as Hegel's declaration that being and nothing are identical, and it is because this supposed unheard of novelty of Hegel's is in reality Aristotelian that Hegel regards the

philosophy of Aristotle as genuinely "speculative." Formless matter, then, is the first term in Aristotle's scale of being. The end, the last term is absolute form, matterless form. Form, for Aristotle, is the same as definition, specification, determination. Absolute form is the completely determinate. And this completely determinate, which is the end of the Aristotelian scale of being, is no other than the absolute concreteness which Hegel also posits as the end, the final category. The scale of being, according to Aristotle, begins with the completely abstract, *i.e.* formless matter, and passes through further and further specifications and determinations, to the completely concrete and determinate, matterless form. This corresponds in all respects to the Hegelian movement from abstract being to the concrete Absolute Idea. And for Aristotle absolute form is the first, is logically prior to formless matter. The end is prior to the beginning. This, too, is Hegel's conception.

150. How, now, does this solve the problem of an undeduced beginning? It solves it because we now see that the category of being is not a mere beginning, planked down, without foundation, without deduction, resting on nothing, hanging in the air. Its foundation is the Absolute Idea. It may be objected that it is not clear what is here meant by the word foundation. The difficulty, it will be said, is that being is undeduced. And the only way in which the problem could be solved along these lines would be to show that the Absolute Idea is the foundation in the sense that being is logically deduced from it. But this is precisely what we do mean by foundation here. Being can be and is deduced from the Absolute Idea, and is for that reason not an undeduced beginning. For deduction means showing that what is deduced is contained in that from which it is deduced. And that being is contained in the final category is obvious, since it has already been shown that the final category contains all previous categories. Being (implicitly) contains the final category; the final category can therefore be deduced from it—through a chain of intermediate categories. The final category (explicitly) contains being; and therefore being can be deduced from it.

We have seen how the species, becoming, is deduced from the genus, being. It is surely obvious that being can be deduced from becoming; for becoming is a species of being and explicitly contains and involves the idea of being. The idea of the genus being is got out of the idea of the species becoming by mere analysis. The idea of the species obviously contains the idea of the genus. There is no difficulty in extricating, *i.e.* deducing, the idea of "animal" from the idea of "horse." Being can thus easily be deduced from becoming, becoming from the next synthesis, and all the categories finally from the Absolute Idea. Being might be deduced from any of the later categories. It is obvious, for example, that it can be deduced from substance. For a substance is a kind of being, and we get the idea of being out of the idea of substance by mere analysis.

151. It would seem then that the deduction of the categories might theoretically begin at either end. Hegel begins with being and ends with the Absolute Idea. Why not begin with the Absolute Idea and end with being? Is Hegel's choice of order merely arbitrary? Is it justified? It is important that we should understand the answer to these questions. In the first place it will be seen that, in order to avoid the enigma of an undeduced beginning, *both* procedures are necessary. If we began with being but could not reverse the process, then being would be an undeduced beginning. If we began with the Absolute Idea, and advanced to being, but could not reverse the process, then the Absolute Idea would be an undeduced beginning. Hegel's solution consists in showing that being is not an undeduced beginning because its foundation is the Absolute Idea; and the Absolute Idea is not an undeduced beginning because its foundation is being. Both orders of deduction are, therefore, necessary.

Why, then, does Hegel, in the Logic, begin with being and proceed in *that* order only, saying nothing of the reverse process? The answer to this is quite simple. All deduction that is worth while proceeds from the implicit to the explicit. In a syllogism the conclusion is implicit in the premises. The object of the deduction is to make explicit what is implicit.

The explicit is the same as the patent, open, and obvious. It is only because the conclusion is not explicit, *i.e.* not obvious, that a deduction is required to make it so. In the same way becoming and all subsequent categories up to the Absolute Idea are implicit in being. But they are not explicit. And therefore, in order to make them explicit, we begin with being and produce them out of it. The reverse procedure is unnecessary because it is obvious, explicit, that the later categories contain the earlier. It is not clear how being involves substance or cause. And therefore a deduction from being to substance, cause, etc., is required. But it is obvious that cause involves being, and therefore it would be waste of time for Hegel to proceed with the deduction in that order.

152. The conclusions at which we have arrived may now be compared with what was said earlier (79 to 82) about the nature of reason regarded as the Absolute. If the absolute *first*, from which the world flows, is reason, is not this reason itself, we asked, an unexplained fact? And we answered that reason is a self-explanatory principle, that it is self-determined, that reason is its own reason. We can now see more fully how true this is. Reason is the system of the categories. It is a self-enclosed, self-determined, sphere. If the final category has for its reason being, yet on the other hand being has for its reason the final category. The whole system of categories returns into itself, is deduced from itself. And this is equivalent to saying that reason is its own reason, that it is self-determined. And hence, because no prior reason can be asked for it, no reason external to itself, it is therefore suited to be the absolute *first*, the principle of explanation of the whole universe.

153. Before leaving this topic, it is worth noting some of its implications regarding the nature of logical deduction. Hegelian deduction proceeds upon the twofold basis that (1) the conclusion, the end, the Absolute Idea presupposes the premise, the beginning, being; and yet, on the other hand, that (2) the beginning, being, presupposes the conclusion. This may appear strange. Yet the same thing is implied in formal Logic. The conclusion of a syllogism presupposes the

premises. Yet the premises also presuppose the conclusion, and this fact is usually expressed by saying that the syllogism is a *petitio principii*. In the syllogism

> All men are mortal.
> Socrates is a man.
> Therefore, Socrates is mortal,

the major premise is only true if the conclusion is true ; *i.e.* the truth of the premise presupposes the truth of the conclusion. If attack is made upon the syllogism on the ground that its premises assume its conclusion, the reply is that they assume the conclusion only in the sense that they have the conclusion implicit in them. Deduction consists in making explicit what is implicit.

Mill assumed, on the contrary, that genuine inference must pass from the known to the unknown, *i.e.* that the conclusion must not be implicit in the premises but must be something absolutely new. His attempt to show how this is possible was a complete failure. By induction, he thought, we pass from the facts that A, B, C, etc., are mortal to the completely new fact that D is mortal. To do this, however, we must assume the truth of the principles of causation and the uniformity of nature. Induction then appears as a syllogism in which one of those principles is the major premise. And in accordance with the general rule that the syllogism is a *petitio principii*, the major premise assumes the truth of the conclusion that D is mortal. From which we see that the Hegelian view is correct ; *i.e.* inference merely passes from the implicit to the explicit.

The contrary view, that the conclusion can be something absolutely new, is a breach of the principle *ex nihilo nihil fit*. Parmenides thought that becoming involves the arising of something out of nothing, and asked how, in these circumstances, becoming can be possible. Aristotle answered the question by formulating the view that becoming does not involve the passage from absolute nothing to absolute being, but from potential being to actual being. The terms potential and actual are identical with the terms implicit and explicit respectively. And just as change, the time-process, meant for Aristotle the passage of potentiality into actuality, so for Hegel the logical process is the passage of implicitness into explicitness. The problem set by Parmenides as regards the nature of change, and the problem how deduction can pass to absolutely new facts, are one and the same problem. And one and the same answer solves both.

J. Divisions of the System.

154. The system of Hegel is divided into three parts:
    (1) Logic.
    (2) The Philosophy of Nature.
    (3) The Philosophy of Spirit.
These three, viz. the Logical Idea, nature and spirit constitute a triad. Logic treats of the Idea as it is in itself. This is the thesis. Nature is the Idea in its otherness. It is the opposite of the Idea in itself. This is the antithesis. Spirit is the unity of the Idea and nature. This is the synthesis.

155. For the sake of simplicity we have hitherto spoken as if the triads followed each other in a simple linear series. This, however, is not the case. Not only does one triad follow another in simple series, but whole series of triads fall within larger triads, and these again within larger. Hegel regards a number of triads as constituting a single sphere of categories or notions. This whole sphere, which may contain many theses, antitheses, and syntheses, is itself regarded as a single thesis. Its antithesis and synthesis will themselves be spheres of categories or notions which contain smaller triads within them. The entire system constitutes a single triad, Idea, nature, spirit. The Logic, which deals with the Idea, is again subdivided into three, viz. being, essence, the Notion. Each of the three terms of this inner triad is again subdivided into smaller triads. Nature and spirit are likewise divided and subdivided. The method followed in this process will be clearer when we come, in the following parts of the book, to the details of the system.[1]

156. The first part of the system, the Logic, deals with pure reason, the system of the categories,—what we have

[1] See also diagram of Hegel's system at the end of the book.

called the first reason of the world. The second and third parts, nature and spirit, deal with the actual world itself. Nature includes space and time, inorganic matter, plants and animals. Spirit means the spirit of man, which is also part of the actual existent world.

157. The system of the categories is the Idea as it is in itself. Nature is the Idea in its otherness. Spirit is the Idea returned from this otherness into itself. To explain what this means we must comment upon the word Idea. The Idea seems at first sight to have two meanings. It is (1) a collective name for the entire system of categories. The Logic has for its subject, we are told, the pure Idea, the Idea as it is in itself. Used in this way the Idea is just the sum of the categories. But the term is also used (2) as the name of the final category in the Logic, or at least as the name of the final sphere of categories. The actually final category itself is called the Absolute Idea, but the sphere of categories to which this belongs is called simply the Idea. Now although we may legitimately distinguish these two senses in which the word Idea is used, the main point for us to grasp is that these two senses, which appear different, are in reality identical. The final category is identical with the sum of all the previous categories, for, in accordance with the dialectical method and its principles, the final category explicitly contains all the earlier categories. It is itself the sum of all the categories. It is their unity. It is, therefore, a matter of indifference whether by the word Idea we understand the final sphere of categories or the entire series from being onwards.

158. Nature as the antithesis of the Logical Idea is the opposite of the Idea. It is *not* the Idea. Yet we have already described nature as the Idea in otherness. Both statements are true. The relation of the Idea to nature is that of thesis and antithesis. Thus it is the same as the relation of being to nothing, the first thesis and antithesis of the system. Nothing is, in the first place, different from being. It is *not* being. It is the opposite of being. In the same way nature is the opposite of the Idea. It is *not* the Idea. But, on the other hand, being is identical with nothing. Nothing *is* being.

In the same way nature is identical with its opposite, the Idea. It *is* the Idea. We have, as usual, identity *in* opposition. And this relation is usually expressed by saying that nature is the Idea in the element of otherness. That it is the Idea—this expresses the identity. That it is in otherness—this expresses the opposition. Such phrases, frequent in Hegel, as that nature is the Idea gone out of itself, that it is the Idea in estrangement from itself, express the same thought.

159. Spirit, finally, is the Idea which has returned, from this otherness and self-estrangement, into itself. This language may be used of the synthesis of every triad. Being goes out of itself into its opposite, nothing. Being is affirmative, nothing the negative of it. Becoming is again an affirmative. It is again being, but being which has now absorbed its opposite into itself. For it is now a being which has nothing in it, the unity of being and nothing. And since becoming is again being, it is the return of being out of otherness into itself. The Idea, likewise, goes out of itself into nature. Spirit is the unity of nature and the Idea, and is therefore the Idea returned into itself. For the Idea is reason. And spirit, *i.e.* the human spirit, is rational. It is the existent reason. As reason it is the Idea. As existent, it is part of nature.

160. Spirit is divided into (1) subjective spirit, (2) objective spirit, (3) absolute spirit. What is meant by these terms will appear in the proper place. Objective spirit contains *inter alia*, Hegel's ethics and his political philosophy. Absolute spirit includes the philosophy of art and the philosophy of religion. Meanwhile it will be seen that spirit, as the final term of the triad Idea, nature, spirit, is the absolute end, and therefore the true beginning, the foundation of all. Just as being has for its proximate foundation becoming, and for its ultimate logical foundation the final category, the Absolute Idea, so the Idea in itself, or, as we shall often call it, the Logical Idea, has spirit for its foundation. And the foundation of spirit as a whole is its third member, absolute spirit. And this means that absolute spirit, as the absolute end of the whole system of triads, is the foundation of the whole, *i.e.* not only of subjective and objective spirit, but also of nature

and the Logical Idea. It is thus the ultimate foundation of the world. It is the Absolute. The Absolute is thus spirit. This, which is a frequent expression of Hegel's, may appear to contradict the previous assertions that the Absolute is the Idea, the system of categories. And the student may be inclined to be puzzled as to what Hegel means. Does he mean that the Absolute is the system of categories, or does he mean that the Absolute is the final phase of the human spirit, viz. absolute spirit? The answer is that the two statements are identical. We have not yet explained what is meant by the category of the Absolute Idea. The accurate specification of this is not possible till we have been through the contents of the Logic. But meanwhile we may say in anticipation that the Absolute Idea is no other than the category of spirit. Just as the category of cause is the abstract thought or concept which applies to those actually existent objects which are causes; so the category of the Absolute Idea is the concept which applies to the highest phase of the human spirit. It is the thought of spirit. Hence the distinction between the Absolute Idea and absolute spirit is the same as that between the category of substance and substance itself, or as that between the category of cause and an actual cause. Now we have seen that although the distinction between the category of substance and substance itself is real, yet there is identity in this distinction. The category of substance is identical with substance itself (101). It is exactly the same here. The category of the Absolute Idea is identical with absolute spirit, and therefore it is indifferent whether we say that the Absolute is the one or the other; just as we saw that it would be indifferent whether we said that the Absolute is the category of substance or substance itself.

161. But although this is so, and although it is true that by spirit Hegel certainly means the human spirit, we must not jump to the preposterous conclusion that, according to Hegel's philosophy, I, this particular human spirit, am the Absolute, nor that the Absolute is any particular spirit, nor that it is humanity in general. Such conclusions would be little short of shocking. Absolute spirit is perfect spirit.

Absolute spirit is certainly in me, this individual me, as my very core and substance, because it is the pattern on which I am made. But I, as this individual with all my irrational caprices, particularities, and selfishness, am but a distortion of absolute spirit. To use metaphorical, *i.e.* religious language, one may say that absolute spirit is nothing less than the spirit of God—the completely rational, all-knowing, all-wise, perfect spirit. And the assertion that absolute spirit is the final phase of the human spirit means no more than that the human spirit is of essentially the same kind as the spirit of God, and that every man is potentially divine. Lastly this metaphorical language concerning God must not be misunderstood. Hegel most certainly did not believe in a personal God in the ordinary crude popular sense in which God is conceived as *a* particular person among other persons. The Absolute is personality—another name for the category of the Absolute Idea—or spirit, but not a particular person or a particular spirit,—which would mean a finite spirit. But these matters can hardly be fully comprehended till we have worked through the system in detail. And we now proceed to the details of the system.

PART II

THE LOGIC

INTRODUCTION

162. Reason, the subject of the Logic, is on the one hand the system of objective categories, and on the other hand it is the system of those subjective categories or concepts by means of which we do our thinking. Objective and subjective reason are identical (140), and the Logic is therefore the science of both. As the science of the objective reason, the Absolute, the supreme reality, it is an ontology or metaphysic. As the science of subjective reason, of the categories with which we think, it is an epistemology. Kant's list of categories is *only* an epistemology because he regarded the categories as purely subjective. Hegel saw that the categories are objective as well, so that his account of them is also a metaphysic, or ontology. And lastly, since it is the science of human, *i.e.* subjective, reason, it is also, in the usual sense of the term, a logic.

163. The Logic falls into three great spheres of categories, viz. the categories (1) of being, (2) of essence, (3) of the Notion. These three spheres constitute a triad. The term being is thus the name of (1) a particular category, *i.e.* being as opposed to nothing, and of (2) a sphere of categories of which this particular category is only one. In this wider sense the sphere of being includes the numerous categories and sub-categories of quality, quantity and measure.

The first sphere, being, is characterized by immediacy. The categories here included, for example being, nothing, quality, quantity, etc., are simple immediate categories in the sense that each sets up to be a self-subsistent concept which stands by itself and does not explicitly refer the mind to, or stand in relation to, any other category. Such concepts as positive and negative are obviously correlatives which **refer to each other**. But being does not expressly refer to nothing. Positive and negative imply each other. Being, apparently, does not imply nothing. It stands by itself, on its own basis. The same is true of quality and quantity. They do not seem to have anything to do with each other. Each of them is what it is quite apart from the other. They do not mediate one another, as positive and negative do. Hence they are called immediate. It is true that, when the categories of the general sphere of being are critically examined, it turns out that they are in fact vitally related to each other. Thus we have already seen how being implies and necessarily involves nothing. And in the same way we shall find that quality and quantity really involve each other. This is the very meaning of the deduction of the categories from one another. The deduction breaks down the supposed self-sufficiency of each category and shows that, though it *purports* to stand alone, it is in reality impossible without the other. But it is this *purporting* to stand alone which constitutes the immediacy of the categories of this sphere. The reference of the categories to each other, their logical implication of each other, is not explicit, as it is in the case of positive and negative. It is implicit, hidden below the surface, and the very purpose of the deduction is to bring it to light, to make this implicitness explicit. Being, nothing, becoming, quality, quantity, etc., are all *apparently* disconnected. This apparent disconnection is their immediacy. Only by means of the deduction is the inner connection between them forced into view.

164. If being is thus the sphere of immediacy, essence, on the other hand, is the sphere of mediation. Mediation in being is implicit. In essence it is explicit. It lies immediately to hand. The categories of essence go in pairs such as cause and effect, action and reaction, substance and accident, identity and diversity, positive and negative. Each category in a pair explicitly refers and points to its correlative category. Each mediates the other. The categories of being are like single stars which *appear* to be self-governed but in reality form parts of one vast system of universal attractions. Their connection

INTRODUCTION

with the others is implicit, hidden. The categories of essence resemble those double stars which are linked together and revolve round each other. In their case the connection is open and explicit. This second part of the Logic is called the sphere of essence because in each pair of categories one is conceived as the essence or ground of the other, as the inner essential reality of which the other is the outer rind or appearance. Thus a substance is conceived as the underlying substratum of its accidents. A cause is the ground of the effect and is manifested in the effect. Identity is thought of as the inner core of reality which manifests itself in diversity and multiplicity,—as we see in all those philosophies which regard the Absolute as a self-identical one which manifests itself in the multiplicity of the phenomenal world.

165. As being is the sphere of immediacy, and essence of mediation, so finally the Notion is the sphere of the merging of mediation. For, on the one hand, the categories of the Notion mediate one another. They explicitly refer to one another. This is the factor of mediation. But these categories which are thus distinguished immediately collapse into a unity. The distinction is no sooner made than it vanishes. The unity in which all distinctions thus disappear is, for that reason, a new immediacy,—an immediacy resulting from the absorption of all mediation. This is the factor of immediacy. Thus, in general, being is immediacy; essence is mediation; the Notion is the unity of immediacy and mediation.

166. In every triad the first term, the thesis, represents the stage of simple apprehension and corresponds to the doctrine of terms in formal logic. The antithesis represents the principle of the understanding and corresponds to the doctrine of judgments. The synthesis represents the principle of reason and corresponds to the doctrine of the syllogism.[1] The

---

[1] These statements may appear to conflict with the passage above quoted from Hegel (141) where he says that the first term is that of understanding, the second that of negative reason, the third that of positive reason. There is, however, no conflict. Both statements are true. The first term viewed by itself in its isolatedness is a simple self-identity—simple apprehension. Viewed in its relation to the second term its very isolatedness implies that it is different, distinct from, the second term. Viewed in this way its principle is *distinction*, which is the principle of the understanding. So

first term is simply apprehended, by itself, as this single term, *e.g.* being. No proposition, no judgment, is as yet framed as regards it. When we pass to the second term, *e.g.* nothing, we now have a judgment, being is nothing. The simple self-identity of the first term has developed a difference within its own substance. Being now splits in twain, it becomes being *and* its opposite, nothing. Here then, in place of simple self-identity, we have difference, distinction, mediation. This is the principle of the understanding. The first term taken alone, before we proceed to the second term, is a self-identity; being is being and nothing more, A is A. The passage to the second term gives us difference. A is not now simply itself; it is something different from A; it is B; hence we have A is B, *e.g.* being is nothing. This is a judgment. The first term is simple identity, the second simple difference. The third term is the unity of the first two, identity *in* difference. It thus corresponds to the syllogism, in which the two extremes, the major and the minor term, are brought together into unity on the common ground of the middle term. This is the principle of reason.

These remarks apply to the three main divisions of the Logic. The doctrine of being corresponds to the doctrine of terms in formal logic. Each of its categories is apprehended simply and immediately as a self-identical, self-subsistent entity standing by itself on its own basis. The doctrine of essence has for its principle mediation and diversity, which are the principles of the understanding. It thus corresponds to the doctrine of judgments. The doctrine of the Notion corresponds to the syllogism inasmuch as its principle is the principle of reason, identity in diversity.

167. We have already seen that, on the one hand, the categories are definitions of the Absolute (102). It is of essential importance to understand that they are also, on the other hand, definitions of, or concepts applicable to, the actual existent universe, the external world of objects. They are just

---

also the second term has two aspects. As distinct from the first term it represents understanding. As identical with its opposite, *i.e.* the first term, it contains the principle of negative reason in the sense described in the passage above (141).

as applicable to this hat, that book, this tree, that star, as they are to the Absolute. They are the concepts by means of which we seek to make the universe intelligible. That we can bring external objects under such categories as being, substance, cause, quality, quantity, etc., is obvious. It is not so obvious, but it is equally true,—and indeed it is the purpose of the Hegelian philosophy to prove—that even the supreme categories are applicable to, and give us the truest knowledge of, the world of objects. For even this crass world of matter essentially is, if we could only see it, nothing else than the Absolute Idea. There is nothing but the Idea. The Idea is all reality. The Idea, we have seen, is spirit. We may now add that the Idea is thought.[1] Just as the category of substance is the thought, the concept, of substance, so the Idea is the thought of thought, the concept of thought. To say that the category of the Absolute Idea, just as much as the categories of quantity, cause, etc., applies even to the world of matter, is equivalent to saying that the material world is, in reality, nothing but thought. The Logic will prove this. And it will prove it in the following manner. If it is admitted of any object, say this hat, that it " is," then it will follow by absolute necessity of logic that it is also " is not," that it " becomes," that it is a " cause," a " substance," and finally that it is thought, the Absolute Idea. This is precisely what the deduction of the categories proves. Being necessarily involves becoming. Therefore if a thing is, it also becomes. Becoming necessarily involves the next category, and therefore if a thing becomes it follows that the next category also applies to it. And so with the next and the next to the end of the Logic. Finally, therefore, to whatever object the category of being applies, the category of the Absolute Idea applies also. In other words whatever *is*, *i.e.* the whole universe, is thought, or, if we prefer to put it so, spirit. The proof of this consists solely in the detailed deduction of the categories. And if each link in the deduction is logically valid, then the proof is absolute and certain.

[1] The precise sense of these terms must be left to be conveyed by the detailed expositions of the Logic and the system generally.

168. We seem to have two distinct points of view. Firstly the categories are definitions of the Absolute. Secondly they are definitions of the existent world. But these two points of view turn out to mean the same thing. For the phenomenal world, the actual universe, is not something different from, and lying outside of, the Absolute. So far as the world is real, so far as it *is* at all, it *is* the Absolute. The Absolute is all that is. And we have already said this when we said above " there is nothing but the Idea. The Idea is all reality " (167). For the Idea and the Absolute are synonymous terms. But although the world and the Absolute are thus identical, it is nevertheless true that within this identity there is a distinction between them. Or, as we said before (158), nature *is* the Idea, and also is *not* the Idea.

169. It follows from what has been said that every category is applicable to every object in the universe. Such concepts as " chair," " green," etc., apply only to some things. But each category is a concept which applies to everything, and this is just what Kant meant by saying that the categories possess universality. It remains to add that the application of some of the categories to all things is not so obvious as the application of others. It may be obvious that quality applies to everything, *i.e.* that everything possesses some quality or other. But it is not so obvious that the categories of the Idea apply to everything, *i.e.* that everything is thought. But that this is true is what the deduction will prove. For it will prove that whatever comes under the category of being, *i.e.* whatever is, comes under all the subsequent categories.

170. The next point is that the Logic gives us a scale of values. The categories are all valid descriptions both of the world and of the Absolute. But the earlier categories, though valid so far as they go, are inadequate. The later categories are progressively more and more adequate. Finally, the category of the Absolute Idea, the last category, is alone the completely adequate and true description of the world, of individual things in the world, and of the Absolute. To apply the category of being to an object, to say that " it is " is to express regarding it the absolute minimum of knowledge. No matter

what the object, merely to know that " it is " is to know next to nothing about it. To know that " it becomes," is to know a little more. For becoming is being with an addition ; it is being *plus* nothing. Each step in the deduction of the categories is a new determination, a new specification of the object, and therefore a new piece of knowledge. And since in this advance nothing is ever lost (144), since the later category contains all the earlier categories, each new category that we apply to the object means that we know that it possesses all the determinations represented by the earlier categories *plus* a new determination. Complete, full, and final knowledge of the object is therefore only given by the final category of the Logic. It is quite true to say of things in the world that they are qualitative and quantitative, that they are causes, effects, substances, and so on. But full knowledge of them only comes when we see that they are the Idea, that they are thought. And this piece of knowledge is complete in itself because it includes all the earlier pieces of knowledge. It is quite true to say of the Absolute that it is being (as Parmenides said), that it is substance (as Spinoza said) and so on ; but all these inadequate descriptions of the Absolute are absorbed and included in the full and final description of the Absolute as the Idea.

171. The categories of being are, roughly speaking, the concepts used by common sense and unreflective consciousness to cognize the world. The categories of essence are those used by science. The categories of the Notion are those used by philosophy. The lowest phase of consciousness, crude sensation, informs us merely that things *are*, are there, are *present* to the senses. This is the category of being. The other categories of the general sphere of being are the various forms of quality, quantity, and measure. That a thing has such and such qualities and is of such and such a quantity, that the universe is composed of quantities of things having various qualities,—this is the common sense way of cognizing the world. Being, too, is the sphere of immediacy, and common sense regards immediacy as the truth of the world. What is immediately there, what is present, this chair, that table—

these immediate objects are what common sense regards as real. And the qualities and quantities of things are just what is immediately perceived about them.

172. We rise from this point of view to that of science. Here of course quantities and qualities are still of importance. But what distinguishes science from common consciousness is that it methodically classifies objects, and thereby introduces a host of distinctions and differences into the world of knowledge. It is only common sense rendered more precise and elaborate. Precision, difference, distinction,—these are the work of the understanding, and characterize the second stage of the triadic movement. Consequently we shall expect to find science using chiefly the categories of essence. The most important categories of essence are the thing and its properties, force and the manifestation of force, substance and accident, cause and effect, action and reaction. And these are precisely the conceptions which are the stock-in-trade of science in its attempt to cognize the world. Science attempts to ascertain what properties the thing has, what its cause is, by what forces it is governed, in what way it is in action and reaction with other things.

173. These categories supersede those of being, and yield a more adequate knowledge of the world, and therefore science is an advance upon unreflective common sense. But completely adequate knowledge is only attained in philosophy, which cognizes the universe by means of the categories of reason, as distinguished from the categories of understanding, which are those of science. The categories of philosophy, of reason, are those of the third sphere of the Logic, the doctrine of the Notion. Here we have the categories of thought, organism, life, teleology, and finally the Idea. That all things are thought, that the universe is a living spiritual organism, that it is governed by intelligence working towards ends, that it is, in the last resort, nothing but spirit, the Idea,— this is the full and final truth about the universe. And the knowledge of this is philosophy.

Philosophy transcends science just as science transcends common thought. It is true that the world is composed of quantities and qualities. It is truer that the world is a system of causes and effects, actions and reactions. It is the perfect truth that the world is spiritual self-conscious thought. But it must not be supposed that the higher truth excludes the lower and opposes it. The higher categories contain the lower absorbed in themselves. Philosophy includes the truth of science. To say that the world is the Idea includes all that science desires to express when it talks of causes, substances, forces and the like. Science and philosophy are not opposed and alternative ways of cognizing the universe. Philosophy admits all that science has to tell us of the world, and supplements this knowledge with a completer view.

174. Just as the series of categories constitutes a series of concepts under which we cognize the external world, a series progressively increasing in value and adequacy as it advances; so, and for the same reasons, it gives us a series of increasingly adequate definitions of the Absolute. The Absolute is being. This is the first and poorest of all definitions. It is true, but totally inadequate. The Absolute is the Absolute Idea (*i.e.* personality, spirit, self-consciousness). This is the last and completely adequate definition. The intermediate categories give us definitions of intermediate value.

Hegel also believed that if we extricate from the various historical systems of philosophy their essential and governing conceptions, we shall find that each such conception is a category of his own Logic; and that the system which presents it appeared, roughly speaking, at a period in history corresponding to the place of that category in the Logic. Thus, apart from the purely physical conceptions of the Ionics, the first definition of the Absolute given in the history of philosophy is that of the Eleatics, *i.e.* the Absolute is being. This is also the first category of the Logic. Immediately after this we have Heraclitus, the central conception of whose philosophy is becoming, which is the second positive category of the Logic.[1] Soon after Heraclitus we have the Atomists. The

[1] As a matter of fact, it can hardly be doubted, I think, that Heraclitus was historically prior to the Eleatics and that Parmenides was acquainted with, and consciously opposed his teachings. But the point is not of much importance here.

central conception of their philosophy, their definition of reality was, according to Hegel, the category of being-for-self, which appears in the Logic a little later than becoming. Later in history we have Spinoza with his philosophy of substance, a category which, in the Logic, appears in the doctrine of essence. It must be admitted that this correspondence of history with the Logic is very rough and ready and cannot be pressed very far.[1] But Hegel bases upon it a new and interesting view of the evolution of philosophies. It is often supposed that systems of philosophy spring up in a haphazard manner, like so many freak speculations, and that they most of them contradict one another. But according to Hegel the history of philosophy presents a definite line of evolution, the principle of which is that the Idea gradually and progressively unfolds itself in time in the successive systems. Hence that history is not merely governed by chance and blind caprice, but is a rational development governed by the Idea itself. The Idea first posits itself in its most inadequate form, that of being. For being, and each of the categories, it must be remembered, *is* the Idea. Being is *implicitly* the Idea. This first phase of the self-positing of the Idea produced the philosophy of Parmenides. The Idea next posits itself, somewhat more adequately, as becoming. Hence arose the system of Heraclitus. And so the development proceeds until the final and completely true conception of the Absolute as the Absolute Idea is attained in the system of Hegel himself.

According to this view the successive systems do not contradict, but supplement, each other. Just as the later categories take up the earlier as factors of themselves, so the later systems take up the earlier into themselves, digest, assimilate, and absorb them. The teaching of Parmenides is true. So is that of Heraclitus. And the latter does not contradict the former. It includes and transcends it. For its governing idea, the category of becoming, includes and transcends the category of being. All philosophies, therefore, are true. But

---

[1] Hegel himself admits this. " To the historian of philosophy it belongs," he says, " to point out, more precisely, how far the gradual evolution of his thesis coincides with, or *swerves from*, the dialectical unfolding of the pure logical Idea " (Wal., *Log.*, § 86 Z). The italics are mine.

INTRODUCTION

some are less adequate, some more so. Finally Hegel's own philosophy is the consummation of the whole historical series. It absorbs into itself all previous philosophies. For it defines the Absolute as the Absolute Idea. And the Absolute Idea is the final category which contains within itself all the others, being, becoming, cause, substance, and the rest.

With this is connected Hegel's entire view of history. The universal history of the world, he thinks, is not the playground of blind chance. Its process is governed by the Idea, that is to say, by reason. History is the progressive self-manifestation of the Idea in time. And this is what is called by theologians " the divine governance of the world." Hegel attempts to carry out this idea in detail in his presentations of the development of philosophy, of art, of religion, and of political history. We now turn to the detail of the Logic.

FIRST DIVISION

THE DOCTRINE OF BEING

INTRODUCTION

175. The general characteristics of the sphere of being have already been described (163. 171). We have seen, too, for what reasons the science of Logic necessarily begins with being (114 to 120). Nothing further need, therefore, be said under these heads. It only remains to say, by way of introduction, that the doctrine of being falls into three spheres of categories, viz. (1) quality. (2) quantity, and (3) measure. We proceed to deal with these in order.

CHAPTER I

QUALITY

176. The specific category of *quality* is not the first in this sphere, but as all the categories in the sphere are, as we shall see, qualitative in character, the term quality is used as the name of the general sphere as well as of the special category. In the same way the term *being* is used in three significations. It is the name of the first category; it is the generic name of the three categories of the first triad; and it is the name of the entire sphere which includes quality, quantity, and measure.

SECTION I

BEING

A. Being

177. **Being** is the first category for reasons already discussed (114 to 120). It is the highest possible abstraction. All character, all determinations of any kind, have been abstracted from. Hence being has no character and is utterly empty.

B. Nothing

178. Because being is thus utterly empty, it is therefore equivalent to **nothing.** The thought of nothing is simply the thought of the absence of all determination. When we think of anything we can only think it by virtue of its having this or that determination, size, shape, colour, weight, etc. What has no determinations of any kind is an absolute emptiness, nothing. And because being is by its very definition the absence of all determination, it is nothing.

This is also evident if we take being as the predicate of a proposition. Reality, we might say, is being. This is only a tautological way of saying, reality *is*. In that form we see that being is not a true predicate, but merely a copula. It does not define reality in any way, but leaves our knowledge of it completely empty. If we are told that reality is, we naturally ask, *what* is it? The predicate being provides no answer. Instead of a proposition in the form S is P, we have one in the form S is —, the predicate being represented by a blank which is equivalent to a cipher. This cipher, which is all being represents, is nothing. Being, then, is nothing. If there were any difference between them it must consist in the fact that being possesses some determination which nothing lacks. But being has no determinations whatever. Therefore there can be no difference. The thought of being and the thought of nothing are the same, and pass into each other.

C. Becoming

179. Thus being passes into nothing. But nothing equally passes into being. For the two as identical are as the two sides of an equation, and every equation may be reversed. If A=B, then B=A. The assertion that nothing passes back into being is apt to puzzle the beginner, even when he has seen that being passes into nothing. This is because the idea of "passage" brings time-associations and images into the mind. We know that, with regard to actual changes of things in time, a change in one direction does not involve a change in the reverse direction. That a leaf turns from green to yellow does not necessitate its changing back from yellow to green. Some such thought puzzles us here. But here the "passage" is only a *logical* or equational transition. It means only that the thought of being is identical with the thought of nothing, and from this it follows that the thought of nothing is identical with the thought of being, *i.e.* that nothing passes back into being. This passage of being into nothing and nothing into being is **becoming.** The passage of nothing into being is **origination,** or coming-to-be. The passage of

being into nothing is **decease**, or ceasing-to-be. Origination and decease may be regarded as sub-categories.

180. Becoming is the concrete unity of being and nothing. It is a unity because it involves their identity. The distinction between them has vanished in the identity. They have collapsed to unity. But the unity is *concrete* because it still contains the difference preserved within it. It is not a mere abstract unity like the ordinary " concept," which includes what is common to the things of a class, but excludes their differences. Becoming includes the differences as well as the identity. Being and nothing are identical, and this gives us the category of becoming. But we must not deny their difference merely because of their identity. They are at once absolutely identical and absolutely distinct. Becoming involves both. The "passage" is only another word for the identity. But were there no difference there could be no passage, no becoming. If A is to become, it must become something different from itself. A cannot become A, for there is no becoming, no change here. It must become B.

Further Explanations

181. The categories of the Logic are successive definitions of the Absolute. The first category is also the first definition given in history. The Absolute is being. This was the definition put forward by Parmenides. The philosophy of Parmenides also involved the category of nothing or not-being, though he denied that reality could be defined by that category. Heraclitus was responsible for the view that reality is becoming,—the second definition of the Absolute.

182. The objections of common sense that, if being and nothing are identical, it is the same whether we have dinner or no dinner, whether we exist or do not exist, etc., are beside the mark. No such absurdities are implied. We have in view here only the empty indeterminate abstractions, being and nothing. Such entities as dinner are not indeterminate. Dinner is, for example, determined as solid, hot, coloured, eatable, and so forth. It is only *pure* being, indeterminate being, which is identical with nothing.

183. We must be careful not to think any *time*-element into the category of becoming. Being and nothing pass into each other logically, not one after the other in time. But, it will be said, the idea of becoming, change, etc., essentially involves time and is meaningless without it. The answer is that becoming involves time only in the same sense that quantity involves matter or at least space. But in thinking the pure thought quantity we have to abstract from the element of space or matter. And in thinking the pure thought of becoming we must abstract from the element of time.[1]

184. Being is not the same as *existence*. To say of anything that " it is " is not the same as saying " it exists." " It is " is an incomplete proposition, a proposition with no predicate. On hearing it we demand a predicate; we ask " *what* is it " ? But " it exists " is a complete proposition. It contains an implied predicate, namely, " in relation with other things." The proposition " it exists " means that " it " is a part of the universe, and that it stands in mutual relations with other things. It means that " it " is a part of that rationally ordered system of entities and relations which we distinguish as real from the entities in dreams, hallucinations, and the like. Hence existence is a much more complicated, rich, and concrete idea than mere empty being, and for that reason existence appears as a category at a much later stage of the Logic (262).

SECTION II

DETERMINATE BEING

185. We are now at the category of becoming. Becoming, as we have seen (180), depends as much upon the difference of being and nothing as upon their identity. A cannot become

---

[1] I am unable to agree with Dr. McTaggart's view (*Com.* §§ 18, 19) that Hegel's category of becoming is not intended to include the conception of *change*. Such a view flies in the face of Hegel's text. The name becoming, the names of the sub-categories origination and decease, the references to Heraclitus, constitute overwhelming evidence that Hegel conceived his category of becoming as change. Such a deduction of change, Dr. McTaggart thinks, would not be valid. Whether the deduction is valid or not may be an arguable question. But that Hegel *intended* to deduce change seems to me indisputable.

A; a young man cannot become young. A must become B; the young man must become old. Hence, if the difference between being and nothing were to collapse, becoming itself would collapse. But the difference *has* collapsed, for being and nothing are identical. Therefore becoming itself disappears and abolishes itself. This thought may be otherwise expressed as follows. Becoming is, firstly, the passage of being into nothing. But nothing *is* being. Therefore becoming is the passage of being into being. But this is not a becoming. Therefore becoming has disappeared. Becoming is, secondly, the passage of nothing into being. But being is nothing. Therefore becoming is the passage of nothing into nothing, which again is not a becoming. Becoming thus collapses.

But the result of this process is not mere nonentity. What we have left is still obviously the unity of being and nothing. All that has disappeared from it is the element of *change*.[1] Hence we are left with the unity of being and nothing now in a state of *rest*. This is clearly a kind of being, for it has being in it. But it is a being which does not *become*, does not at once disappear into nothing. It is no longer true that one may say of it equally either that it *is not*, or that it *is*. It now definitely *is*. It is this *definiteness* of the being which constitutes the new category. It is *definite*, *i.e.* determinate, being, one sort of being as opposed to another. It is being *so and not otherwise*. It is **determinate being.**

The original empty category of being had for its very nature the absence of all determination. We have now arrived at the conception of a being which *has* determination. We cannot as yet say *what* determination it has. We have only arrived at the *general* idea of determination as such. We may know that a thing is coloured, without knowing what colour it is. And we have here in the same way merely the general conception of a being which has *some* determination. This purely abstract idea is the whole content of the category of *determinate being*.

[1] That the element of change disappears is essential to the deduction. But it will be noticed that it infringes the Hegelian principle (144) that as the dialectic proceeds nothing is ever lost.

To me it seems that this deduction is invalid. It appears to derive its force from a play upon the word definite. To say that a thing now *definitely* is, means that it has ceased to chop and change between " is " and " is not." Quite another meaning of the word definite creeps in when we use it as a synonym for determinate. And this is probably why Hegel at this point has recourse to metaphor—" the deus machina of an argument "—to enforce the shaky deduction. " Becoming " he says, " stands before us in utter restlessness. . . . Becoming is, as it were, a fire, which dies out in itself, when it consumes its material. The result of this process, however, is not an empty nothing, but . . . determinate being; the primary import of which evidently is that it *has become*." [1] Sensuous metaphors of this sort should, like the myths of Plato, make one suspicious that they cover up a break in the thought.

Sub-Section I

Quality.

186. We have reached the idea of determinateness as such. And the determinateness which has been thus deduced is quality. This is not at once obvious. It is obvious that quality is a kind of determinateness; but it is not the only kind. The *quantity* of a thing is also a determination of it. How, then, can Hegel, having merely deduced determinateness in general, claim to have deduced the particular kind of determination which we call quality? The answer to this question is as follows. Determinate being is a being which definitely is, *i.e.* does not at once disappear into nothing (185). What prevents it from disappearing into nothing is its determinateness. If it had no determination it would be pure being, and pure being *does* disappear into nothing. Hence the determinateness which we have before us is a kind of determinateness such that the very being of the being depends upon it. Destroy the determinateness and the being itself is destroyed (disappears into nothing). In fact the determinateness *is* the being. For it is only by virtue of its determination

[1] Wal., *Log.*, § 89 Z.

that the being is. The determinateness is part and parcel of the being. They are identical, cannot be separated or regarded as external to each other.

Now this kind of determination, which is identical with the being of a thing, and cannot be separated from it, is quality. The quantity of a thing, on the other hand, is a determination which is quite separable from the being of the thing, and is external to it. Suppose that the thing under consideration is oxygen. It possesses the *quality* of supporting combustion. If this quality were destroyed it would cease to *be* oxygen. The very being of the oxygen *is* its qualities. Alter these qualities and the oxygen as oxygen ceases to exist. Thus the quality of a thing is a determination which is identical with the being of the thing. It is quite otherwise with quantity. You may increase or diminish the quantity of the oxygen to any extent whatever without affecting its being as oxygen in the slightest degree. Quantity is thus a determination which is external and quite indifferent to the being of a thing. Now what we have deduced is, as proved above, determinateness which is identical with being, and with the disappearance of which the being itself disappears. Therefore we have deduced **quality.**

187. Quality, however, splits into two. It may be regarded as either positive or negative. On the one hand the quality of a thing constitutes it what it is, constitutes its being. That a thing has such and such a specific gravity, supports combustion, is colourless, odourless, etc., constitutes that thing oxygen. The quality is, from this point of view, the very being, the **reality** of the thing. On the other hand, since determination is negation, quality also possesses this negative aspect. The qualities which make a thing oxygen also make it *not* hydrogen. Quality is thus also **negation.** Reality and negation are the two sub-categories of quality.

188. Reality, as understood in the last paragraph, is not the same as absolute reality, *independent* being. It was in this latter sense that we used the term reality earlier in this book (12 *et seq.*). By reality in the present context, however, Hegel means simply the fact of a thing being *there*, being *positively*

present. In this sense whatever has determinate being, whatever *definitely* is, is real. This is something more like the popular use of the word real.

Reality is not, of course, the same as pure being. It is *determinate* being. It is only its determinations, its qualities, that make a thing real. And in the same way negation is not the same as nothing. It is not an empty nothing but a determinate nothing. It is the negation of something definite. Nothing negates everything whatever. Negation only negates some definite entity. For example the sea is the negation of the land. But the sea is not nothing.

189. The quality of a thing regarded in its positive aspect (reality) is the inherent character or being of the thing as it is in itself apart from all other things. So considered it is the sub-category of **being-in-itself**. The quality regarded in its negative aspect (negation) is the character of the thing as negating some other thing. It is then a being which stands in relation to (negates) other things. As such it is the sub-category of **being-for-other**.

Sub-Section II

Limit

190. The stage which we have now before us is the category of quality. For we need not consider further the sub-categories to which quality gave rise. Keeping before our minds, then, the idea of quality, we have to deduce from it, *i.e.* show that it necessarily involves, the next category, which is *limit*. This transition is very easy and obvious. For we have already seen that the ideas of determination and limit involve each other (43). The transition really depends simply on the principle that determination is negation. A quality is a determination of a thing, and determination is negation. But to negate a thing is to limit it. Hence a quality is a limit. In this way the category of **limit** is deduced from that of quality.

191. A meadow is a meadow and not a pond because it possesses the qualities of a meadow and not those of a pond. These qualities which it possesses constitute it what it is.

But they also determine it as not being what it is not. Its being a meadow, its possession of the qualities of a meadow, is just what limits it, prevents it from being a pond. Thus its positive quality is also its negation or limit. The word limit is of course here used in a qualitative, not in a quantitative, sense. The physical boundaries of a land limit it in space. They limit its quantity or size. But the qualities of the land limit it in the sense that they define it as this kind of land as opposed to that. Qualitative limits are not physical boundaries in space. But the boundary lines between species and species are qualitative limits. Thus reason constitutes the boundary that cuts off man from the rest of the animals. And the boundaries between species are obviously constituted by their specific qualities. Hence quality clearly involves limit.

The general sphere of categories which come under the title of limit falls into three specific categories:

A. *The Finite*

192. Limit obviously involves **finitude**. For to be limited is to be finite. And the category of the finite implies a further category which Hegel calls

B. *Alteration*

193. For the finite is that which has a limit. And if something is limited, it follows that beyond the limit there must be another something. For a limit or boundary cannot be a boundary of only one thing. It must be necessarily a boundary between two things. To be finite means to be limited *by something else*. There is therefore the " something " and the " other." Or the same result may be reached in another way. It is in its *negative* aspect that quality is limit. The thing which has quality thereby negates; but it does not negate itself; it negates an " other." The quality of light negates darkness. Or lastly, the very notion of limit implies that there must be something beyond the limit. To know that there is a limit is to know that there is something beyond it (66). We have arrived therefore at the conception of " something " and " other." Something is a more advanced con-

ception than mere being. It essentially belongs to the sphere of determinate being. For it means *this* definite being as opposed to *that*. *This* is the " something "; *that* is the "other."

But the other is also a something. There are two somethings. And each something is also an other. There are two others. If A is the something and B is its other, then B is also something and A is its other. It is indifferent which we call something and which we call other. Something and other are therefore identical. Each passes into the other. Thus something becomes other. And this change of something into other, this becoming other, is **alteration** (alter = other).

194. This deduction is apt, like the statement that being and nothing are identical, to be puzzling if the reader fails to keep before his mind the pure abstract categories involved and allows sensuous images to take their place. We saw that the identity of being and nothing did not mean for example, that dinner is the same as no-dinner. So here the statement that something and other are identical does not mean that the something, light, is identical with its other, darkness, or that a pond is the same thing as a meadow. What we have to think is, not these concrete sensuous things such as pond, meadow, light, darkness, but the pure abstract categories " something " and " other." And the point is simply that every other is also a something, and therefore that the pure thought of something and the pure thought of other are identical. Being and nothing, *as such*, are the same. But this special sort of being, dinner, is not the same as nothing. Something and other, *as such*, are the same. But this special sort of something, light, is not the same as this special sort of other, darkness. This point, namely, that in the Logic we are throughout talking only about pure abstract thoughts, and not about sensuous objects, should be carefully kept in mind, not only as regards the transitions of being into nothing and something into other, but as regards all the transitions in the Logic. Failure to understand a deduction will frequently be removed by reflection upon this point. In explaining future transitions we shall not, as a rule, revert to it but shall assume that the reader has made it his own.

195. Finitude, then, necessarily involves alteration. It is for this reason that all things finite change, perish, and pass away. It is no mere accidental fact that the finite is unstable. To be subject to mutation lies in the very notion of finitude itself. For the limit of the finite is constituted by its own inherent positive character, by its quality, and not by anything merely external to it. The meadow is limited by its own being, by the very fact that it is a meadow. But limit is negation. Therefore negation, not-being, are of the essence of finite things. Their very being, *i.e.* positive character or quality—is not-being. They contain within themselves the germs of their death and dissolution.

196. Alteration is not the same as becoming. It is a more concrete, fuller category. Becoming is the passage of being and nothing into each other, as when a thing begins to exist or ceases to exist. Alteration is the passage of one something into another something (not into nothing) as when a leaf changes colour or a man grows old. Becoming is creation or annihilation. Alteration is change of quality.

C. *The Spurious Infinite*

197. Something becomes other. But this other is also a something and therefore in turn becomes other. This other is a third something and again becomes other; and so *ad infinitum*. Hence arises the notion of an infinite series of somethings. This is the popular idea of the infinite, *i.e.* mere endlessness, the unceasing reiteration of the same thing for ever, and is exemplified in infinite space and time and in the infinite numerical series.[1] But it is not the true conception of infinity. It is not the true infinite. It is the **spurious infinite.** For each of the terms of the series, each something and each other, is itself finite. For each is a something which is limited by its other. Thus however far we go, we never get beyond the finite. We have but an endless alternation of something and other, an endless repetition of terms each of which is finite, so that the finite is never got rid of. This is an everlasting

[1] Mr. W. T. Harris (*Hegel's Logic*, pp. 201, 203-4) gives space and time as examples of true infinity. He is clearly mistaken.

attempt to grasp the infinite which however completely evades us. It *ought* to be infinite, but it never *is*. For this reason Hegel calls it the spurious, or false, or negative infinite.

198. " This result," says Hegel," seems to superficial reflection something very grand, the grandest possible. But such a progression to infinity is not the real infinite. . . . When time and space, for example, are spoken of as infinite, it is in the first place the infinite progression on which our thoughts fasten. . . . The case is the same with space, the infinity of which has formed the theme of barren declamation to astronomers with a talent for edification.[1] In the attempt to contemplate such an infinite our thought, we are commonly informed, must sink exhausted. It is true indeed that we must abandon the unending contemplation, not however because the occupation is too sublime, but because it is too tedious . . . the same thing is constantly recurring. We lay down a limit: then we pass it: next we have a limit once more, and so for ever." [2]

Sub-Section III

The True Infinite

199. The endless reciprocal determination of something and other is thus the false infinite. But the other is identical with the something (193). Hence something in being determined by its other, is in reality only determined by itself. This is the **true infinite.** For genuine infinity means self-determination, whereas the finite is what is determined by another. The spurious infinite is merely the unlimited. True infinity is the self-limited.

200. The full riches of this result are seen best by putting the above deduction in another way. Something becomes other. Something and other are opposites. The something is finite. Its other is therefore the infinite. Hence the finite in passing its limit transcends itself and becomes the infinite.

[1] Edification—a favourite *bête noire* of Hegel—invariably used by him in a contemptuous sense, as meaning edifying commonplaces, worthy platitudes.

[2] Wal., *Log.*, § 94 Z.

But this other, the infinite, is itself something, and so again turns into its other, the finite. Thus the finite is never truly transcended, for as soon as we pass to the infinite, this turns out to be only finite after all. Space is an example of this. We may take any point in it as a limit. This side the limit is finite. Beyond the limit is infinite space. But as soon as we get beyond the limit, we find that a further point may be taken as a further limit, and thus the infinite beyond turns out to be finite. This process of laying down limits and then transcending them goes on for ever. This is the spurious infinite.

But, as we saw, when the something becomes other, it only becomes itself. It is self-determined. Thus the infinite is the unity of something and other. But since the something is the finite and its other the infinite, we get this result, that *the infinite is the unity of the finite and infinite*.

The finite and infinite are placed by the understanding in irreconcileable antagonism to one another. The finite, it supposes, is not infinite, and the infinite is not finite. They stand facing each other, the one here, the other there, negating each other, totally opposed. But, says Hegel, this view, which is the common one, " fails to note the simple circumstance that the infinite is thereby only one of two, and is reduced to a particular, to which the finite forms the other particular." [1] The infinite, according to this view, is limited by the finite, and is therefore itself finite. This is the spurious infinite, which only ought to be infinite, but is not, and cannot escape from the conditioning fetters of the finite.

Reason breaks down this absolute opposition. The infinite is not something outside the finite ; it absorbs the finite into itself. The finite and infinite are identical as we see from the very self-contradiction of the view of understanding, which, by making them absolutely opposed, reduces the infinite again to a finite. Even according to this view, the finite and the infinite, are identical. For both are finite. Hence true infinity is the sublation of this distinction, and the recognition of their identity in their difference.

[1] Wal., *Log.*, § 95.

In saying that the true infinite is the unity of finite and infinite, we must be careful to note that it is a concrete, and not merely an abstract, unity. The distinction is not simply abolished. It is retained within the unity.

201. This doctrine of the infinite triumphantly solves the oldest and most formidable difficulty of philosophy and religion. How, it has been asked, can the infinite ever become finite, how can God create a world? How can the infinite issue forth out of itself to the formation of the finite? That it should do so is a self-contradiction. Plotinus, Spinoza, and innumerable others, have struggled with this enigma. The infinite One of Plotinus can have no contact with the finite world, because to do so would limit its infinity. And it is impossible to see how the infinite substance of Spinoza ever came to differentiate itself into the multiplicity of the finite world. The philosophy of Spinoza goes to pieces on this rock, and is convicted of a hopeless dualism.

But these contradictions in all previous philosophy result from the fact that they mistake the spurious infinite, the infinite of understanding, for the true infinite, the infinite of reason. Spinoza, guided by the one-sided view of the understanding, regards the infinite as utterly excluding the finite. Therefore, of course, the finite can never come out of it. The true infinite has the finite within it. It *is* the finite. "The answer to the question, how the infinite becomes finite, is consequently this, that there is no such thing as an infinite, that is *first of all* infinite, and which is afterwards under a necessity to become finite, . . . but it is *per se*, already just as much finite as infinite." "This question, founded, as it is, upon the assumption of a rigid opposition between finite and infinite, may be answered by saying that the opposition is false, and that in point of fact the infinite eternally proceeds out of itself, and yet does not proceed out of itself."[1] It proceeds out of itself inasmuch as it produces the finite; it does not proceed out of itself inasmuch as this finite is itself the infinite so that the infinite remains what it is, abiding in itself.

[1] Wal., *Log.*, § 94 Z.

202. As space and time were examples of the spurious infinite, so thought, in the highest sense, may be taken as an example (indeed the sole example) of the true infinite.[1] For pure thought, as we find it for example in the Logic, *i.e.* the system of reason, is self-determined and therefore infinite. The Idea is infinite. It puts forth the finite, nature, from itself, but in doing so it does not lose its infinity, nor does it pass out of itself. For nature is still the Idea. And the Idea maintains itself in nature, and though it goes forth into nature, yet in nature it is still itself, and abides in itself. Nature is the finite because it is *not* the Idea, because it is the other of the Idea. Yet nature is infinite because it *is* the Idea (158), for the other of the Idea is only itself, just as, at the present stage, the other of the something is only the something itself. Hence the Idea is both finite and infinite. It is therefore the true infinity, for it is the unity in difference of finite and infinite.

SECTION III

BEING-FOR-SELF

203. The true infinite, which we have reached, is self-determined. It is nowise determined by another, for its other is absorbed within itself. Thus its being is wholly in and for itself. It is **being-for-self**. And being-for-self is infinite being.

204. If we consider the three spheres of quality, namely being, determinate being, and being-for-self, we shall see more fully that the last is infinite being. The first sphere is empty being, undetermined, and unconditioned, a mere vacuum. Into this undetermined vacuous being, negation enters. Negation is determination. Negation entering here, therefore,

[1] In reality, of course, every object in the universe is an example of every category (169) and therefore of this category. But some categories are *obviously* applicable to a particular object, while others are not (169). Thus the material world is in reality the Idea (158); but it more obviously comes under such categories as mechanism, causality, etc. So here anything might be given as an example of the true infinite. But the explicit and obvious example is thought. Hegel frequently gives empirical examples of categories, and he is always to be understood in this way.

transforms being into determinate being. This is the first negation. Being is here simply negated, and so determined. Hence we get the categories which are all various expressions of the idea of determination, viz. quality, limit, finitude. In general this sphere is the sphere of being as determined and limited by its other, by what is outside itself; that is to say, it is the sphere of finitude.

The other, by which being is limited, is simply the negation which has entered into it. Determinate being has its negation, in the form of its other, over against it. But in being-for-self this other has been absorbed. The other is seen to be identical with the being of which it is the other. Thus the other, as something over against the being, is here negated. Its otherness is negated, for it is now not the other of the being, but is identical with the being, and the being contains it. The other, which is negation, is itself negated. This is the negation of the negation, or, as Hegel calls it " absolute negativity." Such absolute negativity is the same as infinitude. For what we have here is being which has no other, no external other to limit it. Its other, which determines it, is only itself. It is thus self-limited, self-determined, and to be self-determined is to be infinite.

205. Pure thought, the Idea, was our example of true infinity. It is also, therefore, an example of being-for-self. But this example is truer when the abstract Logical Idea becomes concrete spirit. The highest form of spirit is self-consciousness. This is attained in philosophy, where thought has itself for its object. In this form, since it is its own object, it is *for itself*. It is then being-for-self. The other of the Idea, nature, is here negated, is brought back into the Idea, and ceases to be other. This is the negation of the negation, infinitude, being-for-self.

The same thought is expressed in a different way when Hegel says that the ego is the readiest example of being-for-self. I am not only conscious of external objects. I am also conscious of myself. I as subject have myself as object. I am thus *for* myself. The ego is being-for-self. A stock or stone, on the other hand, is not for itself. It is only for me, *i.e.* it only exists for thought. It is thus being-for-other. Hence it is finite. But the ego, as being-for-self, is infinite.

This example is really identical with the last. The ego, considered at the ordinary levels of consciousness, is not only, not fully, being-for-self. It has its other, the non-ego, outside itself. But in the supreme levels of consciousness, viz. philosophy, the ego finds that the non-ego is merely itself, *i.e.* that nature and the external world are nothing but the Idea, that is to say, thought. In being conscious of the non-ego, thought thus knows itself to be merely conscious of itself. It is pure self-consciousness. Its other is absorbed in it. It is purely and solely for itself, with no external other to limit it. Hence it is pure infinite being-for-self.

The first category is this sphere is

A. The One

206. For being-for-self, as self-subsistent, is a unit, a one. By a one we mean that which is purely for itself, which is related only to itself, and excludes any relation to an other, a single self-subsistent entity. And being-for-self is precisely the being which excludes any relation to an other, for it has absorbed its other into itself. To put it otherwise, in being-for-self the distinction between itself and its other is sublated. The distinction and differentiation, and the multiplicity which they involve, being thus annulled, what we have here is a unity, that is to say, a **one**.

207. In the previous sphere of determinate being the being stood in relation to an other. This relation may be figuratively compared to a ray of light passing out from the being to its other. But now, in the present sphere, the other has been absorbed into the being. Instead of relation to another we have relation to self. The ray of light passing outwards is turned back upon itself, and returns to its source. From this metaphor of light Hegel calls being-for-self "reflection into self." For this reason, though the one is a unity, it is not to be regarded as an empty unity. An utterly empty unity, such as pure being, is not a *unit*. For to be a genuine unit implies self-subsistence. It implies a certain absoluteness, an

independence of anything other than itself. This dependence only on self we find, for example, in the atoms, or units of being, which Democritus took to be the foundation of the world. And for this reason Hegel says that atomism was that philosophy which conceived the Absolute (the real) under the category of being-for-self. The atoms are final, ultimate, indivisible. Each unit is absolute. It does not arise from, or depend upon anything else. It is self-subsistent, a true unit, a one. That it is indivisible means that it is not dependent on composition of parts. It is not an aggregate of many. It is a pure one. It is just the idea of an abstract one, which is not a many, which Hegel makes the content of this category. The atom is a true unit, an abstract one, just because it is not dependent on a multiplicity. There is in it no multiplicity whatever. It is not related to a many, which would be, for it, an other. It is related solely to itself. Hence the self-relatedness, the reflection into self, which we have in being-for-self, gives us the category of the one.

It is important to realize that this idea of reflection into self is necessary for the category of the one. Otherwise we might ask why the one was not deduced much earlier in the Logic. It might be said, for example, that the one could have been deduced from becoming straightaway since that was the *unity* of being and nothing. It might even have been said that the one should have been deduced from pure being, for even that is an empty unity. But the one is not merely a unity; it is a unit. It is an absolute being. Its absoluteness involves self-determination which only emerges here with being-for-self.

208. From the one issues

B. *The Many*

or the many ones. For the self-relation of the one is a negative relation. By a " negative relation " Hegel means a relation to an other, *i.e.* a relation of the being which negates its other. For the self-relatedness of the one exists only by virtue of the fact that it has its other in it. Being has only become being-for-self by absorbing its other. Its self-relation is, therefore, relation to an other. That other is internal to it, yet, because it is an other, it is also external to it. For to be an other means to be external. Or we may put the same thing in another way. That the one is self-related means that the one is related to the one. This involves a distinction between the one which is related and the one to which it is related. The one distinguishes itself from itself. It "repels itself from itself," to use Hegel's own phrase. Thus the one suffers self-diremption into a multiplicity of ones, the **many**. The one repels the one from itself, puts it outside itself. The one which repels is thus distinct from the one which is repelled. There are two ones. And since each of these again splits in two, and so on indefinitely, we have therefore an indefinite multiplicity.

209. From this we pass to

C. Repulsion and Attraction

That the one repels itself from itself—this is **repulsion.** It is that element of *distinction* between the ones which keeps them separate. Each one excludes the other ones from it. It is only by virtue of the fact that it excludes the others that it retains its self-identity and continues to be a one. Each one only maintains itself as one by cutting itself off from the other ones, be enforcing the boundary between them.

But the many are one the same as another. Each is one. Hence they are one and the same. All are identical. This bond of *identity* is the opposite of that element of distinction and mutual exclusion which has been called repulsion. Hence this relation of identity is called **attraction.** We must not be misled into supposing that Hegel is here attempting to deduce the physical forces of attraction and repulsion. The names used are indeed physical metaphors. But they are purely figurative. Repulsion merely means that the many ones exclude each other. Attraction merely means that they are at the same time identical. Repulsion is the mutual exclusion of the ones by each other, whereby they emphasize their *difference.* Attraction is their mutual inclusion and *identity.*

CHAPTER II

QUANTITY

210. At the end of the last chapter we reached the categories of attraction and repulsion. That is the point at which we now stand, and it is from these categories that the notion of the next sphere, that of quantity, must be deduced. The deduction proceeds in the following manner.

The many ones are identical with one another (209). Repulsion is the relation of a one to an other one. But since the first one is identical with the other one, its relation to the other one is a relation to itself. But the relation of identity of the one to itself is attraction. Therefore attraction and repulsion are identical. As this may appear puzzling we will repeat it in other words. The ones are related to each other in two ways. Firstly they are *different* from each other. This is repulsion. Secondly, they are *identical* with each other. This is attraction. Now if we have two ones, the relation between them, since they are different ones, is repulsion. But since they are also identical, the relation of the first to the second is only a relation of the first to itself. Thus it is a relation of self to self, *i.e.* a relation of identity; and this is attraction. The relation between any two ones, therefore, is both attraction and repulsion at the same time. Therefore attraction and repulsion are identical. The relation of one to the other one (repulsion) is only its relation to itself (attraction). The distinction between attraction and repulsion thus collapses to unity. The two coalesce into one. This unity of attraction and repulsion is **quantity**.

The last statement will be more clearly understood, if we

remember that repulsion and attraction are respectively the same as the many and the one. Repulsion is the moment of separation and difference, and is thus the principle of the many. Attraction is relation-to-self, the moment of identity, and is thus the principle of the one. Thus, instead of saying that quantity is the unity of repulsion and attraction, we may say that it is the unity of the many and the one.

This is at once intelligible. A quantity is not an abstract many, or an abstract one. It is essentially a many-in-one. Thus a line is quantitatively measured when we say that it is twelve inches long. This quantity is one—it is one line, or one foot. But it is many inches. A heap of wheat is one heap, but many grains. Neither unity nor multiplicity alone make up the notion of quantity. We must have a unity of both. A quantity is an aggregate of units—many units, one aggregate.

211. There must be mutual exclusion (repulsion), otherwise there can be no many, and no quantity. There must also be identity (attraction). An aggregate, a quantity, can only be made up of parts having a common element, an identity. We cannot add a foot of space to a year of time. We can of course add a man, a cow, and a star, and say that they are a quantity of things. But then they are all *things*. This is the identity. No doubt in this sense we can even add a foot of space to a year of time, and say that they make a quantity of *things* (two). But we can only do this because of their identity as things, their " attraction " as Hegel would call it.

212. Quantity, then, is deduced as the unity of the one and the many, or the unity of attraction and repulsion. But there is another important consideration here. Attraction and repulsion, as the final categories of quality, must contain all the previous categories of quality absorbed within themselves. They must contain the entire fullness of quality. Therefore to abolish attraction and repulsion would be to abolish quality as a whole. Now, in the preceding deduction of quantity, we have just seen attraction and repulsion abolish themselves. For attraction turned into its own opposite, into repulsion. Attraction therefore is not-attraction. It con-

tradicts and abolishes itself. And repulsion likewise abolishes itself because it is the same as attraction and thus contradicts itself. And since attraction and repulsion are thus abolished, and since they contain the whole of quality absorbed in themselves, it follows that quality itself is abolished. Hence the result is a non-qualitative being. And this is quantity. Quantity is indifferent to quality. Quality, as we pointed out (186), is a kind of determination which is identical with the being it determines. But quantity is external to the being of the thing. As far as quantity is concerned it is matter of pure indifference whether the things quantified have this or that quality. Five horses are five horses whether they are brown, or white, or black. A mile is a mile whether it is a mile of metalled road or a mile of telegraph wires. Or again if we alter the quality of a thing it ceases to be the thing it was. But if we alter the quantity it does not change the thing in any way. Thus quantity is external and indifferent to the quality and to the being. Quantity is non-qualitative.

213. Some critics have ridiculed Hegel for deducing quantity merely as not-quality.[1] That quality has abolished itself and that we now, therefore, have not-quality before us, and that not-quality is quantity, this is taken to be Hegel's deduction of quantity. Such a deduction, would, of course, be absurd. A horse is not a pig. But to deduce not-pig would not be the same as deducing horse. The criticism, however, is unintelligent. Hegel does not deduce quantity as not-quality. He deduces it as the unity of repulsion and attraction, and he shows incidentally that this involves its indifference to quality.

214. Quantity, like the other categories, is a definition of the Absolute. That the Absolute is quantity, this is, on the whole, says Hegel, the point of view of materialism. As category, of course, quantity is a pure thought. But matter is essentially the externalization, the outward form, of this category. Quantity is the category of externality; for the essence of a quantity is that its parts lie outside each other. And this externality, this outsideness of part to part, is also the

[1] See, for example, Mackintosh, *Hegel and Hegelianism*, p. 154.

QUANTITY

central feature of matter. Matter is the category of quantity become an object of sense. The materialist's definition of the Absolute as matter, therefore, places its essential character in quantity.

215. The categories of quantity fall into three spheres, pure quantity, quantum, and degree.

SECTION I

PURE QUANTITY

This sphere comprises a single triad of three categories.

A. *Pure Quantity*

216. To speak of quantum here is, properly speaking, an illegitimate anticipation. But for the sake of clearness we may at once distinguish between pure quantity and quantum. A quantum is any definite quantity, such as ten miles, five minutes, twenty pigs, a hundred degrees of temperature. **Pure quantity** is indefinite quantity which is not as yet carved up into quanta. Thus space in general is a pure quantity. When we carve out of space a definite amount, such as fifty feet, this is a quantum. Pure quantity is not necessarily, like space and time, infinite. It is merely indefinite. Thus there are not, as a matter of fact, an infinite number of men. But men, an indefinite number of men, have the character of pure quantity. Carve out of this a definite number, fifty men, or a thousand men, and we have quanta.

At the present stage we are dealing with pure indefinite quantity, quantity in general. That is all that we have reached in the course of the dialectic. We have not yet reached the idea of definite quantities. Pure quantity is the unity of repulsion and attraction.

B. *Continuous and Discrete Magnitude*

217. Quantity has two sources, namely, the identity of the ones, attraction, and the difference of the ones, repulsion. Quantity, regarded under the point of view of attraction, is

continuous magnitude. Regarded under the point of view of repulsion, it is discrete magnitude.

A quantity is necessarily a series of ones, or units. It is one, one, one, one, ... etc. The fact that all these ones are identical (attraction) joins them together, and allows us to pass from one to the other. They make, in this way, a continuity. And as such quantity is **continuous magnitude.** The fact that all these ones are different (repulsion) disjoins them and cuts them off from one another. Quantity, regarded from this point of view, is **discrete magnitude.**

218. It must not be supposed that we have here two different *kinds* of magnitude, as though one quantity was continuous and another quantity discrete. Every quantity is both. These are but inseparable moments or characteristics of any quantity whatever. It would be nonsense to ask, for example, whether space is continuous or discrete. It is both. It is obviously continuous; every part, so to speak, runs into the next. But it is equally obviously discrete, *i.e.* composed of parts, feet, inches, miles, etc.

Continuous and discrete magnitude necessarily involve each other. Continuous magnitude is *ipso facto* discrete, and *vice versa*. Its continuity depends on its discretion. It is obvious that, only by having a plurality of separate ones (discretion) can there be any continuity between them. Continuity is only conceivable as a continuity of discrete ones. Likewise it is obvious that only by having a single continuous series can we chop it up into separate ones. In order to make quantity we must, as already stated, have both unity, or continuity, and difference, or discretion. Thus if we take a man, a cow, a harmonium, and a star, these make a quantity of things. That all are *things*, this is the identity. As so many *things*, it is a continuous magnitude. As so many *different* things, it is a discrete magnitude. Ten feet of space is continuous, because all ten feet are identical; all are space. It is discrete because it is divided into ten *separate* feet.

219. By means of this fact that every quantity is both continuous and discrete Hegel solves at one stroke the ancient and previously insoluble riddle of Zeno about the infinite

QUANTITY

divisibility of space, time, etc. Zeno points out that if we say that space, for example, is infinitely divisible, then any finite quantity, say ten feet, must contain an infinite number of parts, which is self-contradictory. If on the other hand we say that space is not infinitely divisible, then it must be composed of indivisible units having magnitude, and that what has magnitude should be indivisible is a self-contradiction.

But to ask thus whether space is composed of indivisible units, or is divisible *ad infinitum*, is the same as asking the foolish question whether space is continuous or discrete. The question assumes that it is *either* one, *or* the other, whereas in fact it is both. If space were simply discrete, *i.e.* chopped up into discrete ones, then it would be composed of indivisible units. If it were simply continuous then it would be divisible *ad infinitum*. Either of these suppositions is true, but neither is the whole truth. The whole truth is that space is quantity, and quantity is the unity of continuity and discretion.

220. Now quantum differs from pure quantity by the fact that it is definite. To get a quantum we must introduce definiteness, or limits, into quantity. Space in general is quantity. A limited amount of space, *e.g.* ten feet, is a quantum. Hence the transition to quantum must be made through the category of

C. Limitation of Quantity

But the limit must not be merely introduced from outside. It must be deduced from the stage at which we have already arrived. How is this done? Now it is evident that the idea of limit is implicit in what we have now before us. Though continuous and discrete magnitude involve each other, they are yet distinguished. But all distinction involves limit. Moreover this is precisely the limit that we want. A quantum, such as ten feet of space, is a magnitude regarded as discrete from the rest of space. The space on both sides of it is continuous *ad infinitum*. The limits at each end of the ten feet line consist in distinguishing the ten feet quantum as discrete from the continuous quantity out of which it is carved. We can see then that the idea of limit necessarily arises here. It is implicit in the distinction between continuity and discretion. All that is required is to make it explicit. The precise detail of the deduction is as follows.

Quantity arose in the dialectic from the one. The one continues out of itself and becomes many ones *ad infinitum* (208). The many ones are both continuous and discrete By virtue of their continuity we may take any number of ones, say ten, *together*. By virtue of their discretion we may then cut off these ten from the rest, whereupon we have a quantum. This cutting off is the **limitation of quantity.**

SECTION II

QUANTUM

A. *Quantum*

221. Quantity, being thus limited, becomes **quantum**. The quantum is determinate quantity, whereas pure quantity was indeterminate. Hence we have here an advance which corresponds to the advance from pure being to determinate being. Pure being was indefinite. The element of negation, definiteness, limit, was found to lie within it, whereupon it became determinate being. Pure quantity was likewise indefinite, but now introduces into itself the element of negation, or limit, and so becomes definite quantity, or quantum.

The factors of discretion and continuity become, in the sphere of quantum,

B. *Sum and Unity*

222. A quantum is an aggregate, a many, a plurality. As such it is **sum,**—a sum of many ones. This is the moment of discretion. But as continuous these many ones form a **unity**—*one* quantum. These two moments, sum and unity, necessarily involve each other and can no more be separated than discrete and continuous magnitude. Taken thus in their inseparable union with each other they constitute

C. Number

223. For the factors of sum and unity are precisely what make a number. To think the number seven, for example, we must first take an aggregate or *sum* of seven units, and we must then regard them as a *unity*, a *single* quantum. This gives us the **number.**

The category of number is thus the perfect expression of quantum. This may also be seen from the fact that it is by number that we *measure, i.e.* mete, set bounds or limits to, quantity. Suppose we have an *indefinite* number of men. This is a pure quantity. We then count them, and they become a *definite* quantity, a quantum. Thus number is the perfect expression of quantum.

SECTION III

DEGREE

224. The quantum is *extensive* magnitude. That is to say, the constituent units which compose the quantum lie outside one another. In ten feet of space each foot is external to all the other feet. In a hundred men, each man is separate from the others. In a numerical series each number is external to the other members of the series. But now we pass to a kind of quantity where this relation of externality is not found.

Quantum is pure quantity with the addition of limit. The limit of a quantum is what determines its specific character. Thus the limit of the number ten is the tenth one. The limit of the number one hundred is the hundredth one, and so on. Now, since all ones are identical, therefore all the ones in the quantum are identical with the limiting one. Hence they disappear into it, coalesce with it. All of them, therefore, are internal to it, are absorbed within it, and thus the limit, or limiting one, is identical with the whole of the quantum. This gives us the idea of a quantum in which the separate ones do not lie outside each other and outside the limit, but are all internal to the limit itself, and absorbed within its simple unity. Such a quantum is *intensive* magnitude or **degree**.

225. Just as ten feet of space, twenty men, etc., are examples of extensive magnitudes, so a hundred degrees of temperature, or such and such a degree of brilliancy in light, or such and such a degree of intensity in colour, or tone, are examples of intensive magnitude, or degree. Thus if we consider a hundred degrees of temperature, we shall find that it corresponds to the description of intensive magnitude given in the last paragraph. A hundred feet of space lie outside each other. But in a hundred degrees of temperature, the 99th degree, the 98th degree, and so on, do not exist by themselves, nor lie outside the hundredth degree. The hundredth degree is the limit. And only the hundredth degree exists, the others being absorbed within it. Hence the limit, *i.e.* the hundredth degree, is in this case identical with the whole quantum.

Extensive magnitude is a manifoldness. It is " in itself multiple." Intensive magnitude is not thus multiple within itself. It is a simple undifferentiated unity " a simple determinateness."

226. We saw that continuous and discrete magnitude were not two *kinds* of magnitude which could exist apart from each other, but that they imply each other, and that every magnitude has these two aspects. It is the same with extensive and intensive magnitude. In spite of their difference they involve each other, and are, in fact, identical. Every magnitude is both extensive and intensive. This is proved by the following considerations. The intensive magnitude is identical with the limiting one, for the limiting one has, in intensive magnitude, all the other ones internal to it. The twentieth degree contains the other nineteen in itself. Nevertheless, these other ones are, at the same time, also *external* to the limiting one. For although they are absorbed in the limiting one, they are not annihilated but are still real. And this means that they have an existence of their own *apart from* the limiting one. They are *different* and *distinct* from it. They are *other* to it. That they are thus other to it, that they

QUANTITY

exist apart and distinct from it, means that they are *external* to it (not of course external in space, but in thought). Thus the ones are external to the limit and to each other, and to be so constituted is to be extensive magnitude. Intensive and extensive magnitude are therefore identical.

According to Hegel, weight, heat, light, sound, etc., are examples of this identity. A mass, regarded as a *number* of tons, pounds, ounces, etc., is extensive. But as exerting pressure it is intensive. For the quantity of pressure is a degree. Warmth, again, has a degree. But it becomes extensive magnitude when it manifests itself as the expansion of the heated matter. Thus a higher degree of temperature (intensive magnitude) expresses itself as a longer column of mercury in the thermometer (extensive magnitude). In other words an increase in degree is accompanied by a corresponding increase in extensive quantity. Similarly a higher sound-tone, which is degree, is manifested as extensive quantity in the greater number of vibrations.

227. The sphere of degree falls into the three categories, (1) degree, (2) the quantitative infinite progress, (3) the quantitative ratio.

A. Degree

228. The deduction, and also the content and meaning of the category of **degree,** have just been explained. We can pass at once to

B. The Quantitative Infinite Progress

229. The quantum, as we saw, was formed by placing a limit within the continuous indefinite quantity. Now degree is also a quantum. The twentieth degree, for example, is a *definite* quantity and therefore a quantum. But the conception of degree depends upon the factor of continuity by virtue of which the other ones are identical with the limiting one. And by virtue of this same factor of continuity the ones within the limit, *e.g.* one, two, three, etc., up to twenty, are identical with the ones beyond the limit, *i.e.* twenty-one, twenty-two, etc. Thus the limit is broken down and passed

over. The quantum passes beyond its limit into the indefinite quantity beyond. But this indefinite beyond, this indefinite quantity, again of necessity becomes a quantum. We have already seen (220) the dialectic by which every indefinite quantity necessarily becomes a quantum. This new quantum again transcends its limit, passes into the indefinite quantity beyond, which again becomes a third quantum, and so *ad infinitum*. Thus we have an infinite series, and this is the **quantitative infinite progress.**

230. The dialectic here is similar to that by which we reached the spurious infinite in the sphere of quality. There the something passed over into another something and so *ad infinitum*. Here the quantum passes over into other quanta *ad infinitum*. There the something was finite, and therefore its other was infinite, but this infinite in turn became a finite something. Here too the quantum becomes infinite unlimited quantity. But this infinite is spurious. It again turns into a finite because (1) it is limited by the first quantum, and so, being merely the infinite as *against* the finite, it is itself limited by the finite; and (2) because within this unlimited quantity a new limit perpetually arises.

Thus the quantitative infinite progress is not a true but a spurious infinite. It is merely the perpetual see-saw of transcending a limit and then finding a new limit, which again is transcended, and so on for ever. The infinite is never reached. It never *is*. It merely *ought* to be. It is an ever unfulfilled aspiration. And Hegel remarks here, too, as in the case of the qualitative spurious infinite, that there is no true sublimity in it, but merely an endless weariness of meaningless repetition. It is at this point that we see the necessity whereby quantity must perpetually transcend all limits. We know, empirically, that no limit can be set to quantity, and that beyond any limit that we posit there is always more quantity. Thus any conceivable limit to space must have space beyond it. But this is now seen to be not a mere empirical fact, but a logical necessity. It lies in the very notion of quantity thus to exceed itself. The very notion of quantity involves the necessity that any quantum must pass beyond itself into another quantum, and so *ad infinitum*. It is the essential nature of quantity perpetually to extrude itself beyond itself. It not only *does* so. It *must*. That is what quantity *means*.

231. This infinite is spurious, but it is not the same spurious infinite as we had before us in the sphere of quality. The course of the Hegelian Logic is throughout a progress, and there can never be a mere falling back to an earlier category. The former infinite was qualitative. This is quantitative. The former meant that the *quality* of the something was determined by something else and that by something else, so that the qualitative determination of the first something was never complete. This means that the quantity, as independent of quality, infinitely extends itself.

C. The Quantitative Ratio

232. We have arrived, then, at the quantum which passes over into ever other and other quanta and so produces an infinite series. But this infinite is spurious. It is negative. It is merely the not-finite, which as such is limited by the finite, and is therefore itself finite. The transition to the true infinite is accomplished here in exactly the same way as it was in the sphere of quality. There the something became another something *ad infinitum*. But the second, or any subsequent something, was identical with the first something. Therefore the determination of the first something by the others was only determination by itself. It was self-determination, which is the true infinitude. Here the quantum passes into another quantum. But by the virtue of the principle of continuity, the second quantum is identical with the first. In this passage, therefore, the quantum is related only to itself. And with this we reach the **quantitative ratio.** For the conception which we have reached has two sides. It is (1) two quanta which are related to each other; and it is (2) a single quantum which is formed by the coalescence of the two quanta. But these two aspects are identical with each other. For the second aspect, the single quantum *is* the first aspect, the two quanta, except that the two have, in the single quantum, coalesced to one. Hence we have an

equation. On one side of the equation are two quanta related to each other. On the other side is a single quantum. This gives us the arithmetical ratio. Take for example the ratio $6:3$. Here we have a quantum 6, related to another quantum 3, and this relation is equal to a single quantum, the exponent, in this case 2. This gives us the equation $6:3=2$.

CHAPTER III

MEASURE

233. It has been pointed out that quantity is entirely external and indifferent to quality (186, 212). A field may be increased in size without this in any way affecting its quality as a field. Quantity, therefore, is wholly non-qualitative. But in the last category of quantity, namely ratio, quality again emerges, and this is a signal that we are now leaving the sphere of quantity behind. In what way does quality re-emerge in ratio? In what sense can ratio be said to be qualitative?

Quantity is a determination which is external to what it determines. Quality, on the other hand, is an internal determination which is identical with the being which it determines. Self-determination, therefore, has the character of quality, not quantity; for what is self-determined has its determination in itself. It is *internally* determined, not determined by anything outside itself. And such internal determination is quality. Now it was precisely the idea of self-determination, which, appearing in the quantitative infinite progress, changed that category into ratio. One quantum passed into another. But this second quantum is identical with the first, so that the relation of the first quantum to the second is only its relation to itself. It is related to nothing but itself and is therefore self-determined. The appearance of self-determination here is the reappearance of quality. In ratio, to be more precise, quality appears on the side of the exponent.

Thus in the expression 6 : 3 = 2, the side 6 : 3 is an *external* relation of two quanta, and is therefore quantitative. But the side 2 is a self-determined, self-related quantum. For it has been formed by the coalescence of the two quanta into one. Those two quanta were *externally* related to each other. But when they coalesce the relation between them becomes *internal* to the single quantum which is their result. This internal relation is a relation of the single quantum to itself; and because it is self-related it is qualitative.

In more external fashion the same thing may be expressed thus. We have here a self-related being. To be self-related is to be a being-for-self. Being-for-self is a category of quality. Hence we have here a qualitative determination.

This also expresses itself in the ratio as follows. The side of external relation, 6 : 3, can be changed indefinitely without changing the exponent. Thus it may become 12 : 6, or 120 : 60, without altering the exponent, which is still 2. These determinations 6 : 3, 12 : 6, etc., are thus external to the being which they determine, *i.e.* the exponent, and their alteration does not affect its being. And determinations which are thus external to the being of what is determined are, as we have seen, quantitative. But the case with the exponent is quite different. The 2 cannot be changed without altering the other side of the equation correspondingly. It cannot be changed to 3 unless we alter the ratio, say, to 9 : 3. Thus the exponent is a determination which, if changed, likewise changes the being which it determines, viz. the other side of the equation. And determinations which are thus identical with the being, and with which the being varies, are qualitative.

Hence in the ratio we have a combination of quantity and quality. We saw at the beginning of the last chapter (210) that quality, when fully developed as repulsion and attraction, passed into quantity. We see now that quantity when fully developed as ratio, passes back into quality. But this is not a mere relapse to quality. The result is still quantity, but it is a quantity which is also qualitative. It is the unity of quantity and quality. This is a new category, and a new sphere. It is called **Measure**. Measure is the synthesis of the triad of spheres, quality, quantity, measure. Quality was the first affirmation. It went over into its opposite, quantity. Quantity is non-qualitative. It is the negative of quality. It is especially defined as that which is external and indifferent to quality. Measure, then, as the unity of quantity and quality is the synthesis.

234. The English word measure is vague and ambiguous. All that is required, however, to remedy this, is to explain the special sense in which the word is here used. In Hegel the word (*Maass*) implies proportion, balance. We say that language is unmeasured when it is disproportionate to the truth expressed, when it does not retain its sense of balance.

Proportion obviously contains the idea of quantity. Every proportion is expressible as a ratio. We use such expressions as well balanced, well proportioned, both in regard to material and spiritual things. In either case the meaning is that the elements of the thing stand to each other in proper quantitative relations. What is ill proportioned, on the other hand, has quantitatively too much of one element, too little of another; the ratio is wrong. But quality as well as quantity is contained in the idea of proportion. If the proportions of a thing vary beyond a certain limit, the whole character of the thing undergoes change. Its quality is altered. If the ratio of the sides of a square to each other are changed at all, the figure ceases to be a square. In the sphere of chemistry proportion is all-important and quality depends upon it. Water is hydrogen and oxygen combined in the ratio 2 : 1. If we make the ratio 1 : 1, the whole quality of the substance completely changes, and instead of water we have hydrogen peroxide. Measure, therefore, may be defined as *the dependence of quality upon quantity*, or as *quantity upon which quality depends*.

Other examples of measure are the following. The qualitative character of the constitution of a state depends to some extent on the size of its territory and population. The constitution of the Greek city-state cannot be reproduced unaltered in the huge territories of modern nations. The quality (pitch) of a musical tone depends upon the number of vibrations per second. Economy, increased beyond a certain *measure*, becomes avarice. Water, heated beyond a certain temperature, changes its quality and becomes steam; or cooled, becomes ice. Its *quality*, gaseous, liquid, or solid, depends upon the *quantity* of heat.

235. What is present in all these cases is that quality in some way depends upon quantity. And this is the conception of measure. When quantity first came before us in the dialectic it appeared as totally indifferent to quality. It was defined as a determination wholly external to the being (quality) of the thing. It was that which could be increased or diminished without altering the quality of the thing. It was the other of quality, the not-quality. But now the dialectic has shown us that quality and quantity are no more utterly indifferent and independent than being and nothing proved to be. The one involves the other. Each taken separately is an abstraction. The concrete unity in which both are combined is measure, which means the interdependence of quality and quantity. Hence Hegel's definition " Measure is the qualitative quantum." [1]

236. Measure, like other categories, is a definition of the Absolute. Hegel observes, " God, it has been said, is the measure of all things. It is this idea which forms the groundnote of many of the ancient Hebrew hymns, in which the glorification of God tends in the main to show that he has appointed to everything its bound: to the sea and the solid land, to the rivers and mountains; also to the various kinds of plants and animals. To the religious sense of the Greeks the divinity of measure, especially in respect of social ethics, was represented by Nemesis. That conception implies a general theory that all human things, riches, honour, and power, as well as joy and pain, have their definite measure, the transgression of which brings ruin and destruction." [2] The point here is that what in general we may call success, if increased in *quantity* beyond a certain degree, changes its *quality*, and becomes disaster. This is clearly an example of measure.

[1] Wal., *Log.*, § 107.   [2] Wal., *Log.*, § 107 Z.

MEASURE

237. The sphere of measure falls into three categories, viz. (1) the specific quantum, (2) the measureless, (3) the infinite of measure.[1]

A. The Specific Quantum

238. Measure comes before us as the union of quality and quantity. But this unity is, in the first instance, only immediate. By " immediate " Hegel means here that there is no true mediation between quality and quantity. They have the appearance of referring to each other, of being dependent on each other, of mediating each other. But this mediation is only relative and half-hearted. There is no absolute dependence of the terms on one another, such as we find later in the sphere of essence, where positive and negative, cause and effect, etc., have each absolutely no meaning apart from its correlative. Quality and quantity have a certain loose dependence on each other, as we have seen in the examples already given; but they are also relatively independent. Hence, says Hegel, they " are only in *immediate* unity." [2] Complete unity would mean that any change whatever in the quantity of a thing would be followed by a change of quality, and thus the two would be wholly interdependent, completely tied to each other. The present merely immediate unity means, on the contrary, that though to some extent quality depends upon quantity, yet quantity may vary as it pleases within certain limits without any effect upon quality. The connection between the two is loose instead of rigorous. There is a dependence, since quantity cannot vary beyond definite limits without altering quality. But this dependence is only

---

[1] No actual division of the sphere of measure into its separate categories is given in the *Encyclopaedia*. In the greater *Logic* there are thirteen categories of measure but this does not help us, because we are here following the *Encyclopaedia*. And as the division into categories is not clearly indicated, though obviously several categories are involved, the disentanglement of these categories from Hegel's compact paragraphs is a matter of some difficulty. Dr. McTaggart (*Com.*, § 94), proposes the division (1) specific quantum, (2) measureless, (3) the becoming of essence. But it seems to me that the third category is described in § 110 of the *Encyclopaedia*. Hegel there gives it no name. I have accordingly, of necessity, had to invent a name for it. Hence it appears here as the infinite of measure.

[2] Wal., *Log.*, § 108.

an "immediate unity," a loose connection, since within those limits quantity may wander about, up and down the scale, while the quality remains unaltered and so quite indifferent to it. Thus we get the conception of a certain definite quantum which constitutes a limit beyond which change of quality occurs. This is what is meant by **specific quantum.**

The readiest example in nature of the specific quantum is found in the change of water into ice or steam. There is a certain specific quantum of temperature, namely 100° centigrade, beyond which the quality of liquidity disappears. The quantum of temperature may vary as it pleases up to the limit of 100° without the quality undergoing any change. But beyond that limit the quality of liquidity suddenly disappears and the water becomes gaseous. Similarly the specific quantum for the change of water into ice is 0° centigrade.

239. The deduction of the category of specific quantum is noteworthy because it is the first appearance of a type of deduction which is very common with Hegel, of which we shall see hereafter numerous examples, but the validity of which is, in the highest degree, doubtful. This type of deduction always occurs at the thesis of a triad. It consists in pointing out that the particular notion or category concerned, being at the stage of the thesis, is "immediate"; for the thesis of every triad is the phase of immediacy (143). Having pointed out that the notion or category is immediate Hegel then proceeds to deduce the characteristics of the thesis from this immediacy. In the present case the deduction consists in pointing out that measure must be, in the first instance, immediate. There is no special reason for this here. It merely follows from the general Hegelian principle that the thesis must be immediate (143). Immediacy involves absence of mediation or dependence, and so, independence, disconnectedness, between the two terms involved, *i.e.* quantity and quality. It is doubtful whether this deduction is valid because the mere idea of disconnectedness in general hardly gives us the special kind of disconnectedness involved in the specific quantum. The deduction draws its plausibility only from the empirical examples, such as the change of water into steam.

Without this illegitimate appeal to experience the deduction would break down. Yet Hegel frequently uses this type of deduction. For further examples see §§ 256, 280, 323, 328, 351, 361, 369, 392, 419, 420, 450, 460, 472, 497, 498, 511, 578, 639, 726 of this book.

240. However, from specific quantum Hegel passes to

B. *The Measureless*

The deduction from specific quantum to the measureless is accomplished in the following way. What we have in specific quantum is this: that the existence of a certain quality is only possible if a certain quantitative limit is not exceeded. But quantity cannot be thus limited. Apart from all empirical considerations it has been shown to lie in the very notion of quantity that it not only does, but *must*, for ever extrude itself beyond itself (230), and beyond all limits. Hence in the sphere of measure, the specific quantum *must* be exceeded. Therefore the quality which depends upon it must disappear. In empirical examples, such as that of water, we know that a new quality succeeds the old, *e.g.* gaseousness succeeds liquidity. But we have not yet logically deduced this. All that the deduction of specific quantum gave us was, that in specific quantum we have the existence of a certain quality depending upon the non-transcendence of a quantitative limit; but such a limit *must* be transcended because all quantitative limits must be; therefore the quality *must* disappear. Thus we have before us again a free independent quantity with no quality attached to it. Since measure is the attachment of a quality to a quantity this new conception of a quantity which has completely left the quality behind, and become unattached to it, is called by Hegel the **measureless**.

C. *The Infinite of Measure*

241. We have now a free quantity. But we have seen that quantity cannot be thus free. Its indifference to quality has been shown to be a mere abstraction. It necessarily veers round again to quality. Mere quantity has shown itself in the dialectic to return to quality (233). This free quantity,

the measureless, therefore must in turn become qualitative. It cannot subsist by itself. It falls back to quality, and becomes again attached thereto. Its attachment to quality is again measure. Thus the measureless becomes measure. In the world of nature this is seen in the appearance of a new quality when the specific quantum has been exceeded. When water reaches 100° centigrade its liquidity disappears. This gives us the measureless, since the temperature may now vary indefinitely above 100° without being attached to the quality of liquidity. But the truth that the measureless again becomes a measure is seen in the fact that a new quality, gaseousness, supervenes. Gaseousness is dependent upon the temperature-quantum not falling below 100°. And thus we have measure again.

The measureless is thus itself measure. As measure it again becomes measureless. This new measureless again returns to measure, and so *ad infinitum*. Thus we have an infinite series, a spurious infinite, exactly parallel to the spurious infinites in the spheres of quality and quantity. In quality, the finite something became infinite other, and this again became finite something, and so on for ever. In quantity, the quantum overleaps its limit into indefinite quantity, which again becomes a quantum, and so on for ever. In measure, the measure becomes measureless, the measureless reverts to measure, and so on for ever.

In quality and quantity the true infinite was reached by pointing out that the passage from something to an other something, or from quantum to the next quantum, was only a passage of the self-identical into itself, and consequently that in their return-to-self, this purely self-related movement, we have self-determination which is the true infinite. So here too, in the sphere of measure, the measure in passing into the measureless only passes into itself, for the measureless turns out to be itself a measure. This infinity, this being-for-self may be regarded as the true **infinite of measure**.

SECOND DIVISION

THE DOCTRINE OF ESSENCE

INTRODUCTION

242. The deduction of essence from the last phase of being is accomplished by the following reasoning. The infinite of measure, which we have now reached, is the absolute unity of quality and quantity. At the beginning of measure we saw that quality and quantity were there only loosely connected, that their unity was only relative, or, as Hegel called it, "immediate." In the measureless, accordingly, quality and quantity fell apart again. For in the measureless quantity shook itself free of its attached quality. But now, since the measureless is itself measure (241), we see that this freeing of itself on the part of quantity was illusory. Quality and quantity cannot escape from each other. For the measureless, which is quantity freed from quality, again reverts to measure, which is the attachment of quality to quantity. The two factors, quality and quantity, are now therefore finally and firmly bound together. Hence we have reached the conception of the absolute unity of quality and quantity. Such a unity implies, further, that quality and quantity are identical. For quality turns into quantity (210); and quantity turns into quality again (233). Each, therefore, turns into, and is interchangeable with, the other. They are *identical*. But the fact that they change into one another also involves that they are *different*. For the *change* of one thing into another thing implies that the second thing is different from the first. Otherwise there is no change (180, 185).

Thus we have two factors,
(1) The identity of quality and quantity.
(2) Their difference.

And this gives rise to the conception of two strata of being. The lower stratum is a self-identical, self-related, unchanging unity, a single permanent undifferentiated being. This is constituted by the *identity* of quality and quantity. The upper stratum is a diversified being, constituted by the *difference* of quality and quantity; and this stratum is not an unchanging unity, but a diversity in which quality and quantity continually veer into each other. This doubled form of being is **essence**.

243. It will readily be seen that what we have here is the general conception of the sphere of essence. For it involves as it were two layers of being, an outer and an inner. The outer being is the sphere of difference, the inner being is the underlying identity which supports the difference. Being is no longer of one layer, as it has been so long as we considered things solely under the heads of quality, quantity, and measure. There is now a deeper, inner, *essential* being, and an outer rind or appearance. The deeper being is the essence, the outer rind is, in the first instance, regarded as untrue and unessential.

Thus the main character of the sphere of essence in general is that everything is regarded in a double aspect. We no longer take the world at its face value. We distinguish between what it essentially is, *i.e.* what it is in essence, and what it seems. We seek to probe into its inner being. Under the accidents we seek the substance. For every effect we demand to know the cause, and so on. All those categories which imply a dual nature, consisting of a being which supports and a being which is supported, come under the general head of essence, and involve the idea of an underlying substratum beneath the immediate being which is directly presented to us.

244. Essence is the second term in the great triad, being, essence, the Notion, which occupies the whole Logic. Every conceivable phase of being has been passed in review, and now

we enter the wholly new sphere of essence. Being, as the first term in the triad was the sphere of immediacy. Essence, as the second term, is the sphere of mediation. That being is the sphere of immediacy means that all its categories purport to stand alone, to be independent of one another, not mediated by one another. The category of being purports to subsist on its own account, and to ask no help from nothing. Limit has no special correlative on which it depends. Quality seems quite indifferent to quantity, and so on. That this supposed immediacy of the categories of being was an illusion, this it was the object of the doctrine of being to prove. The course of the dialectic consisted in showing that all these categories involve and depend on each other, that they are not cut off from each other, but indissolubly linked together, so that thought can pass along the links from one to the other. But this interdependence of the categories of being was only implicit, and had to be explicated. The connections were hidden and had to be revealed. Hence being was in general the sphere of immediacy.

But in essence the categories explicitly mediate one another, and this is, therefore, the sphere of mediation. Instead of solitary categories, we have now categories which go in pairs, the members of which are indissolubly married, and are never found apart. They explicitly refer to one another. You cannot have a cause without an effect, or properties without a thing, substance without accidents, inner without outer, identity without difference, positive without negative. Each term is relative to its opposite. Essence is the sphere of universal relativity.

The same thing may be expressed by saying that mind, while under the sway of the categories of being, takes immediate existence for the truth and reality of the world, whereas, when it has risen to the stage of essence, it looks behind the immediate presentation and seeks for reality in a deeper ground. This deeper ground is not immediate existence but is what immediate existence points to as its source, and this source is therefore mediate. Qualities and quantities are just the aspects of the world which directly confront us and are immediately known. They are the categories which enter into perception. That a thing is red or big is immediately perceived. But no one can *perceive* that a thing is a cause, or is a positive or a negative. The apprehension of this requires thought and comparison, and all thought and comparison involve mediation.

245. For this reason, too, essence is, in a special sense, the point of view of the *understanding*, whereas being was the point of view of simple apprehension. At the stage of being the mind seizes directly upon what is before it, takes that for a simple unity, an ultimate, independent, absolute being, and rests in that. But at the stage of essence the mind passes beyond the immediate being to a second term and seeks to apprehend the relation between the two. Formal Logic begins with the doctrine of terms. At that stage the mind simply seizes upon a single term, chair, man, table, and goes no further. This is simple apprehension and corresponds to the doctrine of being, in which each category is taken as a final independent isolated entity. Next in formal logic comes the treatment of propositions or judgments. Here the simple term splits into two terms related by the copula. Instead of the simple term, man, we have the judgment, man is mortal. Judgment, then, is the sundering of the previous unity into a diversity of related terms. This is the special work of the understanding, which is the faculty of judgment. This corresponds to the doctrine of essence, in which the simple unity of being has become double. We have no longer single categories but pairs of categories which are distinct and yet related, bound together like the terms in a proposition.

Understanding, we have said, is the sphere of distinctions and differences. Hence the categories of essence are the special instruments of science in its attempt to cognize the world. Its work is to make distinctions, to insist upon definitions and boundaries, to enforce precision, to arrange all things in their proper classes, and to trace the relations between things. That essence is the sphere of relativity, that its categories are all categories of relation, makes it in this last respect too the special instrument of science.

246. It is for this reason, too, that science is traditionally apt to be sceptical in religious matters. Since essence is the stage of mentality at which it has arrived, and since essence has universal relativity for its principle, science therefore is prone to insist upon the relativity of all knowledge and the consequent impossibility of cognizing the Absolute or God. This supposed impossibility arises solely from the exclusive use of the categories of essence. All knowledge which can be obtained by means of these categories *is* relative. Truly to cognize the Absolute is only possible when essence has been transcended by the categories of the Notion, which are the categories both of religion and philosophy.

247. Since essence is the second term in the great triad of the Logic we should naturally expect it to be the opposite of the first term, being. And such is in fact the case. The essential characteristic of being is immediacy, of essence mediacy. And as being is single, so essence is double. Essence is formed by being going out of itself into its other. It has passed over into otherness and is here the double of itself, has come outside itself. Lastly essence comes before us, in the first instance, as the annulment and negation of immediacy, that is of being. Being is what is *there*, directly presented to us. Essence is precisely what is *not* there, not present, but only indicated as the negative source of what is present.

248. Essence is a definition of the Absolute. The Absolute is the essence of the world. It is the veiled being that lies behind the world as its unseen source. Essence is especially the unseen; for what is seen is the immediate. The Absolute, regarded as essence, is the substratum, the underlying unity, the self-identical one, which *manifests* itself in the diversity and multiplicity of the phenomenal world. That the Absolute is essence is the definition given by Hinduism, and by oriental thought generally. For Hinduism has not yet reached the only adequate definition of the Absolute as the Idea, the definition, that is, given by the categories of the Notion.

The Absolute is often described, too, under one or other of the particular categories of essence. It is conceived as the first cause of the world (category of causality), or as a force underlying phenomena (category of force and the expression of force) or, in Spinoza's philosophy, as substance (category of substance), or, by orientals, as the One (category of identity). All these definitions are true, in the sense that they are phases or moments of the truth. But all are false in so far as they are inadequate. For the categories of essence are superseded by those of the Notion which alone are adequate to express the truth about God. As compared with the concreteness of the Notion, essence is a mere abstraction, which is incapable of holding within itself the full riches of the divine being.

249. We have seen that in essence we have two strata of being. The essence is the underlying stratum, the deeper and inner reality. The other stratum is that of immediate being, appearance, the phenomenal world, which is the manifestation of this essence. In the first instance, then, the correlatives come before us as essence and the unessential. The latter is a mere show, a seeming, a hollow appearance, a nullity. This however turns out to be a mistake. For the truth is not merely that the unessential depends upon the essence. The essence equally depends upon the unessential. And therefore the unessential is just as essential as the essence. The essence is no doubt the source of the being of the unessential. But were there no unessential, the essence could not be the source of it, and so could not be essence. If essence is to be essence, there must be a something *of which* it is the essence. Destroy the something and you equally destroy the essence. Therefore the essence depends upon the unessential just as much as the unessential depends upon the essence. The effect no doubt depends upon the cause. But were there no effect there could be no cause. The negative refers to the positive, but the positive equally refers to the negative. The dependence between the terms is not one-sided, but *mutual*.

This *mutual* dependence of the terms on each other is called by Hegel *reflection*.[1] In the sphere of being we have seen the relation of dependence, but not of mutual dependence. The something has its being in an other, and that in another other,

[1] An analogy from light.

and so on. A depends on B, which depends on C, etc. But here A depends on B, and B depends on A. And this absolute dependence of the terms of thought upon each other, this universal relativity, is also the standpoint of reflection, in the sense of reflective thought.

250. The doctrine of essence falls into the three spheres of (1) essence as ground of existence, (2) appearance, and (3) actuality.

CHAPTER I

ESSENCE AS GROUND OF EXISTENCE

251. Essence as ground of existence has three phases, (1) the pure principles or categories of reflection, (2) existence, (3) the thing.

SECTION I

THE PURE PRINCIPLES OR CATEGORIES OF REFLECTION

252. These pure categories of reflection are (*a*) identity, (*b*) difference, (*c*) the ground. They are called principles of reflection, because identity and difference are the two essential principles which understanding, or reflection, enforces. That what is identical is identical, and that what is different is different, this is the point of view of the understanding. The ground also finds its place here, because, as we shall see, it is the unity of identity and difference. We now proceed to the deduction of these categories.

Sub-Section I

IDENTITY

253. The two sides of essence come before us in the first instance, as essence and the unessential. But this, as was pointed out, is erroneous. The unessential is just as essential as the essence (249). Hence the unessential, as being essential, is itself essence. Not only does B depend upon A,

but A equally depends upon B. The relation of A to B is identical with the relation of B to A. Hence what is on one side of the relation is identical with what is on the other. Either side may be taken as essence indifferently. The two sides are not two things, but there is one and the same thing which is now taken as essence, now as appearance. It is the essence that appears, and not anything else, and hence the appearance is the essence.

This perfect equality between the two sides of the relation gives us the category of identity. For essence is only essence by virtue of its relation to appearance. But the appearance is the essence. Therefore the relation of the essence to the appearance is only the relation of the essence to itself. Hence essence is only essence by virtue of this its self-relatedness. Essence therefore is self-relation, and self-relation is **identity**. To be related only to self is to be self-identical.

254. If the essence be called A, and the appearance B, then the relation between them is that of A to B. But since B, the appearance, is itself the essence, A, this relation is properly only the relation of A to A, and this is the relation of identity.

Expressed as a proposition this relation becomes A is A, which is the so-called logical law of identity. According to Hegel, the law of contradiction is the same as the law of identity; only in the former it is negatively expressed. In its positive form we have the law of identity, A is A. The same thought, put negatively, is, A is not not-A, or A cannot at the same time be A and not-A, and this is the law of contradiction.

Since Hegel is popularly supposed to have " denied " the laws of thought, it may be useful to quote here what he actually does say. " It is asserted that the maxim of identity, though it cannot be proved, regulates the procedure of every consciousness, and that experience shows it to be accepted as soon as it is apprehended. To this alleged experience of the logic-books may be opposed the universal experience that no mind thinks or forms conceptions or speaks, in accordance with this law, and that no existence of any kind whatever conforms to it. Utterances after the fashion of this pretended law (A planet is a planet : magnetism is magnetism : mind is mind) are, as they deserve to be, reputed silly."[1]

Hegel's point is, not that this so-called law is false, but that it is a one-sided abstraction. The category at which we have arrived is that of abstract identity, *i.e.* identity which excludes difference. The next category, as we shall see, will be abstract difference, *i.e.* difference which excludes identity. As the first and second members of a triad respectively, each of these is an abstraction which will be shown to have no meaning without the other. The concrete truth will only be found in the synthesis of the two, the unity of identity and difference, which appears in the category of the ground. The laws of thought, however, express only abstract identity and abstract difference, and are therefore not false or simply untrue, but " silly," because one side of the truth means nothing without the other. And Hegel points out in the passage quoted that even ordinary propositions contain more than the abstractions A is A, a man is a man, etc. Ordinary propositions in fact contain the concrete truth. They do not take the form A is A, but rather the form A is B (*e.g.* man is mortal). This implies both identity and difference in combination, not the abstract separation of them as expressed in the so-called laws of thought. For to say A is B implies, firstly, that A and B are different things (man is not the same as mortal) ; and secondly that they are the same, since the identification of the one with the other is precisely what it is the object of the proposition to express.

Sub-Section II

DIFFERENCE

255. The deduction of difference from identity is accomplished as follows. Identity is the relation of essence to itself. But in thus relating itself to itself it thereby distinguishes itself from itself. The self-relation is a negative self-relation (208), *i.e.* the self negates and repels itself from itself. A relation implies at least *two* terms between which

[1] Wal., *Log.*, § 115.

the relation subsists. In the present case the term relates itself to itself. The first " itself " which is related is different from the second " itself " to which it is related. If there were not this inner distinction then there could be no relation. If we express identity in the form A is A, then the A which is subject is different from the A which is predicate. Hence identity necessarily involves **difference.** The reasoning involved in this deduction is really the same as that by which the many was deduced from the one (208).

256. Difference, however, is internally divided into three categories or phases. Its first phase is

A. *Variety*

which is also called *diversity*. For in accordance with the general principle that the first member of a triad is an immediacy, difference, in its first phase, is immediate difference. This means that the differents do not, at this stage, fully mediate one another, are not dependent on one another, but are only loosely connected or indifferent to one another. Where a number of things are all different from each other without standing to each other in any specific relation of opposition we have **variety.**[1] For example, a pencil is different from a camel. But there is no specific relation of opposition. A pencil is not the opposite of a camel; it is merely different, and this is variety. Light and darkness, on the other hand, are opposites. They are positive and negative. And this is *contrariety* as distinguished from mere variety. Contrariety is a category which has not yet appeared and which will be deduced very shortly. But we may by anticipation here distinguish it from variety in order to make the conception of variety clearer. True opposites mediate each other. The positive and negative depend on each other. Each is defined precisely as the opposite of the other. But things which are merely different, *i.e.* exhibit variety, have no such definite relationship. Each is what it is without reference to the other. A pencil is different from a camel, but so is a house, a cigarette, a battle, a star, a trumpet, or anything

[1] See § 239 above.

else in the universe. But in the relation of contrariety, each thing has, not an indefinite number of things opposed to it, but only one thing, one opposite, *its* opposite. Thus the only opposite of light is darkness. And since things which exhibit mere variety, stand in no essential relation to each other, are indifferent to each other, and do not depend on each other, hence they do not mediate each other, but are " immediate." For this reason, difference, in its first phase, as immediate difference, is variety.

B. *Likeness and Unlikeness*

257. The differents, then, are indifferent to one another. Each is what it is on its own account, and its nature is quite unaffected by its relation to the other. Therefore the relation between them is not in the things themselves but is *external* to them. It is otherwise with positive and negative, with true opposites. Here the relation of one opposite to its other is contained in the very notion and definition of each term. The positive only is what it is by not being the negative. Its relation to the negative is part of its own nature, is internal to it. But in variety the relation is not part of the nature of each term, for each term is what it is without reference to the others, and this relation, therefore, is external to it. This means that if the terms be A and B, then the relation cannot be found either in A itself, or in B itself. It can only be found by externally *comparing* them. Such external relations are called **likeness** and **unlikeness.** If we say that A and B are alike, we shall not expect to find this likeness in the nature of A alone, or in the nature of B alone, but only by comparison of the two. A zebra and a horse are different (unlike) yet alike. Yet a zebra is what it is without any reference to the horse, and even if no horse existed in the universe. Hence its quality of being " like a horse " is no part of its own being, but is external to it.

The relation between true opposites is internal to the opposites themselves. But because things which are merely various are indifferent to one another, *i.e.* are what they are independently of the others, therefore variety gives us an external relation between the things. And such external relation is likeness and unlikeness. Likeness is an identity of things which are different. And unlikeness is difference.

258. From likeness and unlikeness is deduced the last phase of difference, which is

C. Positive and Negative

or the relation of *contrariety*. Whereas in variety we had merely the relation of a thing to *any* other, and to any number of others, so that a pen, a camel, a circle, a hair-brush, and a tadpole, are all indifferently regarded as *various* from each other, in contrariety, on the other hand, a thing is regarded as having its own special other, which is its opposite. Difference was, in its first phase, *i.e.* variety, *mere* difference. Now in its final phase as contrariety, it is *specific* difference. It is the positive and negative. Light and darkness, North and South, cold and warm, are examples.

But in what way is this new category deduced from the last? The last category was likeness and unlikeness. Now likeness is identity. And unlikeness is difference. But we have seen that identity involves difference, and that difference involves identity (255). There cannot be the one without the other. Therefore likeness involves unlikeness, and unlikeness involves likeness. They are completely bound together and interdependent. The relation between them is that of "reflection," *i.e.* mutual dependence the one on the other (249). But at the same time likeness and unlikeness are different from one another. Hence we have here a kind of difference, viz. the difference between likeness and unlikeness, in which the two terms are firmly bound together in a complete and mutual dependence on each other. In variety the terms were only loosely connected, or indifferent to each other. Variety was immediate difference. But here we have a kind of difference in which the two terms completely mediate each other, in which each is wholly dependent upon, and relative to, the other. Such difference, as already explained, is **contrariety,** or **positive** and **negative.**

259. It may be objected that this argument begins with an

error. It begins by saying : " Likeness is identity. And unlikeness is difference." That is its first premiss. And to this it may be objected that likeness is not *mere* identity, since things which are alike are always different, always unlike, and that unlikeness is not *mere* difference, since things which are unlike must also be, in some respects, alike ; for if not, we could not compare them. Thus a zebra is like a horse, but it is also, in other aspects, unlike it. A star is unlike a camel, but they are alike at least in this respect that they are both material things, and if this were not so we could not compare them or say that they are unlike.

But to argue thus is simply to play Hegel's game for him. This is precisely his own point. The deduction begins by saying that likeness is identity. But no sooner is this examined than it is seen that, since identity involves difference, it involves unlikeness. And it is precisely on this assertion of the unthinkability of likeness and unlikeness without each other that the whole deduction turns. The argument means that *bare* likeness, taken in abstraction from unlikeness is the same as *bare* identity, taken in abstraction from difference ; and similarly that bare abstract unlikeness is the same as bare abstract difference. And since these bare abstractions of identity and difference have been shown to be false ; since identity and difference cannot be separated, but involve each other ; in the same way likeness is an abstraction if separated from unlikeness. And since the two cannot be separated, since each depends on the other as *its* other, we have the relation of specific difference, opposition or contrariety.

We began with variety, which is immediate difference. We end with contrariety in which mediation and interdependence are fully developed. Contrariety, therefore, is the final and perfected form of difference, and we pass now from the sphere of difference to that of ground.

Sub-Section III

THE GROUND

260. The ground is the synthesis of the triad, identity, difference, and ground. We have now to explain how this category is deduced, and what it means.

The positive and the negative, at which we have arrived, each depend wholly upon the other. The positive is positive only in reference to the negative. The negative is negative only as against the positive. And since they thus bear to each other identically the *same* relation, therefore the one may be substituted for the other. The positive is just as much negative ; and the negative is just as much positive. We may regard the North as positive, in which case the South is negative. But we may equally regard the South as positive, in which case the North is negative. Light is usually regarded as positive and darkness as negative. And here it might seem that the two cannot be transposed. But this is because the sensations (consciousness) of light and darkness are usually confused with the vibration and absence of vibration which are supposed to be their respective causes. But the *consciousness* of darkness is just as much positive as that of light. And darkness may therefore quite legitimately be regarded as the positive of which light is the negative. Or even if we reduce light to vibrations, even so rest (absence of vibration) may be looked on as the positive of which motion (vibration) is the negative.

Hence the positive is the negative, and the negative is the positive. Each is the same thing, namely, absolute dependence on the other. This absolute dependence on the other is the idea of ground. Because the negative depends wholly on the positive, therefore the positive is the ground of the negative. Similarly the negative is the ground of the positive. Each, therefore, is equally the ground. The distinction between them collapses. And their identity is the **ground**.

261. Now, in the course of the dialectic, identity became likeness, and difference became unlikeness. Likeness, in its

turn, became the positive, and unlikeness became the negative. Hence the positive is identity, and the negative is difference. Identity is relation of self to self (253), which thus *affirms* itself and is *positive*. Difference is the distinction of self from self which subsists within this self-to-self relation (255), and it is thus the negating of itself by itself, and so is *negative*. Therefore the ground, which is the unity into which the positive and negative collapse, is at the same time the unity of identity and difference. Thus it justifies its position of arising at this point as the synthesis of the triad, identity, difference, ground.

SECTION II

EXISTENCE

262. The ground is a unity within which, however, there is distinction. For if there is a ground there must be also something which is grounded. That anything is the ground implies that there must be something *of which* it is the ground. Thus the positive may be regarded as the ground, in which case the negative is the grounded. But since the positive and the negative are interchangeable and identical, therefore in the same way the ground is identical with the grounded. There is no distinction between the two. The grounded is its own ground. Or suppose we say that A is the ground, B the grounded. Now the category of ground has only arisen as the unity of positive and negative, in which each side was shown to be grounded in the other. Hence if A is the ground of B, B is equally the ground of A. But if A is grounded on B, and B in its turn is grounded on A, this is equivalent to saying that A is ultimately grounded on A. And similarly B is grounded on B. Or, as we said, the grounded is its own ground.

Thus the category of ground turns out to be empty and useless. It gives, as the explanation, or ground, of a thing, only that very same thing over again. It explains a thing by saying " it is so because it is." We see examples of this frequently. Lightning is explained as being due to electricity.

But to put electricity as the ground of lightning is only to put lightning as the ground of itself. Or the kind of actions a man performs are explained as being due to the kind of character he possesses. But his character is nothing but the kind of actions he performs merely expressed differently as an inward instead of an outward being. Or again, that I am able to think is sometimes explained by saying that I possess the " faculty " of thought. But the " faculty " of thought is only another name for the fact that I think.

Thus the grounded is its own ground. The two are identical. Hence the mediation between the two sides disappears, and we have before us an *immediacy*. The grounded, regarded as an immediacy, as what is immediately present and *there*, is **existence**. The grounded is an existent. But the ground is identical with the grounded. Hence the ground is itself *another* existent. Therefore we have before us the conception of a number of existents which reciprocally determine each other as ground and grounded. " Existence is the indefinite multitude of existents as reflected-into-themselves "—*i.e.* as the groundeds which are their own grounds—" which at the same time equally throw light upon one another "—*i.e.* as having their grounds in one another—" which, in short, are co-relative, and form a world of reciprocal dependence and of infinite interconnections between grounds and consequents. The grounds are themselves existences: and the existents in like manner are in many directions grounds as well as consequents." [1]

263. A beginner is sometimes puzzled to understand the difference between the category of being and that of existence. The difference has already been to some extent explained (184). But it will now be clearer. Hegel uses the word existence to signify that a thing is part of the universe, *i.e.* is in correlation with all other existent things and forms part of the system or network of relations which we call the universe. Existence is not merely being. It is grounded being. For each existent has its ground in another existent, which in turn is grounded in a third existent, and so on. This is a much more com-

[1] Wal., *Log.*, § 123.

plicated and advanced idea than the empty abstraction of being with which the Logic began. Being was completely indeterminate. Existence is determined by grounds. As being a complex concrete idea existence, therefore, rightly comes later in the dialectic than mere abstract being.

The next step in the dialectic is from existence to thing.

SECTION III

THE THING

264. From the beginning of the doctrine of essence we have, in the last resort, been dealing solely with the implications of two concepts which imply each other. These are (1) relation to self, and (2) relation to other. These two concepts have formed the two sides of every pair of categories that have come before us. The relation of self to self gave us the category of identity. But since such a relation also involves the distinction of self from self, this excluding relation, which is in fact relation to other, gave us difference. The like was the side of identity, self-to-self relation, and this in turn became the positive. The unlike was the side of difference, or relation to other, which in turn became the negative. The relation of self-to-self next became the ground, while relation to other became the grounded. The ground and the grounded collapsed together into the immediate unity of existence.

Existence, therefore, contains both sides of the relation. The relation of self to self Hegel calls "reflection-into-self," and the relation to other he calls "reflection-into-another." Hence " existence is the immediate unity of reflection-into-self and reflection-into-another."[1] Each existent then contains these two factors. The first, that of reflection-into-self means that the existent stands on its own basis, as a stable self-identical being, which is independent of other existents, and is what it is, in its own right, apart altogether from them. The second factor, that of reflection-into-another, means that the existent is dependent on others. Now when an existent

[1] Wal., *Log.*, § 123.

is regarded in this double aspect it is then what we call a **thing.** This will be explained in the next paragraph.

Hence in the sphere of thing the first category is the thing and its properties.

Sub-Section I

THE THING AND ITS PROPERTIES

265. For to call anything a **thing** means that it has a certain self-subsistence, even substantiality. If we analyze the popular conception of existence we find that according to it the universe consists of (1) things, which are bound into a network of (2) relations. Popular thought regards the thing as something which has a substantial existence apart from the relations. In order that there may be relations, we say, there must be "things" to be related. Mere relations cannot subsist by themselves, and the universe cannot be composed merely of relations. The " thing " taken apart from its relations is something independent of other things. Apart from all other things and its relations to them, *it is what it is in its own self.* This is exactly the Hegelian idea of reflection-into-self,—the independent, the self-identical. The second element, reflection-into-another, gives the thing's relation to other things; and they are its **properties.**

266. This conception of a *property* needs a little further elucidation. In the doctrine of being we have already dealt with the categories of quality. And it is natural to ask whether a property is not the same thing as a quality. If so we have nothing new here except a new name. And in that case the dialectic is to that extent unsatisfactory, for since the later categories are supposed to be more concrete and of higher truth than the lower, it follows that a category once superseded cannot reappear at a later stage of the dialectic, even if it is concealed under a new name.

Quality, however, is not the same as property. The something has a quality or more properly *is* a quality. For it was an essential in the doctrine of being that quality was a determination which was identical with the being itself (186).

Here, however, the property is not identical with the thing. The thing *has* a property. And this is indicated by the dialectical origin of property as reflection-into-another. This indicates that the property is not part of the thing itself but is rather its influence on other things and its capacity of being influenced by them. For example, water rusts iron. It is a property of water to have that influence on iron. It is a property of iron to be influenced in that way by water. This mutual relationship of water and iron is their " reflection," mutual dependence (249), on one another. And this is what is meant by property. This is a far more complex notion than that of abstract quality, which is identical with the being in such a way that if the quality disappears the being disappears with it.

Objection may be made that it is impossible to distinguish quality and property in this way. Thus the being of red light consists simply and solely in its redness. Redness is a quality. But it may also be looked on as a property since it involves the influence of the light upon the eye. The answer is that every quality may certainly be regarded as a property, but that this involves a new point of view and the application of a new and more concrete category. It is of the very essence of the dialectic that one category turns into another, that what is at first regarded under an abstract category not only may, but *must*, come to be regarded under a more concrete category. What is now regarded as being must next be thought of as essence, and finally it turns out that the Notion is the only category that truly describes it. In just the same way a quality, such as redness, not only may but must come to be regarded, in the course of the dialectic, as a property. So that the mere fact that there is no quality of a thing which cannot also be regarded as a property is no proof that quality and property are the same category.

Sub-Section II

THE THING AND MATTERS

267. We are now at the stage of the thing and its properties. The thing regarded abstractly is reflection-into-self. The properties regarded abstractly are the reflection-into-another. But reflection-into-self and reflection-into-another cannot be regarded thus abstractly. Each involves the other. Each *is* the other as well as itself. For reflection-into-self is simply self-identity, the relation of self to self; and such self-relation equally contains the distinction of self from self, difference (208), reflection-into-another. Hence the property now becomes reflection-into-self and the thing reflection-into-another. So that the thing and its properties change places with each other in all respects. It is now the property, and not the thing, which is self-identical, independent. Formerly the thing was that which is what it is, the " in itself," the self-identical, the inner being, the essence; whereas the properties were the outer being, the inessential. But now the property is the self-identical, independent, inner being, the essence. The property had no existence apart from the thing in which it inhered. The thing alone had independent existence. But now the property has become a thing, *i.e.* an independent existence. Hence the properties are no longer to be regarded as merely *inhering* in the thing. They are themselves solid independent beings out of which the thing is *composed*. They are the materials out of which the thing is made up. The properties have thus ceased to be properties and have become **matters**.

268. It is very difficult to understand what Hegel means by matters here. He says that the matters into which the properties have turned, are independent, and relieved from their attachment to the thing. But they are still spoken of as " characters of the thing," [1] and it is said that " they are not themselves things." [2] They are " entities." [3] The abstract idea and its deduction from property are clear and intelligible.

[1] Wal., *Log.*, § 126. [2] *Ibid.* [3] *Ibid.*

But when we look for examples in the outer world we find that Hegel talks about magnetic and electric matters, caloric matters, odorific matters, and the like. One can see that magnetism, heat, etc., can be regarded as (1) properties of things, and then (2) semi-independent " entities " which are yet not " things." But the conception does not seem happy. There is a passage in the *Phenomenology* where this conception of free " matters " is mentioned, and Mr. J. B. Baillie appends to the word " matters " a footnote to the effect that it is an expression drawn from the physics of Hegel's day.[1] Apparently Hegel mistook an ephemeral and now forgotten scientific conception of his own time for an eternal and necessary category. In any case this category is not the mere idea of physical matter. So far as I can see, the view which regards mind as a compound of cognitions, volitions, and emotions, is an example of the use of the category of the thing and matters. Volition, for example, is first a *property* of mind. The mind wills. But regarded as a semi-independent " entity " volition is one of the constituents, faculties, or " matters," which make up mind. To regard mind in this way is of course to apply a wholly inadequate category to it. But if we do, rightly or wrongly, regard the mind in this way we are applying the category of thing and matters. Thus this category has nothing to do with *physical* matter. To deduce such matter would be wholly out of place in the Logic, which deals only with pure universals. Physical matter is a sensuous universal and its proper place is in the philosophy of nature, and it is there, in point of fact, that Hegel deduces it.

Sub-Section III

MATTER AND FORM

269. The matters treated in the last sub-section were different from each other. There were many matters each distinct from the others. For the multiplicity of distinct matters arises from the previous multiplicity of different properties which

[1] *Phen.*, i. 115.

belong to the same thing. But if we examine this conception we find that the distinctions between the different matters vanish, and that they all coalesce into one matter. The property was reflection-into-another. But this was transformed into reflection-into-self, and when that happened the property became a matter. Each matter, then, is an abstract reflection-into-self. This is the same as self-relation, *i.e.* it is abstract identity without difference. Difference then is excluded from the matters. There is no distinction between them. There is only one matter.

Since the one matter has no distinctions of any kind within it, it is therefore absolutely undetermined, featureless, characterless. For determination and character are only possible through limitation, distinction, and difference.

And just as the matters are the side of abstract identity, and therefore become one featureless matter, so the *thing*, as constituted by matters, is now the side of reflection-into-another, *i.e.* of distinction and difference. All distinction, and therefore all determination and character, therefore fall on the side of the thing and are excluded from the matter.

Thereupon the thing becomes *form*. For form, as here understood, is the principle by which distinctions, outline, character, definition, determination, are imposed upon the featureless indeterminate matter. Thus we arrive at **matter** and **form.**

270. This Hegelian conception of matter and form is simply the Greek conception. Matter is not the matter of the physicist, for this latter is already *formed* matter, such as iron, water, or lead. Matter here is rather the Greek ὕλη, or ἄπειρον, the boundless, the indefinite, featureless, formless substrate of things, common to Anaximander, Pythagoras, Plato and Aristotle. Form, on the other hand, is not merely shape, as in the modern sense; it is the totality of all the characters, the principle of differentiation by which the ἄπειρον becomes limited and defined into a this or that particular sort of thing. It is the εἶδος or μορφή of Aristotle.

CHAPTER II

APPEARANCE

271. The transition from essence as the ground of existence to appearance occurs as follows. The *thing* has, so to speak, fallen into two halves, matter and form. But now it appears that each half is the whole and contains the other. Form includes the whole of matter, and matter includes the whole of form. For matter is the empty self-identical; it is the reflection-into-self of the thing. Form, on the other hand, is the reflection-into-another of the thing. But reflection-into-another is interchangeable with reflection-into-self (267). Therefore, form, as reflection-into-another, is at the same time reflection-into-self, *i.e.* it is matter. And matter, as reflection-in-self, is at the same time reflection-into-another, *i.e.* it is form. Thus the form is the whole thing, for it includes the matter; and the matter is the whole thing, for it includes the form.

Thus the thing is a contradiction. On the one hand it is wholly matter, *i.e.* reflection-into-self, and as such is wholly independent of all else, stands in its own rights as a self-subsistent existence. On the other hand it is wholly form, *i.e.* reflection-into-another, and as such is wholly dependent on another. It is thus an existence whose very independence annuls itself and turns out to be dependence. Existence so conceived is **appearance.**

272. That this definition of appearance is the true one will appear if we illustrate it more concretely. We are familiar with the thought that the sense-world is an appearance. This, however, is a comparatively advanced philosophical concep-

tion. The sense-world does not come before us in the first instance as an appearance. On the contrary it purports to be wholly self-subsistent and substantial. The solid rock, it seems, is something ultimate and absolute, resting wholly in itself. This is the point of view of unreflective consciousness which takes the rock for something absolute. But with the advance of philosophical thought the mind comes to see that this independence and self-subsistence is at the same time wholly dependent on something else, *i.e.* upon the absolute reality, and that it is simply the appearance of that.

It is important to realize that the thing considered as appearance is a *contradiction*. It is something which, to use Hegel's phrase, " sets itself aside." It is not mere dependence on another. To say that the thing has no being of its own but wholly depends on another, would not involve it in any contradiction, but it would deprive the thing of any reality whatever; it would mean that it is utterly empty and void, has no being at all, is merely a show, an abstract nullity. This is not the Hegelian conception of appearance. The thing is not merely dependence—reflection-into-another. It is at the same time independent, a subsistence,—reflection-into-self. It is thus a contradiction. It is an independent which sets its own independence aside and makes itself a dependent. To regard the world as an appearance is to attribute to it an inner contradiction. And in point of fact, though Hegel does not mention it in this connection, this has always been the view of those philosophies which looked upon the world as appearance. Zeno the Eleatic sought to show that the world of sense is an explicit self-contradiction, and that consequently it is an appearance. Kant adopted similar reasoning.

273. Appearance is thus the contradiction of a reflection-into-self which is at the same time reflection-into-another. This identity of reflection-into-self with reflection-into-another gives us the important conclusion that the appearance is identical with the inner being, or essence, which appears. The reflection-into-self is the essence, the inner being. The reflection-into-another is the appearance, the outer being. But these two are identical. Thus the appearance is not a mere

emptiness, an unreality, a nullity. For it is the essence. Essence and appearance are not two things, but one. It is the same thing put twice, now as essence and now as appearance. It is the essence itself which *appears*.

This is a deeper thought than the common antithesis of appearance and reality, according to which the outer being is a merely illusory nothingness, while the inner being alone is real. The Indian describes the world as Maya, mere nothing, non-entity. For Hegel the world is likewise appearance, but the appearance is the essence; *i.e.* it is not less essential than the essence itself. This means that it is essential for the essence to appear; it is its very nature to appear. But in Indian thought it is impossible to conceive why Brahman should manifest himself. For this type of thought the essence and the appearance fall apart, as two quite different things, between which there is no real connection. For Hegel the essence and the appearance are identical, in spite of their difference. The essence has its very being in the appearance; it *must* pass into appearance. It is this conception then at which we have now arrived, and of which we must keep fast hold.

SECTION I

THE WORLD OF APPEARANCE

274. What was formerly a thing has now become an appearance or phenomenon, that is, a thing whose independent existence is contradicted and set aside by its thorough-going dependence. The thing was composed of matter and form. The matter, as the reflection-into-self, was the inner being, or essence of the thing. The form was the reflection-into-another, the outer being. It is the side of reflection-into-another, dependence on another, which now constitutes the phenomenality of the thing. Hence it is the form which now becomes appearance, the matter being regarded as essence. But we have seen that the form embraces in itself the matter, and that the matter is itself part of the form (271). Hence the essence or ground of the phenomenon, *i.e.* the matter, is

equally to be regarded as form, or as part of the form. But form is phenomenon. Therefore the phenomenon has its ground in what is phenomenal, *i.e.* in another phenomenon. This again has its ground in another, and so on. Thus we get a multiplicity of phenomena, all linked and connected together, and dependent upon each other. The totality of these phenomena is the **world of appearance.**

275. In dealing with the category of matter and form we pointed out that it is not to be supposed that what is there deduced is physical matter. A similar word of warning is necessary here. Hegel here introduces the word "world." But it must not be imagined that he has deduced the external universe. Such a deduction finds its proper place in the philosophy of nature. The Logic deals only with pure thoughts. What is here deduced is not the world itself but the *phenomenality* of the world. The two elements of the present category are (1) phenomenality, and (2) the systematic interconnection (of phenomena). The second is the idea of a relation, or system of relations. This is not a sensuous fact, though, like all pure categories, it may be *applied* to sensuous facts. Phenomenality, again, is a pure thought and not a thing. Just as, earlier in the Logic, when we deduced quantity, we were not deducing the sensuous things, stones, butter, space, men, to which quantity applies, but only the pure idea, so here we are not deducing the world of sense itself, or any other world, but only the pure category which the mind applies when it regards the universe as a world of appearance.

SECTION II

CONTENT AND FORM

276. The phenomenon is composed of matter and form. But the matter turns out to be part of the form, and the form part of the matter (271). When so regarded matter and form become **content and form.** In other words, though a distinction is made between content and form, yet each is seen to be substantially the same as the other. The readiest

examples of this relationship are to be found in the sphere of art, though it is by no means confined to that sphere. We separate a poem into its content, the thought or sentiment expressed, and its form, which includes the words which express the thought, the versification, metre, etc. But it soon becomes evident that no such complete separation can be made. It is impossible to say what is content and what is form. For the form makes the content what it is, and the content equally determines the form. If the form of a poem were changed the poem itself, the very content, would be changed too. The form of the poem is not something merely imposed on the content from the outside, so that the form and the content are quite indifferent to each other. On the contrary this particular form is essential to this particular content, and as being essential to the content it is itself part of the content. Form and content are indissolubly fused together, and the one passes into the other.

277. This shows the difference between the categories of matter and form, on the one hand, and content and form, on the other. We might easily imagine that they are the same thing, and that Hegel makes no advance here, but merely repeats himself. In matter and form the two sides are indifferent to each other. The matter is regarded as *formless*, and the form as *matterless*. Each disregards the other. They are separate and merely externally connected. But in content and form the two sides are so far from being indifferent to each other that they completely interpenetrate and determine each other. It is now seen that there is no such thing as formless matter. Even the bare matter has form in itself and when so regarded it is not matter, but content.

SECTION III

RELATION OR CORRELATION

278. In content and form we have arrived at a kind of relation in which the two sides or terms of the relation are identical with each other. Matter and form were separate and

indifferent to each other. But content and form, in spite of the distinction between them, are identical the one with the other. This brings us to a new sphere of categories. The distinctive feature of all the categories in this sphere is that each consists of two sides which, in spite of the two-foldness, are completely equal and identical with each other. The one side is only the other side under a different aspect. The categories which manifest this peculiarity are (1) whole and parts, (2) force and its manifestation, (3) inner and outer.

This sphere is called by Hegel **relation** or **correlation.** It might reasonably be objected that we have been dealing with categories of relation throughout the whole of the doctrine of essence, and further that the mutual dependence involved in reflection is the same thing as correlation. This is no doubt true, but it is a mere matter of terminology. Hegel has now arrived at a sphere in which in each category the two sides are identical. He wants a term to express the general idea. And he arbitrarily selects the terms relation and correlation. The selection may not be a very appropriate or happy one. But as long as we understand the sense in which he uses the words this does not much matter. It is the idea, not the name, which is important. And if he chooses thus arbitrarily to narrow down the term relation to the meaning here assigned, we need not object, and have only to keep in mind the special sense in which he uses it.

Sub-Section I

THE WHOLE AND THE PARTS

279. The first phase of relation is the category of the whole and the parts. The movement of thought in the sphere of relation is essentially similar to that in the sphere of difference (255 to 259), and it will considerably assist the student at this point to keep the sub-section on difference in mind. The deduction of the whole and the parts proceeds similarly to the deduction of variety. The first phase of difference was *immediate* difference, which meant that the differents did not mediate and depend upon one another, but each was indifferent

to the other. Such difference was variety. In the same way here, the first phase of relation is, in accordance with the general principles of the Logic, the *immediate* relation, *i.e.* the relation in which the two terms do not involve each other, but are indifferent the one to the other.

The deduction thus leads us to a relation concerning which we can assert two things; (1) that the two terms are equal to one another, and yet (2) that they are indifferent to one another. This definition is the definition of the relation of **whole and parts.** That relation is the only one which possesses those two characteristics.

Firstly, it is obvious that in this relation the two terms are identical and equal to one another, and this identity is commonly expressed by saying that the whole is equal to the sum of the parts. A heap of sugar consisting of twelve lumps may be regarded (*a*) as a heap, the whole, or (*b*) as twelve lumps of sugar, the parts. It is identically the same thing in either case. The whole and the parts are equal.

Secondly, the whole and the parts do not involve each other. The one is indifferent to the other. And it is for this reason that the relation is an *immediate* one. This is not quite so easy to see as the first point. No doubt parts can only be parts in reference to a whole. But it is indifferent to the part whether it is a part or not; *i.e.* the part is indifferent to whether it stands in relation to a whole or not. It makes no difference to the lump of sugar whether it is a part of a heap, or whether it stands by itself and is not a part. It is the same lump of sugar in any case. And similarly no doubt a whole can only be a whole by having parts. But it is indifferent to the whole whether it is a whole or not. The sugar is just the same whether we pile it in a heap and call it a whole, or whether we scatter it to the four ends of space.

280. The same thought may be expressed in a more familiar form if we say that the relation of whole and parts is a purely *mechanical* one. The whole and the parts are not organically or in any way necessarily connected with each other. And because they are not connected they do not mediate each other but are immediate. It is quite otherwise with organic

relations, as for example those between an organism and its members. It is true that we loosely call the organism the whole and the members the parts. But whole and parts is an utterly inadequate category to apply here just because the organism and its members are not indifferent to one another. A true part, *e.g.* the lump of sugar, suffers nothing by being separated from the heap. But the leg or the hand separated from the body ceases to be a leg or hand, and becomes a mere lump of dead matter. The limb only is what it is when it stands in its proper relation to the others and occupies its due place in subordination to the whole organic system. The body is not a mere mechanical aggregate of parts. But the heap of sugar is such a mechanical aggregate. And it is this latter mechanical relation alone that is designated by Hegel whole and parts. And it is in this way that the whole and the parts are indifferent to one another, and so immediate.[1]

Sub-Section II

FORCE AND MANIFESTATION OF FORCE

281. The whole and the parts are equal and identical. Hence the whole in being related to the parts is related only to itself. And the parts in their relation to the whole are likewise self-related. Thus we have here the moment of self-relation or reflection-into-self. But every self-relation is a negative self-relation, that is to say, a relation which not only affirms itself but also negates itself by distinguishing itself from itself (208). Or again every reflection-into-self is equally reflection-into-another (267). But reflection-into-self is the form of identity, or unity. And reflection-into-another is the form of difference, or plurality. It was for this reason that the thing, matter, content, each of which in turn was found to be a reflection-into-self, were all regarded as unities, while the properties and the form, because they were reflection-into-another, were regarded as pluralities.

We have now before us, therefore, a reflection-into-self which immediately repels itself into reflection-into-another.

[1] See § 239 above.

And this is the same as saying that we have a unity which immediately differentiates itself into a plurality. And since the self-relation, or unity, is the side of essence, whereas the reflection-into-another, or plurality, is the side of outer being, or manifestation, we may say that we have a unity which puts itself forth in a plurality of manifestations.

But not only does reflection-into-self at once become reflection-into-another. Since the two are identical, therefore, reflection-into-another at once passes back again into reflection-into-self. Hence not only have we here a unity which necessarily puts itself forth as a plurality of manifestations, but the many manifestations equally necessarily retire back into the unity. The relation of such a unity to such a plurality is that of **force and the manifestation of force.**

282. It is extremely difficult to believe that this is a genuine deduction of force and its manifestation. It is certainly true, as we shall see, that a force is such a unity, and its manifestations are such a plurality. And this much Hegel has deduced. But that this is all which is contained in the idea of force and its manifestation, is surely not the case. There are other purely empirical ideas involved. Dr. McTaggart suggests that Hegel is under no illusions as regards this.[1] The name of this category—force and its manifestation—is, he thinks, merely metaphorical. Or rather the name of a concrete empirical fact is used, not because Hegel imagines that he has deduced all the empirical material of that fact, but because the pure category which he *has* deduced—namely, the relation of a pure unity which passes into plurality, and a plurality which sinks back into unity—is most clearly exemplified in the outer world by that empirical fact; or in other words because force is the best *example* of such a unity, just as space may be a good example of quantity. Probably this explanation is correct. If so this is a parallel instance to the category of repulsion and attraction, the name of which is undoubtedly metaphorical (209).

283. We have to see, however, that force and its manifestation are examples of such a unity and such a plurality as have

[1] *Com.*, § 146.

been described. This is fairly obvious. We regard a great variety of phenomena as different manifestations of a single underlying force. Thus electricity manifests itself as lightning, as positive and negative electricity, as the sensation received from a shocking coil, and in other forms. Heat likewise manifests itself in a variety of ways. The capacities of a man's character may also be regarded as forces which manifest themselves in his actions.

284. Force not only does, but *must* manifest itself. For it *is* nothing but its manifestation, and without its manifestation it is nothing, merely non-existent. Force is not one thing and its manifestation another. They are the *same* thing. So that if one is taken away, the other disappears with it. Lightning is not something different from electricity. It *is* electricity. And for this reason the attempt to explain things by forces is a futile tautology. It is simply explaining a thing by itself. To explain lightning by electricity is to explain it by itself. The force is unthinkable without the manifestation.

285. And for this reason, too, it is absurd to say, as it is often said, that we can only know the manifestations of force, but that what force is in itself must remain unknowable. It is only unknowable because there is nothing to know. Force, apart from its manifestation, is a nonentity, is nothing but an empty abstraction. It is the empty abstraction of identity without difference, of reflection-into-self apart from reflection-into-another. The very phrase "what force is *in itself*," should teach us this. This "in itself" means that it is regarded apart from any relation to other, *i.e.* as a pure self-relation, or reflection-into-self. But self-relation cannot be thus held abstractly by itself. It necessarily involves relation to other, distinction, difference. There is no such thing as a thing "in itself" destitute of relations to other things. Destroy its relations and you destroy the thing, for the very being of the thing is constituted by its relations. And the necessity of force to manifest itself is simply the necessity of reflection-into-self to pass into reflection-into-another. The necessity, on the other hand, by which we trace back the many manifestations to the unity of a single force, is the return

of the reflection-into-another to reflection-into-self, the grounding of the former on the latter, which as we have seen is a logically necessary movement of thought.

Sub-Section III

INNER AND OUTER

286. Force and its manifestation are identical. From the side of pure thought we reach this result by the insight that force apart from its manifestation, as it is " in itself," is abstract reflection-into-self. The manifestation, on the other hand, is the abstract reflection-into-another. But reflection-into-self and reflection-into-another are identical. Hence force and its manifestation are identical.

Empirically we see the same thing when we reflect that lightning, the manifestation, is not something different from electricity, the force, but that the lightning *is* the electricity; the manifestation *is* the force.

In this relation, the force is, of course, regarded as the inner being, the side of essence. For it is the side of self-relation and identity. The manifestation is the outer being, for it is the side of difference, diversity, reflection-into-another. But as regards its content the distinction collapses, for the content of both terms of the relation is identical. We are left therefore with the empty shell, the formal difference of inner being and outer being. And **inner and outer,** therefore, is the last category of appearance.

287. But even this distinction has only to be mentioned to collapse to unity. The inner is empty ground, the empty form of reflection-into-self. The outer is the empty form of reflection-into-another. And these two are identical. Hence the inner is the outer, and the outer is the inner.

288. The category of inner and outer is not of course to be thought of in the primary acceptation of the words which gives them a purely spatial meaning. It is not, for example, the inside and the outside of a box which is here in view. It is rather the inner and the outer as the essence and manifestation of things respectively. In Hinduism Brahman is the

inner, the world the outer. Or in every-day affairs, the character of a man, his sentiments, intentions, and motives, are the inner, while his actions are the outer.

289. But now we see that the distinction between inner and outer is an empty one. They collapse to unity. To insist on the rigorous opposition of the two, and to ignore their identity is a characteristic of the stiff-necked understanding which leads to endless errors. This is a favourite theme with Hegel. And as the examples which he gives illustrate admirably how powerful the principles of his philosophy become when applied to practical concerns, it may be well to quote some of his own words. Since the inner being of a man is identical with his outer being, " we are thus justified in saying that a man is what he does ; and the lying vanity which consoles itself with the feeling of inward excellence, may be confronted with the words of the Gospel : ' By their fruits ye shall know them.' "[1] And in art too, " if a daub of a painter, or a poetaster, soothe themselves by the conceit that their head is full of high ideals, their consolation is a poor one ; and if they insist on being judged not by their actual works but by their projects, we may safely reject their pretensions as unfounded and unmeaning. The converse case, however, also occurs. In passing judgment on men who have accomplished something great and good, we often make use of the false distinction between inward and outward. All that they have accomplished, we say, is merely outward ; inwardly they were acting from some very different motive such as a desire to gratify their vanity or other unworthy passion. . . . But though it is possible that men in an instance now and then may dissemble and disguise a good deal, they cannot conceal the whole of their inner self, which infallibly betrays itself in the *decursus vitae*. Even here it is true that a man is nothing but the series of his actions.

" What is called the ' pragmatic ' writing of history has frequently sinned in its treatment of great historical characters . . . by this fallacious separation of the outward from the inward. . . . The pragmatic historian fancies himself justified and even obliged to trace the supposed secret motives that lie

[1] Wal., *Log.*, § 140 Z.

behind the open facts of the record. The historian, in that case, is supposed to write with more depth in proportion as he succeeds in tearing away the aureole from all that has heretofore been held grand and glorious. . . . If we have due regard to the unity between the inner and the outer, we must own that great men willed what they did and did what they willed."[1] In this, as in all matters that he touches, Hegel indicates the profounder view and exposes the shallow.

290. Inner and outer is the final phase of correlation. The mediation which was absent, or only implicitly present, in the immediate relation of whole and parts, is now explicit. Inner and outer are not indifferent to one another as whole and parts were. Each completely involves the other and depends on the other; and in this respect they resemble positive and negative in which interdependence was fully developed as against the immediacy and indifference of variety. What is inward necessarily becomes outward, and *vice versa*.

[1] Wal., *Log.*, § 140 Z.

CHAPTER III

ACTUALITY

291. The transition from appearance to actuality is quite simple. We have been dealing with a series of double categories of which, in each case, one was the side of essence while the other was the side of manifestation or appearance. Essence and appearance finally determined themselves as inner and outer respectively. But the distinction between inner and outer collapsed to unity. They turned out to be identical. This means that the distinction between essence and appearance has collapsed to unity. The one is identical with the other. The result, *i.e.* the unity of essence and appearance, is **actuality.**

292. In the doctrine of essence the universe is regarded as double, as having an inner side, which is essence, and an outer side, which is appearance. In particular, each category has its inner and its outer being. But in general, Chapter I., essence as ground of existence, dealt with the inner being, the essence. Chapter II., appearance, dealt with the outer being, appearance, external existence. Actuality, therefore, as the synthesis of the triad is the unity of inner and outer, of essence and appearance.

293. The actual is not merely inner or merely outer. It is both; for, in the actual, inner and outer are no longer separate, but are identical. Yet the distinction, though annulled, is yet preserved, sublated. The actual also has its two sides of inner and outer, but this distinction is *within* its own self-identity. The inner is the outer, and the outer is the inner. The essence manifests itself completely. There is

nothing in the essence which does not put itself forth in manifestation. And this manifestation *is* the essence, and is quite as essential and real as the essence.

294. Hegel uses the word actuality much as other thinkers use the word reality. Hence the position to which this stage of the Logic brings us is as follows. The view that the immediate external world (the outward) is reality, is one-sided. This view is that of common sense, and also of materialism. The view that the external world is a mere show, a nullity, unreality, and that reality lies solely in an underlying essence (the inward) such as the Brahman of the Hindus, or the pure being of the Eleatics, is the opposite one-sided abstraction. The external world is certainly appearance, phenomenon. But it is not a nullity. It is just as essential to reality as the essence is. Were it not so it would be impossible to understand why the essence (Brahman, being, etc.) should ever manifest itself. It does so because it *must*, because it is essential to its own reality that it should do so, because without its manifestation it would itself be unreal. Reality, then, or actuality, is not the essence alone, nor is it the manifestation alone, but it is *the essence which manifests itself.* The external world, the manifestation, is not to be regarded as a veil which hides and obscures the inner being (illusion, Maya, deception), but on the contrary as *revealing* the inner being and bringing it fully to knowledge and light. Thus to know the outer is to know the inner, for the outer is precisely the revelation of the inner. It *is* the inner.

295. If now we ask, what is, in this sense, actual, the reply must be that *only the rational is actual.* Not every existence is actual. For some things which exist, such as evil, are not rational. Hence such things are mere shows, outward nullities which do not reveal the inward reason of the world. Hegel attempts to prove this by arguing that the definition of actuality as the unity of inward and outward involves the idea of *necessity*, and that necessity involves *rationality*. For necessity is the same as rationality (74, 75). Of course not mere external and mechanical necessity is meant, but rather the logical necessity which attaches to the utterances of reason.

That this ink is black is a mere fact. It is so. But for any reason one can see to the contrary it might as well be pink. This fact, then, is a mere fact which is so. It might as well be otherwise. It is contingent. But that two and two make four is a necessity. If it can be shown that to define the actual as the unity of inner and outer logically implies defining it also as what is thus logically necessary, it will then be proved that the actual is the rational. This is the meaning of the famous propositions laid down by Hegel asserting that

What is reasonable is actual, and, what is actual is reasonable.[1]

Since actuality means the unity of inner and outer, these propositions may also be expressed by saying that only what is rational in the outer world is a true revelation of the inward being of the universe.

296. Such a position is really involved in all idealism. For if the Absolute is *reason*, it follows that only the rational in the world truly reveals it. Whether it is not also involved in idealism that everything that exists, including evil and what is generally called the irrational, is, in the last resort, rational, is a question that must be reserved for later treatment (425 to 427). At the moment the only point is that the identification of actuality with rationality and necessity is an essential part of idealism. And therefore its true proof lies in the general proof of idealism, and in all those considerations which were adduced in Part I. of this book. Hegel, however, here attempts an independent deduction of this position by showing that the definition which he gives of actuality implies its necessity and therefore its rationality. Unfortunately this proof is obscure and difficult in the last degree, and is of very doubtful validity. But the main heads of the argument appear to be as follows.

297. We have to show that *actuality is necessity*. The factors of actuality are the inner and the outer. The inner taken by itself is *possibility*. For the inner is reflection-into-self, abstract self-relation, identity. It obeys therefore the law of identity, namely, that it should have no internal con-

[1] *Phil. of Right*, Preface, xxvii, and Wal., *Log.*, § 6.

tradition. And whatever is not self-contradictory is possible. Of course external conditions may render an internally consistent fact impossible. Thus I say it is possible that " the Sultan may become Pope; for being a man he may be converted to Christianity, may become a Catholic priest, and so on."[1] By saying that this is possible what we mean is that there is nothing self-contradictory in such an assumption. From another point of view of course, external conditions may render such an event impossible. But in that case we are considering external conditions, *i.e.* the reflection-into-another, the outer being, of the fact. If we consider merely its inner side, its abstract identity, it is possible. The possibility here in view is of the kind of which it is said that a thing is *in itself* possible, *i.e.* it is possible so long as we leave out of consideration its relations to other things.[2]

If the inner taken by itself is thus the possible, the outer taken by itself is the *contingent*. For, on the one hand, as outward it is an actually existent being, not a mere possibility. On the other hand, since inward and outward are identical, this mere outward is also a mere inward, and as a mere inward is only a possibility. Hence it is an existent being which is yet characterized as not necessary, but merely possible, a thing of which we say " it may be " and therefore equally " it may not be." It is thus an existence for which no reason can be given why it must be, of which the opposite is equally possible. This horse is brown, but it might equally well be grey. This is the contingent.

Rational necessity is that which has its ground in itself, which is its own reason. Hence, for example, we say that axioms are " self-evident," meaning thereby that their reason, or ground, is in themselves, and hence they are necessary. The contingent, on the other hand, is just what lacks this characteristic. It has its ground always in another. The

[1] Wal., *Log.*, § 143 Z.

[2] The introduction of possibility in the sphere of actuality is no doubt partly due to Aristotelian influences. Aristotle contrasted potentiality and actuality. Potentiality is the inward " in itself," mere capacity, which has not yet come forth into actuality. Hegel, with just the same meaning, contrasts possibility and actuality.

greyness of this horse is not grounded in itself, but is the result of external circumstances such as heredity, etc. The ground of the contingent is another contingent, and the ground of that is a third, and so on. But this everlasting system of external determination is the same as necessity, not logical, but merely mechanical necessity. The contingent therefore is necessary in this sense, and hence necessity of this kind is involved in the notion of actuality.

298. So far the argument is clear. It is at this point that it becomes obscure. For Hegel now seeks to pass from mechanical to rational necessity. How he proposes to do this is not very evident. I can do no more than quote from Dr. McTaggart, who is himself merely repeating the interpretation of Noel. " The transition," he says, " seems to consist in the fact that if we all took existence as a whole it would form a necessity which was not contingent, but which had contingency as an element within itself. It would not be contingent, for it would have no ground outside itself. But contingency would be an element in it, because each part of it would be determined by other parts of it. Each part then would have its ground outside itself, and, looked at separately, would be contingent." [1]

299. This is no doubt obscure. But the general position of Hegel as regards actuality is quite clear. Only what is rational is actual. That is the essential point. This position follows from the fundamentals of idealism (296). But Hegel chooses to attempt the proof of it in another way, viz. by showing that the definition of actuality as the unity of inner and outer involves that actuality is the same thing as logical necessity, which is the same as rationality. Taking it for granted, at any rate, that the actual is the necessary and rational we may proceed with the development of this sphere of categories. Actuality develops itself in three phases (1) substance and accident, (2) cause and effect, (3) reciprocity (action and reaction).

[1] *Com.*, § 165.

SECTION I

THE RELATIONSHIP OF SUBSTANTIALITY

300. The inner is the ground of the outer. But in actuality the outer is the same as the inner. The actual, therefore, is what is grounded in itself. But to be thus self-grounded, to be determined by self and not by another, is precisely what is meant by the term **substance.** We call anything a substance when we conceive that it has an independent being of its own. That, on the contrary, whose being is merely dependent on the substance, that which has no separate existence of its own, is the accident of the substance. Thus the first phase of actuality is substance.

Because substance is the ground of itself, it is in that way a self-relation. But self-relation is identity (253), and as self-identical it is a unity. Every such self-relation is a negative self-relation, and by distinguishing itself from itself, puts itself forth to difference and plurality (208). Substance, therefore, similarly differentiates itself into an outward diversity. But what substance puts forth from itself is only itself and therefore disappears again into the self-relatedness of substance. It is a mere moment of substance regarded, for the nonce, as if it were something separate. This diversity of vanishing moments, which substance puts forth from itself only to swallow them up again as passing modifications of its own being, is what we call the **accidents.** Hence we have now before us the relation of **substance and accident.**

301. In outer and inner, we were informed, the duplicity of essence finally disappeared (291). It may therefore be objected to Hegel that substance and accident constitute a duplicity which we are supposed to have transcended. The same remark applies to the other categories of actuality, namely, cause and effect, action and reaction. According to Dr. McTaggart, however, the present duplicity is " no longer the old duplicity which was transcended in inner and outer.... We could, according to Hegel, contrast the reality seen as whole

with the reality seen as parts, for although the content was the same in both cases, whole and parts were two separate forms, under either of which it could be seen. And the same was true of force and exertion. But now it is different. To regard it as substance is to regard it also as accidents, and to regard it as accidents is to regard it also as substance." [1]

302. The category of substance was that under which Spinoza regarded the universe. That the Absolute is substance; this was his definition. That Spinozism was a true philosophy is proved by the arrival of the dialectic at this point. Substance is a necessary phase in the self-evolution of the Idea, and it is a necessary standpoint in the course of the progressive interpretation of the universe. But that this philosophy, and this definition, are still inadequate to the fullness of the truth the onward course of the dialectic from this point will prove. That the Absolute is substance is true. But that it is not merely substance, but rather that it is, when adequately comprehended, subject or spirit, this is the further truth which is yet to seek.

SECTION II

THE RELATIONSHIP OF CAUSALITY

303. Thus substance, being a negative self-relation, puts itself forth as accidents. The accident, being as an *other* to substance, negates it. But substance resumes, or reabsorbs, the accident back into itself. It thus negates its negation, and is therefore absolute negativity (204). The element of negation, however, is activity, creativeness, *power*. Why the element of negation is regarded as power has been fully explained in the first part of this book (43), and need not be repeated here. Substance, as absolute negativity is therefore absolute power, activity. It is an *active substance* which puts forth power from itself.

Substance puts itself forth as accident. But what it puts forth is *itself*. Therefore what it puts forth is substance.

[1] *Com.*, § 166.

Hence the accident is another substance. Thus we have the conception of an active substance which exerts power over a second substance, which is conceived as receiving that power, and so as passive. This is **cause and effect.** The active substance is the cause; the passive substance is the effect.

SECTION III

THE RELATIONSHIP OF RECIPROCITY

304. Causation depends upon the distinction between *active* and *passive* substance. But this distinction cannot be maintained. This passiveness is a mere abstraction. What is passive is also active. We may see this first in the form of pure thought, and secondly in the form of empirical examples.

To begin with pure thought, the effect is, like the cause, a substance. But substance is an absolute negativity, and therefore exerts power, is active (303). The distinction between cause and effect thus collapses. Each is a cause, and each is an effect. Substance A, as active, operates on substance B, as passive. But B as active, equally operates on A. This is **reciprocity,** or **action and reaction.**

305. Empirically we see that if heat melts wax we may, if we like, regard the heat as an activity and the wax as a passive substance. In that case we have a relation of cause and effect. But this effect could not be produced in the wax, were it not part of the nature of the wax itself to be melted. Thus the nature of the wax is just as much part of the cause as the heat is. It is the nature of heat to produce this effect in wax, but it is equally the nature of wax to behave in this way as regards heat. It is really a case of reciprocal activity.

We see the same truth in a more advanced form in the spiritual life of man. We speak of temptations besetting us as if in temptation we remained wholly passive. But it is only because our own feelings and emotions are incited to activity by the outer stimulus that we are tempted. There is really activity on both sides. If we were wholly passive temptation would be impossible.

Reciprocity being a category so advanced that it stands on the verge of the spiritual categories of the Notion, we should naturally expect that it would find its most perfect examples in the spiritual and social life of man. And this is the reason why it is often so difficult, when we come to the arena of history and social conditions, to say which of two phenomena is the cause and which the effect, to say, for example, how far the laws and constitutions of a nation are the effect of the national character or how far the national character is the effect of the laws. What this difficulty really indicates, is that we are moving in a sphere for the comprehension of which causality is an inadequate category. The truer category here is that of reciprocity.

Though reciprocity thus finds its most obvious examples in the higher grades of existence, it is nevertheless, like all other categories, applicable to the entire universe. We have now reached that grade of thought at which the whole universe is regarded as a self-closed sphere of reciprocal action and reaction. Every part of the universe, directly or indirectly, influences every other part.

306. According to Hutchison Stirling,[1] whose interpretation here is at least interesting, reciprocity is the stage at which philosophy had arrived before Hegel. The various phases of the Idea dialectically developed in the Logic unfold themselves also in time in the successive systems of philosophy. In Parmenides and Heraclitus we have the series of categories being, nothing, becoming. The modern pre-Hegelian world of thought was governed by the categories of understanding, and hence their essential concepts are constituted by the categories of essence. In the dialectical development of thought in the Logic, we have the series substance, causation, reciprocity. The historical order is the same. Spinoza represents substance, Hume causation, and Kant reciprocity. What is meant by saying that the essential thought of Hume was causation is fairly obvious,—though the remark is of doubtful value. Kant is said by Stirling to represent reciprocity because the governing idea of his philosophy is that the

[1] *Secret*, vol. i. pp. 217, 218, 219, 245, and other passages.

world of experience as we know it is the joint product of the interaction of things-in-themselves and the subjective forms of perception (space and time) and thought (the categories), or in other words that the essential truth of things is the reciprocal influence of subject and object. The essential category of Hegel, that in which he advances beyond all past philosophy, is found in the Notion.

THIRD DIVISION

THE DOCTRINE OF THE NOTION

INTRODUCTION

307. The Notion arises from the dialectic of reciprocity, the last category of essence. But to understand what the Notion is, and how it is deduced from reciprocity, it will be best to go back to substance and briefly trace the steps of the dialectic from that point.

Substance puts itself forth into accidentality. Since it is *itself* which substance puts forth, the accident is also a substance. Hence the first substance acts on the second substance, and in this relation we have cause and effect, the cause being the active substance, the effect the passive substance. But since the effect is a substance it is also active, and is therefore a cause which reacts on the previous cause. Hence we have reciprocity. In each of these categories we have a self-related substance which puts itself forth into an opposite, first as accident, then as effect, and finally as reacting substance.

Now in reciprocity the substance and its opposite become identical. The distinction between cause and effect is extinguished. For the cause has become effect, and the effect has become a cause. Hence the two substances become one.

We shall fail to understand this if we think exclusively in terms of empirical examples. No doubt it is true that though the sun and the earth react on one another, they do not on that account become identical. But the sun and the earth are much more than cause and effect. The thought of them contains in addition a heap of empirical material. To see

Hegel's point we have to think *pure* cause and effect. Just as the identity of being and nothing does not mean that a particular being, dinner, is the same as a particular nothing, no-dinner, so here it is not meant that a particular cause the sun is the same as a particular effect the earth. We have to abstract from the empirical material, and think pure cause. In this pure cause there is nothing whatever present but its causality. And since the effect is cause, the cause is effect, and there is nothing else in either of them, the two are completely identical. Hence we have now reached the idea of *a being which in passing outwards into its opposite passes only into itself, and this opposite does not become anything different, but remains, even in the opposition, completely identical with itself.* This is the definition of the **Notion.** This being is also an absolute return into itself. For in reciprocity A determines B, but B determines A. Hence in determining B, A only determines itself. And if it goes forth into its opposite, its opposite equally goes forth into it. But since its opposite is only itself, this latter movement is the return of itself into itself. But this being which, while going forth out of itself, yet all the while abides unchanged within itself is no longer substance. It is the Notion.

308. Such is the dialectical derivation of the Notion. But the tyro at Hegel will not be satisfied with this. He will say " cause, substance, quality, quantity—all these are familiar ideas. One knows what is meant by them. But who has ever heard of the Notion ? What *is* the Notion ? We may understand the deduction, but we do not understand what it is that has been deduced." This perplexity is in part due to the fact that the familiar Kantian list of categories contains no division which corresponds to Hegel's categories of the Notion. Hegel's categories of being correspond, roughly speaking, to Kant's categories of quality and quantity. His categories of essence correspond to Kant's categories of relation and modality. There is nothing in the Kantian list corresponding to the Notion. The discovery of the Notion constitutes precisely Hegel's new discovery, his advance beyond Kant.

The first thing to understand is that what is here deduced

is a new sphere of thought which is different both from being and essence. The essential character of being was immediacy. Each category purported to stand by itself as something independent and valid on its own account. The dialectic, indeed, showed that this independence was a mere semblance, that quality so far from being thus isolated, involved quantity, and so on. But it required thought to *force* the categories of being to pass from their isolation into connection with their neighbours. Being was thus characterized as immediacy.

But this kind of being turned out to be false. It passed into essence. The transition to essence proved that it is no longer possible to regard reality as immediacy, but that it must now be viewed as mediation. The categories of essence explicity mediated one another. Each category is mediated by its opposite, identity by difference, positive by negative, cause by effect, and so on. But the point to fasten on here is that each category was mediated, not by itself, but by something different from itself, namely, its *opposite*.

Now in reciprocity this point of view, too, has broken down, for the opposite of the being or substance, which mediates it, has turned out to be no opposite at all but only itself. Reality is now, therefore, regarded as *mediated by itself*. This is the point of view of the Notion. Being is immediacy. Essence is mediation by another. The Notion is self-mediation. The Notion is the idea of *a being which in its opposite remains identical with itself*, and in that way mediates itself.

Since, on the one hand, all mediation has here collapsed to identity, since opposition, which is the same as mediation, has vanished, therefore the Notion is once more an immediacy. But since, on the other hand, the Notion mediates itself, it is, in that way, mediation. Hence it is the unity of immediacy and mediation; it is the synthesis of being (immediacy) and essence (mediation). And it therefore correctly appears here as the third member of the great triad of the Logic, being, essence, the Notion.

309. No doubt the question, " what *is* the Notion ? " still appears to be unanswered. But it must be remembered that we have so far only defined the general sphere of the Notion.

It is impossible to be more definite until we reach the detailed exposition of the categories within this sphere. Then it will be seen that these categories possess the character of self-mediation described. For the present it is impossible to say more than that what constitutes the Notion is the general character of self-mediation. In essence each category was mediated by its opposite. In the Notion each category is still, in a sense, mediated by its opposite, but this opposite is immediately seen to be simply and solely itself. It is seen at once to be a distinction which is no distinction, a distinction of what is at the same time absolutely identical. This is the idea of self-mediation, and if it is understood, then we have grasped the meaning of the Notion.

310. Before we proceed to the detailed exposition of the Notion, there are three general observations which are in point here. Firstly, the Notion is the sphere of *reason*. Being was the point of view of simple apprehension, essence of understanding (245). Essence was characterized by difference, distinction, mediation. The Notion has for its character the merging of mediation, the absorption of all distinctions within an absolute identity, which annuls and yet preserves these distinctions. Its principle is therefore the identity of opposites. The opposites now appear as absolutely distinct and yet absolutely identical. This is the principle of reason.

311. Secondly, as essence was the sphere of necessity, so the Notion is the sphere of *freedom*. For self-mediation is self-determination, and to be self-determined is to be free. Necessity is determination by another. In the sphere of essence the other, in the form of an opposite, stood over against the essence as something different from it which determined it. But the Notion has overcome the opposition, and absorbed its opposite into itself. The opposite which determines it is now seen to be only itself, and as it is not determined by anything other than itself, it is free. Determination by another which constituted necessity has turned into self-determination. This is the meaning of Hegel's phrase, "The truth of necessity is freedom." [1]

[1] Wal., *Log.*, § 158.

312. Lastly, in the Notion thought becomes *infinite*. This also follows from the self-determination of the Notion. Finite thought is thought which is encumbered with an opposite. When it merges this opposite within itself, it ceases to have anything outside it, and is, therefore, infinite. This will become more evident when we reach the final stage of the Notion in the Absolute Idea.

The three stadia of the Notion are (1) the subjective Notion, (2) the object, or the objective Notion, (3) the Idea.

CHAPTER I

THE SUBJECTIVE NOTION

313. The subjective Notion is divided into (1) the Notion as Notion, *i.e.* the Notion " in itself," implicit, *an sich*; (2) the judgment, which is the subjective Notion sundering itself into opposition, the Notion *ausser sich*; and (3) the syllogism, which is the return of the Notion out of that opposition into itself, the subjective Notion *für sich*.

Thus it will be seen that this part of the Logic treats the same material as Formal Logic. But whereas the Aristotelian Logic is wholly empirical, the Hegelian treatment aims at being rational. The common text-books of Logic tell us, *as a fact*, that there are such and such kinds of proposition, such and such figures of the syllogism, and so on. But no reason is given for these assertions. That there are four figures of the syllogism is just as much a blind irrational fact, an absolute contingency, as that there are five continents on the planet. Our only reason for asserting that there are so many kinds of judgment or so many kinds of syllogism is simply that in experience *it is found to be so*. " In this way," says Hegel, " we get an *empirical* logic—surely an odd science, an *irrational* cognition of the *rational*. Logic thus affords a very bad example of obedience to its own lessons." [1]

The Hegelian treatment of the subject proceeds, on the other hand, according to the dialectic method. The different species of judgment and syllogism are not merely asserted but are *deduced*. And in this way Logic is raised from the level of a heap of empirical facts to the level of a rational science,

[1] Macran, p. 163.

which, as the science of reason, it, above all others, surely ought to be.

SECTION I
THE NOTION AS NOTION

Sub-Section I
THE UNIVERSAL

314. The general character of the Notion to which the dialectic has brought us yields us also the factors of the Notion. The Notion is the identity of opposites. Since its opposite is immediately identical with itself, it is, therefore, absolute identity. This unity or identity is the **universal.** Even such common and sensuous universals as man, table, house, exhibit this character, that they are what is identical in the various particulars. But, as we shall see, the universality of the Notion differs fundamentally from these abstract universals.

315. The main thought here, namely, that what is self-mediated is an absolute identity, is easy to understand. But if the universal is simply this identity, it may be asked how the universal differs from the category of identity which came at the beginning of essence. The answer is that that category was *abstract* identity and had over against it *abstract* difference as its opposite. Here, the universal is an identity which includes its opposite within itself. It is not only identical with itself in itself. It is also identical with itself in its opposite. It is thus a *concrete* identity. It is true that the category of identity in essence was also shown to involve difference, but the point is that this had to be *shown*. It was not explicit. But here, as we shall see, the universal is immediately and explicitly seen to *be* its own opposite.

Sub-Section II
THE PARTICULAR

316. Since the Notion opposes itself to itself, it thereby negates itself, determines itself. This element of negativity

determinateness, is difference, *particularity*. It is the *differentia* which determines the *genus* (universal). This gives us the **particular.** The Notion is the identity of opposites. The factor of identity is the universal. The factor of opposition is the particular.

Sub-Section III

THE SINGULAR, OR INDIVIDUAL

317. The Notion thus goes into opposition to itself and this opposition is particularity. But its opposite is only itself. This identity of its opposite with itself constitutes the negation of the negation, and so the return of the Notion into itself. For if the Notion first negates itself and becomes its opposite, this opposition is now again negated to absolute identity. This return into itself of the Notion is therefore the unity of the universal and the particular, or it is the identity of identity and difference, *i.e.* it is the **singular,** or **individual.** Put in another way, this reasoning may be stated as follows. The original Notion in going forth into its opposite develops a duality within itself, but this duality is again immediately annulled; and in the return into itself, it becomes again a unity, but now a determinate unity, since it has determined itself through the particular. This absolutely self-determined unity is the singular.

FURTHER EXPLANATIONS

318. The universal, the particular, and the singular, are not three categories. They are the three moments or factors of the one indivisible category, the Notion. Each moment is itself the whole Notion, and is absolutely identical with the other two. For this is precisely the character of the Notion that, on the one hand, it differentiates itself into its factors, but on the other hand, in these distinctions it remains absolutely identical with itself, so that they in no wise interrupt or disturb its absolutely transparent unity and simple self-identity.

Universality is the original simple self-identity of the Notion.

This is the factor of unity and identity. Particularity is the factor of difference, but although it is thus an opposite, it is identical with the universal. For, inasmuch as the universal is now brought face to face with an opposite, the universal is now itself only *one of two*. It is therefore only a *particular*. Thus the universal and the particular are identical. Singularity, again, is simply the identity of the universal and the particular. And if the universal and the particular be thus regarded as the factors of singularity, then, since the universal and the particular are identical, each of them is accordingly the whole of singularity. The universal, the particular, and the singular, are therefore completely identical with each other. Each, therefore, is the other two just as much as it is itself. Hence each is the whole undivided Notion.

It will be evident that we have now reached the absolute merging of all mediation, the absolute unity in difference and difference in unity which constitutes the very being of reason.

319. The German word for the Notion, *der Begriff*, is the word commonly used to mean " concept." Most Hegelian translators and commentators render it, in the present connection, the Notion.[1] And this translation seems preferable to " concept " because it is of absolutely fundamental importance that the Notion should be clearly distinguished from what is ordinarily called a concept. Ordinarily speaking, any abstract idea, such as man, house, whiteness, goodness, etc., is described as a concept. Such concepts are called universals, and the general sphere of such universals is described as the universal. Now the universal, in this sense, is utterly different from the universal of Hegel's Notion. And if this difference is not apprehended it will be impossible for us to understand the essential characteristics of the Notion. The ordinary concept is an *abstract* universal. Hegel's universal is *concrete*. The former is abstract because it specially excludes from itself, *i.e.* abstracts from, the particular and the singular. But Hegel's universal is concrete because, as we have seen, it contains the particular and singular within itself. " The man

---

[1] Mr. Macran, however, in his *Hegel's Doctrine of Formal Logic*, translates it consistently " the concept."

who wrote this book" is a singular; "man" is the universal; "who wrote this book" is the particular, or *differentia*. The universal, "man," specially excludes all particular determinateness, and is therefore an empty and indeterminate abstraction. But the Notion arose dialectically from reciprocity as self-mediation, as self-*determination*, and therefore as an *absolutely determined self-identity*. In its aspect as identity it is the universal. But this identity is *determined* and is therefore at the same time *particular*. For determinateness is particularity. And the universal which is particular, is the singular. Thus the Notion is no empty abstraction like the concepts of the logic-books, but is concrete out and out.

If then it be asked what examples can be given of true universals, if the ordinary abstractions, man, house, book, etc., are denied that name, the answer is that the categories of the Logic, and also the "notions" of the philosophy of nature and the philosophy of spirit, are such genuine universals. Thus the universal "being" is genuine because it develops its own particularity, "nothing," out of itself, and becomes concrete as "becoming."

320. It is now possible for us to see that the Notion is the very secret, the inner nerve and life-process of the whole Logic. Now we can understand the statement which Hegel makes at the very beginning of the doctrine of being,—"Being is the Notion implicit."[1] We have really been dealing with the Notion throughout the Logic, even in the very first steps of the doctrine of being. But the Notion was there hidden and has only now come to light as the inner truth and meaning of the whole process. Only now is it the Notion *as* Notion. Then it was the Notion as being, or later, as essence, *i.e.* disguised under forms other than its own form. Then it was implicit, now it is explicit.

In each triad of the Logic, the first category is the universal, the second is the particular, and the third is the singular. Being is the universal. This universal is inflected with a negative element, a determination, a difference—nothing. This is the particular. The universal, being, as thus deter-

[1] Wal., *Log.*, § 84.

mined by particularity and difference becomes the singular—becoming. And it is the same throughout the entire process of the Logic, and throughout the rest of the system. The Logical Idea in general is the universal. Nature is the particular, the sphere of difference. The singular is the concrete spirit.

321. Lastly, it should be clear now why this sphere of the Logic is called the *subjective* Notion, or *subjectivity*. What it deals with is essentially *thought*,—concepts, judgments, and syllogisms. The universe is now regarded as subjectivity, as thought. Hegel states that *the ego is the Notion*, or conversely that the Notion is subjectivity. The readiest way of understanding this is by reference to Kant. Kant analyzed consciousness into two halves, the given material and the form. The latter half is the categories, and space and time. These are the work of the ego. They *are* the ego itself. The material content is given from outside and is what is *not* the ego. If then we ask what the ego in itself is, apart from this or that particular content which it happens to have at any time, the answer is that the ego is pure thought, *i.e.* for Kant it is the twelve categories, for Hegel it is the Notion, which is the sum and totality of all the categories, the inner secret of them all. Kant's ego is an abstract universal, a pure self-identity. Hence the question how and why it differentiates itself into the twelve categories remained for him an insoluble problem. For Hegel the problem is solved. The ego, as Notion, is a *concrete* universal which immediately sunders itself into particularity and yet remains universal. As concrete it contains, and *is*, all the categories.

SECTION II

THE JUDGMENT

322. Formal Logic lays down its doctrine of terms—to which Hegel's Notion as Notion here corresponds. It then *asserts*, without rhyme or reason, that besides notions or concepts, *there are* judgments, and it proceeds to classify, arrange,

and divide judgments in the same arbitrary and unprincipled way, treating the different forms of judgment as mere facts, which are so, but for which no reason can be given. And in the same empirical way, having finished its doctrine of judgments, it proceeds to assert that *there are* syllogisms, and that syllogisms are of such and such kinds.

The Hegelian procedure is wholly different. In the spheres of being and essence Hegel did not give, as Kant had done, a mere irrational catalogue of categories empirically picked up and stuck down in any order. He systematically deduced the categories from one another. In just the same way he deduces the judgment from the Notion, and the syllogism from the judgment, and the different kinds of judgment and syllogism are all deduced in their proper places as ascending stages in the self-evolution of the Notion.

323. The Notion, therefore, passes *necessarily* into the judgment. The logical transition from the former to the latter has now to be exhibited. The judgment issues from the moment of singularity. The singular, as the return of the Notion into itself, is the negation of the negation, or absolute negativity. Hence the distinctions of universal and particular are merged and disappear in it, and it is, therefore, an immediacy. As an immediacy it is an *independent* existence, for immediacy is the same as independence (238, 239). The singular is at the same time a totality, for it includes the universal and the particular within itself. It is the totality of the Notion, and is thus an independent self-enclosed whole. But the particular and the universal are each the very same totality, for each of them is identical with the singular. Each is, therefore, an immediate independent totality. Thus the original unity of the Notion suffers diremption into these three totalities, each of which is independent of the others. It is the factor of *independence* which produces this diremption. The moments of the Notion, formerly absolutely identical, have fallen apart into independence of each other. This differentiation, splitting, diremption, of the unity of the Notion into independent totalities is the **judgment**.[1] It should be

[1] See § 239 above.

noted that the differentiation is not introduced into the Notion *by us*. The Notion of its own activity differentiates itself. It is by its own movement that it becomes the judgment, and this, as we have seen, is the proper character of a logical deduction.

This truth is indicated in the German word for judgment, *Urtheil*. Etymologically, Urtheil means the original parting, splitting up, discernment, of a primary unity.

324. What is, in the Notion, merely implicit, becomes explicit in the judgment. The Notion, as we have seen, is constituted by three factors which are both distinct and identical. The element of distinction, the falling asunder of the three factors, is emphasized in the judgment, yet the element of unity is not wanting. Every judgment asserts both the difference and the identity of the factors of the Notion. Thus in the proposition " This rose is red "—" this rose " is a singular or individual, while " red " is a universal. Thus the *logical* content of the proposition, apart from its empirical filling, is :

The singular is the universal.

We have here, first of all, the *separation* and *difference* of the singular and the universal. They are the two extremes of the judgment, and are posited as different from one another. The subject is distinct from the predicate. If this were not so, if no *difference* were alleged, we should have merely an identical proposition such as " the rose is the rose." But while the difference is thus asserted, the *identity* is also expressly stated in the copula. The judgment states that the subject *is* the predicate. Other kinds of judgment, with which we shall shortly meet, give us the truths that " The particular is the universal " and " The singular is the particular." In this way what was implicit in the Notion, namely the difference *and* identity of its factors, is explicitly specified in the ascending grades of the judgment.

325. The present seems a suitable opportunity to clear up a difficulty which is apt to puzzle the beginner at Hegel. We have seen that all the categories in the Logic are said to apply,

not merely to this or that part of reality, but to *all* reality (169). But one might think that the categories of the subjective Notion do not apply to everything, but only to consciousness, or subjective thought. The Notion, the judgment, the syllogism, are, as ordinarily understood, forms of subjective thought, and no more. This, however, is to misconceive Hegel. The categories of the Notion, like all others, are universal in their scope. Hegel expressly states that "all things are a judgment,"[1] and later that "everything is a syllogism."[2] And it is equally true that everything is the Notion. For everything that exists is an individual thing, a singular, and its nature consists in the fact that it is a combination of universal and particular. "This book here before me" is a singular, an individual book. It is a universal for it is a member of the class "book." And it is a particular because it is "here before me." When these factors of its being are explicitly put as separate and yet identical, as when we say "What is before me is a book," it is then a judgment. Similar remarks apply to the syllogism as we shall see in due course.

That everything is the Notion is also implicit in the philosophy of Aristotle, for whom every individual thing (singular) was a compound of matter and form. Matter is the particular, form the universal.

Or it may be admitted that the categories of the Notion apply only to thought and not to things. But in that case it must be added that the very meaning of the doctrine of the Notion is that the universe is no longer regarded as a collection of *things*. We have passed the stage of science with its categories of thing, force, matter, and the like. All existence is now viewed as being essentially and inherently nothing but *thought*. This is the essential point of view of the Notion, which is the stage, not of science, but of philosophy. Every category gives us a definition both of the world and of the Absolute. The definitions which issue from the Notion are that the world is thought, and that the Absolute is *subject*. Hence the forms of thought, the Notion, the judgment, the

[1] Wal., *Log*, § 167. [2] Wal., *Log.*, § 181.

syllogism, are essentially the forms of all reality and of the Absolute itself.

326. The judgment develops itself through four ascending stages, (1) the qualitative judgment, (2) the judgment of reflection, (3) the judgment of necessity, and (4) the judgment of the Notion. (It will be noticed that Hegel here abandons the usual triadic division.)

Sub-Section I

THE QUALITATIVE JUDGMENT

327. In the judgment the factors of the Notion have fallen asunder. They are now independent and indifferent to one another. Thus the judgment is the going forth of the Notion into otherness. In the syllogism it returns to itself and the factors are there clasped together again in an absolute identity. The different kinds of judgment, therefore, constitute an evolution, a gradual movement from the complete independence of the notional factors, with which we begin, back to their self-identity which is finally reached in the syllogism.

The first form of judgment is, therefore, that in which the factors of singularity and universality, the subject and the predicate are independent, unrelated, and indifferent to one another. This is the same as saying that we begin with the *immediate* judgment. This is the **judgment of quality**. It is, firstly,

A. *The Affirmative Judgment.*

328. The general form of this judgment is

The singular is the universal.

Both terms are immediate. The immediate singular is an individual object, such as "the rose." The immediate universal is the universal which is not mediated, which does not contain the particular and the singular; hence it is the *abstract* universal. And because it is a universal which is isolated and not truly related to the subject, it is accordingly some isolated property or, *quality*, of the subject. Hence at this stage we get such a judgment as

The rose is red.

The redness has no necessary or intrinsic connection with the rose. It is merely an accidental property which is, so to speak, *stuck into* the rose as a matter of chance, and inheres in it. There is no *necessity* why the rose should be red. The notions of rose and redness have no logical connection with each other, and it is here that the *immediacy* of this kind of judgment comes to light, since between the subject and predicate there is no real relation.[1] This is the **affirmative judgment.**

B. *The Negative Judgment.*

329. The affirmative judgment *asserts* that the singular is the universal. But since they have in fact proved to be quite unconnected with each other, or to be connected only by an external tie of inherence, since they lie thus apart and isolated, the assertion of their identity, which is the essential meaning of the affirmative judgment, turns out to be false. Hence the truth rather is that

The singular is not the universal,

e.g. that the rose is *not* red. This is the **negative judgment.**

Not-universal, or not-red, cannot be taken here in the barren and empty sense of the logical contradictories of universal and red,—as when we say that the mind is not-red. It must mean " not red, but some other colour." And this gives us the judgment that " the rose is *some* colour," which is equivalent to

The singular is the particular.

The necessity of taking the not-universal in this sense lies in the fact that we are not now in the sphere of empty names, but in that of the concrete Notion. If the singular is not the universal, it cannot be the empty contradictory not-universal, for that would place it outside the sphere of the Notion

---

[1] See § 239 above.

altogether. Hence if it is not the universal it must be the other factor of the Notion, the particular.

Thus the negative judgment is just as much an affirmative judgment, or is capable of being expressed in the affirmative form, the singular is the particular.

C. *The Infinite Judgment.*

330. Because the negative judgment is also an affirmative judgment, it is therefore just as false as the affirmative judgment, and for the very same reason. It is now asserted that the singular is the particular, but these extremes, though asserted to be identical, are in fact unrelated. It is not now said that the rose is red. But it is alleged that the rose is coloured. But its colour is just as much a mere accidental quality of the rose as its redness was. We now merely assert of the rose the general sphere of colour without naming any individual colour. But this does not affect the indifference and irrelevancy of the predicate to the subject.

The affirmative judgment asserted some individual quality (redness) of the subject. The negative judgment negated this individual quality, but still allowed that the general sphere to which that quality belonged (colour) might be predicated of the subject. But since the negative judgment turns out to be as false as the affirmative, what we have now before us as the proximate truth is that some general sphere, some universal, is totally denied of the subject altogether. The subject will be, as before, an individual object. The predicate will be some universal which has absolutely no connection whatever with the subject, and which is utterly incompatible with it. This is the **infinite judgment,** such as " The mind is not an elephant," " A lion is not a table," " The mind is not red."

331. The infinite judgment is the last form of the judgment of quality. But before we pass to the next sphere of judgment, it may be useful to illustrate, with Hegel's own examples, the fact, already stated, that the judgment applies not only to subjective thought, but to all reality, so that " everything is a judgment." The negative judgment and the infinite

judgment differ in this, that the former denies only a particular quality of the subject while admitting the general sphere to which that quality belongs, whereas the infinite judgment denies even the general sphere. Crime, according to Hegel, is an infinite judgment, whereas a cause of action in a civil suit is a negative judgment. Thus in a civil dispute as to the ownership of a land the complaining party does not deny the law of ownership in general; on the contrary he asserts that law, and bases his claim upon it; but he denies the particular right of the defendant. But the thief, on the other hand, negates the law of ownership altogether, and his act is therefore an infinite judgment.[1] Similarly disease is merely a negative, while death is an infinite judgment. "In disease merely this or that function of life is checked or negatived: in death, as we ordinarily say, body and soul part, *i.e.* subject and predicate utterly diverge."[2]

Sub-Section II

THE JUDGMENT OF REFLECTION

332. The infinite judgment now purports to be the truth. But the fact is that, so far is it from being a true judgment, that it is not a judgment at all. It is a mere nonsensical conglomeration of words. Empirically this appears as the utter triviality and senselessness of saying, for example, that the mind is not an elephant. But that the infinite judgment is, in fact, not a judgment at all, is more evident if we consider it abstractly as pure thought. For it expresses only total opposition between subject and predicate, between singular and universal. The subject has now no connection whatever with the predicate. And the predicate having thus broken completely loose from the subject, the subject is left standing by itself, isolated, a mere self-related singular, which utterly excludes its other from itself. But a judgment must assert *some* relation between subject and predicate. And as there is here no relation at all, this is a judgment which is no judgment.

[1] See also § 548 below.   [2] Wal., *Log.*, § 173 Z.

This self-contradiction of the infinite judgment forces us onwards to a new sphere. Since the subject is now an isolated individual, what it excludes, namely the predicate, is something completely *other* than itself. But even exclusion is, after all, a *relation*. So we reach the idea of a judgment the predicate of which expresses the relation of the subject to what is *other* than it. And since this otherness is not determined as any particular other, it can only be otherness in general,—a world of other objects. This is the judgment of reflection. Its predicate, instead of being some isolated quality, such as red, hot, scented, etc., is such an adjective as "useful," "dangerous," "wholesome," etc. Such predicates express the relation of the subject to other things, or to the world in general. If we say "this house is useful," this expressed the relation of the house to human needs. And the same is true of such a proposition as "This body is heavy"—which means that it possesses a gravitational relation to the earth. Because such judgments express relativity, connectedness of things, mediation, in place of the immediacy of the qualitative judgment, they therefore correspond to the sphere of essence and are called **judgments of reflection.**

A. *The Singular Judgment.*

333. The subject of the qualitative judgment was the singular. In the above transition to judgments of reflection it is only the predicate which has undergone any change. Hence the subject remains the same as it was, the predicate, however, now expressing relativity. This gives us the **singular judgment** which applies such a predicate as "useful" to a single individual. "This house is useful." This again has the form "The singular is the universal."

B. *The Particular Judgment.*

334. The singular judgment is false for precisely the same reason as the affirmative judgment was false. Both state that the singular is the universal. But "useful," "heavy" and the like are just as much accidental qualities of the

object as redness, or sweetness. There is no necessary connection between subject and predicate. If we are to attain truth, the predicate must state the essential inner nature of the subject, so that the connection between the two is immanent and necessary. The subject will then be a singular and the predicate will be the same thing, *i.e.* the inner nature of the thing, expressed, however, as a universal, and the two terms will be thus genuinely identical as the judgment states them to be. But at present this statement that the judgment makes is untrue. " Usefulness " and " heaviness " are no more the essential nature of the object than redness is. Hence it is not true *at this stage* that the singular is the universal. The truth rather is, again, that the singular is *not* universal. Then what is the universal, if it is not the singular ? It must be the particular, and this gives us

The particular is the universal,

e.g. Some houses are useful. This is the **particular judgment.**

335. It will be noticed that, whereas in the qualitative judgment, when it was found that the first form of it was false this negation attached to the predicate, now the negation is said to attach to the subject. In qualitative judgments when it appeared that the singular is not the universal, we deduced the judgment that the singular is the particular (329). Now, on the same ground, we deduce that the particular is the universal. Formerly from " the rose is not red " we concluded that " the rose is some other colour." But at present from " This house is not useful," we deduce " Not this, but some other houses, are useful." The negation in the negative judgment changed the predicate from universal to not-universal, *i.e.* particular. Here the negation changes the subject from singular to not-singular, *i.e.* particular.

336. As I am unable to understand the justification for Hegel's apparently arbitrary procedure here I give it in his own words. In the *Greater Logic* he says " since the reflective judgment is not merely an affirmative one, the negation does not directly affect the predicate, which does not inhere but is the *intrinsic*. It is the subject instead which is liable to

alteration and determination."[1] In the *Encyclopaedia* he says, " To say ' This plant is wholesome,' implies not only that this single plant is wholesome, but that some or several are so. We have thus the particular judgment (some plants are wholesome. . . . etc.)."[2]

337. According to Dr. McTaggart [3] the reason why Hegel now regards the change as affecting the subject instead of the predicate is as follows. In the qualitative judgment we found that, though it stated that the singular is the universal, this turned out to be false. We therefore altered the predicate to try and make it fit the subject. This has now been found to be fruitless. It has not yielded us the correspondence of the terms which we seek. Accordingly, we now, in the judgment of reflection, try the experiment of progressively altering the subject to try and make it fit the predicate. But the objection to this explanation is that the dialectic is not, or ought not to be, a progress brought about by experiments made *by us*. No doubt it is the self-contradiction of a category which forces us onward to the next category in which that contradiction is resolved. But the new category must not be merely *found* by a subjective casting about on our part for a category which *happens* to solve the contradiction, and which *we* therefore *bring* from outside to meet the case. The old category must itself *produce* the new one. And it is this latter point which is the difficulty here. Dr. McTaggart's interpretation may correctly represent Hegel. But if so Hegel has not given a genuine deduction.

C. *The Universal Judgment.*

338. The particular judgment is as much negative as positive. " *Some* men are happy " implies that some men are not happy.[4] Therefore this proposition gives no information about the individual, for any individual man may belong either to the some who are happy or to the some who are not. Now

---

[1] Macran, p. 207. [2] Wal., *Log.*, § 175 Z. [3] *Com.*, § 198.

[4] Whether " some " is to be taken as meaning " some only," as Hegel here takes it, is a disputed point in the ordinary text-books of logic. Most writers disagree with Hegel.

the problem here is to make the singular fit the universal. Because the singular does not, as given in the singular judgment, fit the universal, we raised it to particularity. And as it now appears that the extension of the singular to the particular fails to solve the problem, we must again extend the particular in turn to the universal. This gives us the **universal judgment,**

" *All* men are mortal, unhappy, fallible, etc."

SUB-SECTION III

THE JUDGMENT OF NECESSITY

339. The subject of the judgment is now marked by universality or *allness*. As it first appears (1) this universality is merely subjective, that is to say, it is merely *we* who collect all the individuals of a class together, and label them " all." But (2) this universality is in reality objective, for it constitutes a *genus*, and is as such the essential nature, the foundation, of the individuals, without which the individuals could have no existence. All men, it seems, possess a characteristic which the lower animals lack, *i.e.* they have ear-lobes.[1] But the possession of ear-lobes by Smith or Brown is evidently a mere accidentality which has no connection with their essential characteristics. They would still be essentially what they are, namely men, even if they had no ear-lobes. But the universality which is implied in such a phrase as " all men " is different. Smith and Brown could not be pious, musical, rational, brave, etc., if they were not *men*. To be men, this is their essential inner nature, and this universality is not merely something external which we subjectively attach to them. It is, on the contrary, their essential objectivity; it is that whereby they *are*. This change from subjectivity to objectivity is indicated in language when instead of saying " all men " we say " man "—Man is mortal, fallible, etc.

[1] This illustration is, I am informed, incorrect. The higher anthropoid apes possess ear-lobes. But the ear-lobe attains its greatest development in size in the human being. Presumably this is what Hegel refers to. In any case, of course, the incorrectness of Hegel's illustration does not affect the validity of his argument.

This gives us a new kind of judgment in which the subject is a *species* such as man, rose, etc., and the predicate is a *genus*. Examples of such judgments are, The rose is a plant, The lion is an animal.

This is the **judgment of necessity.** In the qualitative judgment, and even in the judgment of reflection, we saw that the predicate was attached to the subject by no necessary bond of connection, but in a merely contingent and accidental manner. It may be a *fact*, that the rose is red, but no one can see any essential reason for it. But the rose *must* be a plant, for if not it could not be a rose. It might well be a rose without being red, but it could not possibly be a rose without being a plant. To be red is a mere chance character of the rose. To be a plant is its essential nature. We have here a great advance in the evolution of the judgment. All judgments *assert* the identity of subject and predicate. But as the judgment first came before us this assertion was untrue. In the qualitative judgment the factors of the Notion lay apart, indifferent to one another. The rose and its redness have no real relation to each other, much less identity. Hence that kind of judgment was false because it asserted a relation between a subject and a predicate which are really unrelated. But now, in the judgment of necessity, the subject and predicate have become more closely knit in a relation of necessity. The rose and its redness are indifferent to one another. But the rose and its being a plant are essentially connected, and nowise indifferent.

340. The first form of the judgment of necessity is

A. *The Categorical Judgment.*

The **categorical judgment** simply asserts the necessary connection between species and genus, *e.g.* " the rose is a plant."

B. *The Hypothetical Judgment.*

341. Because the relation between the subject and the predicate is now a bond of *necessity*, therefore the latter *depends* upon the former. Hence the judgment may now be

stated "*If* there is a rose, there is a plant"—or in general, *If A is, B is*. This is the **hypothetical judgment**.

C. *The Disjunctive Judgment.*

342. What is really stated in the hypothetical judgment is that the existence of the *genus* depends on the existence of the *species*. If there is a rose, there is a plant. In other words, the genus has no existence *apart from* its species. The universal only exists *in* the particular. Plants are not something different from roses, lilies, daisies, etc. The *same* thing is taken now in its universality (genus) and now in its particularity (species). This brings out the essential defect of the hypothetical judgment, which is that it asserts the dependence of the genus on only *one* of its species, instead of on all. If there is a rose, there is a plant. But it is equally true that, if there is a lily, there is a plant. The existence of plants does not depend on the existence on *one* species, the rose, but upon the existence of all the species.

The recognition of this defect gives us at once the **disjunctive judgment** which states that the genus is the same thing as the sum of its species. Plants are roses, lilies, daisies, etc. Or, a plant is either a rose, or a lily, or ... etc. A is either B or C or D.

What has especially to be noted here is that the identity of subject and predicate, which all judgments *assert*, is for the first time *true* in the disjunctive judgment. The subject is the genus, the predicate is the sum of the species. But the genus is the same thing as the sum of its species. The same thing is twice put, once in its universality in the subject, and again in its particularity in the predicate.

Sub-Section IV

THE JUDGMENT OF THE NOTION

343. Because the subject and predicate are now identical in their difference we have before us again the genuine unity in difference and difference in unity—in a word, the Notion.

The factors of the Notion which had fallen asunder have now returned to self-identity.

But the disjunctive judgment, although it exhibits the identity of the universal and the particular (genus and species), has the defect that it leaves the singular out in the cold. It shows that the universal has its being only in the particulars, but we have still to see that its being descends even into the single individuals. In other words we have still to find a universal predicate which is absolutely identical with the singular subject, *this* rose, *this* picture. The judgment which performs this work is the judgment of the Notion. Such a judgment must have a singular for its subject and a universal for its predicate, yet the two must be identical. The predicate must be the same thing taken in its universality as the subject was when taken in its singularity. In other words the predicate must be simply the essential and universal nature of the subject. The judgment must state the agreement or disagreement of the subject with its own essential nature—with its universal concept, with what it *ought to be*. It must show that the individual, which is the subject, is in harmony or out of harmony with its *proper* character. The predicate is thus the *ideal* to which the subject, if it *is* what it *purports* to be, must conform, and the judgment states whether it does so conform or not. Thus the essential universal nature of man is his *reason*, and a judgment which states that a man is or is not rational, will tell us whether he is what the essential notion of him implies that he must be; it will tell us whether this man is *truly* a man. That a man is snub-nosed is irrelevant to his manhood. He is still a man, snub-nosed or not. But that a man is irrational destroys his essential manhood, because reason is the very essence of man. Hence to say, " this man is rational," is the same as saying, " this man is a man,"— not in the sense of an empty identity, but as importing his conformity with his ideal. But in saying that this man is a man we are saying that *this* man (singular) is a *man* (universal). Thus the subject and predicate are distinct as being respectively singular and universal. And yet they are absolutely identical since it is " man " that appears both as subject and predicate.

Hence in the **judgment of the Notion** the predicate is always a term which implies conformity with a rational ideal—this picture is (or is not) *beautiful*, this action is (or is not) *good, just, noble*.

344. The judgment of the Notion appears first as

A. *The Assertoric Judgment.*

The **assertoric judgment** simply asserts conformity or non-conformity with the ideal. This action is good, bad, right, etc.

B. *The Problematic Judgment.*

345. The assertoric judgment merely *asserts* that the subject is or is not what it ought to be. But no ground for this assertion is given. This picture *is* beautiful, but I cannot say why. It is merely my opinion. Hence it is at once confronted with the contrary assertion: this picture is ugly. This contrary judgment has as much right to be asserted as the original judgment, because, in truth, neither of them has any right, both being mere assertions. It is, therefore, *doubtful* which judgment is true, and this gives us the **problematic judgment,** *e.g.* this picture *may* (or may *not*) be beautiful.

C. *The Apodeictic Judgment.*

346. The subject of the problematic judgment is a *contingency*. It may or may not conform to the ideal. Hence it becomes evident that it only conforms or does not conform because it contains within itself some ground in the nature of its constitution for this conformity or non-conformity. Hence we get such propositions as, This action, being so and so constituted, is right, This picture, being thus and thus painted is beautiful. The subject is now raised from *contingency* to *necessity*. The picture *must* be beautiful *because* it is thus and thus painted. Or to put it otherwise the beauty of the picture is grounded in the nature of the picture itself. It is self-grounded. And to be self-grounded is to be necessary. Hence such a judgment is an **apodeictic judgment**.

This judgment asserts that the singular (this picture) **is** identical with the universal (beautiful) through and by means of the particular (being thus and thus painted). It contains, therefore, the three factors of the Notion, distinct and yet merged in absolute identity. Hence it is the perfect judgment, the truth of judgment in general.

SECTION III

THE SYLLOGISM

347. The singular is now identical with the universal *through and by means of* the particular. Thus the particular appears as a middle term which mediates between the two extremes, singular and universal. This is the first form of the **Syllogism.** Every syllogism contains three terms. Of these the one that is widest in its scope is the universal. A narrower term is included within the wider and this is the particular. A still narrower term is subsumed under the particular, and this is the singular. Thus in the syllogism

Green is pleasant,
This fruit is green,
Therefore, this fruit is pleasant,

the widest term, pleasant, is the universal, green is the particular, and this fruit is the singular. Thus, using the symbols S, P, U, for singular, particular, and universal respectively, this syllogism may be represented as

$$P - U.$$
$$S - P.$$
$$S - U.$$

The particular is the middle term which mediates between the singular and the universal, and unites them in the conclusion. The same thing may be more briefly expressed in the formula, $S - P - U$, which Hegel adopts.

348. In the Notion as Notion we had the factors of singularity, particularity, and universality, lying in a primitive and as yet undifferentiated *unity*. In the judgment the Notion differentiated its factors into *diversity*. In the syllogism the moment

of diversity is preserved in the fact that the moments of the Notion appear as the extremes, while their unity is posited in the middle term. Thus the syllogism is the synthesis of the Notion and the judgment.

349. The judgment, from the emphasis it laid on difference and diversity, was recognized as the product of the *understanding*. The syllogism, as expressing the unity of the extremes, or, in other words, the identity of opposites, is the special form of *reason*. But it is not to be regarded as a merely subjective form of thought. Like the judgment, it is objective. Everything is a syllogism. Or, more correctly, because the syllogism is the form of *reason*, therefore everything *rational*, *i.e.* everything *actual*, is a syllogism. Thus the syllogism, like every other category, is a definition of the Absolute. The Absolute, or God, is a syllogism. God, regarded as abstract universal, is the Logical Idea. But God is not merely this empty abstract universal. This universal goes out of itself into particularity, which is *nature*, and returns to itself in the singularity of concrete *spirit*. Similarly such actualities as the infinite, the unconditioned, the supersensuous, freedom, right, and duty, are syllogisms because they do not remain empty and abstract universals, but differentiate themselves, and appear through particularity as *this* freedom, *this* duty, *this* right, etc.

350. The phases of the syllogism are (1) the qualitative syllogism, (2) the syllogism of reflection, (3) the syllogism of necessity. As these names indicate, the evolution of the syllogism is largely parallel to the evolution of the judgment.

Sub-Section I

THE QUALITATIVE SYLLOGISM

351. The syllogism first appears as *immediate*. Hence though it *asserts* the identity of its extremes through the mediation of the middle term, this identity is in fact delusive, and the terms remain mutually indifferent and unrelated.[1] Such a syllogism is the **qualitative syllogism**.

[1] See § 239 above.

A. The First Figure, S – P – U.

352. As already explained (347) the syllogism first appears under the schema S – P – U, where the particular is the middle term. This is the **first figure.** The singular is subsumed under a wider term, the particular. This again is subsumed under the universal, giving us the conclusion that the singular is subsumed under the universal. Or,

P is U,
S is P,
Therefore, S is U.

The singular and universal find their identity in the particular. For in relation to the universal the particular is the *subject* (*i.e.* in the major premiss) and is therefore singular. In relation to the singular it is predicate (in the minor premiss) and is therefore universal. Thus as being both singular and universal it is the unity of the extremes.

Because this is the *immediate* syllogism, therefore, just as in the case of the qualitative judgment, its terms are indifferent and unrelated in spite of the relation which the syllogism alleges (327, 328). The singular is an individual object, this rose, that house. The particular is some isolated quality which *happens* to inhere in this individual, its redness, its odour, its shape. The universal is again some isolated quality which *happens* to attach to the particular. Hence we get such a syllogism as

Green is pleasant,
This fruit is green,
Therefore, it is pleasant.

It is a mere fact that the fruit is green. There is no necessary or logical connection between the colour and the fruit. And it is a mere fact that green is pleasant, and there is no essential reason for it. All the terms are mutually indifferent.

B. Second Figure, P – S – U.

353. The defect of this first figure is that it thus asserts a relation between unrelated terms. Hence it is a matter of

mere chance which one of the many isolated qualities of the subject I pick out to act as a middle term, and it is equally contingent which quality of the middle I pick out as the predicate with which it is to connect the subject. By choosing the greenness of the fruit as the middle term and the pleasantness of green as the predicate I arrive at the conclusion that the fruit is pleasant. But by choosing some other qualities I might equally have proved that it is unpleasant. *E.g.*

>Poisonous things are unpleasant,
>This fruit is poisonous,
>Therefore, this fruit is unpleasant.

The whole procedure is utterly capricious. If pleasantness were the essential nature of green, instead of being a mere chance character of it, then green things would, in *all* circumstances, be pleasant. Then our syllogism would be true. But, as it is, the chance character of pleasantness is liable to be destroyed by any other chance quality, such as being poisonous. Hence it is the fact that there is no real connection between the terms that is the defect here. Hence our middle term, green, or poisonous, or whatever it be, though it *purports* to be particular, is in fact treated by this syllogism as a detached quality, a single isolated immediacy, a singular. Hence the truth of this syllogism will be better expressed by frankly admitting the middle term to be what in fact it is, a singular. This will give us a new syllogism, P – S – U. This is the **second figure.**

The same result is evident from another consideration. In the first figure the conclusion S – U is not an immediate connection of S and U, for it has been mediated by P. But the premisses, which are S – P and P – U, have not been mediated by anything and are merely immediate connections of these terms. Such immediate relations are inconsistent with the nature of syllogism, the essence of which is that in it any two factors of the Notion are mediated by the third. Hence the premiss P – U must be mediated, and as the only factor available for the purpose is S, the syllogism will run P – S – U, which is the second figure. The other premiss S – P must be mediated by U giving the syllogism S – U – P, which, as we shall see, is the third figure.

The necessity for thus mediating the premisses of the first figure is usually expressed by saying that the premisses of a syllogism themselves require proof, *e.g.* may themselves be the conclusions of anterior syllogisms.

The middle term is now the singular. Each of the other two terms, therefore, is wider than the middle term, and each premiss will therefore state that the middle term is subsumed under one of the other two. Hence the singular will in both cases be the subject thus:

$$S - U.$$
$$S - P.$$
$$P - U.$$

Now this only alters the order of the terms, and not their character as merely immediate contingencies. The singular will as before be an individual object, and the other two terms will be random qualities which happen to be united by both inhering in the same subject thus:

This fruit is pleasant,
This fruit is green,
Therefore, green is pleasant.

It will be observed, as regards the order of the terms, that this Hegelian second figure is not the second, but the third, figure of Formal Logic. The conclusion P is U, since its subject is the particular, indicates the common rule of the third figure in the text-books, namely, that the conclusion in this figure must be particular.

The conclusion of this figure is the major premiss of the first figure, " Green is pleasant," or P is U. Thus this figure remedies the defect of the former figure that in it the relation P – U was unmediated.

C. Third Figure, *S – U – P.*

354. The second figure has a mediated conclusion P – U. Its major premiss S – U is also mediated, for S – U is what

was proved in the first figure by the mediation of P. But its minor premiss S – P is still unmediated. It can only be mediated by U, and this gives us the **third figure** S – U – P.

We may arrive at the same result by considering the content instead of the form. The second figure concluded that because two qualities, such as green and pleasant, both inhere in the same subject, such as this fruit, therefore they inhere in each other. Thus the middle term is regarded as what is merely common to the extremes. It is not this fruit in its full concreteness, with its multitudes of other qualities, that we have before us, but a mere abstraction, which drops out the manifold of qualities and is merely an abstract meeting place of these extremes. And because it is this abstraction, this mere common element, it is therefore not a true singular at all, but an abstract universal. Hence the syllogism P – S – U *purports* to have the singular for its middle but this singular is really the universal. And this result will be expressed by explicitly putting the universal as the middle term, which gives us the third figure S – U – P.

This will yield such a syllogism as

>   Green is pleasant,
>   This fruit is pleasant,
>   Therefore, it is green,

which, as far as the order of its terms is concerned, will be recognized as the second figure of Formal Logic. The above syllogism is invalid, because in this figure one of the premisses and the conclusion must be negative, to avoid an undistributed middle. This fact openly exposes the defect of the qualitative syllogism as a whole. This syllogism could only be valid if we could say, not merely that green is pleasant, but that green is the only thing which is pleasant, *i.e.* that everything pleasant is green. That we cannot do so is due to the fact that greenness and pleasantness have no *necessary* connection with each other, *i.e.* it is due to the immediate character of the qualitative syllogism as a whole. Not only this figure but all the figures suffer from the same defect, which has to be remedied in a latter phase of the syllogism.

D. The Mathematical Syllogism, U – U – U.

355. The singular, the particular, and the universal have each in turn appeared as the middle term. Each figure has for its conclusion one of the premisses of the other figures. Thus each figure presupposes the other two. This may be regarded as removing that defect of the qualitative syllogism which consists in the fact that though its conclusion is mediated its premisses are not. But the vital defect of this kind of syllogism still remains. It is a matter of perfect indifference which term is made the middle, for in each case the same defect, the utter disconnectedness of the terms, appears. The three factors from this point of view are all the same as one another, are identical, since each can replace the other, and this leads to a syllogism in which this pure indifference of the three terms to each other is fully expressed as merely mathematical equality. Since it makes no difference which term is made the middle or which the extremes, we can abstract from their qualitative difference altogether and regard them as three counters, any one of which can be indifferently substituted for any other, just as in dealing with actual counters we should abstract from the fact that one might be red, another green, and another blue, and regard them all as simply counters, as identical.

When all qualitative difference is thus neglected we get simply mathematical equality

$$A = B,$$
$$B = C,$$
$$\text{Therefore, } A = C.$$

or, as it may otherwise be stated, " If two things are equal to a third they are equal to one another." Hegel expresses this relation by the schema U – U – U, and calls it the **mathematical syllogism.**

Though Hegel treats this syllogism under the head of the qualitative syllogism, it does not properly come under that head, and he himself calls it elsewhere the quantitative syllogism. He also refers to it as the fourth figure. But it has of course no connection with the fourth figure of Formal Logic, which it will be remembered does not appear in Aristotle but is a later addition. Hegel, following Kant in this respect, repudiates the ordinary fourth figure of the syllogism as meaningless and futile, because it is merely an inversion of the first figure.

Sub-Section II

THE SYLLOGISM OF REFLECTION

356. The mathematical syllogism, with its utter emptiness of notional content, is merely the *negative* result of the dialectic of the qualitative syllogism. But there is also a *positive* result. The three terms of the qualitative syllogism were isolated, disconnected, and exclusive of each other. They were merely abstract singularity, abstract particularity, abstract universality. Now each of these abstract forms has alternately been put as the middle, and each has failed to fulfil the function of the middle, namely, to be the *concrete* unity of the extremes; so that the extremes still remain indifferent to each other. The positive result of this process is therefore that we must put as the middle, not any mere abstraction, but the concrete unity of the extremes. And as the extremes are, in the first instance, singularity and universality, the middle will be a particular which combines in itself singularity and universality. Such a syllogism will be **the syllogism of reflection** because the factors of the Notion will not remain mere abstractions, but will genuinely mediate each other in the middle term. The first phase of the syllogism will be

A. *The Syllogism of Allness*,

which Hegel also calls the syllogism of complete extension.

357. In the **syllogism of allness** the middle term will be a particularity which consists of *all the singulars*. It will be such a term as *all men*. Because every individual man is denoted by this term it therefore contains *singularity*. Be-

THE SUBJECTIVE NOTION 255

cause it contains *all* the individuals it is thereby *universal*. And because in such a syllogism as

All men are mortal,
Socrates is a man,
Therefore, Socrates is mortal,

the middle term is subsumed under the higher universal "mortal," it is therefore the particular. Hence the schema of this syllogism will be that of the first figure S – P – U.

This syllogism remedies the defect of the qualitative syllogism. In that syllogism the middle term was a mere abstraction, a single quality of a concrete object, which had an indefinite number of other such qualities any one of which could be taken as the middle with the most contradictory results. The fruit was pleasant because green, and unpleasant because poisonous. But here the middle is no such single quality but is a totality of concrete objects, all "men," all "green things," etc. This middle, therefore, can only connect the subject with a universal which all subjects of that species possess, and no contradictions can arise. It is perfectly true that green is pleasant, but green is a mere abstract quality. If instead we had said "All green things are pleasant" we should immediately have thought of the poisonous fruit, green snakes, etc., and seen at once that this premiss is false. And so we should have been saved from the contradictions into which we then fell. This is precisely what is done in the syllogism of allness, which consequently removes the defect of the earlier syllogism.[1]

---

[1] Dr. McTaggart (*Com.*, § 215) argues that the supposed defect of the qualitative syllogism, whereby it leads to applying contradictory predicates to the same subject, is not a defect at all, because what is really meant by "Green is pleasant" is "All green things are pleasant," which is, of course, false. But if the syllogism is stated in Dr. McTaggart's form it is not the qualitative syllogism at all, but the syllogism of reflection. That the syllogism put in that form has not this defect is precisely Hegel's point. The qualitative syllogism as given by Hegel certainly has the defect of which he accuses it. Dr. McTaggart says that the conclusion that the fruit is pleasant requires the premiss "All green things are pleasant." This is just what Hegel says too. And it is because it has not got the premiss it requires that it is defective. And it is because the syllogism of allness supplies the required premiss that it removes the defect. Dr. McTaggart seems to have been misled by supposing that the first figure of the qualitative syllogism corresponds in all ways to the first figure in

B. *The Syllogism of Induction.*

358. But the syllogism of allness has a defect of its own. Just because its major premiss alleges its predicate of *all* the singulars it thereby begs the question, and assumes the truth of its conclusion. To say that *all* men are mortal assumes that Socrates is mortal, for if he were not, then it would not be true that all men are mortal. The only remedy for this defect is to go through all men individually and show that each is mortal. We have to show that Caius is mortal, Cassius is mortal, Caesar is mortal, Brutus is mortal, and so on throughout the human race, and when this process is complete we shall then be able to assert that all men are mortal. This is inducton, and put in the form of a syllogism, it is P – S – U, – the second figure. More accurately it is

$$\begin{array}{c} S \\ S \\ P-S-U \\ S \\ S \end{array}$$

ad infinitum.

Here S stands for an individual man. P of course is the species (particular) man, while U is the higher universal, mortal. The two premisses will be

$$(1) \quad P-S \begin{array}{c} S \\ S \\ S \\ \end{array}$$

etc.

i.e. All men are Caius, Cassius, Brutus, etc. *ad infinitum*; and

$$(2) \quad S-U \begin{array}{c} S \\ S \\ S \end{array}$$

formal Logic. But the actual correspondence is confined wholly to the order of the terms. It is rather the syllogism of allness which really corresponds to the first figure in Formal Logic, as will be seen by the example given in this section—which is obviously a syllogism in *Barbara*.

i.e. Caius is mortal, Cassius is mortal, etc. The conclusion will be P – U, or, all men are mortal.

It will be noticed that the singular is here the middle, and that whereas the syllogism of allness was of the first figure S – P – U, the **syllogism of induction** is of the second figure, P – S – U. Nevertheless this singular is not the abstract singular of the second figure of the qualitative syllogism. For although it is singular, it is at the same time universal, because it comprises all the singulars.

C. *The Syllogism of Analogy.*

359. The syllogism of induction removes the defect of the syllogism of allness, but again develops a defect of its own. For it is obvious that it requires the complete enumeration of all the singulars *ad infinitum,* and this is impossible. Hence it assumes, after observing that all men so far known have died, that no exception can arise in the incompleted series to contradict that experience. But this can only be the case on the assumption that the genus man has mortality, not as a contingent quality, but as a necessary and essential part of his nature, that, in fact mortality is involved in the very notion of manhood. We must believe not merely that all the men observed happen, as a matter of fact, to be mortal, but rather that *man* is mortal *because* he is man. This gives us the **syllogism of analogy,** *e.g.*

> The earth is inhabited,
> The moon is an earth,
> Therefore, it is inhabited.

This argument rests upon the assumption that the earth is inhabited, not for any accidental reason, but *because* it is an earth, from which it will follow that any other earth, such as the moon, will also be inhabited. This particular example of analogy is of course so superficial as to be wholly absurd. The fact that the earth is inhabited depends, not on its simply being an earth, but on its atmosphere and other circumstances which are absent in the moon. But the *principle* is correct. A better example would be

> I who talk and act am conscious,
> Caesar is a being who talks and acts,
> Therefore, he is conscious.

Now the syllogism of induction was in the form P – S – U. In the syllogism of analogy the middle term is still a singular, *e.g.* the earth, but it is now a singular taken in its universal nature. The earth is not merely inhabited as being this individual earth, but as being *an* earth, *i.e.* a member of a genus, whose essential character it is to be inhabited. Since the singular has here, therefore, a universal significance, the middle term may be explicitly stated as what it essentially is, a universal. Hence the schema of this syllogism is S – U – P, – the third figure. Yet it is no longer an abstract universal, as in the qualitative syllogism, but is rather concrete inasmuch as it is also essentially singular.

In the three phases of the syllogism of reflection, then, as in the qualitative syllogism, the middle term is alternately the particular, the singular, and the universal.

Sub-Section III

THE SYLLOGISM OF NECESSITY

360. The syllogism of analogy has a defect similar to that of the syllogism of allness. Its conclusion is S – P, *e.g.* the moon is inhabited. But its major premiss is also S – P (*e.g.* the earth is inhabited). It is true that the singular which is the middle term and subject of the major premiss (in this example the earth) is taken in its universal nature, for which reason we have counted it as U. But it may equally be insisted that it is singular, and in that case, since the conclusion is S – P, and the premiss is S – P, the premiss asssumes the truth of the conclusion. Or if we were explicitly to set this term in its universality, and say "All earths are inhabited," then the syllogism would be a syllogism of allness which, as we have already seen, assumes its conclusion.

The syllogism of analogy comes under the schema S – U – P. But the defect pointed out means that the middle, though put as a universal, constantly relapses into singularity. This defect can only be removed by a syllogism of the form S – U – P in which the middle is out and out universal. Now we have already seen that in the syllogism of analogy the middle as the universal *necessarily* connects itself with the extremes. That syllogism rests upon the belief that, in the example chosen, the earth is inhabited, not for any extraneous or contingent reason, but necessarily, *because* it is an earth, because to be inhabited is necessarily involved in the notion of earth, and is part of its essential nature. The new syllogism S – U – P will therefore have for its middle an out and out universal to which the extremes belong as a necessary part of its essential nature, and not as a mere contingent fact, so that this universal is in truth the foundation and very being of the extremes—in a word it will be the *genus*. This is the **syllogism of necessity.**

A. *The Categorical Syllogism.*

361. The first phase will be *immediate*. Although the extremes are *necessarily* connected with the middle, yet in this relation some element of immediacy, *i.e.* of contingency, will still linger.[1] The one extreme, as immediate, will be, as before, a concrete single object. If the middle is the genus man, this extreme will be some individual, *e.g.* Socrates. What is contingent here is that there is no reason why I should hit upon Socrates rather than any other individual member of the genus. What is necessary is that the genus man is the very foundation of the individual Socrates, without which he could not be what he is. To be a man is the essential nature of Socrates, which determines his whole being. It would have been different if we had subsumed him under some universal other than his essential genus, *e.g.* under "snub-nosed beings," for he could well be rational, brave, noble, free, without being snub-nosed, but he could be none of these

[1] See § 239 above.

things without being a man. The other extreme will be some characteristic which necessarily belongs to the notion of man, such as rational, or free, or morally responsible, or capable of religion or art. The necessary connection here is obvious, and the contingency again lies in the fact that there is no reason why this rather than any of the other essential characters of man should be chosen.

This procedure yields the **categorical syllogism**, for example,

>Man is rational,
>Socrates is a man,
>Therefore, Socrates is rational.

The general schema of the syllogism of necessity is S – U – P. The middle term in the above syllogism, man, is a universal of the kind required. But in the categorical syllogism this universal appears as subsumed under a wider universal, in this case, rational. Hence in relation to this latter universal it is particular, and the special schema of the categorical syllogism will be S – P – U, which is the first figure.

B. *The Hypothetical Syllogism.*

362. The real result of the categorical syllogism is that the conjunction of the extremes depends upon the middle term, that, for example, Socrates is only rational in virtue of being a man. Since rationality is the *special* character of man as distinguished from the brutes, it is only if he is a man that Socrates is rational. This is explicitly stated in the **hypothetical syllogism,**

>If Socrates is a man, he is rational,
>He is a man,
>Therefore, he is rational.

Here the middle term is not the genus man, but *the fact of being a man* as we see more clearly if we cast the syllogism in the awkward form

>Being a man is being rational,
>The being of Socrates is being a man,
>Therefore, etc.

Because the middle is a *fact*, it is therefore an immediacy, and as an immediacy may be regarded as a singular, so that the schema of this syllogism is P – S – U, which is the second figure.

C. *The Disjunctive Syllogism.*

363. The hypothetical syllogism states that the individual and the species *are the same thing* as the genus. Being a man and being rational are one and the same thing. Or again, the very being of Socrates *is* the being rational. But when it is stated in this form the defect of the hypothetical syllogism is exposed. No doubt the genus is the same thing as the species, but it is only identical with *all* its species taken together, not with one of them alone. And the species again is identical with *all* its individuals. This gives us the **disjunctive syllogism** in which the middle term is the genus (U) distributed into its species. The extremes are the species (P) and the individual (S). The syllogism is thus of the form S – U – P, which is the third figure.

To give an example of this, rational is the genus, man the species, Socrates the individual. The genus being wider than the species we must assume, for the sake of the example, that there are other rational beings besides men, *e.g.* angels. Our syllogism will then be

>Rational beings are either men or angels,
>Socrates who is a rational being is not an angel,

Therefore, he is a man.

Or it will be

>Rational beings are either men or angels,
>Socrates who is a rational being is a man,

Therefore, he is not an angel.

CHAPTER II

THE OBJECT, OR, THE OBJECTIVE NOTION

364. The factors of the Notion appeared first, in the Notion as Notion, in undifferentiated unity. In the judgment they fell asunder. The syllogism exhibited their mediation and return to unity. In the disjunctive syllogism this return to unity was completed. For firstly, the middle term is no longer an abstract universal, particular, or singular, but it is all these; it is the concrete totality of the Notion. It is the genus, or universal, which explicitly states itself to be at the same time the totality of its species, or particulars—A (genus) which is B and C and D (species). And since this is also given in the form " A which is B *or* C *or* D," since, therefore, the species are given as mutually exclusive units, they are therefore at the same time the totality of the singulars. This syllogism contains, therefore, in its middle term, the absolute collapse of the factors of the Notion to unity. And their mediation has sunk to *immediacy*.

In the second place, in the syllogism

> A is either B or C or D,
> But A is B,
> Therefore, A is not C or D,

we find that A is the subject in each premiss and in the conclusion. In the major premiss it is the universal, the genus, and is identified with the totality of its particulars. In the minor premiss it is a particular, a species. In the conclusion, because it is this individual A which excludes C and D, it is the singular. This syllogism thus exhibits A as the totality of the Notion.

The mediation, which is the essential character of the syllogism, is thus merged, and in its place we have a being which is now *immediate*. Immediacy thus forms the fundamental characteristic of the new sphere. Moreover the factors of the Notion, in the sphere of subjectivity, mediated, and in that way were dependent upon, one another. Each was only through the other. But now since mediation is annulled, dependence is also annulled. Hence we have a being which is *immediate and independent*. This is the category of the **object**.[1] Whatever is (1) *immediate*, is there, and confronts thought as (2) an *independent* being, is described as an object. From subjectivity we have passed to objectivity.

365. According to Dr. McTaggart[2] subjectivity and objectivity are not here used in the sense of inner and outer, of what is thought and what is not thought. Subjective, he thinks, means capricious, contingent, while objective means universal and necessary. Without denying that these meanings may have significance here, it does not seem to me that they are the most important. Subjective, he urges,[3] cannot mean merely the inner side, the side of thought, of the self as against the not-self, because Hegel expressly states that the categories of subjectivity, such as the judgment and the syllogism, apply not only to thought but to everything. "Everything is a syllogism." But the answer is that, from the point of view reached in the Notion, everything is thought. The first two divisions of the doctrine of the Notion, viz. the subjective Notion and the object, are, it must be remembered, one-sided and abstract, the concrete truth being reached only in the third division, the Idea. In the subjective Notion we reach the view that everything is thought, is subject. In the present division, we pass to the opposite view that everything is object. In the Idea, as we shall see, the truth emerges that everything is at once subject and object.

It must not, of course, be supposed that in passing from subject to object we have left thought behind, and that we are no longer dealing with thoughts or categories. We have not here a transition from pure thought to the outward material

---

[1] See § 239 above. [2] *Com.*, § 233. [3] *Ibid.*, § 184.

world in the sense in which such a transition occurs at the end of the Logic, where we pass over to nature. We are still in the sphere of the Logical Idea, of pure thoughts or categories. And objectivity, as Hegel points out, is just as much a thought as subjectivity.[1] What we are now dealing with is the universal and necessary idea of objectivity, the *thought* of the object.

It may be objected that the transition to the object involves the abandonment of the point of view reached in the Notion, viz. that the universe is no longer regarded as a collection of *things* but as inherently nothing but *thought*. To regard the universe as object, and not as thought, is a return, it might be said, to the points of view of being and essence, to such categories as the thing and its properties. But an *object* is not the same as a *thing*. A thing, for all one could say to the contrary, might exist unrelated to a subject, as it is supposed to do in the theory of materialism. But the very word object means essentially the object *of thought*. The general point of view of the Notion is that the world is thought. But thought has two terms, subject and object. To complete the truth that the world is thought, it must be conceived as object quite as much as subject. And this is the point of view we have here reached. To say that a thing is an object means that it essentially exists only for a subject. And this is to say that it is thought, which is the point of view of the Notion.[2]

366. This consideration may also help us to understand the transition from the disjunctive syllogism to the object,

---

[1] Cf. above § 100, " Atoms are thoughts."

[2] There is a passage (Wal., *Log.*, § 193) which seems, at first sight, to tell against this interpretation. "That the object is also an object for us," says Hegel, there " will be more precisely seen, when it puts itself in contrast with the subjective. At present ... it is only immediate object and nothing more, just as the Notion is not describable as subjective, previous to the subsequent contrast with objectivity." This only means, however, that when the object first appears on the scene, we, as having left the subject behind, regard the object in its pure abstraction from the subject. It is impossible, however, to remain at this attitude of abstraction, and the contrast with subjectivity immediately reasserts itself. The last words of the quotation clearly show this. If the Notion is not describable as subjective till it is contrasted with objectivity, neither can the object be described as an object till it is contrasted with the subject. See also footnote to § 366 below.

which certainly, at first sight, seems very puzzling. Granted that in the disjunctive syllogism we have a collapse to immediacy, why, it might be asked, should this immediacy be regarded as the object? In the course of the Logic we have had numerous examples of the merging of mediation and the consequent emergence of immediacy. Why should not any of those immediacies have been construed as the object? Nothing whatever seems to be deduced here except the bare idea of immediacy, which has been deduced many times before. If immediacy was not the object then, why is it so now? What is the difference between this immediacy and those?

The difference, we may answer, is that we have now, in the Notion in general, reached the sphere of thought, which we had not reached earlier. This immediacy, therefore, is the immediacy of thought. It is the immediate element in thought, and that is the element of objectivity. Kant, it will be remembered, divided experience into what is contributed by the activity of the subject, and what is *given* from the outside. Now what is *given* is precisely the immediate element in thought, and its source is the object. All else is contributed by the connecting and mediating functions of the subject. Hence the immediate element in thought is the element of objectivity, mediation being the work of the subject. Now the subjective Notion, in its categories of Notion, judgment, and syllogism, is in general the sphere of mediation, and hence is rightly described as the subject. And the transition to immediacy, because it occurs here in the sphere of thought or the Notion, is essentially a transition from the mediating moment of thought (subject) to the immediate moment of thought, that is, the object.[1]

---

[1] The reference to Kant is, of course, merely illustrative. It is not to be taken as a justification of the Kantian dualism. The illustration is, however, instructive in other respects. Kant's distinction attributes the *form* of knowledge to the subject, the *matter* to the object. The highest connective unity of form is the pure ego, the subject itself, the "transcendental unity of apperception." This proceeds—though how it does so Kant cannot explain—to differentiate itself into the twelve forms of the categories, which are also the forms of the faculty of judgment. Now Hegel (321) identifies the Notion as Notion with Kant's pure ego. But Hegel, unlike Kant, does, as we have seen, explain how the Notion as Notion, or the ego, differentiates itself into the judgment, and, further,

367. The object, like other categories, gives us both a description of the world and a definition of the Absolute. Firstly, everything is an object. And this involves that there is nothing which is not related to thought, to the subject. There is no unknowable entity wholly cut off from the subject, like the Kantian thing-in-itself. Secondly, the Absolute is object. God is absolute object. When this point of view is taken abstractly, as meaning that God is not also subject, it gives rise to the view of God as " a dark and hostile power " over against the subject, confronting him as something utterly alien to his own life and subjectivity, a mere external power which has nothing in common with him and which is therefore to be feared, but cannot be loved. This is the point of view taken by superstition and slavish fear. When we reach the higher truth that God is not only object, but also subject, then as subject God is no more a mere external power confronting us, but is also our own true and innermost self and is seen to dwell " in our hearts." This is the point of view of Christianity.

368. As it first comes before us the object is abstract object, divested of subjectivity, the mere empty immediacy of the not-self. The Idea, as the synthesis of the triad, is the unity of subject and object. The process of the object within itself will therefore be a graduated return to subjectivity. In accordance with the universal principles of the Hegelian method the subject goes out of itself into its opposite, the object, and then returns into itself in the synthesis. This graduated return of the object into subjectivity exhibits three stages (1) mechanism, (2) chemism, (3) teleology. In the last we are clearly returning to the view of the object as governed

---

into the syllogism. All this shows that Hegel adopted the Kantian view that pure subject means the *formal* part of knowledge, object the material part. There is a passage (Macran, p. 283) where he expressly identifies the formal element in knowledge with subjectivity. But whereas Kant regarded form and matter as arising from different sources, Hegel sees that the matter of knowledge arises out of its form, and his exposition of this constitutes the transition, here expounded, from subject to object. These considerations should render the meaning of the transition clear. They should also finally dispose of Dr. McTaggart's view that subjective and objective only mean contingent and necessary, and do not refer to the inner and outer sides of knowledge.

by thought, by purposes, by subjectivity, and this forms the transition to the Idea.

SECTION I

MECHANISM

369. As it first meets us the object is one, a *single* object, the single immediacy into which the moments of the Notion have collapsed. But this unity nevertheless has in it the diverse factors by the merging of which it has arisen. And each of these factors is not a mere factor, but is itself the whole. For this is the result reached in the syllogism, namely, that each factor of the Notion is itself the whole Notion, is itself the totality of all the factors. For the same reason the object splits up into a multiplicity of objects. Each is itself a totality, and an independent whole, and each therefore is an object. Hence what we have before us is a world of objects.

Now the first phase of the object will be the object in its *immediacy*. And this means that each object is an independent being totally indifferent to the others. Its being, therefore, is in no way affected by the being of the others. Consequently the only relations between them will be purely external relations, which do not touch in any way their inner natures. These relations will be no true part of the objects themselves but will be merely attached to them from the outside, or as we say, mechanically. When the universe is thus viewed as a mere aggregate, or heap, of indifferent objects, connected by no inner relationship, but merely externally added together, and externally connected, we have arrived at the category of **mechanism**.[1]

370. The essential point of this mechanical view of the universe is its *externality*. All mechanical theories of the world have this as their central idea. Thus what is called the mechanical theory of quality, which was first vaguely indicated by Empedocles and developed by Democritus, views quality as founded upon quantity, *i.e.* upon externality of

[1] See § 239 above.

parts to parts. The Atomists, again, explained everything by the impact and concussion of atoms. The inner nature of the atom itself is in no way affected by its external relations. Again, our knowledge is said to be mechanical "when the words have no meaning for us, but continue *external* to sense, conception, thought. . . . Conduct, piety, etc., are in the same way mechanical, when a man's behaviour is settled for him by ceremonial laws, by a spiritual adviser, etc., in short, when his own mind and will are not in his actions, which in this way are extraneous to himself." [1]

371. Mechanism has, of course, its rights as a category. It is chiefly suitable to describe the relations of inert masses of matter in the inorganic world, though even here it is only the most abstract relations of matter which obey the laws of mechanics. But in the organic world, and even in the realm of mind, mechanism plays a part, though it becomes an increasingly trivial part as we rise in the scale of being. Purely mechanical operations are, as Hegel notes, important to the development of memory. But the category of mechanism is a superficial one wholly inadequate for the thorough comprehension of the organic world. And many popular modes of thought are vitiated by the application of the category of mechanism where it is wholly unsuitable. Thus the statement that man consists of body and soul contemplates a purely mechanical relationship between the two. The same remark applies to the division of the soul into "faculties."

Sub-Section I

FORMAL MECHANISM

372. **Formal Mechanism** is simply the category of pure, unrelieved, bare mechanism. When the universe is regarded as a collection of objects external to each other, side by side, each of which is what it is independently of all the others, and which are connected by purely external relations which do not affect their inner natures in any way, then we have the category of formal mechanism. Take, for example, the remark quoted above, that man consists of body and soul. This

[1] Wal., *Log.*, § 195.

implies that the body and the soul are two independent objects which have, in their inner nature, no connection with each other, and are merely mechanically conjoined. It implies that this independent object, the soul, is what it is, and would be what it is, quite apart from the body. Thus whether it stands in relation to a body or not in no way affects its own inner and essential nature. In the one case as in the other, it is what it is quite on its own account. And the body too is regarded as likewise a quite independent object indifferent to its connection with a soul.

Thus the essential ideas of pure mechanism are (1) that the relations between objects are purely external, (2) that each object has its own nature entirely in itself, which nature remains untouched by its relations to other objects.

Sub-Section II

MECHANISM WITH AFFINITY

373. Formal mechanism breaks down and refutes itself because it is impossible to keep up the absolute separation which it involves between the inner nature of the object and its external relations. No matter what its external relations the object is supposed to remain *in itself* unaffected, unaltered, immobile, inactive. It is thus the prey of external forces. It passively allows itself to be completely determined from the outside and it itself takes no part in the moulding of its situation. But that it remains passive and unresisting under the pressure of other objects, that it allows itself to be completely determined by them, this very fact, after all, can only be due to its own internal nature. This, in fact, *is* its inner nature. Hence all these external objects could not thus determine it but for its own inner nature, and since to that extent the external determination is due to itself, such external determination is really self-determination. Thus the object forms a centre which determines itself by determining the other objects to determine it. Hence the object is not merely externally related to other objects, nor is its inner nature indifferent to them. It is connected with them by its inner

nature; it exhibits a bias towards them, an inner bond of unity, a sort of "affinity," or leaning towards them. Hence this category is called **mechanism with affinity.**

Sub-Section III

ABSOLUTE MECHANISM

374. Absolute mechanism is simply the full development of the last category. Not only is the particular object, which we happen to be considering, a centre having a core or inner nature connecting it with external objects, but these external objects are all of them similarly such centres. Each object in the universe may therefore be regarded in turn as such a centre and all the rest as its satellites. The whole universe is a system of such centres. This is **absolute mechanism.** It is still mechanism, because the relations between the objects are still purely external, but these external relations are seen to be not indifferent to the inner nature of the objects. Gravitation may be regarded as an empirical example of such reciprocal centrality.

SECTION II

CHEMISM

375. Although Hegel called the last category absolute mechanism, it is clear that the pure and undiluted conception of mechanism is found rather in the category of formal mechanism, and that the progress of the last section thereafter involves a gradual departure from the pure idea of mechanism. Mechanism means essentially an absolute externality of relationship between objects which are independent of, and totally indifferent to, each other. This independence and indifference undergoes a progressive breakdown in mechanism with affinity and absolute mechanism. There we see that the inner nature of objects, so far from being unaffected by their relations to other objects, is profoundly modified thereby. We have but to develop this new aspect of objects to its legitimate conclusion and we have the category of chemism.

The inner nature of the object is no longer indifferent to its outward relations. It exhibits a leaning or affinity towards other objects. In pure mechanism each object is what it is in its own self, and quite independently of all others. But now we see that this inner nature of the object only is what it is in and through the other object. Its being is the being of the other object. Consequently the being of the two objects becomes identical. They coalesce into one object, which Hegel calls the neutral product. In this the separate inner natures, *i.e.* the specific characters and qualities, of the two objects, are merged and disappear. This conception is **chemism.**

As being a unity into which its factors have disappeared the neutral product is undifferentiated, and "has sunk back to immediacy."[1] Apparently for this reason—though Hegel's argument here is not clear to me—the neutral product is capable of disintegration, and splits up again into the original two objects, which again coalesce, sunder, and so *ad infinitum.*

Examples of this category are, according to Hegel, not only the well-known processes of chemical combination of elements from which it takes its name, but also the "meteorological process," the sexual relation of plants and animals, the spiritual relations of love and friendship. It has to be confessed that the whole of this section on chemism is apt to appear fanciful.

SECTION III

TELEOLOGY

376. It was observed (368) that the evolution of objectivity would exhibit a return to subjectivity. The object, it must be remembered, is the antithesis in the triad of the Notion. Although therefore, it is itself the Notion, and although it is *thought*, it is yet at the same time the Notion, or thought, in the form of otherness, it is the other of thought, and is

[1] Wal., *Log.*, § 202.

therefore *not* the Notion, and *not* thought. This is expressed by saying that it is not subjectivity, but objectivity. Or we may say that the Notion, by passing into objectivity, becomes sunk, submerged and lost therein. And just as being disappears in nothing, so that nothing is *not* being, while at the same time it *is* being, so the object, as essentially the Notion, becomes the opposite of itself, is *not* the Notion, while at the same time it *is* the Notion. At the heart and core of it there is hidden, no doubt, the Notion. But as it immediately reveals itself to us the Notion is lost in it. This disappearance of the Notion manifested itself as the *externality* which is the essential characteristic of formal mechanism. For what the Notion means is *internality*, or to be more precise, the unity of opposites (310). It is that whose distinctions are at the same time no distinction, the distinguished factors being as absolutely identical as they are absolutely distinct. Now in formal mechanism we have the very opposite of this, viz. a world of objects which are absolutely distinct but have no identity or unity. Each object is what it is, solely in itself, and is completely indifferent to all others. Thus it is a crass plurality with no unity. This, evidently, is the very opposite of the Notion. Or as the Notion as it is in itself (*an sich*) is the same as subjectivity, we may also say that formal mechanism is marked by the complete absence of subjectivity.

In mechanism with affinity and in absolute mechanism the total indifference and externality of the objects to each other is modified. They have become dependent upon one another. Here, therefore, unity begins to reappear amid difference. It is the first sign of returning subjectivity—for subjectivity, as just observed, is the same as the Notion, *i.e.* unity in difference.

In chemism the different objects explicitly coalesce to unity. In other words we have unity in difference, *i.e.* the Notion, or subjectivity, clearly emerging from the object in which it has been buried. But the release of the Notion from bondage in the object is only completely seen in teleology.

In chemism the different objects merge their differences, and lose their specific characters in the neutral product. Hence what we have before us is the negation of the immediacy and externalism of objectivity. And since this immediacy is the essential character of objectivity (364) we have arrived at the negation of objectivity itself. And that which here negates the object is just the Notion, which has reappeared. And since the Notion now negates the object, it is therefore independent of the object, has entered on a free existence of its own, like a soul which has escaped from the body in which it was imprisoned.

The Notion, as thus free, stands in opposition to the object and the object to the Notion. The object is what is *not* the Notion, not what it *ought* to be. Consequently the Notion can only stand to the object in the relation of an ideal which it ought to aim at, an *end*. This is **teleology**.

377. Hegel proceeds to distinguish between what he calls " external and finite design " (teleology) on the one hand and " inner design " on the other. By external and finite teleology he means the view which regards means and end as quite distinct objects each of which is capable of existing by itself apart from the other. Thus money may be used as means to procure bread. The bread and the money are quite distinct objects. Bread could exist without money, and money without bread. Similarly the moon has sometimes been regarded as having been created to give light to man by night. But man and the moon are distinct and indifferent objects which do not exist in and through each other.

By " inner design," which is the *true* form of teleology, is meant, on the contrary, a relation of means and ends where each exists solely in and for the other, where the one could not exist without the other, and where, in the last analysis, the one is identical with the other. This is best understood by reference to Aristotle's conception of life, to which Hegel himself refers here. According to Aristotle, the life or soul is the " form " of the body. " Form " includes function, end, and organization. The living organism has not its end outside itself. It is its own end. As end it is the form, the organizing principle, or unity. As means it is the matter which is moulded into this form. Now the " form," which is the factor of unity, the universal, is precisely Hegel's Notion. For

Aristotle the form is the end, for Hegel the Notion is the end. The "matter," which is the factor of plurality, is Hegel's object, which, as we shall see, becomes the *means*.

The living organism thus provides the best example of inner design, or true teleology. It does not consist of two separate objects which stand to each other as means and end. The means and the end are but two aspects of one object, namely the organism itself. All the organs, or separate parts, work in subordination to the purpose of the whole. This purpose of the whole is simply the life of the whole itself. It is not anything outside the organism. The organism exists for itself. The parts are for the sake of the whole. The parts, therefore, are the means, the whole is the end. But the parts and the whole are one and the same thing, now viewed as a plurality, now as a unity. So that here the means and the end are the same thing. The organism, regarded as a plurality, is a means. Regarded as a unity it is an end. Means and end are not two objects, but two aspects of one object.

The same thing may be seen in the state. The state may be regarded as the end of the individuals. But at the same time the state *is* the individuals.

That this is the true view of teleology is not mere assertion on Hegel's part. This definition of teleology is what has been *deduced* from chemism. Chemism gave us the unity of a plurality of objects. The factor of unity is the end as here described; the factor of plurality is the means.

But this complete view of teleology does not emerge till we reach the last category of the section, viz. realized end.

Sub-Section I

THE SUBJECTIVE END

378. Teleology will only be seen in its complete truth when, as stated above, the end and the means are seen to be identical. At first, however, they are not so. The Notion has now freed itself from the object, and stands in opposition to the object (376). The Notion is the end, the object is the means.

THE OBJECT; OR, THE OBJECTIVE NOTION 275

Hence the means and the end confront each other in opposition. The object has not coalesced with the Notion, or in other words the end is still unrealized, unaccomplished. It stands before the object as a mere ideal which the object has not yet reached. And as the end has thus not yet *objectified* itself, but is merely an idea, is merely *subjective*, it is therefore only the **subjective end.**

Sub-Section II

THE MEANS

379. Because the object is still distinct from the Notion, or end, it is therefore *related* to the end. The relation which passes from the object to the end is the purposive action by which the end must be realized, or in other words by which the separation between the object and the end must be annulled. This is the **means.**

Sub-Section III

THE REALIZED END

380. When the separation between object and end is annulled, the end has ceased to be merely subjective, and has become objective, *i.e.* has realized and accomplished itself by coalescing with the object. This is the **realized end.**[1]

381. The process from subjective end to realized end is not, of course, a process in time. Hence the view of the universe at which we have arrived in this category does not mean that the end takes time to objectify itself. The view that it does so, the supposition that the purpose of the universe is not yet accomplished, is due to our using lower and inadequate categories. "The consummation of the infinite end," says Hegel, "consists merely in removing the illusion which makes it seem yet unaccomplished. The Good, the absolutely Good,

---

[1] I am not satisfied with this exposition which, it will be seen, gives no real deduction at all. I am free to confess that Hegel's meaning is here obscure to me, but I doubt whether it was clear to himself. Nor am I satisfied with any other explanation, *e.g.* Dr. McTaggart's, that I have seen.

is eternally accomplishing itself in the world : and the result is that it needs not wait upon us, but is already by implication, as well as in full actuality, accomplished. This is the illusion under which we live."[1] But Hegel does not mean that this is a mere subjective illusion. It is itself the work of the Idea, and is necessary for the fulfilment of the end, and is therefore real. For Hegel proceeds, " In the course of its process the Idea creates that illusion by setting an antithesis to confront it ; and its action consists in getting rid of the illusion which it has created. Only out of this error does the truth arise," (arise, that is, objectively not merely subjectively in our minds), . . . " Error, or other-being, when superseded, is still a necessary dynamic element in the truth : for truth can only be where it makes itself its own result."[2]

[1] Wal., *Log.*, § 212 Z. Compare with this " The Idea is not so impotent as merely to have a right or obligation to exist without actually existing " (Wal., *Log.*, § 6). There are numerous such passages in Hegel. The thought which they express, though possibly somewhat vague, is perhaps one of the most profound insights in his philosophy, involving the clue to the solution of the problem of evil. The existence of evil, error, imperfection, is no mere subjective illusion. These are real, yet they are compatible with the fact that the absolute Good is already, now and always, accomplished, and that the universe, therefore, is perfect. See also below, § 403.

[2] *Ibid.*

CHAPTER III

THE IDEA

382. The doctrine of the Notion has for its first phase subjectivity. The nature of reality, of the Absolute, of the world, is there defined as being essentially *subject*. This is the thesis. The second phase of the doctrine of the Notion is objectivity. Reality is now defined as the opposite of subject, namely, *object*. This is the antithesis. The synthesis will accordingly define reality as being, not one-sided and abstract subject, or one-sided and abstract object, but the unity of subject and object. This is the Idea. The Idea may be defined as the unity of subjectivity and objectivity.

383. The transition to this final phase of the Notion is found in the category of teleology. According to the perfected conception of teleology, as found in realized end, means and end have coalesced to unity. Now the means is the *plurality* of objects; the end is their *unity* (377). For example, in the organism the separate organs are the means of the life of the whole, while the end is simply the organized unity, the whole itself. The means and end are thus identical, the means being the organism viewed as plurality, the end the same thing viewed as unity. Now the factor of plurality, the means, is the side of objectivity. The factor of unity, the end, is the side of subjectivity. To be a mere unorganized plurality of objects, without unity, such as we found in formal mechanism, was recognized (376) as the essential character of objectivity when completely divested of subjectivity. The factor of unity which began to reappear amid plurality in mechanism with affinity, absolute mechanism, and chemism, was recog-

nized (376) as the element of subjectivity. Hence when means and end coalesce to unity in the category of realized end, what has really happened is that subject and object have coalesced, and have been recognized as identical. Hence we have arrived at the idea of the unity and identity of subject and object. And this is the **Idea.**

384. The general point of view of the doctrine of the Notion is that all things are thought. But thought has the two sides, or terms, subject and object. At first, therefore, one term is abstractly emphasized, and the universe is declared to be subject. Next the other term is, equally one-sidedly, put forward, and all things are seen to be the object of thought. Finally, this abstraction and separation is annulled, and the nature of the universe is declared to be thought which is neither simply subject, nor simply object, but subject and object in one. The precise meaning of this will only be fully realized when we reach the final phase of the Idea, the category of the Absolute Idea. Meanwhile the general point of view of the Idea has been indicated.

385. There is a misconception possible here which must be carefully avoided. The identity of subject and object, which we have now reached, is not an empty identity. The unity is not an undifferentiated unity. It is not a homogeneous unity in which all difference is annihilated. As always in Hegel, the differences are retained within the unity, which is, for that reason, a concrete unity. The distinction between subject and object is sublated in the Idea, that is, it is superseded and yet preserved. The two sides remain distinct within their identity.

The identity of subject and object is not a mere neutral point between the two. Hegel points out that the definition of the Absolute which we have now reached in the Idea is sometimes expressed by saying that it is " the *unity* of thought and being, of finite and infinite, etc." [1] (Thought and being are here used as equivalents for subject and object respectively; further, the infinite is identified with the subject, the finite with the object.) Such an expression is correct, but may

[1] Wal., *Log.*, § 215.

become entirely incorrect, if interpreted to mean that the Absolute is a neutral which is *neither* subject nor object, thought nor being, infinite nor finite. In that case, " the infinite would thus seem to be merely *neutralised* by the finite, the subjective by the objective, thought by being. But in the negative unity of the Idea, the infinite overlaps and includes the finite, thought overlaps being, subjectivity overlaps objectivity. The unity of the Idea is thought, infinity and subjectivity and is in consequence to be essentially distinguished from the Idea as *substance*."[1] This passage is of profound importance. Its meaning is sometimes also expressed by saying that thought overreaches the distinction between itself and its object.

Hegel is, in this passage, delivering a counterblast to the views of Schelling, according to whom all distinctions, including that between subject and object, totally disappear in the Absolute, which is conceived as a completely undifferentiated homogeneous unity, a total blank, which is neither subject nor object, but is, as regards this and all other distinctions, completely neutral, empty of all differentiation and therefore of all character.[2] The substance of Spinoza was also, like Schelling's Absolute, conceived as neither thought nor being. And this explains the reference to substance in the last clause of the passage quoted.

386. The true point of view here may be indicated by remembering that the object, as it came before us in the last chapter, is not merely the opposite of the subject. It is not simply not-thought. The object itself is thought (365). And therefore the distinction between thought and being, subject and object, is not an absolute one. Being is thought. Object is subject. The object is the subject in the form of otherness. Even when subject passes over into its opposite, the object, yet it still remains subject. Hence the subject overlaps the object, thought overlaps being. Or we may say that the Notion first posits itself as subject. The second phase is the

[1] *Ibid.*

[2] Cf. Hegel's famous remark that Schelling's Absolute is like " the night in which all cows are black." (*Phen.* i. 15.)

object, which, however, has not totally broken loose from the subject, but still remains the product of subjectivity, so that in it subjectivity is still present, though veiled and hidden. The third phase is the return of the subject out of its otherness into itself. It is the return to subjectivity. The Idea, therefore, is essentially subject, thought, and is no mere neutral emptiness. But it is not the abstract subjectivity which we met with in the first phase of the doctrine of the Notion, and which has the object over against it. It is subjectivity which has absorbed its opposite, the object, has taken it into itself and reconciled the distinction between them. It is thus *concrete* subjectivity. And it is in this sense that the saying of Hegel is to be understood that the Absolute is not substance, but subject.[1] Just as the true infinite was seen (200, 201) to mean, not the negative and abstract infinite which has the finite as something over against it, but rather the unity of the negative infinite and the finite, an infinite which has absorbed the finite into itself and so is no longer opposed by it, so here the subject has taken the object up into itself, and when it has done so, it is the Idea.

387. At this point, too, we are in a position to understand the true case as regards the identity of knowing and being which was provisionally explained at an earlier stage (99). Knowing is the subject; being is the object. It was there pointed out that knowing and being, that is, subject and object, are identical and yet distinct. The opposition and distinction is universally recognized and is generally assumed to be the whole truth. Hence we there insisted more emphatically on the identity. Now we see that the identity and the opposition are equally fundamental and important. If Hegel were asked for proof of his doctrine of the identity in difference of knowing and being, he would have pointed to the present chapter in the Logic. The full proof consists in the whole of the dialectic of the Logic from pure being to the present point.

Unreflective common sense supposes that subject and object, thought and being, are entirely separate. It sees their distinction but has no suspicion of their identity. This

[1] *Phen.* i. 15.

THE IDEA

is because common sense is governed by the categories of the understanding, and never rises to a point of view more advanced than that of essence. Science, which likewise uses as its instruments chiefly the categories of essence, also looks at the matter in the same way. So long as we view the universe only in the light of the categories of being and essence, the separation of knowing subject from known object must appear absolute. It is only philosophy which, by penetrating beyond essence to the Idea, and by viewing the universe under the categories of the Idea, is able to see that the object of thought is itself thought, is itself subject, because the whole universe is nothing but thought, and that thought overreaches the distinction between itself and its object and includes the latter within its own unity. Precisely how it does so has now been explained by the advance of the dialectic to this point. Nevertheless this point of view cannot be made completely intelligible till we reach the category of the Absolute Idea.

388. The Idea has three stages, (1) life, (2) cognition, (3) the Absolute Idea.

SECTION I

LIFE

389. In realised end we reached the identity of means and end. The means appeared as plurality, the end as the unity which binds the plurality into one. The means or plurality were regarded as existing solely in and through the end or unity. The unity exists solely in and through the plurality. Neither could exist by itself. Each is wholly what it is through the other. Moreover they are not two beings but only two aspects of one and the same being. The plurality and the unity, the parts and the whole, are identical and yet distinct.

This conception of a unity whose whole nature consists solely in its differentiation into the plurality which is subsumed under it, and a plurality whose whole nature consists solely in its forming that unity, constitutes the category which

Hegel calls **life.** In order to think the category of life all we have to do is to think such a plurality in unity as is defined in the last sentence. This is not, to be sure, all, or anything like all, that is usually imported by the word life. But whatever additional meaning we ordinarily attach to that word must be carefully discounted as an empirical content, which is not deduced by Hegel, and which is not included in the meaning of the category. This, like force and its expression, is one of those categories which Hegel *names* after an empirical fact, because it is most nearly and clearly exemplified in that fact, without, however, supposing that he has deduced all the empirical content of that fact as found in experience. And organic life is undoubtedly such a plurality in unity, or at least more nearly approximates to it than any other fact of experience. To be such a plurality in unity is, in fact, *the* essential character of living organisms. An organism is composed of parts, or organs, which are what they are only in relation to the other organs and in subservience to the life of the whole. The hand cut off, as Aristotle observed, ceases to be a hand. That is to say, the essential nature of this organ consists solely in its relation to the whole of which it is a part. Destroy its connection with that whole and you destroy its essential nature. The parts of the living body, then, are a plurality whose essential nature consists in being combined in the unity of the organism. Conversely the unity of the organism has no meaning or even existence except *in* the plurality of its organs.

390. The living body is not, however, a perfect example of Hegel's category. This category imports that the plurality and the unity could have no existence at all apart from each other. This of course is not the case in the organic body. The hand cut off ceases to be a hand, but it does not cease to exist. Nevertheless we have but to carry the idea of the unity in multiplicity, as actually found in organic life, to its logical conclusion, and we have Hegel's category of life. It will be well to remember that empirically life does not in itself include or imply consciousness. Plants are living organisms but do not possess consciousness. And here too we must

not think the idea of consciousness into Hegel's category of life. Cognition appears in the next section as a higher category than life. Hence as examples of Hegel's category of life we should take plants rather than animals.

391. Hegel calls the element of plurality the body, the element of unity the soul. These names, like the name life itself, are rather to be taken metaphorically than literally.

That life is the unity of subject and object will also be evident. For the living organism is both a subject and an object.

The sub-divisions of life, which are confused and unsatisfactory,[1] are (1) the living individual, (2) the life-process, (3) the kind.

Sub-Section I

THE LIVING INDIVIDUAL

392. The first phase of life is *immediate*, *i.e. this* life, the single organism, the **living individual.**[2]

Sub-Section II

THE LIFE-PROCESS

393. The body and soul, that is, the plurality and the unity, are, in the living individual, in immediate unity. Nevertheless they are distinct. Hence the relation of the soul to the body is a negative self-relation. For, inasmuch as the two are identical it is a relation of self to self. And inasmuch as they are distinct it is a relation of the self to what is other, what stands over against it and confronts it as not-itself. This latter or negative element in the self-relation gives us the idea of a something confronting the organism which is not itself, not-organism, and therefore an inorganic nature. This inorganic nature which confronts the organism is, however, only the organism itself, and has proceeded from itself. The

[1] For which reason I have summarised them in the briefest manner possible, omitting the very doubtful reference to sensibility, irritability, reproduction, etc.

[2] See § 239 above.

organism, therefore, strives to overcome the opposition and to reabsorb the inorganic into itself (a process which Hegel, surely fantastically, compares to assimilation). The struggle to do this, the consequent action and reaction between the two sides, the organic and the inorganic, is the **life-process.** It is impossible to expound these reasonings so as to show them in the character of a rigorous *a priori* deduction; for they hardly possess such a character and seem to depend almost wholly upon elements empirically gathered.

Sub-Section III

THE KIND

394. By means of the life-process the organism reabsorbs the inorganic into itself. In doing so, according to Hegel, it ceases to be the individual, and becomes the universal, the genus, the Kind. "The living individual," he says, "which in its first process comports itself as intrinsically subject and Notion, through its second assimilates its external objectivity and thus puts the character of reality into itself. It is now, therefore, implicitly a **Kind,** with essential universality of nature."[1] It is difficult to extract much meaning from this. But apparently Hegel's idea is that so long as the organism has the inorganic over against it, it is merely one of two, *this* as against *that*, and is in that way *particular*. By absorbing its other into itself it ceases to be one of two, ceases to be particular, and is now, therefore, *universal*. And the organism, regarded in its universality, is the Kind. It is difficult to take such a deduction seriously.

SECTION II

COGNITION

395. The organism, having merged the inorganic into itself, is now a self-contained totality, having nothing outside it or

[1] Wal., *Log.*, § 220.

over against it. It is, therefore, related, not to its other, but only to itself, for there is nothing other than itself to which it could be related. Nevertheless, just because it is this self-relation, it therefore distinguishes itself from itself, (208) and puts itself forth again as an element confronting itself. This element, which has proceeded from itself and now confronts it, is the external world. Thus we have two results. (1) The living individual is confronted with an external world; (2) the external world is, nonetheless, not only thus outside it, but also *within* it. For although the external world is now its other, it has proceeded from the organism. What is put forth by the organism is thus only the organism itself and remains therefore *within* the organism. These two results follow respectively from the two factors of the self-relation which we have seen the organism to be. These two factors are the factors of identity and diversity. The organism is related to itself. That to which it is related, as being identical with itself, is not outside it, but in it. But again, that to which it is related, as being distinguished from it, is other than it, and is, in that way, external to it.

That the organism is confronted by an external world, which external world, however, appears within the organism as internal to it,—this is the definition of **cognition.** That I cognize the world means, firstly, that there is a world external to me, but secondly that this world also appears, in the form of presentation, *within* my consciousness, within me.

396. That cognition rightly appears as a category of the Notion is evident from the fact that the general point of view of the Notion is that the universe is thought, and cognition is a form of thought. That it rightly appears as a category of the third phase of the Notion, namely the Idea, is evident from the fact that cognition implies the unity of subject and object. That these two sides in cognition are distinct goes without saying. But it is evident that they also form a unity, since that subject and object come together is the very meaning of consciousness. This is the identity in difference of being and knowing.

397. In cognition, then, the external world, or object,

becomes internal to the subject. Now this may happen in two ways. On the one hand the subject may be regarded as passive, and as receiving the external world into itself. This is cognition proper. It is the object which here modifies consciousness, not consciousness which modifies the object. The aim of knowledge (cognition proper) is to know the world as it is. It does not seek to alter the world, but passively accepts it. Or, on the other hand, the subject may be regarded as *active* and as seeking to mould the world in order to bring it into conformity with the subject. This is volition, the principle of action, as distinguished from knowledge. Action does not, like knowledge, passively accept the world. It seeks to alter it to bring it into unison with its own ends and purposes. Cognition in general, as here defined by Hegel, means that the discrepancy and division between the subject and the world are abolished so that the two are at one. The discrepancy may be abolished either by the subject conforming itself to the world, which is the case in *knowledge*, or by the subject conforming the world to it, which is the case in *action* by the *will*.

Thus cognition has the two sub-divisions (1) cognition proper, (2) volition. The triad is incomplete. There is no third. Hegel here abandons the triadic method. Nor is any explanation of his having done so forthcoming.

398. The word cognition, as ordinarily employed, does not include volition, to which, in fact, it is usually opposed. Hegel, however, uses the word to include both cognition proper, *i.e.* what is ordinarily called cognition, and will. Dr. McTaggart suggests that the word consciousness would have been more suitable than cognition.[1]

Sub-Section I

COGNITION PROPER—THE TRUE

399. **Cognition proper** has for its object the **Idea of the True.** It is also called the Theoretical Idea.

Since in cognition proper the subject is regarded as passively

---

[1] *Com.* § 278.

receiving the object into itself, the object is consequently regarded as not being the product of the subject, but as a *datum*, which exists on its own account, is *given* from the outside, and is received into the forms of subjectivity. This, for example, is the point of view of Kant. The fact that Kant regarded the forms of subjectivity, *i.e.* the categories, as spontaneous *activities* of the subject, does not alter the truth of this. The point is that the *external world* is taken as already existing, as given, as presented from the outside to the subject which, therefore, passively receives it.

400. This cognition is essentially *finite* cognition and is capable of apprehending only finite truth. Its finitude consists in the fact that it is not itself all reality but, on the contrary, has the world as a given something externally confronting and limiting it. Hence this kind of cognition sticks fast at the point of view of the separation and division of subject and object, and fails to comprehend their identity. It is in general the kind of cognition which emphasizes diversity and distinctions and ignores identity. Hence it is the cognition of *understanding*.[1] If it should be asked why consciousness adopts this form the answer is found here. The cognition of understanding is here *deduced*. It exhibits itself, therefore, at this stage in the dialectic, as a *necessary* stage in the self-evolution of thought.

401. The forms of subjectivity into which, in this finite cognition, the external object is received, are universals, (*e.g.* Kant's categories). They are, moreover, empty and abstract universals. For the concrete universal is the universal which produces the particular and singular out of itself, and thus generates its own filling. But the universal of finite cognition receives its filling from the outside, in the shape of an already existing *datum*, and is thus in itself empty and abstract.

[1] The beginner may possibly be puzzled by wondering why, if this cognition is the finite cognition of the understanding, it appears here in the doctrine of the Notion, which is the sphere of reason and the infinite, instead of in essence, which is the sphere of understanding and the finite. The answer is that the category of cognition gives us the point of view that the universe is essentially cognitive thought. The point of view of essence, on the contrary, was that the universe consists of "things," "forces," "substances," etc. Because the present category regards the universe as *thought*, it necessarily belongs to the doctrine of the Notion.

Hence the first method of thought to which this finite cognition gives rise is what Hegel calls the *analytic* method. Its aim is to subsume the individual object under its appropriate abstract universal. It thus begins with the individual object and rises to the universal. This is the method of induction. Empiricists, like Locke, regarded all thought as thus analytic.

Finite cognition may, however, reverse the process and begin with the universal in the form of a definition. It then descends through the particular, as a middle term, to the individual. This, which Hegel calls the *synthetic* method, is the method of geometry. Geometry begins with universals, *i.e.* definitions and axioms, and descends through demonstration to the individual case, or to the less general truth which it desires to prove. Spinoza attempted to introduce the synthetic method into philosophy.

Neither the analytic nor the synthetic method, however, is suitable to philosophy. For both are forms of finite cognition which presuppose the object as something given, and are thus devoid of necessity, since what has a presupposition lacks necessity. The true philosophical method is the dialectic method, which is also called the absolute method. This has no presupposition since its beginning, the category of being, is not a *mere* beginning, but is founded on its end, the final category, the Absolute Idea. The dialectic method is both analytic and synthetic in every step of its progress. It is itself the synthesis of both methods. Because it advances from the abstract universal, through further and further specification, to the concrete *singular*, it is synthetic. And because it begins with immediacy, and advances through mediation to the concrete *universal*, which contains the previous immediacy under it and within it, it is analytic.

Sub-Section II

VOLITION—THE GOOD

402. Cognition proper thus gives rise, on the one hand, to demonstration by the synthetic method. Now such demon-

stration has the character of *necessity*. The conclusion in a demonstration follows necessarily from what preceded it. In fact, demonstration consists in nothing else than showing the necessity of the conclusion. But with the emergence of the element of necessity we have passed beyond the sphere of cognition proper. The essential character of that cognition was that it passively accepted the world as given from the outside. But necessity cannot be given from the outside. What is simply given exists as a mere fact, as a contingency, for which no reason is given and in which, therefore, no necessity can be seen. Of what is *given* we say " it is," but we can never say " it *must* be." This necessity, therefore, is not externally presented to the subject, but is, on the contrary, the spontaneous activity of the subject.[1] Hence we have left behind the conception of the passive subject accepting the world, and have advanced to the conception of the active subject moulding the world into conformity with itself. But the subject, as active, as moulding and altering the world to suit itself—this is will, **volition.** We have passed from the Theoretical Idea to the Practical Idea. And as cognition proper has the true for its object, so the will aims at **the Good.**

403. Volition, like cognition proper, is finite, and for the same reason. Although it is active and seeks to mould the world, it still regards the world as given from the outside, as an already existing material upon which it has to exercise its powers. The world is still an alien being which confronts it and limits it. It is because of this finitude of the will, because of the absolute separation which it still holds to exist between subject and object, between means and end, between what is and what ought to be, that it still regards the good as unexecuted and as awaiting accomplishment in the world. What is, is the factor of being, the object. What ought to be, is the factor of the Notion, the subject (376). Finite cognition, including will, has not yet reached the point of view of the absolute identity of subject and object which is completely

---

[1] The line of thought here is identical with that of Kant, who argued that the elements of universality and necessity in consciousness cannot arise, as Hume showed, empirically in experience, and must, therefore, be due to the activity of the subject.

attained only in the Absolute Idea. Hence what is and what ought to be appear as quite different things, and the action of the will takes the form of an infinite series of endeavours towards the good, which, however, is never accomplished. The truth, however, as will be seen in the category of the Absolute Idea, is that the object, or what is, and the subject, or what ought to be, are at once identical and distinct. In other words the good is just as much executed as not executed, and " the final purpose of the world is accomplished no less than ever accomplishing itself." [1] Unreflective consciousness does not penetrate beyond the rind of the world to its inner essence. It applies inferior categories. But the philosophic mind rises to the point of view of the category of the Absolute Idea. It then sees that all things *are* the Absolute Idea, that what the world veritably *is*, is nothing but the Absolute Idea. As such there is no distinction in the world, thus seen in its truth, between the means and the end, the object and the subject, what is and what ought to be. The world in its essence *is* nothing but the good, and therefore the good is already and eternally accomplished. It is only the finite intellect, the understanding, which puts a gulf between subject and object, " is " and " ought," and so regards the good as a far off and impotent ideal in the future or in some other world.

SECTION III

THE ABSOLUTE IDEA

404. The will is finite. It is still opposed by the object which it regards as something alien to it, something which is not itself, confronting it. Hence there lies in the will the contradiction noted above. It sets before itself a purpose which must be carried out. This purpose is the good. And will looks upon the good as, on the one hand, the sole reality and essence of the world; and the object, in so far as it diverges from the good, is regarded as mere semblance and

[1] Wal., *Log.*, § 234 Z. Cf. *supra* § 381 and footnote.

unreality; while on the other hand, will regards the good as an unreality, since it lies in the future, since it is not executed, since it is not yet in objective existence. This contradiction manifests itself in the infinite progress of the endless labours of the universe to reach the good, which is yet never attained.

This contradiction is the defect in the category of volition which forces it onwards to the Absolute Idea. The root of the contradiction lies in the fact that in volition subject and object still confront each other as unreconciled, that the object is still an alien material presented to the will from the outside. Therefore the contradiction can only be removed by a category in which the object is no longer alien from the subject which wills but is identical with the subject itself.

The struggle of thought to attain this reconciliation expresses itself as *action*. The will aims at the good. But, because the good is unexecuted in the external world, it is, therefore, not objective, but a mere subjective ideal. The will accordingly *acts*. It seeks to force objectivity to coincide with this its subjectivity. It strives to make subjectivity and objectivity identical, and thus to overcome its own finitude, and to render the object no longer alien to itself. In doing so will recognizes its own inadequacy.

In this way the category of will returns to the category of cognition proper. It recognizes that the truth cannot be merely this contemplation of a good which is only subjective. The will itself requires that the good shall be objective, shall actually exist in the world. And when it so exists as an actual object, the attitude of the subject towards it will again be the attitude, not of will, but of cognition proper. For the subject will then no longer strive for a good which is not (volition), but will actually cognize a good which *is*, a something which is *present* (cognition proper). Hence volition necessarily involves cognition proper, and can only overcome its own contradictions by combining itself with cognition proper. Hence the new category will be the unity of volition and cognition proper.

In this new category, therefore, the good is regarded as eternally executed. What *ought* to be, also *is*. The two sides are identical. What *is*, however, is the side of the object. What *ought* to be, is the side of the Notion, the subject. Hence the subject and the object are now identical. The thought involved here is in its essence the same as the thought (377) that in the realized end we have the unity of means, which is the object, with end, which is subject. The end and the good are of course cognate conceptions, the category of the good being merely a further specification and definition of the end. End and good are both the side of the Notion, or the subject. And the objectified good, therefore, means the identity of the subject with the object.

This absolute identity in difference of subject and object is the **Absolute Idea.** What it immediately means is that the subject, instead of having the object as something alien and outside it, now recognizes that the object is only itself. The object is the subject. The subject has for its object only itself. Philosophy, in attaining to this category, sees that the whole universe of planets, stars, men, and things, is not something " given " to mind from an external source but is only mind itself. Mind, or the subject, thus duplicates itself, puts itself forth as its own object in the form of an external world, and in contemplating that world contemplates itself. It is mind which knows itself to be all reality. It is thus the thought of thought, thought which thinks, not an alien object, but only itself. It is the νόησις νοήσεως of Aristotle. The same thing is sometimes expressed by saying that the Absolute Idea is the category of *self-consciousness*, or *personality*, that is, the consciousness, or thought, which has itself for its object.

405. The Absolute Idea is the absolute truth. It is the final, complete, and adequate definition of the Absolute, or God, and of the universe. God is the thought of thought, the absolute subject-object. The world, seen in its truth, is nothing but the Absolute Idea. When we look upon the world as a system of " matter," governed by " forces," controlled by " causes," and the like, we are seeing it in its untruth, in the light of inadequate and onesided categories. The full truth, here attained is, firstly, that the world is thought (the doctrine

of the Notion in general) and finally that it is the thought of thought (Absolute Idea) or personality.

406. The Absolute Idea is the absolute *infinite*. For it has overcome all opposition. It is subjectivity which has merged its opposite, objectivity, into itself, and, being now confronted by no new rival, is coextensive with all reality. For the same reason, while the cognition which gave rise to the analytic and synthetic methods, was finite cognition, philosophical thought, which has penetrated to the Absolute Idea, is infinite cognition. Common cognition has an external object, a house, a tree, a star, which determines it. Philosophical cognition knows that its object, be it house, tree, or star, is only itself, and that it is therefore solely self-determined and therefore infinite.[1] The common saying that the mind of man is finite is false, for philosophical cognition is infinite thought which is therefore capable of apprehending the infinite. And it is itself the infinite which it apprehends.

407. Hegel says also that the *content* of the Absolute Idea is simply the system of Logic which is now closing. This is readily intelligible. As we have so often seen, every category contains explicitly within itself all previous categories merged in its unity. The Absolute Idea as the final and absolute reconciliation of all differences has within it all previous categories, the whole Logic. The Absolute Idea, however, is both subject and object. As subject it is the *form* of the Logic, for the form of thought is the side of subjectivity (366 *f.*). But the form of the Logic is simply the dialectic method. Hence the Absolute Idea, as subject, is the dialectic method. As object, as content, it is the categories of the Logic. But this form and this content, subject and object, are not, as in finite cognition, external to one another.

---

[1] Failure to remember this is responsible for Dr. McTaggart's argument that philosophical knowledge is not an empirical example of the Absolute Idea. For " Knowledge," he says (*Com.* § 295), " exemplifies the Idea of the True—the category in which the universe is determinant of the harmony." This identifies knowledge with cognition proper, which, as determined by an alien object, cannot exemplify the Absolute Idea. But knowledge cannot be thus limited. Philosophical cognition is knowledge, and is infinite, and knows that its object is itself. Hence it truly exemplifies the Absolute Idea. It is an urgent necessity to cut away the roots of Dr. McTaggart's mystical distortion of the Hegelian Absolute as Love.

Hence the dialectic method is not to be regarded as an alien form externally imposed upon an indifferent material, as the method of formal logic is imposed upon its objects, but as out and out identical with its content.

408. With the category of the Absolute Idea the Logic closes. For the absolute Idea exhibits no defect which requires it to pass, within the sphere of pure thought, into a higher category. It is not a one-sided abstraction. It is the concrete whole. It is the final truth. We pass therefore from the sphere of the pure Idea, Logic, to the sphere of Nature.

PART III

THE PHILOSOPHY OF NATURE

PHILOSOPHY OF NATURE

409. There has never been any difficulty in understanding what it is that Hegel is attempting to do in the Logic. The Logic is concerned with pure thoughts or categories, and its object is to deduce these pure thoughts from each other. But what Hegel is attempting to do in the philosophy of nature and in the philosophy of spirit has not always been so clearly understood. There is no doubt that in passing from the Logic to nature and spirit, we do, in some sense or other, leave behind the sphere of mere *thoughts* and come to the consideration of concrete *things*. The philosophy of nature considers no mere abstractions such as being, cause, or substance, but actually existent things, matter, plants, animals. The philosophy of spirit, too, is concerned with actual things which exist in the world, the actual minds of men, human institutions, the products of art, religion, and philosophy. The transition from Logic to nature is, therefore, a critical point in the system. It is the point at which the system passes from thoughts to things. And since this transition has all the appearance of a logical deduction, similar in all respects to the deductions within the Logic itself, it is sometimes said that we have here an impossible leap from thoughts to things. Nothing, it is urged, can be deduced from a thought except another thought. To suppose that one can deduce a solid thing, a table or a chair, from a system of abstract thoughts, is equivalent to supposing that by mere thought we can *create* these solid things out of nothing. It may be admitted, for the sake of argument, that all the deductions of category from category, which the Logic contains, are valid. So long as thought keeps within its own sphere, so long as it merely

attempts to deduce thought from thought, its procedure may be legitimate. But to suppose that any process of logic can deduce an existent thing from a mere thought is an insane delusion. And it is supposed that Hegel made this attempt in the transition from Logic to nature.

410. Without denying that there may be difficulties in this transition, it must be said that any such account of the matter as that just given is wholly illusory. This transition is not a leap from thoughts to things in the sense supposed by these objectors. It is, like every other deduction, a transition from one thought to another. The philosophies of nature and spirit are still concerned, not with things in their crass particularity, but solely with thoughts. If Hegel appears to deduce nature from the Idea, what he actually deduces is not nature itself, in the absurd sense supposed, but the *thought* of nature. If, within the philosophy of nature he seems to deduce animals from plants, what he is really doing is to deduce the thought " animal " from the thought " plant." If, within the philosophy of spirit, he seems to deduce civil society from the family, and the state from civil society, what he is actually deducing is the *thoughts* of these things. Everywhere, throughout the entire system, he is concerned solely with thoughts, and there is nowhere any attempt to do anything except deduce one thought from another.

411. All this is perfectly clear from the explicit statements of Hegel himself. The thoughts which he deduces in the second and third parts of his system are called by him " notions." And his procedure is to deduce one notion from another, the notion of civil society from the notion of the family, the notion of the state from the notion of civil society, and so on. The dialectic method is as applicable here as elsewhere. To deduce civil society from the family means to show that the notion, thought, or idea, of the latter implicitly contains and involves the notion, thought, or idea of the former; just as the deduction of nothing from being consisted in demonstrating that the thought being contains the thought nothing. Hegel explicitly and repeatedly tells us that the philosophies of nature and spirit deduce only *universals*; they do not

deduce this particular pen or that particular grain of sand. Now universals are concepts or thoughts. And it is surely obvious that to deduce " plant," " animal," "family," " state," and the like, is to deduce nothing but concepts, *i.e.* thoughts, since all these terms apply, not to one thing, but to whole classes of things. Here, just as in the Logic, we are concerned solely with concepts and the deduction of concepts from one another. There is nothing absurd or illegitimate in such a procedure.

412. To this the objection may be taken that, if this is a true interpretation of Hegel's system, then that system, since it never leaves the sphere of abstractions, has, or may have, no application to things at all. It is a mere system of empty thoughts, constructed in the air. Whatever Hegel's procedure may be, actual things, it may be said, exist; there *is* this solid world, this table, that chair, my hat, your boots. And if philosophy is to explain the universe it is these actual things it has to explain, not mere abstractions and universals. And since to explain a thing means to show that it flows from a reason, is the logical consequent of a logical antecedent, since in fact explanation means deduction, philosophy must, on Hegel's own principle, deduce actual things, not mere thoughts. If it does not do so it fails to show why anything should exist at all. Granted that all these notions follow logically from one another, what reason is there why they should not remain mere notions, mere thoughts? How is it that corresponding things actually exist?

413. The answer to this is simply that things *are* thoughts and nothing but thoughts (95, 100, 101), and that to deduce the thoughts is therefore the same as to deduce the things. This actual piece of paper is nothing but the universals whiteness, squareness, etc. There is nothing in the paper but universals. And to suppose that there is anything other than universals is to believe in the existence of an unknowable entity completely outside the range of thought. To deduce all universals would therefore be the same as deducing all actual things in the universe.

414. Now I shall argue shortly that Hegel himself did not

fully grasp this, but that, in spite of his frequent reiteration of the doctrine that thought is all reality, he nevertheless allowed himself to be seduced by a lingering trace of the idea which he had himself explicitly repudiated, that there is some mysterious entity in or behind things in addition to the universals which compose all we know of them. And I shall attempt to show that it is this inconsistency which lies at the root of the whole famous difficulty about the transition from Logic to nature, as well as of the difficulty of explaining the place of " contingency " in his philosophy. In the meanwhile it will be well to turn to certain other aspects of the same problem.

415. We may first clear up an apparent inconsistency in what has already been said. We began by observing that all deduction is from thoughts to thoughts, that the attempt to deduce actual things from thought would be illegitimate, and that Hegel made no such attempt. But we went on to say that, since things are nothing but thoughts, the deduction of thoughts is the same as the deduction of things, and therefore that Hegel does deduce, and so explain, the actual world. Do not these two positions contradict each other? The answer is that what is illegitimate—and indeed quite absurd—is to suppose that our subjective deductions and thoughts can produce actual facts. It would be ludicrous for Hegel to suppose that he, Hegel, could, by writing down deductions, create a world. In this sense he does *not* deduce things. But the Hegelian deduction is no mere subjective process. It is the discovery of an objective reality. And the logical transition from the Idea to nature means that nature exists because there is the Idea, because the Idea is objective and real,—not because Hegel happens to think the Idea. It is not Hegel who deduces nature from the Idea. It is the Idea itself, the objective Idea, not the Idea in Hegel's brain, which produces nature out of itself.

416. The Logic deals with thoughts. The philosophy of nature, too, as we now see, deals with thoughts. But, in that case, it may be asked, what is the difference between the Logic and the philosophy of nature? Is not the latter merely

a continuation of the former? The Logic ends with the Absolute Idea, which is said to be the highest category. But if our interpretation is adopted, will it not follow that the lowest notion with which nature begins is simply a higher and further category than the Absolute Idea? And will this not destroy the whole fabric of the Hegelian system? I answer that in one sense it is true that the philosophy of nature is merely a continuation of the Logic. It is certainly not cut off from it by any such absolute gulf as has been supposed to be implied in the impossible leap from thoughts to things. It is an integral part of the same system. But it is a new sphere of the system which is clearly distinguished from the sphere which preceded it, the Logic; just as, within the Logic, the doctrine of essence is a continuation of the doctrine of being, but is also clearly distinguished from it. The categories of being are thoughts which all have this in common, that they are characterized by immediacy. The categories of essence are also thoughts. But they are a different kind of thoughts. For they are all characterized by the opposite of immediacy, namely mediation. Now the entire Logic deals with thoughts. And the entire philosophy of nature deals with thoughts. And because both deal with thoughts it is legitimate to regard one as a continuation of the other. But they are nevertheless fundamentally different and opposed. The difference consists in this, that the Logic deals with *categories*, a special kind of universals whose peculiarity is that they apply to everything, are universal in their scope. The philosophy of nature deals with other universals, universals which are not categories, universals which apply only to some things and not to all. Everything in the universe has being, has qualities, is a cause, or an effect. Being, quality, cause, effect, are therefore categories, and fall within the sphere of Logic. But only *some* things are plants, only *some* are animals, only some are inorganic matter. "Plant," "animal," "inorganic matter," are therefore universals of a kind wholly different from categories, and they therefore fall outside the sphere of the Logic.

417. The distinction between the categories and the uni-

versals of nature may also be expressed by saying that the categories are pure non-sensuous universals while the universals of nature are sensuous universals. The factor of sense simply means that what is sensuous has not merely universality but particularity also. It is *this* as opposed to *that*. A sensuous universal is therefore the same as a universal which applies to *these* and not to *those*, to some things (moment of particularity) and not to all. We may therefore characterize the transition from Logic to nature in the following manner. The Logic gives us the first reason of the world, consisting of pure universals. We have now arrived at the stage at which, our account of the first reason of the world being complete, we proceed to its logical consequence, the world itself. The actual transition is from the general sphere of pure universals to the general sphere of sensuous universals.[1]

418. We have to distinguish carefully between the two questions, (1) whether the attempt to deduce nature from the Idea is legitimate, and (2) whether Hegel's attempt succeeds, *i.e.* whether the actual deduction given by him is valid. To the first of these questions we answer that the attempt is not only legitimate but absolutely necessary. It is legitimate because it is not, in the absurd sense usually supposed, a transition from thoughts to things, but only a transition from one kind of thought to another. And no one has ever doubted that it is legitimate to deduce thoughts from thoughts. The deduction is also necessary because it is the only possible way of explaining the universe. It is necessitated by the entire body of considerations which have been adduced in the third chapter of the first part of this work. What we have there seen is that to explain means nothing else than to deduce. All idealism is based upon the idea that the first principle of explanation of the universe is a *logical* principle, that it is the universal, and that the universal is the reason, or logical antecedent, of which the world is the consequent. This can mean nothing else than that the world is to be deduced from the Idea. We saw, in the first chapter of this book, that the relation between the Absolute and the world is a logical and

[1] On this question see also the last part of § 95.

not a time-relation. The Greeks, especially Aristotle, saw this. The Aristotelian principle of form is prior to the world, the end is prior to the beginning, not in time, but in logic. What the Greeks did not yet realize was that this thought, when fully developed, can mean nothing except that the Absolute is related to the world as the premises of a syllogism to its conclusion, and that therefore the world must be deduced from the Absolute. It was precisely the failure to realize this which resulted in the hopeless dualism of the systems of Plato and Aristotle. The very critics who now castigate Hegel for attempting to deduce nature from the Idea are also those who complain that Plato and Aristotle were guilty of an unreconciled dualism between matter and thought. Monism means that there is only one absolute reality and that all else is produced by this reality. For Plato and Aristotle, and for idealists in general, the absolute reality is thought. Therefore they must show that matter is produced by thought. Plato and Aristotle did not show this. Therefore they left matter as an ultimate underived principle, an independent being, an absolute reality, alongside of thought,—dualism. For this they are blamed. But when Hegel attempts to reconcile this dualism in the only possible way, namely, by deducing matter from thought, he is considered to be doing something ludicrous. But the critics cannot have it both ways. Unless they are to rest in an unreconciled dualism, they must admit either that thought produces matter or that matter produces thought. In the latter case they are materialists. In the former case, they have admitted the position of Hegel. If we admit the general position of idealism, that thought is the Absolute, then we must show that thought produces matter. If not, we are landed in the dualism of Plato and Aristotle. And there are only two ways in which it is possible to conceive that thought produces matter. Either thought, the Absolute, is prior to matter in time, and produces it as a cause produces its effect; or the Absolute is logically prior and produces matter as its logical consequent. The former alternative is, as these critics would admit, out of the question. The latter means that the world must be deduced from the Idea. If we are to adopt neither of these alternatives, if the Absolute produces the world neither as its effect in time, nor as its conclusion in logic, these critics may fairly be asked in what other manner they propose that we should conceive the relation of the Absolute to the world.

419. Coming now to the actual transition which Hegel makes from the Idea to nature, we find that, in the final sections of the larger Logic, he says: "Since the Idea posits itself as the absolute unity of the pure Notion and its reality, and consequently assumes the form of immediate being, it is, as the totality of this form, nature."[1] Hegel proceeds to make a number of remarks upon this deduction, but this is all he gives us for the deduction itself. The corresponding passage in the *Encyclopaedia* tells us nothing further. This deduction appears to mean that since all mediation is absolutely merged in the Idea, the Idea is therefore an absolute immediacy. But what is absolutely immediate is *there*, is present, is simply *given*. And the character of being immediately given, presented to us from the outside, is the essential characteristic of the external world, *i.e.* of nature. To be immediate is the same as to be *given*. For what is given is a mere *fact*, a fact which simply *is so*, without any reason being given for it. It is that which is not mediated by a reason. It is the immediate. Hence the Idea as immediate is something simply externally presented as an immediate fact. And this is precisely the character of the external world of nature.

420. This deduction is invalid, or at least insufficient. We have on innumerable occasions already seen mediation collapse to immediacy. Each or any of these immediacies might, for all that we can see to the contrary, have been taken as a transition to nature, if, as Hegel would have us believe, the mere fact of immediacy is sufficient to afford a transition to nature. All that can be said by the most hopeful Hegelian is that possibly Hegel's transition affords a clue to the truth

---

[1] The translation which I have used of this passage, and the passages subsequently quoted, is that given by W. T. Harris on pp. 398-9 of his *Hegel's Logic* (Chicago, 1895).

which some subsequent thinker may follow up to find a valid deduction.[1]

421. But after this deduction Hegel proceeds to comment upon it. " This," he says, " is not a becoming or a transition as above, when we took the step from the totality of the subjective Notion to objectivity, or when we passed over from subjective end to life ... It (the Idea) is not subject to any more transitions; its simplicity is perfectly transparent and has the form of the abiding Notion." But if the transition to nature is not a transition similar to previous logical deductions, what is it? Hegel replies that it " means that the Idea emits itself with freedom in the form of nature," and he goes on to speak of the " resolve of the pure Idea to determine itself as external Idea," *i.e.* as nature. And in the *Encyclopaedia* he says: " Enjoying however an absolute liberty, the Idea does not merely pass over into life, or as finite cognition allow life to show in it: in its own absolute truth it resolves to let the moment of its particularity, or of the first characterization and other-being, the immediate Idea, as its reflected image, go forth freely as nature." [2] It is to these phrases that Schelling and others have objected that they are a mere tissue of metaphors which cover up an absolute break in the system. The Idea in its absolute " freedom," in its " liberty," " resolves " (makes up its mind?) to let the moment of its particularity go forth freely, as its " reflected image," as nature. These are clearly poetic metaphors and no more. But the critics of Hegel have almost invariably failed to note the important fact that these poetic phrases are not part of the deduction itself, but only appear as a commentary upon it. The deduction itself is contained in the single sentence quoted in § 419, and is of purely logical character.

422. It is clear that Hegel here asserts that the transition to nature is not of the same kind as the transitions within

[1] See § 239 above. No doubt the immediacy of the Absolute Idea differs from the immediacy of previous categories in that, according to Hegel, the Absolute Idea for the first time achieves absolute stability, and does not give rise to any contradiction which necessitates the passage to a higher category. But this does not seem to me to render the deduction any more valid.

[2] Wal., *Log.*, § 244.

the Logic. It does not necessarily follow from this that he meant to deny that it is a logical deduction of any kind. Within the limits of the Logic itself Hegel distinguishes various kinds of logical transition. In the sphere of being, he says, transition consists in a passing over of one term into another. In the sphere of essence it is not a passing over but a reflection of one term on another. In the sphere of the Notion he says " the onward movement of the Notion is no longer either a transition into, or a reflection on, something else, but *development*. For in the Notion the elements distinguished are without more ado at the same time declared to be identical with one another and with the whole."[1] Thus we see that as each of the three great divisions of the Logic makes its appearance, Hegel informs us that the deductions by which it is characterized differ in character from those in the preceding division. Hence the mere fact that he now tells us that the transition to nature is not like the transitions in the Logic does not of itself prove that the passage into nature is not a logical deduction at all. The transitions in the spheres of being, essence, and the Notion, are said to be different from each other, yet they are all logical deductions. Possibly Hegel means that the transition from the Idea to nature is a fourth kind of logical deduction. But if so, it must be added that it is quite impossible for us to make out what kind of logical deduction is meant. The language used to describe it is mere poetry and may not unfairly be said to mean nothing in particular.

423. Two things, at any rate, are certain. Firstly, whatever Hegel intended to do, he *ought* to have deduced nature from the Idea. Such a deduction is essential to the system, is essential to any explanation of the world, as has already been shown. Secondly, whatever Hegel may have said or meant in a contrary sense, the passage in which he actually makes the transition, *is* of the nature of a logical deduction. The actual transition is not made in the poetic passages about the Idea resolving in its freedom to let its moment of particularity go forth as nature. These passages are merely descriptions

[1] Wal., *Log.*, § 161.

of the transition which has *already* been made in the single sentence previously quoted, but which we will quote again: " Since the Idea posits itself as the absolute unity of the pure Notion and its reality, and consequently assumes the form of immediate being, it is, as the totality of this form, nature." This means that the thought of the Idea contains and involves the thought of immediacy; that the thought of immediacy is the same as the thought of givenness, externality; and that this is the thought of nature. To show that one thought contains and involves another thought is to deduce the second from the first. This *is* a logical deduction, whatever Hegel meant it to be. It is a deduction of a special type which first made its appearance at the category of specific quantum, which we there specially commented upon (239), and of which we have since seen numerous examples. The fact that it is an invalid or insufficient deduction does not, of course, affect the point in question.[1]

424. Possibly, as we have seen, Hegel's statement that this is not a transition like those in the Logic merely means that it is a logical deduction of a new kind. But if it be considered that he did really mean to deny that it is a logical deduction at all, then we have to conclude that Hegel was wrong, and in that case it only remains for us to explain the error. The error, if it existed at all, is, in my opinion, due to the fact that Hegel had never completely rid himself of the phantom of the thing-in-itself; and this notwithstanding his repeated attacks upon the thing-in-itself. If a material object, say a stone, is nothing but universals, thoughts, then there is no reason why it should not be deduced. For to deduce thoughts from thoughts is admittedly legitimate. But if it contains any element which is *not* thought, then that element would be undeducible and unknowable. It is possible that Hegel was still confused by traces of this idea, believed nature to contain some undeducible element, and so hesitated and fumbled over the transition from the Logic to nature.

425. And this would explain, too, the extraordinary position

---

[1] For an expression of the view that the transition from Logic to nature is not a deduction, see Macran, pp. 79 to 85, especially p. 84.

he takes up on the question of the *contingency* of nature. It appears that a certain Herr Krug, supposing Hegel to be attempting in the philosophy of nature to deduce all actual existent objects from the pure Idea, enquired whether Hegel could deduce the pen with which he, Herr Krug, was writing. Hegel demolishes the unfortunate Krug in a contemptuous and sarcastic footnote, in which he states that philosophy has more important matters to concern itself with than Krug's pen. And the general position he takes up is that the philosophy of nature cannot and should not attempt to deduce particular facts and things, but only universals. It cannot deduce *this* plant, but only plant in general; and so on. The details of nature, he says, are governed by contingency and caprice, not by reason. They are irrational. And the irrational is just what cannot be deduced. It is most improper, he tells us, to demand of philosophy that it should deduce *this* particular thing, *this* particular man, and so forth.

426. This position will not bear examination. If there is in this stone, or this man, nothing but thought, nothing but universals, then it ought, theoretically at least, to be possible to deduce this stone or this man. If it is not possible, the impossibility can only arise because the stone contains some element which is not universal, and which, as absolutely particular, is outside the reach of thought altogether. What is outside the reach of thought is unknowable. It is the Kantian thing-in-itself. Thus Hegel's position as regards the contingency of nature lends some colour to the suggestion that he was still, in spite of all his assertions to the contrary, infected with the Kantian idea of the unknowable. And this in turn would explain his fumbling over the transition from Logic to nature.

427. In my opinion Hegel was wrong, and Krug right, as regards the question of the pen. And Hegel's ill-tempered petulance is possibly the outcome of an uneasy feeling that Krug's attack was not without reason. If we are to have an idealistic monism it must explain everything from its single first principle, thought. And that means that it must deduce everything. To leave anything outside the network of

deduction, to declare anything utterly undeducible, is simply dualism. It implies that something exists which is not the product of thought, which is outside thought altogether, which is an ultimate underived absolute being. This is an outcrop of that same dualism which was so plain in the systems of Plato and Aristotle. No doubt it is true that, in Hegel's system, nature must be regarded as, in some sense, mindless and irrational. The Idea is reason. Nature is the opposite of the Idea. Nature, therefore, is irrational. And since rationality is the same as necessity, nature must be governed by the opposite of necessity, viz. contingency. There is no necessary logical reason why anything in nature should be as it is; it simply is so. But it is likewise an essential feature of the Hegelian system that any two terms which are opposites are also identical. There cannot be an *absolute* separation between the rational and the irrational. The irrational must be also, at the same time, rational. It must be shown that it is rational that the irrational should exist. Now if Hegel had asserted that any particular object, say this stone, is, on the face of it, something irrational; but had further gone on to show that this very irrationality was a product of reason, that, when the true essence of the stone is revealed it is found that its centre and core is thought, reason,—this would have been in consonance with the essentials of his sytem. This would, moreover, have been to deduce the stone. But to say that the stone is something so utterly irrational that it lies wholly outside the Notion, that it cannot be deduced, this is to admit an absolute separation and opposition between the rational and the irrational, an opposition within which there is no identity, an opposition so complete that it introduces a fatal dualism into the system. For it means that there is in the universe a division which cannot be healed, an absolute cleavage into two incommensurable halves, each of which is an absolute and independent being. There are, on this view, two kinds of reality. It is useless for Hegel to assert, as he does, that what is not rational is not real. This leads to a contradiction which we also find in Plato. The Platonic " matter " is declared by Plato to be absolute not-being. But the truth is that this "matter," since it is an entity which Plato does not derive from the Ideas, is really an absolute being. It is the same with Hegel's contingent and irrational. He declares it to be an absolute unreality. But since it exists, and since it is not deduced, not derived from thought, it has therefore an independent being of its own. It is an absolute reality.

428. An idealistic philosophy, to be complete, must accordingly deduce every detail in the universe. This means, of course, that it never can be complete. Infinite knowledge, omniscience, would be required to complete it. And the position which Hegel ought to have taken up, and which any reasonable Hegelian now must take up, is to admit that the system is not and cannot be complete. This, however, is what Hegel would not do. There was undoubtedly a kind of arrogance about him which prevented it. He wears always an air of omniscience. The system is to be complete, absolute, final. It is to solve all problems. To take up the position that a complete philosophy must deduce everything, and to admit in consequence that his own system, however great—and it *is* great and magnificent, the greatest system that any human brain has produced—was after all but a candlelight in the immense darkness of the universe,—this humility did not suit Hegel's mood. For the rest, it is important for us to bear in mind, as we proceed with the details of the rest of the system, that Hegel did, rightly or wrongly, adopt the view that particular things cannot be deduced; that nature is governed by caprice and contingency; and that he is to deduce only the universal genera of nature and spirit. We cannot even expect, he thinks, to deduce all natural species. For nature runs riot here too and blindly multiplies species without reason. In the infinite welter of forms which nature produces reason is completely lost. This endless extravagance of natural production is, according to Hegel, a sort of madness, the absolute unreason of nature. And he observes that this so-called "wealth" of nature, her infinite variety, which is so much admired, is in truth far from admirable. It is the 'impotence of nature," her powerlessness to keep within the

bounds of reason. This mad productivity on the part of nature is a sort of running amok, a Bacchantic dance in which nature revels uncontrolled by reason.

429. The questions so far discussed in the present chapter are controversial in the sense that various critics take various views both as to what Hegel meant and as to the legitimacy of his proceedings. On these questions I have now expressed my opinions. The rest of this chapter will be concerned with the exposition of the actual contents of Hegel's philosophy of nature, regarding which there are no differences of opinion.

430. Nature is the antithesis of the triad which is constituted by the Logical Idea, nature, and spirit. It is, therefore, the opposite of the Idea. It is the Idea gone out of itself into otherness, into self-estrangement. It is for this reason that, as the opposite of the Idea, which is reason, nature is irrational. Nature too is the moment of particularity which the Idea allows to escape from itself. In accordance with the general principles of the dialectic method, the Idea is the universal (for the Logic deals only with pure abstract universal thoughts); nature is the particular; spirit is the singular, concrete individuality.

431. Just as the Idea is a sphere of many thoughts, so nature is a sphere of many things. And just as Logic begins with the emptiest and most abstract thoughts, and therefrom deduces a series of more and more concrete categories, so the philosophy of nature will begin at the bottom with the emptiest and most abstract things and will present us with a logical triadic evolution of more and more concrete forms. It begins with empty space. Space is utterly empty and abstract. It has within itself no character, no features, no determinations of any kind. It is the formless. It is an absolutely homogeneous continuous emptiness in which there is no differentiation. It corresponds to the category of being which is likewise a homogeneous emptiness destitute of all determination and differentiation.

432. Thus the lowest term of nature is space. At its other end, at its highest term, it passes over into spirit. Spirit is reason. It is the Idea returned into itself. But the ascending

stages of nature constitute the *gradual* return of the Idea into itself, and the completion of this process is spirit. When, in the Logic, the subjective Notion passed over into the object, this new sphere began with that which was most destitute of subjectivity, namely, mechanism. The successive categories of this new sphere constituted the gradual return and emergence of subjectivity. Subjectivity, which was lost and buried in mechanism, made its definite reappearance in teleology, and with that the object passed over into the Idea. The progress of the ascending stages in nature is in all respects comparable to this. Nature begins with that which is most mindless, most irrational, space. The Idea, reason, is here almost wholly lost and buried. In the succeeding stages of nature, reason gradually reawakens. And with the final stage, the animal organism, nature attains consciousness, and is ready to pass over into spirit, the rational spirit of man.

433. Space is thus that which is most empty of mind, of thought, of reason. Nature is, in space, in its most extreme opposition to the Idea. Space is, in general, the extreme opposite of thought. For thought is absolute internality, space absolute externality. The parts of thought do not lie outside each other as the parts of space do. In fact it is only by a metaphor that we can speak of the " parts " of thought. Things in space, and space itself, have parts; which means precisely this, that externality is the character of space. The parts of space are only parts because they are external to, and lie outside of, each other. This externality is the essential of space. Space in fact *is* externality.

The very essence of thought, on the other hand, is internality. We may say, if we choose, that the Idea is composed of parts, namely, the various categories of the Logic. But to describe the categories as *parts* of the Idea is only a metaphor. They are not really parts because they essentially do *not* lie outside each other. On the contrary, they are *inside* each other, and to prove this is the very purpose of the deduction. Nothing is *within* being. And it is only because being has nothing *in* *it* that deduction can produce nothing out of it. All the succeeding categories are implicitly within being. All the preceding categories are explicitly within the Absolute Idea. An intermediate category, such as substance, explicitly contains all the categories which precede it, and implicitly contains all those that follow. Thus every category contains every other category *within* it. This is the absolute internality of thought, which is the extreme opposite of the externality of space.

434. The philosophy of nature presents us with a doctrine of evolution, a progress from lower to higher forms. But it should be carefully noted that no time element is involved here. One phase succeeds another, not in order of time, but only in logical order. Hegel lived in pre-Darwinian days, and he was not aware that evolution is a fact in time as well as a process of logical thought. In fact he expressly denied the theory of an historical evolution. "Nature," he says, "is to be regarded as a system of grades, of which the one necessarily arises out of the other, and is the proximate truth of the one from which it results,—but not so that the one were *naturally* generated out of the other . . . It has been an inept conception of earlier and later 'Naturphilosophie' to regard the progression and transition of one natural form and sphere into a higher as an outwardly actual production . . . Thinking consideration must deny itself such nebulous, at bottom sensuous, conceptions, as is in especial the so-called *origin*, for example, of plants and animals from water, and then the origin of the more highly developed animal organizations from the lower."[1]

We may no doubt smile at Hegel's description of the most fruitful of subsequent scientific discoveries as an "inept conception." But it should be carefully noted that his mistake in no way affects the value of his philosophy of evolution as such. In the first place, Hegel's actual aim is to explain the phenomena of nature by deducing them in logical order. And it is quite irrelevant to his purpose whether events in time happen to correspond with that order or not. The explanation, *i.e.* deduction, of the forms of nature will be the same in either case. But apart from this, the great value of the

[1] *Encyclopaedia*, § 249. The translation is that given by Stirling in the *Secret of Hegel*.

Hegelian conception is that it gives the clue to a rational justification for the belief that some forms of nature are higher than others. We believe that a horse is a higher being than a worm, and that a man is higher than a horse. But the mere scientific theories of Darwin and Spencer afford no justification for this. They do not give us a rational scale of values. The development from some ape-like being to man is not, for anything that biology can show, a change from lower to higher, but only a change from one indifferent thing to another. It might just as well have been a change from man to ape.

Change can only become *development* in the true sense by being viewed teleologically in relation to an *end*. Unless nature is moving towards an end there can be no advance, and therefore no higher or lower. To say that anything is higher can have no meaning unless it refers to some standard of perfection, some perfect end, towards which the world-process is moving. Now modern science does not supply the conception of such an end. But to Hegel the end is the actualization of reason, the Idea, in the world, and this end is, at least proximately, reached in man, for man is a rational being. That form is higher in nature which more nearly approaches this end. It is a further development of reason than the lower form. And the mere order of deduction in the philosophy of nature proves that the later grades are higher than the earlier grades. For the process here is the same as in the Logic. The latter stage is explicitly what the earlier is only implicitly. The earlier is the mere potentiality of what the later is in actuality. The later therefore contains and is all that the earlier contains and is, *and more also*. It is a fuller, completer, more adequate version of the earlier. It is what the earlier was only trying to be. The Logic gave us a series of categories of increasing value. And the philosophy of nature gives us a series of natural forms of increasing value. And just as in the Logic the later categories take up the earlier into themselves, so that nothing is lost, but with each triad something new is added; so it is in the philosophy of nature. So that Hegel's system gives us a genuine basis for a philosophy of evolution. And all this is quite unaffected by the blunder which he happened to make on the question of the evolution of species in time.

435. It is not necessary for the student to enter elaborately into the detailed deductions of the philosophy of nature. It is almost universally admitted, even by the most ardent Hegelians, that this branch of the system, depending as it does upon physical science for its data, is now out of date owing to the strides which physical science has made since Hegel's day. Nor will anyone now dispute that, even in his own time, this philosophy of nature was, as regards the details of its deductions, mostly a failure. To deduce the forms of reason, which is the work of the Logic, was a not impossible task. But to deduce the forms of nature, infinitely manifold, tangled, and confused, this was a task at which even the genius of Hegel broke down. His deductions in this sphere depend mostly upon far-fetched and fanciful analogies, and sometimes upon erroneous scientific information.[1] It would be useless to reproduce them here. Nor do I pretend to be competent to expound them. They cannot be regarded as a living part of philosophy. They are of no more than historical interest.

It is, however, profoundly important that the general idea of the philosophy of nature should be understood, for it is an organic part of the Hegelian system. Unless we understand what function it performs, what position it occupies in the system, the Logic and the philosophy of spirit are left hanging in the air. Its general function and position in the system have now been explained, and it only remains to give the briefest possible outline of its actual contents.

436. Nature exhibits a triad of three stages, which are treated of respectively in (1) mechanics, (2) physics, (3) organics.

(1) *Mechanics.* This is the first phase of nature, the thesis. The Logical Idea, the realm of thought, was internal to itself. This internality passes into its opposite, the absolute externality which is the system of space, time, and matter. This

[1] See Croce, pp. 185 to 191.

appears at first sight as an absolute outside-itself-ness, a complete indifference of part to part, a blind and endless multiplicity lacking in any principle of unity. Nature here is governed by sheer mechanism which, as we have seen, is the absence of unity, of subjectivity, of the Notion, of reason. Nevertheless it is not wholly so. The striving after unity, which is the principle of reason, of subjectivity, appears in the form of gravitation. Gravitation, because it seeks to draw this blind multiplicity into a system and a unity, exhibits even here the governance of thought, the principle of internality.

(2) *Physics.* In mechanics, however, matter is regarded abstractly. It has not yet become this or that individual thing, having qualities and a character of its own. Thus, in astronomy, it is not this particular planet, the earth, which is considered. Any physical body could be substituted. It is not the earth, the sun, the moon, that are dealt with, but only the abstract geometrical and mechanical relations of those bodies. In physics the philosophy of nature rises from this abstract view to the consideration of material objects as individual entities, as possessing qualities and character. This gives rise to the study of the forms and species of inorganic nature.

(3) *Organics.* Here we pass from inorganic to organic nature. The transition is effected through the chemical process. Organic matter passes through three stages.

(a) *The geological organism*, comprising the mineral kingdom. The geological earth is to be regarded, not indeed as a living being, but as a sort of huge corpse.

(b) *The vegetable organism.* The plant is a living organism and exhibits the partial reduction of the multiplicity of nature to a systematic unity. Nevertheless the parts are not held firm within this unity. They are largely indifferent to one another. One part of the plant may perform the functions of another part. There is not that systematic differentiation and integration which is found only at last in

(c) *The animal organism.* In animals the return of subjectivity makes itself definite in the form of consciousness.

And in man this subjectivity becomes free ego. Hence the animal organism is the final form of nature, and constitutes the transition to spirit.[1]

[1] Some further sub-divisions of the philosophy of nature will be found in the diagram at the end of the book.

PART IV

THE PHILOSOPHY OF SPIRIT

INTRODUCTION

437. The German word for spirit here is *Geist*. Some English writers translate it spirit, others mind. We shall, as a rule, use the former rendering; but it will occasionally be useful to use the latter. And in any case the two translations of the word should be remembered. We have seen that the Absolute Idea is the category of spirit. But it may also be called the category of mind, or thought. The Logic is a description of the absolute mind, the primal intelligence which was before the world, God as He is in Himself before His manifestation. But this mind, which the Logic describes, is an entirely abstract mind. It does not *exist*. It has not manifested itself. In nature this abstract mind has gone over into its opposite, the mindless, the irrational, the crass externality of nature. Now, in the philosophy of spirit, we see its return into itself. What we have before us is no longer mindless. It is once more definitely mind, spirit. But it is no longer abstract. It is the living concrete spirit of man. It is mind or reason in manifestation, mind which has now come to *exist* in the world.

438. Spirit, as the synthesis of the triad, is the unity of the Idea and nature. Man is, on the one hand, an integral part of nature. He is an animal. He is an external material existence subject to the dominion of natural laws. He is, on the other hand, a spiritual being, a living embodiment of reason and of the eternal mind. The Idea is the abstract genus. Nature is the differentia. Reason, now determined by the differentia, the Idea flecked with nature, this is the species, the spirit of man. The pure Idea had in nature gone over into its opposite, become estranged from itself, become the

mindless, the idealess. In spirit it returns into itself enriched from its own opposition. The Idea was, in nature, imprisoned in the mindless. In spirit it frees itself from this bondage, comes to exist as free spirit. The philosophy of nature exhibited the gradual steps of the evolutionary process by which the Idea disengages itself from absolute mindlessness. This evolution from inorganic matter to animal organism is the gradual return of the Idea, from its absolute self-contradiction in crass matter, to itself, to rationality. Spirit is the completion of this process.

439. Nevertheless, just as there are grades in the realm of nature, so there are grades in the realm of spirit. The Absolute comes to itself in man, but only by means of a long and arduous dialectical development. Spirit does not posit itself forthwith as absolute spirit. It begins with a low stage of itself, and only gradually attains its complete self-fulfilment. To trace out this gradual evolution, stage by stage, is the task of the philosophy of spirit, and the dialectic method is the instrument which Hegel uses here as elsewhere.

440. The philosophy of spirit falls, accordingly, into three main spheres which constitute a triad. The first phase in its self-evolution is entitled subjective spirit. Its content is the human mind viewed subjectively as the mind of the individual subject. Its sub-divisions are therefore the successive stadia of individual consciousness, such as sense-perception, appetite, intellect, reason, imagination, memory, and the like. Spirit thus considered is spirit in itself, implicit. Spirit proceeds out of itself into otherness in the second main division of the philosophy of spirit, *i.e.* objective spirit. The essential inwardness of spirit as subjective here passes over into its opposite, into external objectivity. Just as the Idea in general passed into externality and so created an objective external world, nature; so now the subjectiveness of spirit creates an objective world external to itself. But this is no mere world of crass matter. It is a spiritual world. It is the world of spiritual *institutions*. These are the institutions of law, morality, and the state. These are objective; they are just as much outward objects as a stone or a star. But

they are also identical with the I to which they are thus external. They are nothing but the objectification of myself. They are not indeed the objectification of my single self, of me as a peculiar individual with my personal eccentricities and caprices. But they are the objectification of my universal self, my reason, of what I have in common with all humanity, of the universal spirit of man. For example, the laws of the state are not, or ought not to be, merely the embodiment of the whims, the prejudices, or the interests, of any individual or class. They embody the rational and universal life of the community. These institutions are thus, on the one hand, objective and outward. And, on the other hand, they are clearly spiritual; for they are the manifestation of mind, intelligence, purpose. And for this reason they fall here under the head of the philosophy of spirit. This part of Hegel's system gives us his ethics and political philosophy.

441. The third main division of the philosophy of spirit is called absolute spirit. This is the human spirit in its manifestations in art, religion and philosophy. And this division of Hegel's work comprises, therefore, his aesthetics, his philosophy of religion, and finally, to use a phrase which Hegel himself does not use, his philosophy of philosophy. Absolute spirit is the unity of the subjective and the objective spirit. And it is only here that spirit becomes at last absolutely free, infinite, and fully concrete. In its final phase, philosophy, spirit knows that it is itself all reality. For the philosophic spirit sees the world as merely a manifestation of thought, that is, of itself. The world is only itself. Its object, *i.e.* the world, is identical with itself, with the subject. Subject and object are, therefore, in philosophy, identical. Or in other words, philosophy is the final unity of subjectivity and objectivity. It is for this reason that absolute spirit is the synthesis of subjective spirit and objective spirit. And in philosophy the return of the Idea into itself is complete. For philosophic man is the supreme manifestation of reason, *i.e.* of the Idea, in the world. The more exact meaning of these teachings must be left till we come to deal with absolute spirit in detail.

442. That the Idea should return into itself,—this is the

end, the purpose, of the world-process. We saw that a philosophy of evolution must justify the values of higher and lower, and that it can do so only in relation to an end, only if the world is regarded teleologically (434). The whole progress of the evolution which is begun in the philosophy of nature and completed in the philosophy of spirit is determined by this end. The Absolute is the logical Idea, reason as it is in itself. But the logical Idea is merely abstract reason; it is reason which does not exist, has not manifested itself. The purpose of the world is the self-manifestation of reason; reason must come to *exist* as a concrete being in the world. The Absolute must manifest itself. This end is attained in man, for man is a reasoning being. And *philosophic* man is, in theory at least, the completely rational being, the complete manifestation of the Absolute. Higher and lower in the scale of evolution mean respectively nearer to and further from the attainment of this end.

443. As in the Logic and the philosophy of nature, it must of course be understood that the successive phases of the evolution of spirit do not constitute a time-series. The process is a purely logical process. And the transition from one phase to the next is a logical deduction. Just as the category nothing is deduced from the category being, so here objective spirit is deduced from subjective spirit, religion from art, philosophy from religion. Or at least, this is what Hegel aims at. Whether the deductions are in fact valid and successful is of course another question. But because we have here, in theory at least, a chain of deductive reasoning stretching without a break from the first page of the Logic to the last page of the philosophy of spirit, and because this systematic development comprises everything in the universe, material or spiritual, therefore, in this way, the entire universe is *explained*, *i.e.* shown to be the necessary logical consequence of its first reason, which first reason is the consequence of itself (self-determined).

FIRST DIVISION

SUBJECTIVE SPIRIT

INTRODUCTION

444. The sphere of subjective spirit is the sphere which is generally understood to be dealt with by the modern science of psychology. Its subject matter comprises all the grades, functions, and "faculties," of the individual mind of man, from the lowest forms of instinct, feeling, and sensation, to the highest forms of reason, intellect, and practical activity. Its subject is thus the whole range of mind or spirit, regarded as *inward*, *i.e.* as not yet having put itself forth in an *outward* and external form in the shape of *institutions*. The institutions of law, custom, morality, political organization, and the like, constitute an external world which is not, like nature, merely mindless, but is, on the contrary, the very substance of mind become outward, the objective realization of reason and spirit. These institutions, therefore, constitute objective spirit. But what we now have to deal with is subjective spirit, the mind of the individual as individual, my mind, your mind, etc.

445. But we must be careful to avoid the mistake of supposing that by individuality, in this connection, is meant merely personal peculiarities or oddities that attach to one individual mind and not to another. It is certainly the structure of your mind and my mind which Hegel is here seeking to deduce, but only in so far as our minds are *universal* in their character. It is only what is essential to mind, not what is accidental and contingent, that is to be deduced.

Thus memory, reason, self-consciousness, desire, are universal characters of mind. But the fact that I dislike the colour yellow, or that you exhibit a passionate love of horses, the facts that one man prefers beef to mutton and another mutton to beef—these are no universal characters of mind as mind, but are merely the accidental, meaningless, and contingent eccentricities or foibles of the single self. These have no place in the philosophy of spirit. And these remarks apply, of course, not merely to the sphere of subjective spirit, but to the philosophy of spirit as a whole. It is only mind as mind, spirit as spirit, the universal and essential in the spirit of man, that we anywhere consider.[1]

446. The subject matter of the division which deals with the subjective spirit is thus the same as the subject matter of psychology, namely, mind regarded as inward. This does not mean, however, that we are about to enter upon a discussion of psychology in its ordinary sense. Psychology is an empirical science. But what we have here is philosophy. The subject matter of philosophy in general is the same as the subject matter of the empirical sciences, namely, the universe in which we live. But philosophy is nevertheless distinct from geology, botany, chemistry, physics, etc. And so here, too, it is not the empirical science of mind that is to occupy us, but the philosophy of mind. Empirical psychology simply picks up its facts as it finds them, takes them for granted, and asks no questions. Philosophy has to *deduce* its facts. Psychology will be content to say that the mind, as a matter of fact, *has* memory, reason, desires, etc. Philosophy seeks to show that the mind *must* have these phases by deducing one from the other.

447. The word psychology is nowadays used, and has been used by us in the last three paragraphs, to mean the empirical science of the whole of subjective mind. Hegel himself, however, uses the term in a much narrower sense, for he has applied it only to the last of the three divisions of subjective spirit. When it is thus narrowed down it has for him a specialized meaning which we shall come to understand in the appropriate

[1] On this subject see §§ 425 to 428 above.

place. But it may be useful to remark that Hegel's terminology, here and everywhere, is largely arbitrary. In the Logic he discovered so many categories that the naming of them became a matter of great difficulty. There were not enough terms to go round. Sometimes he invented new terms, sometimes he was forced arbitrarily to assign special meanings to familiar words. It is just the same in the philosophy of spirit. It is, as a rule, of little use to puzzle ourselves as to why Hegel used such and such a term for such and such a meaning. We have to recognize that his language is largely arbitrary, and simply to learn his meanings for words. And from a philosophical point of view (whatever the literary artist may think), there is no objection to this, provided we find that Hegel consistently uses his terms with the same meanings. In the main he does so.

448. Subjective spirit exhibits the three stadia (1) anthropology—the soul, (2) phenomenology—consciousness, (3) psychology—mind. Every one of these terms is used in an arbitrary way which differs from the common use of the words. Their precise meanings can only be explained in the course of the dialectic. But by way of anticipation it may be said in general that by soul Hegel means the lowest conceivable phase of mind; a stage so rudimentary that it has not yet even reached sense-perception, but is still a vague dim semi-consciousness, which realizes nothing, which is still in bondage to nature and to the body, which is scarcely yet recognizably human, and is barely above the level of animality. The term anthropology means the study of the soul in this sense.

When we thus speak of the various stages which spirit passes through, as soul, consciousness, understanding, desire, reason, etc., it must not of course be supposed that we are dealing with so many separate " things," or even " faculties." The soul is not something different from the mind, nor is reason anything different from understanding. Nor has the spirit a number of different " faculties " in the way that the body has two legs or two eyes. Spirit is an ideal unity, and soul, consciousness, mind, etc., are but different stages or aspects of the one life that pulses undivided through them all.

CHAPTER I

ANTHROPOLOGY—THE SOUL

449. The soul, which is the subject of anthropology, passes through three phases, (1) the natural soul, (2) the feeling soul, (3) the actual soul.

SECTION I

THE NATURAL SOUL

450. Spirit posits itself first as the **natural soul.** Its characteristics are deducible from the fact that it is the absolute *beginning* of spirit. It is therefore *immediate*, and because it is immediate, it has for its sole characteristic mere *being*.[1] Nothing can be said of it except that it *is*. For the absence of all mediation in it means (1) that it is not mediated by itself, *i.e.* that it has no distinctions within itself, but is completely undetermined, empty, homogeneous, and (2) that it is not mediated by anything outside it, such as an objective world over against it, and therefore that it is not characterized by any *relation* to anything; and hence the categories of essence, which is the sphere of *relation*, do not apply to it, but only the category of being. Just as the first category of Logic was being, a homogeneous emptiness of thought, and the first phase of nature was space, an external emptiness, so now the first phase of spirit is, so to speak, a mere homogeneous blank in the sphere of spirit.

Here at the beginning of spirit we stand on the topmost rung of the ladder of nature. And we may ask ourselves how

[1] See § 239 above.

far above nature the natural soul rises. The answer to this question is given in what has just been said. Because the natural soul is this mere blank of spiritual *being*, completely lacking in any definite spiritual determinations, the measure of its advance upon nature may be said to be so far nil. It is still almost completely entangled in nature, and in bondage to it. It is for this reason that it is called the *natural* soul.

Sub-Section I

PHYSICAL QUALITIES

451. The life of the soul is thus, at this stage, still one with the life of nature. It is completely determined by its environment. This environment is, as we know, the surrounding world of natural objects. But though *we* know this, the rudimentary soul which we are studying does not know it. These natural objects exist *for us*, but not *for it*. It is still a long way off from the stage of being conscious of external objects. And since there is for it nothing external to itself, it is for itself therefore the totality of all existence. Whatever is, therefore, must be *in* it. Hence the various modes in which it is affected by its environment are not, for it, affections by external objects, but appear within it as modes of its own being, that is, as qualities which it *has*. And since its whole life is still a mere partaking in the common life of nature, these qualities will be *natural* or **physical qualities**—qualities which are just as much part of its animal body as of its soul. Here we are again speaking in terms intelligible to us, but which have no meaning for it, since as yet the distinction between body and soul is foreign to it.

452. These physical qualities are tabulated by Hegel as follows. The soul (1) " takes part in the general planetary life, the periods of the day, etc. This life of nature for the and feels the difference of climates, the changes of the seasons main shows itself "—*i.e.* in us, in fully developed man—" only in occasional strain or disturbance of mental tone. In recent times a good deal has been said of the cosmical, sidereal, and telluric life of man. In such a sympathy with nature the

animals essentially live." [1] In the case of civilized man, Hegel goes on to say, these points of sympathy with nature are almost completely overwhelmed and submerged under the superstructure of thought, reason, and mind, which the higher faculties have developed. "The response to the seasons and hours of the day is found only in faint changes of mood, which comes expressly to the fore only in morbid states." [2] But among savages this kind of sympathy with the life of nature is sometimes exhibited in an almost uncanny way.

(2) Differentiation of the geographical spheres of the terrestrial globe give rise to differences of race and of the various racial or national minds.

(3) The differentiation of man into different types of racial mind proceeds further to the differentiation of individual minds, distinguished by their special temperaments, characters, talents, etc.

453. Whether or not Hegel's reasoning is to be regarded as a rigorously valid deduction, one can at any rate trace the thread of logical thought running from the idea of the immediacy of the natural soul, through the affections of it by its environment regarded as *in it*, to the general conception of these as physical qualities which it *has*. But the rest of the detail tabulated by Hegel, and the examples given, seem to be entirely undeduced, arbitrarily and empirically picked up and foisted in here. The amount of empirical material which Hegel surreptitiously introduces into the philosophy of spirit is far greater than in the Logic.

454. It is of vital importance to remember that we are here, and for some time to come, dealing with confessedly *abstract* states of mind. They are abstractions just as what has been called "bare sensation" is an abstraction. Sensation as a mere receptivity, completely divorced from all intellective activities, does not exist. Even in the lowest kind of perceptual knowledge, categories, such as those of resemblance and difference, are present. The natural soul is an even thinner abstraction than bare sensation. It does not exist, at any rate in man. It might perhaps be said to exist

[1] *Phil. of Mind*, § 392. [2] *Ibid.*

in an amoeba, though even in the consciousness (if we could use such a term) of the amoeba the categories must be implicit. But this is not of course to be made a ground for criticism of Hegel. He perfectly realizes it. He does not for a moment suppose that these rudimentary forms of mind exist separately on their own account. But just as geometry rightly considers shapes in abstraction from things, and psychology rightly considers sensation in abstraction from intellect, so philosophy here exercises the same right. But whereas everyone recognizes the element of sensation in himself, most of the phases of mind dealt with in Hegel's anthropology are so abstract and so rudimentary, that we have some difficulty in recognizing them in ourselves at all. They have long since become submerged in sub-consciousness. Nevertheless they do make their appearance " in faint changes of mood " and " in morbid states " as Hegel himself points out.

455. It is of course essential to Hegel's position, and in accordance with the fundamental assumptions of the dialectic method, that all the later stages of spirit, even the highest, are implicit here in its lowest forms. If this were not so, it would be impossible to deduce the higher from the lower, since such deduction simply means showing that the higher are in the lower (122, 153). This principle is, in fact, the same as that which is asserted by psychologists and others when they point out that " bare sensation " is an abstraction. What they mean is that even in the crudest possible sensation higher forms of mind, categories, reason, conceptual thought, are implicit.

Sub-Section II

PHYSICAL ALTERATIONS

456. The physical qualities of the soul now become **physical alterations** such as the changes involved in the passage through childhood, youth, manhood, etc. So far as I can see no genuine deduction is attempted here. The transition in Hegel occupies only one sentence : " Taking the soul as an individual,

we find its diversities "—*i.e.* its physical qualities—" as alterations in it, the one permanent subject, and as stages in its development."[1] The very use of the words "we *find*" implies that the alterations are not deduced, but are empirically found existing. No doubt the idea is that the differentiation at which we have now arrived, in the shape of *various* physical qualities, involves diversity and alteration from one to another. But although change certainly implies diversity, diversity does not necessarily imply change,—which would be necessary to Hegel's deduction.

457. The details of these physical alterations also appear to be, except in one case, undeduced. Hegel gives them as (1) *childhood, youth, manhood, and old age,* the essential characters of which he describes, (2) *the sexual relation,* the alteration involved in the individual seeking and finding itself in another, and (3) the changes of *sleeping and waking.* Of the essential features of this last Hegel gives a deduction. Whereas on its first appearance the natural soul was entirely empty and homogeneous and so without internal distinctions, there is now within it the implicit distinction between itself, *i.e.* the homogeneous blank with which we began, on the one hand, and the affections of its environment which appear in it as physical qualities and alterations on the other. The former Hegel calls its "immediate being," the latter we may call— though the term is not used by Hegel—its content. When the individuality now distinguishes within itself its content from its mere immediate being we have the state of *waking.* Sleep, on the other hand, is its relapse into the state of its immediate being. This immediate being is an "undifferentiated universality," which when it becomes specialized and differentiates itself gives rise to its content, its physical qualities and alterations. Sleep is, so to speak, the loss of this content, the return to homogeneous universality. In it the soul has returned to its first phase, mere being. It may be regarded as consciousness robbed of all content, *i.e.* consciousness of nothing, unconsciousness.

[1] *Phil. of Mind,* § 396.

Sub-Section III

SENSIBILITY

458. The implicit internal distinction between the immediate being of the soul and its content also gives rise to sensation or sensibility. For the soul now distinguishes its content, its affections, from itself. Hence instead of being its qualities they are now its *sensations*. For because they are something distinct from itself, they are therefore something *found*, something which seems to have a subsistence apart from the soul itself. They are therefore not part of it, as its qualities are, but are affections which exist in it as something other than itself, *i.e.* sensations. The possession of such sensations is **sensibility**.

But it must be carefully noted that although the sensations have thus a kind of semi-independence, they are still within the soul itself. The soul is still for itself the totality of all existence, outside which there is nothing. There is as yet no external *object* over against the subject. This sensation is not something other than the soul itself; it is only an aspect of itself which, as such, it distinguishes from itself. The distinction is still one which the soul makes *within itself*, not a distinction which it makes between itself and something else. Sensations which we do not attribute to any external source, but have within ourselves, such as hunger, fatigue, internal pain, perhaps constitute examples of what Hegel means. Such sensations are distinguished by me from myself. " I " am not my hunger. Nevertheless they are within me. It is not objective sensations, such as those of seeing a tree or a house, that are here in view, but purely *subjective* sensations. There is as yet for the soul no such thing as an external object.

It is precisely this which makes the distinction between the sensibility deduced here and the sensuous consciousness, or sense-perception, which will be deduced in the next chapter under the head of phenomenology. Sensuous consciousness means for Hegel the consciousness which the senses give us of external objects. And this does not exist as yet.

SECTION II

THE FEELING SOUL

459. We have arrived at the existence of sensations in the soul. These may be regarded from two points of view which have already been indicated. On the one hand, they are distinguished from the soul itself, and on the other hand they are within it and are therefore parts of itself. As distinguished from the soul, they are found existing by it, and from that point of view it is they which *affect* the soul, *i.e.* they are active while the soul is passive. But since, on the other hand, these sensations are within the soul, are part of itself, it follows that what is thus active in affecting the soul is only the soul itself. The soul is therefore active. Its sensations are its own act. It is the soul which *feels*, and the soul so viewed is the **feeling soul**.

Hence the distinction between sensation, which was the subject of the last sub-section, and feeling, which is the subject of the present section, is simply that sensation emphasizes the passivity of the soul in its affections, whereas feeling emphasizes its activity. The soul itself now feels, or is *sentient*.

Sub-Section I

THE FEELING SOUL IN ITS IMMEDIACY

460. Although the feeling soul is, as such, active, yet in the first phase of its immediacy, its activity is not realized as such, but appears, on the contrary, as passivity. For the fully developed idea of the activity of the soul involves its realization of itself as a *self*. It involves the sense of self, the distinct feeling that it is " I " who act. This again involves the distinction between the " *I* " who act and the somewhat upon which I act. Now this distinction is already implicitly made inasmuch as the soul distinguishes its immediate being from its sensations. But Hegel apparently thinks that, because the first phase of the feeling soul must necessarily be the phase of *immediacy*, the mediation which is

involved in this distinction between the self and its sensations must be regarded as not operative. Hence it is not yet the " I " which feels, but the soul rather has its " I " outside itself in another soul, which feels for it, and whose feelings it receives in passive sympathy as from an outside source. It is then the **feeling soul in its immediacy**.[1] The most important examples which Hegel gives of this state are the conditions of the soul in the child still in its mother's womb, and the condition of the soul in the state of hypnosis. The feelings of the child in the womb are indeed not its own feelings but its mother's. It is *her* self which governs and controls the soul of the foetus, so that in truth the latter is a mere passive recipient of the states of her soul. The child has not a soul of its own. Its soul is her soul. In hypnosis the soul of the patient is similarly merged in and determined by the soul of the operator and is a merely passive recipient of the latter's states of mind. It is not the soul of the patient which itself, of its own activity, feels. It is the soul of the operator which, so to speak, feels in the soul of the patient.[2]

Sub-Section II

SELF-FEELING

461. Self-feeling, or the sense of self, is implicit in the preceding states. The soul now explicitly distinguishes its sensations and feelings from itself. They are therefore recognized as merely *particular* aspects of itself. They are therefore *its own* sensations and feelings. And with the consciousness that these feelings are *mine* I am *ipso facto* aware of *myself*. This is the sense of self, or **self-feeling**.

462. Hegel further remarks that the failure to keep the *particular* aspects of self in proper subordination, and the tendency to let one particular aspect subordinate all others to

---

[1] See § 239 above.

[2] Cf. Addington Bruce, *The Riddle of Personality*, 2nd edition, p. 21. " Dr. Esdaile ... demonstrated the possibility of ' community of sensation ' between the operator and his subject. This he did through a young Hindu ... while in the hypnotic trance. In turn Dr. Esdaile took in his mouth salt, a slice of lime, a piece of gentian, and some brandy, and the Hindu ... in every case identified the taste."

it, and so govern the whole life, is insanity. These remarks, however, appear to be parenthetical, and to have no connection with the course of the dialectic.

Sub-Section III

HABIT

463. The soul is now distinguished into "itself," its immediate being, which is undifferentiated homogeneous universality, on the one side, and its content, consisting of sensations and feelings, which is a multiplicity of diversified particulars, on the other. These are, so to speak, two halves of the soul. But the former is, by itself, a completely empty *form* of universality. The latter is by itself a blind medley. Hence the one is just as essential as the other, and the two cannot exist apart. Thus the empty universality must, in order to exist, embody itself in the particulars, and exist in and through them. In doing so it stamps its own universality upon these particular sensations, impressions, etc. This universality, which now appears in the particulars, is, according to Hegel, only a "reflexive universality," *i.e.* a mere numerical universality which consists in the same thing getting itself repeated time after time in a series. When the particular sensations, activities, feelings, etc., thus repeat themselves, they constitute **habit**. Habit is thus the form of universality, which is one half of the soul, realizing itself in the particulars, which are the other half.

464. The deduction here is somewhat subtle. We may be inclined to object that it is performed by using the word universality in two senses, first as the universality of class, the universal which is the same as a concept or an abstraction, and secondly as meaning simply totality, the sum of a series of similar things, heaped together, and called "all." The universality with which we begin is the universality of form, of the "immediate being" of the soul, which is a class-universality reached by abstracting from the particular contents of the soul. From this we pass to the mere numerical universality which, in habit, appears as the continual repetition

of the same unit. These, it may be said, are quite different ideas, and we have no right to pass from one to the other as if they were the same.

But it may be answered that class universality is simply an abstract idea, and the only way in which such an idea can *manifest* itself in the real world is through the numerical universality involved in a repetition of units. For example, "man" is an abstract idea, a class universal. This can only manifest itself in the real world in a multiplicity of units which repeat themselves in a series which runs, this man, this man, this man ... etc. That is to say, class-universality is *ideal*. Its realization in the world is numerical or "reflexive" universality. We have, therefore, not two different kinds of universality, but one universality, now ideal, and now real, *i.e.* in manifestation.

Now the essential point of the Hegelian deduction here is that the formal universality of the ego has to manifest itself in the particulars. It can only become manifest as a numerical universality, *i.e.* as a repetition of units of sensation, feeling, activity, etc. This is habit.

SECTION III

THE ACTUAL SOUL

465. In the last sub-section we have seen the two halves of the soul coalesce to unity. The universality *appears* in the particulars and exists only in them. The particulars again have no meaning except in the unity. The result of this coalescence is the single self or subject, which Hegel calls the **actual soul.**

Formerly the soul distinguished itself from its content. Now it is seen that without its content it is nothing, a mere blank, so that its content is also *itself*, is just as essential to it as its universality. This single whole of universality and content, moulded into each other, each as essential as the other, is the actual soul. Or, to put it in another way, the state of mind which is called the actual soul is the realization by the soul that its content is not something alien to it, and that it itself is not merely one half, but is both halves.

466. Why is this called the *actual* soul? This is in accordance with Hegel's invariable use of the word "actuality." Actuality, as defined in the Logic (291) meant the unity of inner and outer, of essence and manifestation. The one half of the soul, its universality, is here regarded as the inner. The other half, the particular content, is regarded as the outer. The point of view which we have reached is that the real soul is neither the inner by itself, nor the outer by itself, but is the unity of inner and outer. The inner side is not hidden or veiled behind the outer; on the contrary it *appears* in it, is *revealed* in it. The particular content of the soul is the very stuff of its universality. The two are one. This is therefore the "actuality" of the soul.

467. This is the final phase of the "soul" as that term is used by Hegel. We now leave "soul" behind, and pass to the more developed form of spirit which Hegel designates by the word "consciousness." We pass from anthropology to phenomenology.

CHAPTER II

PHENOMENOLOGY [1]—CONSCIOUSNESS

468. In the stage of " soul," the mind was still a monadic individual, which contained within itself its entire universe, all its sensations, impressions, and feelings, being purely subjective. No world of objects, no external universe, existed for the soul. The next stage at which mind arrives has for its general character the fact that it has now become aware of an object external to it, of which it is conscious. The pure subjectivity of soul now undergoes diremption into the two sides of subject and object. This phase of mind is called by Hegel *consciousness*, and the study of it *phenomenology*.

469. The deduction of consciousness consists merely in making explicit the distinction between the soul and its content which was implicit in the previous chapter. The soul there distinguished its content, consisting of its sensations, feelings, and impressions, from itself. But at the same time this relation of otherness was also a self-relation. Its content was identical with itself. Now, however, the factor of distinction is alone explicitly emphasized. The soul closes with itself, and leaves the sum total of its sensations, feelings and impressions, standing outside it as an external object. These sensations and feelings, although a mode of its own life, were after all something which it distinguished from itself, something *other* to it, which confronted and opposed it. It only requires that mind should explicitly *realize* this externality of its content,

---

[1] This term is used in a much narrower sense here, *i.e.* in the *Encyclopaedia*, than in the *Phenomenology of Mind*. The following account is, as usual, based on the *Encyclopaedia*, but I have supplemented it from the fuller explanations given in the *Phenomenology of Mind*.

for its content to become a definitely external world of objects. When this has occurred we pass to the phase of **consciousness.**

470. A further result follows from these considerations. Up to the present the ascending grades of the soul have appeared as what they are, viz. changes or developments in the soul. Since, in the sphere of anthropology, the soul comprised within itself all existence, therefore any changes that occurred fell necessarily within the soul, for there was nothing outside the soul to which these changes could be attributed. Thus in the passage from sensibility to feeling, or from self-feeling to habit, it was the soul itself which underwent development, for there was nothing outside the soul to develop. Now, however, something other than the subject, namely, the object, has come upon the scene. And the successive steps which consciousness now makes seem to it to be changes, not in itself, but in its object. This must be so. For the whole wealth and variety of content which was formerly inside the soul has now been, so to speak, turned out of doors, thrust out of it to take up an independent existence of its own in an external world. This wealth and variety of content being gone, the subject is left contentless, a mere formal universality and abstract self-identity, which has within itself no inner distinctions. All distinctions, and therefore all changes— since changes involve distinction—now fall, not within the subject, but within the object. Hence in the ascending phases of consciousness, the thinking subject itself seems to remain always unchanged as the same abstract universality. The object seems to change. The phases seem to consist merely in the fact that the thinking subject becomes successively aware of various objects, or of various phases of the object. This, in general, is the point of view of ordinary unreflective common sense. At one moment, it seems, I am aware of a house, at the next of myself as an ego, at the next of some other person as an ego, and so on. It is not I, so it seems to common sense, who change. Only my objects change.

The philosophic mind may know that what thus seems a change in the object is in reality a change in the subject. For the philosophic mind knows that the external world is not really an independent reality, but is only the product and projection of mind itself, and that whatever happens is but the result of its own spontaneous activity. But this is not the point of view of the stage of consciousness at which we have arrived. For consciousness, it seems to be the object which undergoes change.

SECTION I

CONSCIOUSNESS PROPER

471. The object has now emerged from the recesses of the subject and taken up an independent position confronting it. It is this *independence* of the object which first gets recognition. The object is not-me, is something alien, in which I have no part. It is not yet realized that the object is, in its truth, only a projection of myself. It is at first seen as completely external, independent, and alien from the subject, an absolute other over against it. This is the position of **consciousness proper.** It exhibits three stages, (1) sensuous consciousness, (2) sense-perception, (3) intellect.

Sub-Section I

SENSUOUS CONSCIOUSNESS

472. The first phase of consciousness is, of course, *immediate*. This means (1) that the object is itself an immediacy, and (2) that the relation of subject to object is an immediate relation. The immediacy of the object constitutes it a singular, an individual object, a "this" or "that." The immediacy of the relation of subject to object involves that the object is directly presented to consciousness, *i.e.* immediately apprehended as *there*. There is no mediating or intervening link between the thinker and his object as happens when the existence of the object is *inferred*. Its existence is not now an inference for consciousness but a *presence*. Such immediate apprehension of an individual object is **sensuous consciousness.**[1]

[1] See § 239 above.

473. All that sensuous consciousness knows about its object is that the object *is*. It attributes *being* to the object and nothing more. For if it had any further knowledge of the object this would involve mediation, of which there is as yet no trace, and which would contradict the immediacy of this kind of apprehension. It knows nothing of any distinctions within the object, nor of any relations between objects. For all such distinctions and relations involve mediation. Thus the object stands for it in absolute isolation, unrelated to anything. This type of consciousness is, therefore, simply the abstraction of " bare " sensation, sensation as distinguished from sense-perception. The latter involves the apprehension of relations and universals. I " perceive " this chair. But I perceive it *as* a chair, *i.e.* as a member of the class of things designated chairs. Such perceptual knowledge involves comparison, the application of concepts, the relationships of similarity and difference which the chair bears to other objects. In the bare sensation which is now before us there is no such advanced content. The object is not linked up to other objects by a network of relationships. It stands in sheer isolation as an absolute immediacy, an absolute atomic unit of sensation. It is a mere *thereness*. Consciousness knows that it is, and knows no more about it. It is thus the crude sensation, the raw material of knowledge, which has as yet no shape and no form. Such a state of mind does not exist in man as a separate state. It is a mere abstraction. Any state of mind experienced by us is higher than this, and yet every state of mind has this as its foundation. That consciousness should begin with such a mere abstraction is, of course, inevitable for Hegel. Concrete states of mind emerge only later.

Sub-Section II

SENSE-PERCEPTION

474. The transition from sensuous consciousness to sense-perception is accomplished by means of the abstract character of the former which has just been noticed. Because it is abstract it is inadequate and untrue, and this constitutes the

dialectic by which it rises to perception. For **sensuous consciousness** exhibits this inner contradiction with itself, that whereas it purports to seize and be aware of the " *this*," this latter which it purports to know turns out to be meaningless, unknowable, and non-existent. It purports to be " *this*,"— an absolutely unrelated, unmediated, isolated sense-unit. But what is " this " ? Whatever we say in answer to this question invests the " this " with a universal character, the very opposite of what it is supposed to have. To say that it is " here " or " now " is at once to apply concepts, or universals, to it; for " here " and " now " are both universals. Even to say it is "this" leads to the same result; for "this" is likewise a universal. Everything is a " this," so that the term " this " is a general term which applies to everything. Everything belongs to the class of objects which are called " this." Hence " this " is a *class*-name and imports a universal. There is no such thing as the absolutely isolated particular which sensuous consciousness *purports* to apprehend. If there were it could not even be a " this," since to call it " this " is to class it with all other objects which are " thises," *i.e.* to know it as a universal. Thus the completely isolated unmediated " this " does not exist and has no meaning.[1]

Thus sensuous consciousness refutes itself and breaks down. It is now seen that what alone the senses can apprehend is the object leavened with universality. It apprehends " this " as what it is, *i.e.* as a member of the class of " thises." It apprehends the chair, the table, the man, the star, as what they are, members of the various classes of objects to which they belong. That is to say it apprehends them in their class nature, their universal nature, as mediated and related to other objects. This sensuous apprehension leavened with universality—a universality which, no doubt, is introduced by the spontaneous activity of the mind—is **sense-perception**.

475. The above is the argument as given in the *Phenomenology of Mind*.[2] The deduction which Hegel gives in the *Encyclo-*

[1] The line of thought here is the same as that already fully developed at § 6 above. It is also identical with Aristotle's assertion that formless matter is not-being.

[2] *Phen.* vol. i. chap. i.

paedia seems to be somewhat different. There he says " The *sensible* as somewhat becomes an *other* : the reflection in itself of this *somewhat*, the *thing*, has *many* properties ... The muchness of the sense-singular thus becomes a breadth,—a variety of relations, reflectional attributes, and universalities."[1] This means that whereas sensuous consciousness seeks to apprehend the object as a simple undifferentiated " one," such a point of view turns out to be impossible, for the " one " develops internal distinctions and inner variety in the form of its many properties. Such inner distinction and manifoldness of course involve mediation, whereas sensuous consciousness purports to apprehend the object as absolutely immediate. Instead of immediacy we have now mediation, instead of unrelatedness we have internal relations, and therefore we have universality. And such universality being introduced into sensation, we get perception. The argument, at bottom, however, is the same as that of the *Phenomenology*. It rests, as did the latter argument, on the principle that the completely unmediated, unrelated, undifferentiated, is unthinkable, and that we must, in order to mean anything, have mediation and therefore universality. But the first argument emphasizes chiefly the external relations of the object, *i.e.* its relations with other objects of its own or different classes, while the second argument emphasizes chiefly the internal relations involved in the inner distinction of the object into a manifold of properties.

The matter may be put in a nutshell by saying that the search for immediacy is futile, and that however low we descend in the scale of consciousness we never find bare sensation, pure immediacy, but always mediation is at work. This fact, as well as the distinction between sensuous consciousness and perception, are very well illustrated by Mill's assertion that when a man says " I saw my brother " the statement is incorrect. All he really *sees* is " a certain coloured surface," and the consciousness that this is his brother is not a direct observation (immediacy) but is an inference (mediation).[2] But if we suppose that by descending to " a certain coloured

[1] *Phil. of Mind*, § 419.   [2] Mill, *Logic*, Bk. iv. ch. i. § 2.

surface" we have reached immediacy we are much mistaken. "Coloured" and "surface" are both universals. Nor does it help us to talk of "visual sensations." "Sensation" is a universal. Pure immediacy is absolutely unreachable. Even the lowest sensation involves mediation and universality. And when we have realized this we have grasped the Hegelian deduction. The lowest conceivable sensuous consciousness has *in it* mediation, and therefore perception. The deduction consists in just this—that the consequent (perception) is implicit in the antecedent (sensuous consciousness). This is the logical character of all deduction.

SUB-SECTION III

INTELLECT

476. Sense-perception in its turn exhibits itself as self-contradictory and is accordingly superseded. The contradiction which it develops is that between the individual and the universal. What is perceived is, or purports to be, an individual, a "this." But at the same time its only truth and meaning have already been shown to consist in the fact that it is *not* an individual but a universal, or if we prefer it, a congeries of universals. What is perceived is at once an individual and not an individual. The result is that the object of perception turns out to be "a tissue of contradictions."

This contradictory character of the object of perception develops itself more particularly in the following manner. The object is no longer a single sensation or impression, but is now, for perception, a "thing." Owing to the mediation and differentiation which have now been introduced, the "thing" has "properties." If we consider the "thing" and its "properties" in abstraction from one another, we may say that the "thing" is the factor of isolatedness, unrelatedness, and immediacy, whereas the "properties" are the universals with which, at this stage, the individual is now leavened. For the properties are precisely what we classify the thing by. It is a chair, for example, because it has qualities in common with other objects which are also called chairs, and because it has not the qualities or properties of a house or a table. "Being used to sit on," "having four legs," etc., are the universals by means of which we apprehend the object as a chair. That it has these universals, or properties, and not such universals as "being alive," "conscious," etc., is what makes it a chair and not, say, an animal. The side of universality, mediation, relatedness, then, lies in the "properties." The side of isolated particularity lies in the "thing," for the "thing" without its properties is precisely that unreachable immediacy of which we can say nothing, since even to say that it is "this" would imply that it has the universal, or property, of "thisness."

Now the object as a "thing" is a "one." As having "properties" it is a "many." But to be both one and many is self-contradictory. It is a futile expedient to say that there is no contradiction because "from one point of view" the thing is one, while "from another point of view" it is many. This implies that the object is not really *in itself* many or one but that its manifoldness or unity are merely our subjective way of looking at it, and lie, not in the thing itself, but in us. We first attribute the unity to the thing itself, and believe that the thing itself is "one," and that its manifoldness is not in it, but is a mere appearance which is due to our point of view. We then reverse the process and say that the thing itself is many and that its unity is merely our way of looking at it and lies in us. Any such procedure is futile, and we have to realize that the thing itself is both many and one.

For, in fact, its unity involves its multiplicity, and *vice versa*. Thus suppose we begin by saying that the thing is "one" and disregard the manifoldness of its properties, we shall soon see that we cannot thus leave out its manifoldness which is implied in the very fact of its being "one." For it is only "one" by virtue of excluding others from itself. But it only excludes others by means of its properties. Thus the chair only excludes the table, *i.e.* is different from it, by reason of its possessing the properties of a chair and not those of a table. Thus it is only enabled to be a "one" by having properties, that is, by being a "many." It is impossible to avoid the immanent contradiction which the object has in itself by any subterfuges about the point of view from which it is regarded. The contradiction does not arise from the point of view of consciousness, but exists in the object itself.

It is only another form of the same contradiction when we say that the object has, on the one hand, an essential nature which constitutes what it is in itself, while, on the other hand, its relations to other things are an external and unessential character which is no part of its true internal being. Apart from all other things, we say, it is what it is in its own self, and thus its essential character is unaffected by its external relations to other things. But a moment's thought will show that it only distinguishes itself from, and relates itself to, other things, by means of its inner nature. And conversely it is only what it is in its inner nature by virtue of its distinctions from other things. Its being-for-self and its being-for-other are identical. Its external nature is part of its internal nature, its unessential being is just as essential as its essential being. This is, at root, the *same* contradiction as that between the " many " and the " one." For its internal nature is just the side of its " oneness," the side of the " thing," its external nature is constituted by its " properties," which are its relations to other things.

Thus the object of perception is, apart from all questions of " point of view " or *our* way of looking at it, " a tissue of contradictions." All these contradictions are, however, at bottom, merely deductions from and developments of the one fundamental contradiction which exists between the object as universal and the object as a single individual. As universal it has " properties," is in relationship to other things, has being-for-other. As a single individual it is the " thing," the " this," cut off from other things, shut up within its own being-for-self. All sense-perception involves this absolute contradiction between a universality and a singularity which subsist in the same object and are yet absolutely incompatible. I see this chair. On the one hand, it is simply and solely this single individual chair. But on the other hand, it is a universal, a " chair," and if it be regarded simply and solely as an individual, as non-universal, then it ceases to have any meaning or even existence.

Sense-perception cannot avoid this contradiction, quibble as it may about points of view. Therefore consciousness must rise above sense-perception to a new attitude of mind. This it does in the following manner. Sensuous consciousness had for its object the bare unmediated singular. This becoming impossible, it rose to sense-perception, and took for its object, no longer the bare singular, but a compound of singleness and universality. The truth, it sees, is not singleness but universality, which alone gives meaning to the single "this." But its object, as perception, is not pure universality, but universality mixed with singleness. Now it finds, however, that this is an incompatible combination and gives a contradictory object. The truth is neither bare singleness (sensuous consciousness) nor a mixture of singleness and universality (perception). The truth, therefore, can only be pure universality with the element of singleness dropped out altogether. Hence consciousness now takes pure universality for its object, or, to put it otherwise, the object itself changes, ceases to be an individual thing, and becomes a pure universal.

This involves a change in the kind of universality in view. For perception, universality means only sensuous universals, such as "chair," "house," "river," "star," "tree," *i.e.* universals which are concepts of sense-objects or of qualities sensuously perceived. Were it otherwise, we should not, of course, be dealing with *sense*-perception. But in rising beyond perception, the mind necessarily passes to those universals which are not *perceived*, *i.e.* to non-sensuous universals. These, as we shall see, are such universals as "force," "gravitation," "one," "many," "law," etc. These belong to a class of universals distinct from those with which perception is concerned. For we can see a "chair" with our eyes, we can touch a "tree" with our fingers. But we cannot see, touch, or otherwise sensuously preceive "law," or "gravitation," or "unity," or "multiplicity." These are pure universals. When the mind takes for its object such pure universals it has become **intellect**.

477. We can now indicate the general attitude to the object which *intellect* takes up. Its point of view is that the true object, or the object when it is really understood in its truth, is the pure universal. That is to say, it regards the universal as the *reality*. But it does not thereby cease to be *aware* of the single individuals of sense. It regards them, however, as not being the *true object*. In other words, it regards them as *appearance*. The multiplicity of the sense-world is thus conceived as a veil, behind which is the true world, which is a super-sensuous world of universals.

Now the universal stands to the individual sense-objects as unity to multiplicity. Even with sensuous universals this is so. There is but one concept " chair," while there are many individual chairs. Thus the true super-sensible world is regarded by intellect as a world of unities which manifest themselves in the multiplicities of the sense-world. And the typical view of intellect is that which regards the universal as a " law," and the supersensuous world as a " kingdom of laws." Thus we have the single law of gravitation. In the sense-world this manifests itself in an endless multiplicity of individual gravitational phenomena. Or again the universal is the law of electricity which appears in the sense-world in an infinity of forms and particular electrical phenomena, all of which are mere " examples " of the one law.

478. Intellect is the attitude of mind adopted by most of the empirical sciences. It imagines that it can " explain " phenomena by referring them to their " laws." No doubt science does not realize the fact, but in doing this it is implicitly adopting the view that the universal, or the law, is the true and only *reality*, and that individual phenomena are mere *appearances*. For it finds the *truth* of all particular things and events in the laws which are said to " explain " them. That which " explains " is *ipso facto* regarded as a self-subsistent and independent being, *i.e.* as *reality*, while that which is explained is regarded as dependent for its being on the underlying essence which explains it, *i.e.* as *appearance*. Thus, for example, electricity itself is regarded as a reality, while lightning is only one *form* of electricity, *i.e.* one shape in which

it *appears*. The lightning is a mere form, or shape, or guise, under which the reality is hidden. And so the same reality appears in many different shapes, for example, as positive and negative electricity, as the invisible current in the telegraph wires, as the visible lightning, as magnetism, and so on. These are merely so many outer disguises or mere appearances. The true reality is the one force, identical in all these diverse forms, which remains hidden behind. But this one force which is identical in all its diversity of forms, is not itself any single individual thing or event or phenomenon. It is a universal. This is the point of view of science.

479. The German word for Intellect here is *Verstand*, the same word which is elsewhere rendered *understanding*, as distinguished from *reason (Vernunft)*. The special characteristics of understanding as distinguished from reason are hardly emphasized by Hegel here under the head of intellect. None the less the connection is clear. Intellect puts the multiplicity of sense on one side as appearance, and the universal on the other as reality. It puts them in two different worlds. This separating and distinguishing character of intellect is what has elsewhere been recognized as the special mark of understanding. Moreover, the point of view of intellect is fundamentally the point of view of the categories of essence. According to that point of view we find essence and appearance set over against each other as opposites. For intellect the "realm of laws," the supersensible world of universals, is the essence, while the sense-world is the appearance. Thus it would not be entirely misleading to translate *Verstand* at the heading of this sub-section by the word understanding.

SECTION II

SELF-CONSCIOUSNESS

480. The distinguishing feature of consciousness proper, which included sensuous consciousness, sense-perception, and intellect, was (471) that the object was by it regarded as *independent* of the subject, as an impenetrable and alien

existence, as simply and finally describable as the negative of the subject, as the *not-self*. The distinguishing feature of the new phase of consciousness, to which we now turn, is that it sees in the object, not an alien being, but simply itself. The object *is* itself, and when consciousness recognizes this it is self-consciousness. We have seen (470) that in the sphere of phenomenology the development of consciousness appears in the guise of a development or series of changes in the *object*.

Thus the object first appeared as an isolated unit of sense, then as a compound of universal and singular, and lastly as the pure universal in the form of a " realm of laws." A further change now takes place. The supersensible world of universals, which was still, in intellect, a *not-self*, undergoes transformation and becomes subjectivity or self. Consciousness has already recognized that the truth and reality of the sense-world is the supersensible world of universals. It now takes a further step and recognizes that this world of universals is nothing but itself or its own subjectivity, and that in being conscious of an external world it is really only conscious of itself. The object is still an external object, but this external object is nevertheless itself. This new phase is accordingly entitled self-consciousness.

The transition from consciousness proper to self-consciousness takes place as follows. Intellect finds the truth about the object to be that it is a pure universal. Now a universal is a thought. The object, therefore, is thought, and is of the nature of the subjective thinking self. But this is not all. Intellect, in regarding the multiplicity of the sense-world as appearance, and the unity of the universal as reality, is placing reality in the " one " and appearance in the " many." These it separates and keeps apart in two different worlds. But this separation turns out to be illusory. For the " one," or the universal, thus emptied of all particular content, is a mere blank. So far is it from being, as intellect supposes, the fulness of reality, that it is rather, on the contrary, a mere vacuum, or at best an empty form. And the " many " of sense, thus separated from the universal, is a blind and unintelligible medley. The phase of intellect is again only another attempt to avoid the contradiction of the object as a many-in-one by placing the many in this world and the one in that. Intellect believes that, if they are thus shut off from each other in different worlds, they cannot fight. But it is now evident that the one cannot exist without the other. Consequently the object has at last to be recognized as a one which is in itself many, or, what is the same thing, as a universality or unity, which of its own motion undergoes diremption into diversity. But the universal which splits itself into particularity, the " one " which puts itself forth from itself as an other, and yet remains in that other identical with itself, so that it gives rise to a distinction which is no distinction,—such a universal is neither more nor less than the Notion (307, 314 to 318). The Notion, however, is essentially subjectivity (321). Hence the object is now subjectivity. In other words, the subject sees that what is real in the object is simply itself. It sees its own pure image and reflection mirrored in the object. It finds there, no longer, an alien not-self, but its own very being. This is **self-consciousness.**

481. The reasoning of the last section will be made clearer by reference to the " explanations " of phenomena through their laws which, we have seen, are offered by science. It is obvious that such " explanations " are entirely tautological. To explain a phenomenon by a law is merely to explain it by itself. For the event, stated in a universal form, is the law. Asked why a particular event happens, this kind of explanation merely says that it happens now because it *always* happens. Or again, to explain lightning by electricity is to put it as its own explanation. For lightning *is* electricity. And all the other various manifestations and forms of electricity *are* electricity. If electricity is not *identical* with its various forms, then it must be possible to say what electricity is apart from the forms in which it appears. But apart from these forms it is evidently nothing whatever. Now this means that the " one," electricity, or force, or the law, or the universal, is not, as intellect supposes, something separate from, but is *identical* with, the " many," the multiplicity, the individual phenomena in which it manifests itself. Thus we get the same

result as before, viz. that the "one" *is* the "many," that the object is a universal which undergoes self-partition into particularity, and so is the Notion, or subjectivity. Thus the truth about the object is not that it is the empty abstract universal of understanding (intellect), but the concrete universal, the Notion, which is identical with subjectivity.

482. A crude but possible misunderstanding may here be avoided. When we say that the mind now recognizes the object as itself, it is not of course meant that the *individual* mind recognizes the object as a replica of its *individual* self. John Smith, looking at a house, has no right to say "That house is simply John Smith." It is mind in general, or considered in its universal aspects (445) which sees universal mind in the object. So far as the universal mind is in John Smith he can indeed see himself in the house. But the part of him which he recognizes there is not his personal peculiarities, not what his mind is as *this* mind, but what mind is as mind.

483. Self-consciousness undergoes development in three phases, (1) appetite or desire; (2) self-consciousness recognitive; (3) universal self-consciousness.

Sub-Section I

APPETITE OR INSTINCTIVE DESIRE

484. Self-consciousness does not immediately and explicitly appear as what it is. It takes the form, in the first instance, of appetite or desire. For consciousness now recognizes that the object is itself. The object, however, still remains an external object, a part of the external world, a physical thing. But consciousness feels that this physical thing is, at bottom, itself. This situation involves a contradiction and a disharmony. For on the one hand the object is I, while on the other hand it is not-I. On the one hand it is identical with me, on the other hand it is something independent of me, having a self-subsistence of its own. Thus the attitude of mind, at this stage, is composed of two factors, which are not in harmony with each other: (1) since the object of mind is simply mind itself, the attitude of mind is self-consciousness; but (2) since

the object is still an independent external thing, *i.e. not* mind itself, mind to that extent still occupies the position of consciousness proper. Hence mind has not yet completely emerged from its lower form of consciousness proper. Self-consciousness has not fully developed, but is still only *half* self-consciousness and half consciousness proper.

Self-consciousness must, therefore, more fully develop itself; it must become *pure* self-consciousness. It can only do so by getting rid of its lower factor of mere consciousness proper, which is, so to speak, dragging it down. Now this aspect of it as consciousness proper, of which it has to rid itself, is due to the fact that its object is still an independent not-self. On the one hand the object is identical with the self which thinks it, but still, on the other hand, it retains its independence as an external object. Self-consciousness, therefore, can only overcome this inner contradiction, can only develop itself into full self-consciousness, by *abolishing this independent self-subsistence* of its object. The *impulse*, which is thus generated, to abolish the independence of the object, is **desire** or **appetite**. And it carries out its purpose by destroying and *consuming* the object. Thus, in the simplest form of appetite, that of *hunger*, the object, *i.e.* the food, in the first instance stands over against me as an independent object. By consuming it I destroy its independent existence in the world, I make it part of myself, and it ceases to confront me as a not-self. Though this is most obvious in the case of hunger, all other desire or appetite has, according to Hegel, the same essential inner nature. It consists in the impulse to abolish the independence of its object, to destroy its self-subsistence by making it a mere satellite of myself and so a part of me and my world. In its most simple form it takes the shape of actually destroying the object.

Sub-Section II

SELF-CONSCIOUSNESS RECOGNITIVE

485. In the phase of desire, the object is still regarded as a lifeless physical thing, *e.g.* food. The individual ego has not

yet come to recognize the existence of other egos in the world. Its objects have, through the entire development of mind up to the present, been *things*, not persons. Its position is, so to speak, solipsist. Nothing exists for it except itself and the physical objects which circle round it as their central sun. These objects it has recognized as being, at bottom, nothing other than itself, and any appearance of independence of itself it has, in desire, sought to destroy.

The new phase of mind to which we now turn recognizes at last the existence of other selves in the world. Its object is now another self. It sees itself, not now in a mere physical object, but in another similar self. Since the other self is a reduplication of itself, since in this other it still sees itself, it is thus a mode of self-consciousness. And since it recognizes, what it did not recognize before, namely, the existence of other selves, it is called self-consciousness recognitive.

486. How is this phase of mind deduced? Since, in the sphere of phenomenology, all changes appear to be changes in the *object*, and not in the subject, the transition will be made from the object of desire to the new object, viz. the other self or selves. The physical object of desire will be seen to undergo transformation into a conscious ego. This may appear fantastic, but if the nature of Hegel's procedure here is grasped it will cease to appear so. Its seeming fantastic is due to the fact that we are apt to forget that it is only a logical transformation, and not a transformation in time, that is in view. It is not meant that, for example, a piece of bread ever actually, as a historical fact, *turns into* a person! What is meant is that the idea of another self is implicit in the idea of a desired object, and may be logically deduced from it. The existence of desire is familiar to everyone as a *fact*. What Hegel has so far attempted to do is to bring to light the universal character of desire, the essence of what in its hidden nature it is. And what he now proposes to do is to prove that when this essential inner nature of desire is understood it is seen to involve the further idea of the existence of consciousnesses other than the one who is subject to the desire.

487. The actual deduction or transition is, however, not

very easy. It is most clearly explained in the *Phenomenology of Mind*. The purpose which appetite has in view in consuming its object is to destroy the independence of the object which appears to rival its own independence. The position occupied by self-consciousness at this stage is that the object is itself, has no independence of it, and consequently that it is itself the only independent self-subsistent being in the world. And because the object obstinately persists in maintaining that *it* also is an independent being, the ego proceeds to destroy it. In doing so it seeks to attain complete satisfaction of its sense of self, *i.e.* its sense that it alone truly *is*. But now a new difficulty arises. The very fact that the ego can only attain this triumphant sense of self by destroying the object shows that it is *dependent* on the object for its self-satisfaction. For if the object had not an independent existence the ego could not destroy its independence, and so could not attain self-satisfaction. Hence the ego is dependent on the object, and the object has again to that extent an independent being. In the very act of having its independence destroyed the independence of the object thus crops up again. The ego negates the object but is unable to get rid of it, or to attain its full sense of self, its feeling of being the sole independent occupant of the universe. Hence, if the self-consciousness of the ego is to develop to its full height, since the ego cannot negate the object, the object must negate itself. But when the object negates itself, it has become a consciousness, another self. For " since the object is in its very self negation and in being so is at the same time independent, it is consciousness." [1]

It is this last step in the argument which it is so difficult to follow. The statement is that what " negates itself " is consciousness. Apparently the idea is that consciousness is what puts itself forth from itself as an object. It thus makes a distinction within itself and gives rise to an *other*, the object. The object is then *there*, outside mind. But it has still to become *known*. By the act of *knowing* it the subject again brings it back into itself and so abolishes the distinction which

[1] *Phen.*, i. p. 173.

it made. In abolishing the distinction it negates the otherness of the other, it negates the other, and since the other is also itself, it thus negates itself. When the object of desire comes to negate itself, it is, in this way, consciousness. And so the object of desire undergoes transformation into another conscious self, and we have **self-consciousness recognitive.** The transition is, however, extremely obscure. But the language of the *Encyclopaedia* seems to me to bear out this interpretation (*Encyclopaedia*, § 429).

488. But although the ego is now forced to recognize the existence of other egos, it must not be supposed that it at once *accepts* them into its world. The aim of the ego at present is to see in itself alone an independent self-subsistent being, and to destroy any independence that claims to rival it. The other ego, just because it is an ego, claims an equal independence with the first ego. Each therefore seeks to destroy the other ego in order to retain its sense of being all reality. There follows a life and death struggle. But it soon becomes apparent that for one ego to destroy the other by death would defeat its own object and lead to a new contradiction. For self-consciousness is only self-consciousness in virtue of the fact that in the other self it contemplates its own self. To destroy the other self entirely would, therefore, be to destroy its contemplation of itself in the other, and in doing this, self-consciousness would destroy itself and so contradict and frustrate its aim of being the *only* self-consciousness. Therefore, instead of destroying the other self entirely by death, it now seeks to destroy only the independent selfhood of the other, and to reduce it to absolute dependence on itself. This result appears in history as the institution of slavery, in which the master alone retains independence, the slave being reduced to the level of a " thing."

It will be observed that, in order to reach this result, there is necessary the condition that one ego is more powerful than the other, thereby attaining the mastery and reducing the other to slavery. Hegel makes, so far as I can see, no attempt to deduce this inequality, but merely empirically foists it in. Moreover it was impossible that, on his own principles, he ever could deduce this inequality. For such inequality is the result of the individual peculiarities of the antagonists, and forms no part of the universal essence of mind as mind, upon which alone the philosophy of spirit can dwell.

489. Hegel remarks [1] that, in this institution of lordship and bondage, we have the emergence of the beginnings of man's social life. It rests upon *force*. Social institutions, therefore, begin in force. This does not mean, however, that society is *founded* on force and has force for its principle. The origin of a thing—this is one of the great lessons of idealism in general—gives no clue to its essential nature. Force is merely the "external commencement of states, not their underlying and essential principle." [2]

If these remarks were intended as a contribution to history, they might perhaps be criticized on various historical grounds. That the actual origin of social institutions is to be found in slavery is probably not true. But such a criticism would indicate a confusion as to Hegel's method and meaning against which continual warning is necessary. Hegel is deducing the *logical* order of the phenomena of mind. The historical order may possibly be different.

Sub-Section III

UNIVERSAL SELF-CONSCIOUSNESS

490. We have now reached the stage at which one self-consciousness recognizes itself as alone independent and negates and abolishes the independence of the other. The slave, because his independence is abolished, is not a self-consciousness, but remains only at the stage of consciousness proper. For independence consists in seeing that there is no genuine other to oneself, but that the supposed other is, at bottom, only one's self. And this also is self-consciousness, being conscious of one's self in the other. Hence, self-consciousness and independence being the same thing, the slave in losing the latter loses the former also. His position, therefore, is merely that of consciousness. And his object, consequently, is not

[1] *Phil. of Mind*, § 433. [2] *Ibid.*

another self, but only inanimate things to which he takes up the position of appetite. Yet he does not, for that reason, destroy the object, but now works on it and moulds it by his labour for the enjoyment of his master.

Two results follow from this. In the first place the self-consciousness of the master finds that its independence is dependent upon the slave. For it is only by negating the independence of the other ego that it retains its independence. This independence, therefore, contradicts itself, and turns out to be a dependence.

Secondly, the slave through work and labour, attains to independence and self-consciousness. For in moulding the object he alters it by putting *himself* into it. It is no longer a mere independent object but is what his will makes it. It is now dependent upon him. And in abolishing its independence he attains self-consciousness, for it is the independence of the object which constitutes consciousness proper, and the abolition of this independence which brings about the development of self-consciousness. In putting *himself* into the object he sees himself there, and this awareness of himself in the other is self-consciousness.

Thus the master finds that his own independence is dependent on the slave. This very fact proves the independence of the slave; and the master in being forced to recognize his independence recognizes him as another self-consciousness. For independence and self-consciousness are the same. The slave also now knows himself as a self-consciousness. Hence each now recognizes and accepts the other as a self-consciousness. The position to which mind has now attained is therefore this, that instead of the ego recognizing only itself as the sole self-conscious independent being in the universe, it now recognizes other egos as self-conscious beings. This mutual acceptance of all egos by each other is **universal self-consciousness.**

SECTION III

REASON

491. The ego now recognizes the independence of other egos. But since the other ego is for my self-consciousness another self-consciousness, it is therefore simply and solely myself. Ego has ego for its object. In contemplating the other it contemplates only itself. There are, therefore, two factors present here. Firstly, the object is an independent other. Secondly, the object is only myself, *i.e.* is not an independent other. The subject admits the distinction between itself and its object, but yet asserts that this distinction is no distinction, that the distinction is *within* itself. The subject has the object over against it but yet overlaps and overreaches the object and keeps it within itself. This is the point of view of **reason** (*Vernunft*). For reason is the principle which while admitting the distinction sees also the underlying identity. It is the principle of the identity of opposites. The object is now both distinct from the subject and yet identical with it.

It will be observed that reason, as the third member of the triad,—consciousness, self-consciousness, reason,—is the unity of the other two. The position of consciousness is that the object is independent, is distinct from the subject. The position of self-consciousness is that the object is identical with the subject. Reason combines these two abstract positions in a synthesis. The object is now both distinct from the subject and identical with it. It is identity in difference.

CHAPTER III

PSYCHOLOGY—MIND

492. The *soul*, which was treated in anthropology, was a monad which included in itself all existence and had nothing outside it. This, however, was only because nothing else, no *object*, had yet come into existence. In phenomenology the mind, now as *consciousness*, underwent diremption, split in two, put forth part of itself as an external object confronting it and conditioning it. Thus the *soul* was the subjective spirit in a state of implicitness, of undifferentiated simple unity. It was the subjective spirit " in itself." *Consciousness* was the putting itself forth of the subjective spirit into otherness, into opposition to itself in an object. It was the subjective spirit " out of itself." *Mind*, as treated in *psychology*, is the return into itself of the subjective spirit, its return enriched from its going forth in consciousness. It is the subjective spirit " in and for itself."

493. For we have already reached, in reason (491), the position that the subject overlaps the object, takes it back into itself, abolishes its externality and otherness. Spirit, when it thus sees that its object is no independent reality, but is nothing but itself—spirit, when it thus knows itself to be all reality, is the truth and highest phase of the subjective spirit. It is **mind**. The whole struggle of the ego, within the range of consciousness, was to know itself as the sole reality. But this it at first attempted to do by denying, ignoring, or destroying, the independent object which set up to be a reality in opposition to it. Finally, however, it was led to accept the object by the knowledge that this object is not an

independent reality but is its own self. Thus the object returns into the subject. The distinction becomes a distinction *within* the compass of the subject itself, so that once more the subject alone is what is. This is mind. And the treatment of it is what Hegel calls psychology.

494. The word for mind here is *Geist*, which is equally well translated spirit, and is the same word which is used to describe the subject matter of the philosophy of spirit in general. Thus the word mind or spirit has two meanings for Hegel, a wider and a narrower, which must be kept apart. Firstly, it signifies in general the spiritual being whose development begins in anthropology and is continued throughout the whole philosophy of spirit. Secondly, it signifies in particular the highest phase of subjective spirit with which we are about to deal in this chapter. We have already seen instances of similar double uses of words by Hegel—for example, Idea may mean in general the subject matter of the whole Logic, or it may mean the last sphere of the categories of the Notion. Words standing for categories or mental states are not sufficient to go round. Hence one word has sometimes to be used twice, or even thrice, over.

495. Mind is now no longer confronted with an alien object. Hence it is no longer sensuous perception or any kindred state. For such phases of mind are fettered to an external world. This is obviously true of sense-perception. It is also true of that kind of self-consciousness which has other selves for its object. For these other selves are part of the external world. Now, however, it is the *free* acts of the mind itself, mind which has risen above the external world and operates in *a world of its own*, which we shall have before us. Such acts are those of representation, thinking and willing. What in this sphere corresponds to sensuous perception is *representation*, the reproduction of mental imagery, etc. The object of the mind in such imagery is not an external object, but a mental picture or image, which is *within* the mind, and is its own free activity. Thinking and willing, likewise, are free acts of the mind which has risen above the external world and now operates in its own sphere.

496. Mind, as the subject matter of psychology, falls into three sub-divisions: (1) theoretical mind, *i.e. cognition*, (2) practical mind, *i.e. volition*, (3) free mind. The transition from theoretical mind to practical mind will be given in its place. But meanwhile the necessity of the development of both within this sphere is foreshadowed in the notion of mind itself which has just been given. For the mind is, as stated, not now dealing with any alien object, but with what is *its own*. This content, which is its own, in the first place *is*, has *being*. The mind, so to speak, comes across or *finds* this content within itself. It thus has the aspect of dealing with something that is already in existence and which it finds, and this aspect of it is *cognition*. But secondly, this content is *its own*, and as such is not something simply *found* by it, but is, on the contrary, something *made* by it. This making and moulding of the content as its own is the *practical* side of mind, its aspect as *volition*.

SECTION I

THEORETICAL MIND

497. Theoretical mind is mind in its *immediacy*. For although the content of mind is its own, it does not at first realize this. In the first instance its content simply *is*. It is there, has immediacy, *being*, is found existing. And the attitude of intelligence to what it finds already before it can only be the attitude of coming to *know* this something which it finds there, *i.e.* knowledge, cognition or **theoretical mind**.[1] The phases of its development are its gradual elevation to the realization that its content is *its*. These phases are, (1) intuition, (2) representation, (3) thinking.

Sub-Section I

INTUITION

498. The first phase is of course the phase of immediacy.[2] We shall find no mediation in it. But at the same time it is

[1] See § 239 above. [2] See § 239 above.

essentially *cognition*, a free act of mind which, as such, will have something of the nature of judgment or thinking, though these are not yet developed. Such immediate cognition, such a judgment which is yet not a judgment, is intuition. It cannot be a judgment because judgment involves mediation. And yet it is a cognition. It will therefore be a *feeling*, based on no grounds—for to be based on grounds is to be mediated —that a thing *is so*. It is the instinctive feeling, the intuitive perception of a fact. We all experience instinctive feelings, that such and such a fact is true, though we can assign no reasons for it. This may apply in the moral, religious, political, or any other sphere. This is **intuition**.

499. Intuition is often supposed to be something very exalted and grand, something far more sublime than the work of thinking. And at the present day there are not wanting even philosophers who apparently take this view. But here we see that Hegel gives intuition its place as the very lowest of the free acts of mind. And he indicates at the same time the characteristic defect of intuition, its subjectivity. An intuition may contain the truth, but it exhibits it in the form of untruth, in the form of something peculiar and private to the intuiting ego. It is merely a subjective impression of the individual, and lacks all universality.

500. According to Hegel intuition involves two factors which are of importance in the further development of mind. Firstly, it involves *attention*, which is the fixing of the direction of the mind,—the direction in which the ego collects itself together and concentrates itself in a special way. Attention comes to light for the first time here because it is a free act of mind, and therefore has not been involved in the previous phases of soul and consciousness. It is only now, in the sphere of psychology, in the treatment of mind (in the narrower sense) that free acts of mind, such as attention, have place.

Secondly, the *feeling* which constitutes intuition is, like all mere feeling, something subjective and merely inward. But because intuition is a form of *cognition*, a feeling that such and such a thing *is so*, it is not purely subjective but involves a reference to objectivity, to an outward. It thus implies the outwardization of the inward feeling, its projection into time and space, as something *existent*. Thus intuition is not solely feeling. It is only when the two elements of attention and outwardization are present that it is a fully developed intuition.

Sub-Section II

REPRESENTATION

501. Intuition is thus something both outward and inward. But the outwardness is the result of the activity of the mind itself. It is the mind which has itself outwardized the feeling. This outward is therefore *its own*, or in other words, it is an inward. The intuition thus freed from the external reference and made inward is **representation** (*Vorstellung*).[1] Representation passes through the three phases of recollection, imagination, and memory.

A. Recollection.

502. The outward has become inward. What was, therefore, in external time and space, now passes into an inward or subjective time and space. It is then an *image* or picture. Thus the actual rose is in outward space. But my mental image of a rose is pictured as in a space which is just as imaginary and inward as the representation of the rose itself. Thus we have **recollection**.

503. The image is transient and disappears (this fact Hegel does not deduce but merely asserts). But it is not thereby obliterated from the mind. It is stored up in the sub-conscious ready to reappear at any time. Hegel explains this by the contrast of implicit and explicit, potential and actual. The ego which, *in itself*, in its implicitness, is a blank and empty universality, is yet, because it is the Notion (321) a self-differentiating universality, and as such is the potentiality of its specific contents. The disappeared image has retired into the black pit of the mind's potentiality. Hence to talk of images, ideas, etc., as actually " existing " in the sub-conscious

---

[1] This is the only meaning, vague and doubtful though it may be, that I have been able to extract from the extremely obscure passage in which Hegel makes this transition (*Phil. of Mind*, § 450).

is as foolish as to suppose that the oak exists in the acorn in the sense that a powerful enough microscope would reveal the actual parts and members of the oak.

The image, being a picture of the thing as removed from its relations and connections with other particular things, loses its particularity, and takes on a universal character. It becomes a generalized image stored up in the sub-conscious. When we receive a new impression it is subsumed under the appropriate generalized image, and this act constitutes remembrance (or perhaps we might simply call it *recognition*).

B. Imagination.

504. The mind thus continually produces from the subconscious a flow of such images and remembrances. When it does so we have the reproductive **imagination**.

These images, however, are representative, or universal in character, and each fresh impression as it comes into the ego is subsumed under such a universality. The particular image thus comes to *stand for* something more than itself, namely, the universal. Thus the particular image of the lion becomes the *sign* of lions in general. There thus arises a system of *signs*, which when fully developed, becomes *language*.

C. Memory.

505. In language the word, which is a vocal sign, or sound, is a *thing* which exists in the external world. It is an outward. But by being received into consciousness it becomes an inward. It itself becomes an image. By becoming an inward which is fused with the universal for which it stands, the name or word, comes to be used *by itself* in intelligence, and itself does the work which was formerly done by a flow of imagery. When we thus come to think in names, **memory** is fully developed. " Given the name lion, we need neither the actual vision of the animal, nor its image even : the name alone, if we *understand* it, is the unimaged simple representation. We *think* in names." [1] Thus pure memory tends to become, in a

[1] *Phil. of Mind,* § 462.

sense, meaningless. "A composition is, as we know, not thoroughly conned by rote, until one attaches no meaning to the words." [1]

Sub-Section III

THINKING

506. Memory constitutes the transition from mere imagery to thought proper. When the image, as an image, is suppressed, what is left is a **thought.** Thus we see in the passage quoted above that "the name alone, if we *understand* it," is sufficient. This *understanding* of it, without images, is *thinking*. This does not mean, of course, that, as a psychological fact, thought is never accompanied by images. That would be contrary to obvious facts. But though thought may be, and usually is, *accompanied* by imagery, the very fact that it is so *accompanied* means that it itself is not the imagery, *i.e.* that it is itself imageless.

507. The process of transition to memory and thinking has taken place by the fusion between the universal for which the word stands and the particular representation which is subsumed under it. In this fusion the representation, *as* a representation, *i.e.* as an image, has disappeared. Its immediacy, or particularity, however, remains in the product, thought, which is accordingly a unity of the universal with the immediate. And since immediacy as such is being, is what is *there*, what is *this thing*, a thought is accordingly a unity of universality and being. Being is the side of objectivity. Hence the characteristic of thought is that it overlaps the distinction between itself and being, between subjectivity and objectivity. "It knows that what is *thought, is*, and that what *is*, only *is* in so far as it is a thought." [2] Thought is itself the unity of thought and being, of itself and its other. So that the position is again made explicit that thought sees in its object only itself. Hegel remarks that this position, which has already occurred at the end of the sphere of consciousness, must needs continually reappear, because it is the essential truth of philosophy.

[1] *Phil. of Mind*, § 463. [2] *Ibid.* § 465.

508. Thinking has its content, which is the side of immediacy or being. Considered in abstraction from this content, *i.e.* as being mere universality, it is formal identity, that is to say, it is (*a*) *understanding* which works up its material into species, genera, laws, etc. But because this content is essentially itself, it is therefore thought itself which splits itself in twain, and puts forth this content. As being this *partition* (*Urtheil*) thought is (*b*) *judgment*. But finally as superseding and abolishing the distinction, as bringing it back into unity with itself, it is (*c*) reason.

SECTION II

PRACTICAL MIND

509. Thought now knows that its content is itself, and therefore that it *determines* its own content. The world is therefore no longer regarded as a hard mass intractable and alien to thought, but on the contrary as essentially made what it is, moulded, acted upon, and determined by thought. The subject thus moulding the world by its own activity is **will**, or **practical mind**. The transition here is at bottom the same as the transition in the Logic from cognition proper to volition (402), except that there is no reference here to the element of *necessity*.

510. Will undergoes development through the phases of (1) practical sense, or feeling, (2) the impulses and choice, (3) happiness.

SUB-SECTION I

PRACTICAL SENSE OR FEELING

511. Though intelligence, as will, knows its object as itself and as wholly determined by itself, and though it is, as such, free and infinite, it does not in the first instance attain to that position. It appears first as practical feeling.

In the sphere of consciousness, the ego was confronted with an object. In the present sphere, that of mind (psychology), the object has, in general, been absorbed into the ego, and appears within it, as its *content*. Now will has arisen dialectically from cognition, or theoretical mind. And it takes over from cognition the content of the latter. The difference between will and cognition is that the content in cognition is not determined by it, whereas intelligence as will determines its content. In its first phase, however, will is *immediate*. And it therefore *finds* its content, as something already given to it.[1] No doubt this content is now determined by it, and so conformable to, and in harmony with it. But this conformability is not its own *act*, but is merely found to be so. Hence will appears here merely as the *feeling* that the existent fact, the content, is, or is not, conformable to it. This is the feeling of the *pleasant* or *unpleasant*.

As such it is, of course, an *instinct* to action. But it is only an instinct. It has not yet actually issued in action. And, moreover, because it is immediate, it is not governed by any universal rule or principle, since such universality involves mediation. It is not a decision to act upon a principle, but, in its absolute particularity and immediateness, it is a mere feeling or instinct towards this or that immediate object. This is **practical feeling.**

Such feeling may appear in the moral, religious, or political spheres, but in such cases it is the instinctive and unreasoned (unmediated), or intuitive, feeling that the subject should act in such and such a way.

512. Hegel here introduces a diatribe against those who appeal to mere feeling, the "heart," the breast, inspiration, intuition, and so on, against the utterances of reason and the practical dictates of a rationally controlled will and intelligence. Such disputes between the "heart" or feelings, on the one side, and reason on the other, involve at least two fallacies. In the first place they involve the abstract separation of the mind into "faculties." Feeling cannot be thus set up against reason when once it is realized that feeling and reason are not two things, but one thing in different phases of its development. The mind or spirit is not a pack of externally connected "faculties" feelings, will, reason, etc.

[1] See § 239 above.

"We must not imagine that man is on one side thinking and on another side willing, as though he had will in one pocket and thought in another."[1] Mind is a single being appearing in serially developed phases, will, thought, feeling, etc. It is absurd, therefore, to ask whether feeling is right or thought is right, for feeling and thought are the same thing in different forms. But secondly, if we must prefer one to the other, it is certainly to rational cognition, rather than to feeling, that we must award preference. For reason stands to feeling as the more to the less developed phase of spirit. Because feeling is immediate, it lacks universality. Thought on the other hand is essentially the universal. That which lacks universality cannot be a law, for it is characteristic of law to be universal. Hence my feelings are a law to no one but myself. They are merely private and subjective, whereas my reason is also the universal reason of all men, of all rational beings. Hence attempts to found morality, political institutions, and the like, upon the feelings, are foredoomed to failure. How, for example, can morality, which is not a mere private affair of my own, but is essentially a *law*, and a law for all, be founded upon feelings which have no validity outside the sanction of my personal consciousness?

513. Nevertheless it is, of course, possible that in a particular instance a man's feelings may be right where his reasoned conclusions would lead him wrong. One remembers the advice given by an experienced official to a raw one: "act as you think right, but do not give your reasons. For your instinct will be right, but your reasons will be wrong." Such human phenomena, however, are due to the fact that feeling is *implicitly* thought, and is therefore guided by unrealized reason. The lower phase, here as in the Logic, always contains the higher phase implicitly. The feelings are implicitly universal and contain thought as their inner substance. But this universality is here hidden under the guise of particularity and immediacy. The undeveloped human being, therefore, following his instincts and feelings, may often act rationally, because instinct is the highest phase of reason which he has yet

[1] *Phil. of Right*, § 4 Addition.

developed. Whereas, if he attempted to move upon the higher plane of rational cognition he would inevitably go wrong, just because such cognition *is* a higher plane, a plane on which he has not yet learned to move. Thus, though it may often be a good piece of practical advice to tell a certain type of man to trust his instincts, or his " heart," rather than his " head," this provides no justification whatever for attempting philosophically to found morals or politics upon the feelings, or to exalt feeling above reason. Reason, the universal, is, in fact, the foundation of the world, and it is the foundation of all forms of spirit, including the feelings themselves.

Sub-Section II

THE IMPULSES AND CHOICE

514. Practical feeling contains a contradiction, which is its dialectic. For, on the one hand, it merely *finds* its content conformable or not conformable to itself; but, on the other hand, it is essential to it as a mode of will that this conformability should be its *own act*. It is contrary to the very nature of will that it should merely find the world and leave it as it is. Its essence is rather to mould the world into conformity with itself, to act, and in acting to alter and shape its object. It develops, therefore, propensities for such action, and these propensities are what are called the **impulses**. Impulse, inclination, interest,—are so many different names for this phase of intelligence. If the intelligence throws itself wholly into the fulfilment of *one* impulse, to the exclusion of all others, this impulse is then called a *passion*.

515. Hegel here makes the important remark that the impulses should not be excluded, as was done by Kant, from the moral life. Kant supposed that duty must be done solely for duty's sake, out of respect for the law, and never from inclination. Even if an act were in itself good, yet, if it were done from inclination and not from duty, it lost, in Kant's opinion, all moral value. " But," says Hegel," impulse and passion are the very life-blood of all action."[1] " Nothing

[1] *Phil. of Mind,* § 475.

great has been and nothing great can be accomplished without passion."[1] Kant's false and abstract view is based upon the separation of the mind into independent "faculties." The "practical reason," the "categorical imperative" is here on the one side. The impulses and inclinations are over against these on the other side, usually warring against the practical reason, but in any case quite independent of it. But as soon as it is seen that these very impulses have the "practical reason" implicit in them, are themselves only an inchoate and undeveloped form of it, such an abstract view becomes impossible.

516. There is a multiplicity of impulses. Each is a *particular* impulse. But the will is one and universal. It therefore distinguishes itself, as one and universal, from its diversified content, its impulses, as multiple and particular. It now, therefore, stands above them, and *chooses* between them. This is the element of **choice** in the life of will. In order fully to understand this it is necessary again to advert to the unity of mental life and the fallacy of splitting it up into faculties. It might be objected to the deduction of choice, just given, that the will *is* the impulses, and that it is not the will which stands above them and contemplates them, but the I, the pure ego, which is cognitive rather than volitional. The answer is that the will *is* the I, the pure ego. The I thinking is cognition. The I acting is will. It is one and the same I which is both.

Sub-Section III

HAPPINESS

517. The will is universal, because it is the I, and the I is a pure identity or universality represented by the equation $I = I$. The satisfaction of the will, the accomplishment of its work, consists in conforming its content to itself. Therefore, since the will is universal, its satisfaction can only be attained by making its content universal. Each impulse, however, is nothing but a particular impulse, and its object is a particular object. Therefore intelligence, as will, does not find satisfaction in the gratification of these particular impulses and

[1] *Ibid.* § 474.

inclinations. Unsatisfied by the gratification of one impulse, it plunges at once into the next impulse, seeking satisfaction there but only finding the same result. There results a progress *ad infinitum.* Hence the will is led to seek a universal satisfaction, which is not to be found in any particular impulse. This universal satisfaction which it seeks is **happiness.**

SECTION III
FREE MIND

518. Will now finds that its object must be universal. But in happiness no *true* universality is found. For although the will has now abandoned the belief that it can attain satisfaction in any particular impulse, yet the universal satisfaction which it seeks in happiness can only be pursued through and by means of the particular impulses. For the will has no other content. And however much it may seek to attain happiness by postponing or preferring one impulse to another, by subordinating this inclination to that, by systematizing and controlling its interests, yet in the end it is only this or that particular impulse which is preferred and followed, and which does not yield satisfaction.

This lack of satisfaction the will can only remedy by taking as its object a genuine out-and-out universal. But it is itself universal. Hence its path will now lie in making itself its own object. It must put itself forth into the world and there contemplate itself in objectivity. This process is not completed till we pass to objective spirit. But the phase of transition Hegel calls the **free mind.** What is essential to the free mind is that it is will which has itself for its object. As such it is *free* will. For freedom consists in not being limited by an other. In impulse the will is not free because its impulse and its object, which determine it, are something other than itself. But free mind knows its other, its object, to be itself, and knows itself, therefore, as self-determined, and self-limited, *i.e.* as free. And because it is self-determined it is also infinite.

SECOND DIVISION

OBJECTIVE SPIRIT

INTRODUCTION

519. Subjective spirit meant the spirit considered as inward. Objective spirit means the spirit which has issued forth from its inwardness and subjectivity, and embodied itself in an external and outward world. This external world is not the world of nature, which is already found existing by spirit. It is a world which spirit creates for itself in order to become objective, existent, and effective in the actual world. It is in general the world of *institutions*. This means, not merely the positive institutions of law, society, and the state, but includes also customs and manners, the rights and duties of the individual, morality and ethical observance. In what order and in what way these various kinds of external institutions develop themselves we shall see in the sequel. The present remarks are merely anticipatory. These institutions are essentially intelligence, *i.e.* spirit, solidified in the world, and hence they are objective spirit.

520. The deduction of objective spirit, *i.e.* the proof that subjective spirit must now pass over into objectivity, is implicitly contained in the idea of *free mind* with which the sphere of subjective spirit closed. The will is universal, for it is simply the ego in its phase of *acting*, just as cognition is the ego in its phase of *thinking*. The ego, however, is the I = I, a simple unity with itself, an abstract self-identity. As such self-identity it contains within itself no diversity or particularity. And as not yet having sundered into particularity it is simple universality. And since the will, *i.e.* the I *acting*, can find no satisfaction in any *particular* impulse

(517), it must in consequence will the *universal*. But in spite of its universality it is itself an individual. As subjective it is simply *this* I. In willing the universal, therefore, it wills what transcends its mere subjectivity; it wills the *objective*. For what is universal stands opposed to what is merely private and personal to me as an individual. Thus universality and objectivity are equivalent terms. (This can be very clearly seen by anyone who will study the period of the Sophists and Socrates. The principle of the Sophists was that what I, in my mere particularity, think, is the truth *for me*. They denied any universal criterion of the truth. And hence, since the truth is not subject to any universal standard, it is merely the private and personal affair of my subjectivity. Socrates saw that to deny universality meant denying objectivity. Only if the truth is regarded as universal can it be objective. What is true merely *for me* is subjective. But the truth which is sanctioned by a universal criterion is independent of my individual views and personal impressions, and is therefore objective.)

521. Thus objective spirit is based upon the activity of the will. Institutions are the work of the will putting itself forth into the world, moulding the crude material of the world into a new world of mind. And in this activity the will has two aspects. Firstly in willing the universal, it wills *itself*. For universality is its very substance. It is for this reason that the new world which it creates is not merely objective, but is *spiritual* (objective *spirit*). It is *itself* which the spirit puts forth into the world. This spirituality or, what is the same thing, this universality of the institutions which intelligence sets up are seen in the very fact that their essence is to be universal. Thus morality is no private affair of mine; it is a *law*, *i.e.* a universal. The state, again, has as its very essence the universality of purpose and interest which stand opposed to the particular and private purposes of individuals. The very meaning of an institution is that it is something universal. But universality is the mark of mind or spirit. And hence the institutions of morality, the state, etc., are essentially a manifestation of spirit.

522. If the first aspect of the activity of the will, in this

sphere, is that it wills *itself*, its second aspect is that it wills what transcends itself, and what is, therefore, not merely subjective, but objective. The will is, on the one hand, universal; it is the I = I. On the other hand it is individual; it is *this* I. In willing the universal, it, as universal, wills itself; and in willing the universal, it, as individual, wills what transcends itself, the objective. For its aspect as individual is the aspect of its subjectivity. Hence, combining these two aspects, what the will produces by its action is (1) spiritual, (2) objective. It is thus **objective spirit**.

523. Because it wills itself it is essentially *free will*. Objective spirit, therefore, is founded on the notion of free will. Institutions are the embodiments of freedom. Laws are the conditions of freedom. In being governed by the law I am being governed by the universal, and by the universal which I myself have projected into the world; and I am therefore governed by myself, and am free. In actual history, of course, there have been and are bad and unjust laws. Such laws, however, are not an embodiment of the universal, and are consequently manifestations of unfreedom. Thus a law made solely in the interests of a particular *class*, or even of a particular individual (*e.g.* the king in an undeveloped primitive despotism may make laws to benefit only himself), do not proceed from the universal essence of spirit as spirit. On the contrary they embody the private and particular aims of individuals which are opposed to the universal. In obeying such laws, therefore, I am not governed by myself, but am in bondage. But the inherent nature of law, as true law, is to embody universality, *i.e.* to embody myself.

524. Hegel's treatment of objective spirit thus covers those parts of philosophy which are usually called ethics and politics. It also contains a philosophy of law. But his ethical and political theories differ from those of most other philosophers in this, that they are not regarded as detached portions of philosophy, but are developed in their proper places in the organic unity of the system. Another philosopher might produce a metaphysic, and then an ethic, and then perhaps an aesthetic,—as if all these were separate subjects, or at best as

if they were connected merely by some loose bond of analogy or similarity of procedure. To go about things in this purely empirical way, pecking here and there at bits of the universe, considering isolated problems and producing isolated solutions, is of course abhorrent to the systematic procedure of Hegel. For him everything must be deduced, and its necessity shown. Everything must appear—not hanging in the air—but in its proper place in the organic whole which is the universe. The philosophy of objective spirit, therefore, does not take up institutions, laws, moral codes, etc., haphazard as they chance to present themselves. It deduces them from one another in their proper order.

525. To deduce an institution is to show its *necessity*, to show that there is a logical necessity, a necessity of reason, that it should arise at the place and in the way in which it does arise. Hence all the institutions which we study in objective spirit are regarded by Hegel as the necessary forms in which reason embodies itself. From this point of view it is seen that all theories which regard laws, morals, social institutions, etc., as mere shifts, mechanical contrivances introduced for the sake of expediency or convenience, are shallow and worthless. That there should be the institutions of property, contract, law, government, family, etc.—this is a rational necessity. None of these things are mere expedients and contrivances for bringing about adventitious ends. Each and all of them are the essential and necessary forms in which spirit embodies itself in the world. They are the manifestation of reason. They are phases of the necessary self-evolution of the Idea. They are steps in the progress by which the Absolute becomes, in the world-process, conscious of itself and of what it is. They are themselves manifestations of the Absolute, and, as such, have absolute validity. They are not merely human *devices* for securing unessential ends, for satisfying subjective wants which have no meaning in the world-process. The view which thinks that human beings *happen* to be here, and *happen* to be constituted in such and such a way, and to have such and such needs for the securing of which they " invent " morals, laws, society, etc., but that all this is

indifferent to the essential purpose of the world—if it has any purpose—such a view Hegel regards as false and worthless. Institutions are not "invented." They necessarily are; they arise from the very nature of things, and express the inner meaning of the universe. The views that the state is a mutual agreement of all with all for the protection of life and property, that punishment is justifiable only as a deterrent, that morality is based on expediency and utility, are from this point of view, seen to be essentially worthless.

526. The general view of ethics here developed may profitably be compared with the ethics of Kant. Kant saw that morality, as being a universal and a law, cannot be founded upon what is *not* universal, upon feelings, private intuitions, empirical standards of utility, etc. It must be founded upon the universal element in man, that is, upon *reason*. But reason, for Kant, meant the abstract understanding whose canon is empty identity. Hence his principle of morals was that the individual must act upon universal maxims and rules. He must so act that he could, without self-contradiction, will the maxim upon which he acted to be a universal law. Thus a man must not break his promise, because if the breaking of promises were erected into a universal rule, promises themselves would cease to exist, and we should thus have a self-contradiction. All this amounts to, however, is that right action is defined as *self-consistent* action, action which does not contradict itself. Therefore, if a man could contrive to be consistently evil he would obey the Kantian maxim. Mere consistency, obedience to the formal laws of identity and contradiction, can never yield a concrete moral code, any more than mere consistency in logic can yield material truth. It is impossible to extract from this abstract universal any *content* whatever. No doubt, for example, to break a promise is self-contradictory, *if* the institution of promises exists in the world. But why should this institution exist at all? Kant's principles afford no answer.

Hegel, like Kant, founds morality upon reason, upon the universal. But the universal in his case is not the empty and abstract universal of the understanding. It is the concrete universal, the Notion. The concrete universal produces its content, *i.e.* its differentia and species, out of itself. It is, therefore, capable of yielding, not merely an empty principle of identity and consistency, but the concrete body of institutions which make up the content of morality and the state. It tells us, not merely that *if* there are promises, they must be kept, but also how and why there must be promises. The institution of contract (promise) is *deduced*. And so with the institutions of property, marriage, criminal law, etc. Thus the Hegelian ethic contains all that is true, good, and noble, in Kant's ethical system without its defects. What was great in Kant was that he repudiated shallow utilitarian views which would make the moral law conditional on circumstances, which would make it a mere human contrivance without any foundation in the essential being of the universe, and exhibited it instead as having an absolute and unconditional validity in this or any rational universe. His defect was that the idea of morality remained in his hands an empty abstraction, without body. Hegel is equally the champion of the claim of morals to essential nobility, to absolute validity, but with him morality is no longer an empty name, but is replete with content. Kant's absurd view that duty must be done without passion or inclination is due to the same defect of abstraction, and is equally impossible for Hegel.

527. The freedom of the will is likewise vindicated by Hegel. But, as with Kant, freedom is not interpreted as mere caprice, motiveless action, but as autonomy, self-determination. The will is free if and so far as it wills the universal. That is to say, if its acts are in accordance with right, with the law (moral or legal), it is free. For the law of right is its own law. It is its own universality which it has produced out of itself and erected in objectivity. The universality of the ego is, subjectively, merely the self-identical $I = I$. When this is made objective, it can only appear as an objective universal, *i.e.* a *law*. In obeying the law I obey only my essential and true self. But if the action of the will is contrary to right, if it contradicts the universal, and proceeds merely according to its private, particular, and selfish, interests, it is then not free.

For these selfish interests are not the embodiment of the true self whose essential is universality. They belong to man as a part of nature rather than as a spirit. And the will is, in such case, rather to be regarded as still in bondage to nature. And this is genuinely bondage, unfreedom, because to be ruled by nature is to be ruled by the external world, by what is *not* me.

528. If it be asked what justification there is for distinguishing between the " true " self and any other part of the self, and why its aspect of universality should be regarded as " true " rather than its aspect of particularity, the answer is simple. Feeling, appetite, impulse, have been deduced in their proper places in the foregoing pages. In the dialectic development of subjective spirit it will be seen that these particular and immediate aspects of spirit appear early, and that the universal aspects of spirit, both as cognition and as will, are the last to appear. The later phase in the dialectic is always the " truth of " the earlier. The true self is therefore the self as universal, whether in will or in thought.

529. In objective spirit human freedom objectifies itself in the external world. To enable it to do this there must be an external world to provide it with the material upon which it is to work, and which it is to mould into its own forms. The existence of such an outward material has already been deduced in the sphere of subjective spirit. As soul (anthropology) the spirit had private and personal needs, physical qualities and conditions, and these of course still subsist. As consciousness (phenomenology) it developed out of itself a definite external object. As mind (psychology) it had its own content which, though internal, was yet external to it. All these forms of externality constitute the material which the will now works up into a world of objective intelligence, and in which it embodies itself.

530. Objective spirit is regarded by Hegel as the sphere of " right " or " law." Right or law is the objective universality of the will in general. The term therefore includes legal right, moral right, and state right.

Objective spirit develops itself through the three phases of (1) abstract right, (2) morality, (3) social ethics.

CHAPTER I

ABSTRACT RIGHT

531. The will, conceived in the first instance as merely implicit, as "in itself," as not yet having gone forth into externality, is simply the abstract ego, the I = I. This is a pure self-identity; it refers to nothing outside itself, but is simple self-reference. As such it excludes from itself all otherness. It refers to and returns only upon itself. As excluding all others, it is a self-enclosed unit, a "one." As a "one," it is an individual, a single self. But because in referring itself to itself, it thereby distinguishes itself from itself (208), it therefore has itself for its object. It is *self*-consciousness. It is not merely I. It is I = I. It is not merely consciousness or a bare ego. But, in addition to this, it *knows* itself as ego. As a single individual which is conscious, not merely of the external world, but of itself as an ego, it is a *person*.

Not every consciousness is a person. That animals, though conscious, are not persons, goes without saying. And in Roman Law slaves were not regarded as persons but as things. A person, as such, has rights, whereas a thing has no rights. The Roman slave had no rights, and the animal may also be regarded as having no rights.[1] So far all this is mere assertion. It is to be deduced, however, in the following way.

532. The self-conscious I = I is a self-enclosed unit. It refers only to itself, *and is therefore infinite*. As infinite it is an absolute end, and cannot be used as a means. Hence one person cannot treat another person merely as a means to his

---

[1] It might be said that the animal has the right to be kindly treated. It is doubtful, however, whether this can be regarded as a right in the animal, although it is no doubt the duty of man to treat animals well.

own ends, but is bound to treat that other person as, equally with himself, an end. This gives me, as a person, my rights, and also my duties to other persons. The general law of right therefore is: "Be a person and respect others as persons." [1]

Thus what constitutes a person and gives him rights is not mere consciousness, but self-consciousness. For consciousness as such is limited by its object, and is therefore finite. But the object which limits self-consciousness is only itself, and to be self-limited, or self-determined, is to be infinite. And *it is on the infinitude of the self that its personality and rights are founded*. And it is for this reason that "things" have no rights as against persons, and are therefore subject to the wills of persons. Persons as such have an absolute right over things.

533. The sphere of **abstract right** is the sphere of those rights and duties which accrue to human beings, considered abstractly, *i.e.* simply as persons, and not yet as citizens of states. Apart altogether from my rights as a citizen, I as a human being, as a person, have rights. It is these that are here considered. It may be objected that the institutions which Hegel deduces under this head, namely property, contract, and punishment of wrong, all imply a settled social state, and could not exist without such a state. This is true, but irrelevant. It is equally true that sensation cannot exist without thought. Yet sensation was deduced very early in the sphere of subjective spirit, and long before thought made its appearance. Hegel's method is to deduce first the abstraction and afterwards the concrete state in which alone the earlier abstraction finds its true being. It may be true that property, contract, punishment, can only exist in a definite and intelligible way in an organized society. But this does not alter the fact that these rights are based, not upon the state, but upon the single person. The right to possess property is inherent in the person as such, and exists by virtue of his mere personality. The fact that he cannot in practice effectively exercise this right until the state is developed makes no difference to this truth.[2]

[1] *Phil. of Right*, § 36.
[2] In the *Phenomenology of Mind* the "person" is also deduced. But person there seems to have a different signification from person as treated

Abstract right develops itself through three phases: (1) property, (2) contract, (3) wrong.

SECTION I

PROPERTY

534. The subjective will is confronted with an external world (529). Its task, as we have already seen, is to embody itself in this external world, to mould this material into the likeness of itself. The will, however, is now a *person*, and the external object is, correspondingly, a *thing*. The person has a right over the thing (532). This is the institution of **property**.

A person is an absolute end, who cannot be used as a means. But the thing, just because it is not a person, is not an end, but may be appropriated by the person as a means to his own satisfaction. This is the rational basis of property. " Every man has the right to turn his will upon a thing or make the thing an object of his will, that is to say, to set aside the mere thing and recreate it as his own . . . Only the will is unlimited and absolute, while others things in contrast with the will are merely relative. To appropriate is at bottom only to manifest the majesty of my will towards things, by demonstrating that they are not self-complete and have no purpose of their own." [1]

535. It is not merely property, but *private* property, which is here shown to be a necessity of reason. For the right of property springs from and inheres in the *single* individual person. Hegel is therefore opposed to schemes for the abolition of private property. But it is worth remarking that his teaching is not really inconsistent with modern socialistic ideas. The true essence of socialism, if it understands itself,

here in the *Encyclopaedia* and the *Philosophy of Right*. In the *Phenomenology* the person is deduced after the state and civil society, and means the person as legally invested with rights by positive law. (*Phen.* ii. pp. 478-485.)

[1] *Phil. of Right*, § 44, Addition.

is not an absolute objection to private property as such, but to the inequitable *distribution* of private property. No scheme of communism can ever really get rid of the necessity of private property. For even if wealth become nominally the property of the state, it must at last be divided among individuals, appropriated and consumed by them. Food can only be eaten by individuals, whatever the form of Government, and in eating it they make it their absolute private property. Even a public park can only be enjoyed by individuals, and the action of the state in nationalizing it does not really abolish private property in it. It merely distributes it among *all* the individuals instead of allowing this or that person to exclude others from their share. The necessity of private property in this sense of the appropriation of things by individual persons is all that really follows from Hegel's deduction, though he may have imagined that he deduced more than this. He remarks that, if exceptions to the rule of private property are to be made, the state alone can be suffered to make them.[1]

536. The question of the alleged "equality of all men" also falls to be considered here, for it is sometimes interpreted to mean that property should be equally divided among all men. It is true that all men, as being *persons*, as absolute ends, are equal. And it is just for this reason that one person cannot be subordinated as a means to another. And since every man is a person it may be deduced from this that every man has the right to own property. But the question of the *amount* of property that each may own cannot be decided on this basis. For each man is, it must be remembered, much more than a mere person. He has in addition certain definite capacities, abilities, character, and so forth. Individuals differ in these respects, and there will be corresponding differences in the amount of property which each may own. Individuals are all the same, *i.e.* equal, inasmuch as each is an $I = I$, a person. In other respects they are different, *i.e.* unequal.

537. Property involves three different species of right on the part of the will, namely (*a*) the act of possession, (*b*) the

[1] *Phil. of Right*, § 46, Addition.

use of the object, (*c*) the right of relinquishment. These may be briefly discussed.

(*a*) If my will is to embody itself in an outward object, it is not enough that I merely inwardly and subjectively will the object to be "mine." Such a mere intention remains subjective, and the task of will here is to objectify itself. There must be, therefore, a positive act of possession. Such an act may be performed either by simple bodily grasp, or by working upon the object and fashioning it into the shape which I will it to have, or by merely designating or marking the object. The act of possession further serves to signify to other persons that the object is mine, and not theirs, that I have set my will in it and that it is thus already appropriated. For since the right of property is a right which inheres in the single self, it equally involves the right to exclude other selves. And it also involves their duty to respect my property. For my property is now an objectification of my will, and to lack respect for it is to lack respect for me as a person.

(*b*) The right to use property follows from the conception of it as a mere *thing* which has no rights against the owner as a *person*. It is, therefore, rightly treated as a *means*, *i.e.* used.

(*c*) Since a person, as such, has the absolute right to set his will upon an object, and so make it his own, he has equally the right to withdraw his will from it. He has the right, therefore, to relinquish his property.

538. Since property is only property by virtue of an exercise of the will, if the will ceases to be exercised towards the object it *ipso facto* becomes ownerless. This is the rational basis of the law of prescription. Thus prescription is deducible from the Notion, and is to be regarded as a necessity of reason, and not as a mere social expedient.

539. My life may be regarded as my property. But the right of relinquishment does not apply to life, *i.e.* suicide is not justifiable. For all rights of property are based upon the right and necessity of the will to objectify and realize itself. The right of relinquishment exists because it is a manifestation of will in the world. Suicide, however, is so far from

realizing and manifesting my will that it negates and abolishes it. And therefore no right of suicide exists.

SECTION II

CONTRACT

540. Contract is conceived by Hegel as transfer of property. And no doubt all contract is, at bottom, essentially of that nature. For property, in Hegel's terminology, includes not only material things, but labour, services, etc. I have the right of property over my labour. And therefore even a contract of personal service is an exchange of property.

541. The transition from property to contract is based upon the right of relinquishment. Two persons owning property have each the right to relinquish his property in favour of the other. This is **contract**.

542. It might be objected to this that it only proves that the person *can* transfer his property, not that he *must*, and that what the dialectic has to show is not the arbitrary possibility of contract, but its absolute necessity. The objection is not well founded. We are here in the sphere of *rights*. What the dialectic has to show is that the person *necessarily* has the *right* of contract, not that the person is compelled to exercise it. And this has been shown. The deduction is a genuine one. It has been proved that the notion (*Begriff*) of *person* necessarily involves the notion of his right to property. This necessarily involves his right to relinquishment, which in turn involves contract. What has been proved is that the notion of property contains the notion of contract implicit in it, and that the latter is thus produced out of the former. This is the nature of all deduction.

543. Just as a subjective intention is not a sufficient manifestation of the will in the sphere of property, but requires to be objectified by the act of possession, so here in contract an outward act is also necessary in addition to the internal intentions of the parties. This outward act is *performance*.

544. Marriage, it will be seen, is deduced, not here, but in the third division of the objective spirit, *i.e.* social ethics. From this it follows, and Hegel specifically remarks,[1] that the view of marriage as simply a civil contract (popular with all who wish to weaken the marriage tie), is false and inadequate. Of this, of course, no proof can be given at this stage, and the remark is merely to be regarded as an anticipation. Its proof can only consist in the deduction of marriage in its proper sphere.

545. For the same reason the view of the state as a "social contract" is to be regarded as false.[2] The state also appears later on in the sphere of social ethics. "Contract arises out of the spontaneous choice of the persons. Marriage, indeed, has that point in common with contract, but with the state it is different. An individual cannot enter or leave the social condition at his option, since everyone is by his very nature a citizen of a state; if there is no state, reason claims that one should be founded."[3]

SECTION III

WRONG

546. Right is the objectification of the universal will. By universal will here is not meant the common will of all, or of a majority, or anything of that kind.[4] It may even be that the will of a single individual alone embodies the universal will, while all others are opposed to it. Not a mere extrinsic

---

[1] *Phil. of Right*, § 75, note.

[2] This, of course, does not mean merely that there never was historically such an event as the conclusion of a social contract. That goes without saying. What is here regarded as false is the view that, whatever its historical origin, the state is, in its essential nature, a contract. No doubt it may sometimes be useful and justifiable to use the category of contract in reference to the state (cf. Burke's famous dictum), just as it may suit us to say that God is being, or substance, instead of Absolute Idea. But God is much *more* than being, or substance, and the state is much *more* than a contract. Such views are not wholly false, but are utterly inadequate and fall short of the complete truth.

[3] *Phil. of Right*, § 75, note.

[4] "Rousseau ... conceives the will only in the limited form of the individual will, ... and regards the universal will not as the absolutely reasonable will, but only as the common will." (*Phil. of Right*, § 258, note.)

universality of allness, but the *intrinsic* universality of the will, the will which wills the intrinsically universal, *i.e.* the *rational* will, is the source of right. The *rational* will is the universal will. Now contract brings to light the full possibility of *voluntary acts* of individuals in the disposal, exchange and acquirement of property. The individual is intrinsically universal. He is the I = I. But in addition to this he is, as already deduced, a being of impulses, private interests, particular appetites, and the like. Hence arises the possibility that the voluntary acts, of which we now see that he is capable, may be dictated by these private ends, and may be opposed to the universal will, or to the law of right. This is **wrong**.

547. It is not, of course, necessarily the case that a man, in following his private interests, does wrong. For the content of what he, from private interest, wills, may be in accordance with the universal will; as happens, for example, when a man is honest merely because honesty is good policy. But if a man, pursuing his private interests, does an act which is not in accord with the universal will, then his act is a *wrong*.

548. There are three degrees or species of wrong. We are not, of course, here concerned with wrong in the sense of moral evil. Morality has not yet been deduced. The right which we have been considering is not moral right, but legal right, *e.g.* the rights of property and contract. So, too, the wrong here deduced is legal wrong, breach of legal right. The first degree of wrong is (1) *unpremeditated wrong*. This forms the subject-matter of civil actions. Such wrong arises because several individuals may claim mutually inconsistent rights of property or contract. Hence arise collisions. The essential point of the wrong here is that the doer of it believes himself to be acting under the law of right. He does not, as the criminal does, repudiate right altogether. On the contrary he affirms it, and appeals to it. It is only the particular right of the other party which he negates. And his very act is, or is intended to be, an affirmation of right in general.

(2) The second degree of wrong is *fraud*. Here the individual *purports* to act under the law of right, but in fact consciously acts against it. The other party is imposed upon

and made to believe that he gets his rights. But the supposed right which is done is a mere appearance, an unreality.

(3) The highest degree of wrong is *crime*. Here the individual does not admit the law of right at all. Nor does he even purport to act under it. He openly negates it. And what he negates is not the particular right of the individual, but the universal law of right as such.

549. In wrong, right is outraged and negated. Right, however, is the positive existence, wrong a mere negation and unreality. Right, therefore, must restore itself by negating this negation. In civil wrong it does so by compensation, restoration, or other means. The universal negation of right, however, which constitutes crime, is negated by *punishment*. In punishment right restores itself and is strengthened and confirmed.

Crime is an "untrue," because a self-contradictory, existence. It, of course, exists. But it is an unreality, a mere appearance, a nullity. It is self-contradictory because it is an act which contradicts the essential notion of the will and the true conception of human action. The essential notion of the will is its universality, and it is precisely this which the crime negatives. It is, therefore, an act of the will which contradicts the will, and is accordingly not anything positive, but a meaningless act which is a mere nullity. Its essential nullity is exposed when the day of **punishment** comes.

550. Punishment is, therefore, an absolute act of justice. To regard it merely as a deterrent, or even as intended essentially to reform the criminal, is to take a shallow view of it, for it is to regard it as a mere means to a further end. Justice is, however, an absolute end in itself. No doubt it is a good thing if punishment deters people from committing crimes, or if it helps to reform the criminal, and no one can be blamed for taking account of these excellent ends. But to place the essential nature and the justification of punishment in these ends is wrong. Apart from all such utilitarian purposes which punishment may incidentally serve, it is the absolute law of right that pain and punishment must follow

upon crime. It is not a human contrivance for securing property or life. It is rather a law of the universe, a necessity of reason, which springs from the central heart of things.

551. Equally objectionable is the theory which regards punishment as a safety-valve for feelings of private revenge, or as regulating and legitimatizing revenge. Private revenge may, as far as its *content* goes, execute justice on the criminal. But true justice is an act of the universal will, that is to say, an act of right. Revenge, on the other hand, springs from the particular motives of the particular will. It is, therefore, a new wrong. Justice abolishes the crime and restores right. But revenge merely adds a second wrong to the first. This new wrong again calls forth vengeance, and so we have an infinite progress—the vendetta. But justice, because it is not a new wrong, but a restoration of right, does not call forth a new act of wrong; it concludes the matter.

552. An animal may be beaten or otherwise made to suffer in order to deter it from objectionable actions, as when men, in training their pet dogs, are compelled to beat them. This, however, is not intended as an act of justice, but is a mere deterrent. And the deterrent theory of punishment, in fact, puts men on the same level as the animal. The difference, however, is this. The criminal is a rational being, whose essence is universality; the animal is not. It is, therefore, the inherent right of the criminal to be treated as a rational and universal being. Hence the crime cannot be regarded as a mere objectionable act, as a dog's delinquencies may, but must be viewed as an affirmation of a law which the criminal wills to be universal. Violence, therefore, must be punished by violence. For the criminal has, by his own act, asserted the law of violence. It is his right as a rational being that his act should be taken as importing a universal, as erecting violence into a law. It is the criminal, therefore, who punishes himself. It is his own will. He has asserted violence as *his* law, and the application of this law to himself is justice. In the beating of the animal, on the other hand, there is no element of right or justice. It is a mere act of expediency. The deterrent theory of justice treats man as an irrational

being and forgets his essential dignity and grandeur, in which the criminal, too, shares, so that punishment is his inalienable *right*. And in this connection Hegel remarks that "the desire of Beccaria that men should consent to their own punishment is reasonable, but the criminal has already yielded consent through his own act."[1] He has yielded consent not, of course, for the trivial reason that he knows when he acts what justice ordains and voluntarily takes the risk, but because his act is in its very nature an appeal to violence, an *assertion* that violence is the *law*, that violence is *right*. It is by this assertion that he has already yielded consent to the application of force to himself.

553. It was Beccaria, too, who argued that capital punishment is unjustifiable because the social contract cannot be supposed to contain the individual's consent to his own death. Hegel replies that that state is not a contract, nor is the protection and security of the individual its unconditional object. On the contrary the state is a higher end than the individual, and the life of the individual may on occasion be rightly sacrificed for the ends of the state. Hegel, therefore, supports capital punishment. But he is in sympathy with its further restriction. He thinks that Beccaria's attack on capital punishment did good, because it induced moderation, enabled men to see what crimes deserved death and what did not, and made the death-penalty far less frequent, as should be the case with the extreme penalty of the law.

554. The vindication and restoration of right, through punishment, closes the sphere of abstract right. We next pass to *morality*. Before doing so, however, it will be fitting to point out how far Hegel has wandered, in the present section, from the strictest interpretation of the dialectic method. We have passed through the triad, (1) property, (2) contract, (3) wrong. It is quite impossible to see any sense in which contract can be said to be the opposite of property. And it is equally impossible to regard wrong as the unity of property and contract. It is true that in the *Encyclopaedia* what appears to be deduced is not wrong itself, but the con-

[1] *Phil. of Right*, § 100, Addition.

flict between right and wrong. For which reason the section [1] there is headed "Right versus wrong," whereas the corresponding section in the *Philosophy of Right* is simply headed "Wrong."[2] But this does not appear to help the matter at all. It is just as difficult to view the conflict as the unity of property and contract as it is to regard wrong itself in that light.

[1] *Phil. of Mind*, § 496.   [2] *Phil. of Right*, § 82.

CHAPTER II

MORALITY

555. Abstract right is the *outward* objectification of freedom. Freedom embodies itself in a *thing*—property. We are not, in the sphere of abstract right, concerned at all with the *inward* state of the will, or the subjective consciousness of the individual. We do not, for example, consider questions of motive, purpose, intention. Morality, however, is not an outward *thing*, like property. It essentially concerns the state of the soul. It is an affair of the individual's inward conscience. Hegel uses the word morality in a restricted sense peculiar to himself, the import of which will be explained shortly. But for the moment the essential point to grasp is that the chief difference between abstract right and morality is that the former has its being and embodiment in the external world, while the latter is an affair of the internal consciousness.

556. The transition from abstract right to morality is brought about through the consideration of crime and punishment. Wrong, and in particular, crime, reveals for the first time the fact that a distinction and opposition has arisen between the particular will of the individual and the universal will. In crime the individual will pits itself against the universal will. But the notion of the will is to be universal. Its essential nature, its true self, is its universality. Therefore the individual will, in opposing itself in crime to the universal will, is putting itself in opposition to its own true self. *Such a will does not coincide with the notion of will.* There is a breach, a disharmony, between the will as it *is* and the

will as it *ought* to be.[1] This " ought " is in general the element of obligation in morality, and it attaches to the inward being of the subject. It is *he* who ought to be different from what he is. So that here already we have the inwardness which is the characteristic of morality as distinguished from abstract right. But this is not yet the complete deduction of morality. We have deduced the existence of a discord between the will and its notion. This discord, however, is a mere negation. The particular will, in opposing itself to the universal will, negates the latter, and in so doing negates right. Punishment, however, is the negation of this negation. It is this negation of the negation which gives us the positive idea of morality. For the breach between the will and its notion is the negation ; it is the negating of the universal will, or right, by the individual will. The negation of the negation is, therefore, the negation of this breach, *i.e.* it is the idea of the will of the individual in harmony with the notion of the will. And for the individual will to be thus in accord with its notion, to be what it ought to be, is **morality**.

557. This process is described by Hegel as a turning back of the will into itself. In abstract right the will passed out of

[1] This passage will not be intelligible unless the reader has clearly grasped the meaning of the word notion (*Begriff*) as used by Hegel. The fact that Hegel uses this word with three different applications is apt to be most confusing to the beginner. Firstly, there is *the* Notion, the category of pure Logic which supersedes essence, and has been fully treated in its place. Secondly, any of the categories of the Logic are referred to as 'notions.' Being, becoming, appearance, are notions. These are pure thoughts which differ from Plato's Ideas only because they are non-sensuous, universal and necessary, and because they are not *abstract* universals, but self-generating universals which give birth to their own differentiae and species. Thirdly, Hegel speaks of the notions of particular things, the notions of man, of freedom, of the plant, the animal, or, as here, the notion of the will. This kind of notion differs from the second kind of notion, viz. pure categories, only in this that they are thoughts, universals, which do not apply, as the categories do, to everything in the universe, but only to specific things, man, animal, will, and so on. The notions of these things are their concepts, the general ideas of them, just like Plato's Idea of the man, Idea of the plant, etc. But they differ from Plato's Ideas in the following respects. Plato's Ideas are reached by mere empirical induction, and hence do not possess necessity. Hegel's notions are deduced, and are therefore *necessary* concepts. Plato's Ideas are abstract, and therefore sterile and motionless. Hegel's notions generate their opposites, and so their differentiae and species, out of themselves. But, like Plato's Ideas, the notions are *definitions* and give the essential nature of the thing, what the thing *ought* to be. Hence here we find that the notion of the will is what the will ought to be.

itself into externality; it embodied itself in external *things*, which became property. Property is freedom, or the will, become outward. In morality the will returns into its own subjectivity. It is no longer the *thing* which is to embody my will. It is now *I*, the inward ego, which is to embody its own freedom in itself, in its inward state, as a moral I.

558. Because the term morality, as used by Hegel, applies exclusively to the inward state of the will, it is much more restricted in its scope here than it is in popular parlance. Morality is, for Hegel, something purely subjective. It therefore excludes all positive duties connected with the family, society and the state, all of which are objective institutions. Even what is especially regarded in popular speech as morality, namely chastity, does not fall, for Hegel, under the head of morality at all. For sexual relations are an affair which concerns the family. The family, society, and the state are not yet in existence. They have not been deduced. They come later under the head of social ethics. Hegel cannot be criticized adversely on this account. He does not, as we shall see, disparage the duties of the individual in the family and the state by not including them under the term morality. Very much the contrary. It is a mere matter of terminology. He chooses to use the word morality in a sense more restricted than its common use. So long as we understand the sense in which he uses the term, no harm is done.

559. Morality, like abstract right, is one-sided. Abstract right is purely objective, centred in an outward thing, and the inward state of the subject, his motives and aims, are indifferent to it. Morality is the other one-sidedness. It is purely subjective. It never gets itself actualized in the world in the form of objective institutions, or, when it does so, it has ceased to be morality and has passed into social ethics. Social ethics is the concrete unity of subjective and objective in the sphere of objective spirit. And it may even be said in a sense that morality itself does not come to exist until it has passed beyond itself into social ethics. For if morality be defined as the concord of the existent will with its notion, *i.e.* with the universal will, then we find that this concord is

not actually brought about till we reach the stage of social ethics. Only then is the will completely coincident with its notion. The development in the present sphere, that of morality, is the process of reaching that coincidence, of overcoming the breach which has arisen between the will and its notion. And it is for this reason that morality is the sphere of what *ought* to be but is *not*.

560. Morality is the return of the will upon itself, its retirement from the outward world of things into its own self-centred inwardness. For this reason the will is here infinite and self-determined. And the same result arises from the consideration that in morality we have the negation of the negation (556). Negation is in general the sphere of finitude. Negation of negation is the infinitude which has absorbed its opposite into itself (204). In morality, therefore, the will, as self-determined, is a law unto itself. In abstract right it was determined by the outward thing, property. It had the outward thing as its object. Now, however, the will, which has returned upon itself, has itself for its object. And the fact that in morality the will is a law unto itself gives us in general *the right of the subject*. Legal or abstract right gave rise to commands and prohibitions which were imposed upon the will from an external source, the thing. The position of the will in morality is that it recognizes no mere external authority as binding upon it, but only the dictates of its own reason (*conscience*). I, as a rational being, cannot be subjected to the imposition of commands which I do not myself recognize as right and reasonable. Only what is approved by my own conscience can be a law for me. This is the right of the subject. It is the source of the idea of democracy and also of that " right of private judgment " which is often stated to be the guiding principle of Protestantism.

As morality is a one-sided abstraction which has to be corrected by social ethics, so the right of the subject is itself one-sided, a half-truth, if taken in abstraction from the equally important *right of the object*. This latter makes its appearance in social ethics, where the objective institutions of the family, society, and the state, appear as having rights of control over the individual subject. Man, as rational and infinite, must be self-determined, and can tolerate no determination from an external source. The commands of the family and the state are indeed external to the individual. They are the side of objectivity in the ethical sphere. But it will appear in due course that this objectivity is itself nothing but a projection of subjectivity out of itself, that the object is but the subject which has put itself forth into objectivity, so that the subject, in being governed by this objectivity is governed only by himself. I, in obeying the rightful commands of the state, am obeying only my true self, *i.e.* myself as universal. But if this half-truth, the right of the subject, is taken in separation from the right of the object, and treated as if it were the whole and final truth, then it becomes in principle bad. The individual subject then claims that he alone is the absolute law-giver to himself, that he is subject to no control whatever, and is at liberty to act as he pleases, to set up his own whims, fancies, or capricious self-will, as his sole authority. In the political sphere this is the root-principle of anarchism, which puts exclusive emphasis on the right of the subject and denies any function to the state.

561. Morality passes through three stages, (1) purpose, (2) intention and well-being, (3) goodness and wickedness. It is only in the last that morality can properly be said to have come into existence. The first two are mere factors of the third.

SECTION I

PURPOSE

562. The will is essentially the I as *acting*, and is thus distinguished from cognition, which is the I as *thinking*. And because morality is an affair of the will, it is an affair of action. The will must put itself forth in action. Now the will can only act upon external objects in the external world, and its action consists in bringing about change in this external material. But because no external object is isolated, but

every object is linked to all other objects by causation and necessity, my action necessarily sets on foot a chain of consequences. And because this external world is the sphere of contingency and unreason, I cannot foresee all the consequences of my act. In acting I, so to speak, put forth part of myself into the infinite stream of outward events, which may carry it away into remote and strange regions. But, in the sphere of morality, I, as self-determined, admit nothing as binding upon me which does not issue from myself. Only what the will willed binds the will. For it to be bound by what it has not willed would be to be determined by what is not itself. I, therefore, cannot impute to myself all the unforeseen consequences of my act. To assume responsibility for an event is to admit it as binding upon me, and I cannot admit this as regards any event which was not in my consciousness when I acted, and which, therefore, did not issue forth out of me myself. To do so would be an infringement of my self-determination, an infringement of the right of the subject. Thus the right of the subject, which is the foundation of morality (as distinguished from social ethics), is that the subject should be held *responsible* only for what is in his **purpose**.

SECTION II

INTENTION AND WELL-BEING

563. The words purpose and intention are commonly used as synonymous. Hegel, however, decides to use the latter in a special sense.

The foundation of the subject's right to repudiate those consequences of his act which he could not foresee, consists in the fact that those consequences are the result, not of his will, but of external forces which have carried away the act of his will into unexpected trains of events. These unforeseen consequences are, as far as the subject is concerned, accidental, capricious, contingent. They may be anything. My eating an oyster might conceivably exercise an influence in the destruction of an empire. Any ingenious person could invent the intermediate links in the chain of events. It is because they are *accidental*, and not *necessary*, that I am not responsible for unforeseen consequences. But this involves the result that I am responsible for the *necessary* consequences of my act, and must be held to have intended them, even if, through my folly or ignorance, they were not foreseen by me, and not in my *purpose*. This is true in all cases save those of lunatics, children, etc., who, though potentially rational beings, are not actually so, and cannot be treated as such. The necessary consequences of an act are to be regarded as part of the act itself. For they are *my* act, since I am responsible for them. They constitute indeed the *universal and essential* inner nature of the act. If I hold a pistol to a man's head and pull the trigger, the necessary consequence —apart from unforeseen counteracting causes—is that the man will be killed. The mere pulling of the trigger, which is all *I* do, is in itself a trifle. The essential nature of my act, however, is that it is murder, and this lies, not in the act itself, but in the consequence. I *ought* to know the necessary consequences of my acts. I ought to know their essential character. And this essential nature of the act, when willed by me, is what Hegel calls my **intention.** Purpose comprises all the foreseen consequences of the act. Intention comprises, of the foreseen consequences, only those that are necessarily bound up with the act and constitute its special character.

564. The individual, besides being universal, is also this particular individual, and, as such, has his particular desires, aims, needs, etc. It is his right to satisfy these by his action, so long as their content is not contrary to the universal will. Hence, in addition to purpose and intention, every act has its particular *end*. If I shoot a man through the head, my *purpose* includes all the consequences of the act that are foreseen and accepted by the will. The *intention* is the universal character of the act, the necessary consequence, namely, the death of the man, murder. But I do not commit murder for the sake of murder. I do it for some particular

end which appears to have value for me as an individual subject, *e.g.* to get rid of a rival in love. My end may be either good or evil. But the distinction between good and evil is irrelevant for the moment. It does not make its appearance till the next section.

These subjective ends may be co-ordinated, or one end may be subordinated to another and made a means towards that other. When comprehended in a single general aim they constitute **well-being.** Well-being is the same as happiness, which has already been deduced under the head of practical mind (517), except that well-being, appearing, as it does, in the moral sphere, has a moral element, whereas happiness had none. The subject has a *right* to seek his well-being, and this right is the moral aspect of it. The kind of view which disparages the great deeds and productions of great men, and seeks always to attribute them to petty and selfish motives, vanity, and the like, is essentially shallow and worthless. For in the first place, the subjective satisfaction of the individual in his work, the gratification of his needs and aims, the fulfilment of his well-being, are his right, and are therefore perfectly legitimate. And, in the second place, these particular ends do not alter the fact that in performing a great work the individual is also seeking a universal end. While quite admitting that the poet may not be without thought for his personal fame, or even for money, it is psychologically false to suppose that this is his only motive, and that his poem is not for him an absolute end in itself, an end universal in character and having absolute value.

565. The view that morality must carry on a continual warfare against the satisfaction of oneself, and that one ought "to do with aversion what duty requires"[1] arises from the same abstract way of regarding the matter.

---

[1] A line of Schiller's intended to be a parody on the Kantian view that a good act loses its moral value if done from inclination instead of from duty.

SECTION III

GOODNESS AND WICKEDNESS

566. We have now developed the factors of the will in moral action, viz. purpose, intention, and well-being. But morality itself is still lacking. The point at which we began, in this chapter, was the contradiction, which made its appearance in crime, between the will and its notion, between the individual will and the universal will. We have now seen that the individual must act, and his act must have purpose, intention and end. If we combine these considerations we get the result that the ends, aims, and intentions of the individual will must coincide with the ends of the universal will. This is morality. The coincidence of the will with its notion is the *good*. The will which coincides with the notion of will, *i.e.* its universality, is in a state of **goodness.** The will which opposes itself to the universal will is in a state of **wickedness.** It sets up its mere caprices, whims, self-will as the law in opposition to reason and the universal. These caprices and whims are, in their essence, particular, and possess no universality. They are purely and solely *my* ends, *my* caprices, *my* will. They, therefore, have no validity as laws. What is universal in my will is not these particular ends, but the element of *reason*. Reason, as universal, is capable of being made a law. My will, as rational, is universal, is identical with the universal will. My will, as capricious and irrational, is a private affair of my own. Hence the will that wills rationally, that wills reason to be done in the world, is the good will. In fact the expression " the universal will " means nothing more nor less than the reasonable will. So far as my will is reasonable it is not merely my will but is universal; for reason *is* the universal; it is common to all rational beings, whereas my self-will and my whims are merely my own. Hence when I will reasonably my will coincides with the universal will; it coincides with its notion, and is, therefore, good. When it wills merely private ends, which are unreasonable, it is evil. As we have already seen,

the mere fact of willing my private ends is not in itself evil. For those ends may be essentially reasonable and therefore universal, notwithstanding that I seek them for my personal well-being. It is only when my ends are solely *my* ends, when they are in their nature intrinsically opposed to the universal, that I do evil.

567. Morality, therefore, consists in willing and doing the universal, the rational. Good action is rational action. But this, so far, gives us a merely empty and abstract formula. It provides no answer to the question, *what* acts, *what* ends, are reasonable and universal. The position at which we have arrived is, in fact, the same as the Kantian position. For Kant too what was essential to moral action was its universality. That an action must be capable of being universalized into a law was, for him, the test of its being moral. But this means, as we saw, merely that logical consistency in action is the test of goodness. Logical consistency, observance of the laws of identity and contraction, was the highest idea Kant could form of reason. For his philosophy was still governed by the understanding, and what he called reason was the mere identity and absence of contradiction which are the laws of the understanding. Hence to act without contradiction was for him to act rationally, and so, to act morally. Up to the present, therefore, the Hegelian maxim of morality is the same as the Kantian : act rationally, act universally. But Kant never got beyond this. Out of mere consistency nothing *new* can ever come. Hence it was impossible for him ever to deduce from his principles any positive duties, or to say *what* acts are rational and moral.

568. The Hegelian principle of reason is not mere consistency, but is the self-differentiating universal. Hence for Hegel it is possible to deduce positive duties from the maxim, " act rationally." But up to the present this has not been done. We are still left with an empty command to act the universal. The positive duties which flow from this do not make their appearance in the sphere of morality at all. They only appear under the head of social ethics.

We must not expect then, in the present chapter, to get any

deduction of positive duties. We must not expect to get beyond the general maxim, act universally and rationally. *What* acts are considered universal and rational, and *why* they are so, will be considered in the sphere of social ethics.

569. Meanwhile, one other remark is here to be made. The position of morality, as distinguished from social ethics, is the position of the *right of the subject*. The subject here claims to be absolutely self-determined, to be a law unto himself. This means that to answer the question *what* acts are universal, rational, and good, I will appeal only to myself. I will search within my own breast for the answer. Since I am a rational being, I claim that I can know with absolute certitude what is rational, universal and good, from the inner resources of my own consciousness alone. This attitude is the attitude of *conscience*, which accordingly makes its appearance here in the sphere of morality.

570. To sum up the present discussion. The good is defined as the coincidence of the will with its notion. The notion of the will is the will as universal. What alone is universal is reason. Therefore goodness consists in rational action. When the will wills rationally it is, *ipso facto*, not merely the individual will. It is then in itself the universal will. And this identity of the particular will with the universal will, *i.e.* with the notion of the will, constitutes the good. Evil or wickedness is the decision of the will to follow its own irrational caprices and private ends in opposition to reason, *i.e.* to the universal will. Since the essential nature of the will is its universality, the will which wills evil is out of accord with its true self, and is a self-contradictory existence. Conscience is the claim of the individual, as a rational being, to be self-determined, to find within his *own* reason the universal reason, the law of good.

CHAPTER III

SOCIAL ETHICS

571. The deduction of *social ethics* from *morality* is, as given by Hegel,[1] extremely obscure. But the meaning of it, if I understand it rightly, is as follows. We have now arrived at conscience on the one hand and the good on the other. But the good is utterly empty and abstract. It possesses no filling. It is merely the empty form of universality. Universality in action is its definition. But what particular acts possess this universality it is impossible to say. Thus the good, in itself, is not any particular concrete act or thing at all. It is a mere general idea, an abstraction. It is a universality which is equivalent to nothingness, for it has no content. Conscience, on the other hand, is just the same empty universality. It, likewise, does not know *what* its duties are. It merely knows in general that, *if* it has any duties, it is out of itself that they must be produced, and that it alone is the judge of what they are. But *what* these duties are, it, as yet, cannot say. Hence conscience, like the good, is void of content, empty, a mere abstraction. And it is not merely empty; it is also an empty *universal*. For it is the ego; it is the $I = I$; and the ego is essentially a universality. Thus nothing whatever can be said of the good, save that it is empty universality, mere vacuity. And nothing whatever can be said of conscience, save that it, likewise, is a vacuous universal. And as neither of them has any further determination, it is impossible to assign any difference between them; for to assign a difference is to state a determination which is

[1] In the *Phil. of Mind*, § 512, and in the *Phil. of Right*, § 141.

possessed by the one and not by the other. What we have, therefore, is the absolute *identity* of conscience and the good.

Now, in the moral sphere, conscience is the side of subjectivity, the good is the side of objectivity. That conscience is pure subjectivity is obvious. And the good is objective because it is the object of the will, because it is what the subject is to *do*, to put forth, by means of action, into the objective world. Hence the identity of conscience and the good, which we have reached, is the identity of the subjective and objective in the moral sphere. This identity of moral subjectivity and moral objectivity is the **Ethical System,** consisting of the family, civil society, and the state, which is the subject of **Social Ethics.** The particularization of the ethical system into family, civil society, and the state, has, of course, not yet taken place. They are reached by further detailed deductions, and are mentioned here merely by way of anticipation. All we have to grasp at present is that the idea of the identity of subjective and objective here deduced is, in general, the idea of the sphere of the ethical system. For the ethical system consists of *institutions* which, as such, are definitely established and existent in the outward world, are objective. But at the same time, these objective institutions constitute no mere alien otherness subsisting in absolute opposition to the subject. They are essentially the product of the subject himself, the projection of himself, and his reason, into the outward world. They are the putting forth of himself into objectivity. They are, therefore, subjective as well as objective, and this unity of subjective and objective is just what has been deduced. This deduction, however, gives us merely the idea of the general sphere, not the particular institutions, which are yet to come.

572. The ethical system, as the synthesis of the triad, is the unity of abstract right and morality. Abstract right was purely objective, morality purely subjective. The ethical system is the unity of the subjective and objective in this sphere.

573. The ethical system is the identity of the will with its notion, an identity which was sought but not found in

morality. There the identity of the particular will with its notion, *i.e.* with the universal will, was merely an obligation, something which ought to be, but was not. Here it actually *is*. It is *there*, positively existent in the world in the form of institutions. These institutions are the universal will become actual; they are rationality objectified. Hence these institutions embody the true self of the individual. For the true self of the individual is his universality and rationality. The family and the state are, therefore, something higher than the individual in so far as he exists in separation from them, *i.e.* in so far as his will deviates from the universal will. The essential truth of the individual is the state. It is only the untruth of the individual which can be in opposition to the state—assuming, that is, that the state is a genuine one, an embodiment of freedom, and not a mere embodiment of the selfish interests of some particular class or individual, as sometimes happens in actual history. The state is a higher end than the individual, and may, in certain circumstances, rightly demand the sacrifice of the individual to its ends.

574. This view is sometimes quoted as proving that Hegel was a reactionary, always ready to suppress the individual in favour of the state. If we persist in regarding the interests of the individual as necessarily opposed to the interests of the state, this will be a correct deduction. But for Hegel the state is the true self of the individual. His very individuality only finds its perfect expression in the state. For the state is simply his true self, *i.e.* his universality, objectified. The interests of the state are, therefore, the true and essential interests of the individual, and the sacrifice of the latter to the state is only his sacrifice to his own higher self, not to some external and alien authority.

575. For the same reason the duties which are imposed upon the individual by his membership of the family, society, or the state, are to be regarded, not as limitations of his freedom, but, on the contrary, as the embodiment of it. Freedom does not consist in being governed by no law, nor in the absence of all restraints. It consists in being self-determined, governed by one's own law. But the laws of the

state, the edicts of the family, are precisely the establishment in objectivity of the true self of the individual. In obeying them he obeys only himself, and finds therein his freedom. A duty is a limitation only of the natural will, of the caprices, selfish whims, and non-universal impulses of the individual, and these constitute the untrue side of his nature. To regard marriage, for example, as involving a loss of freedom, is a false view. In it, on the contrary, the individual finds his liberation.

576. It was said in the last chapter that the positive duties of man, which are lacking in the empty universality of subjective morality, would make their appearance under the head of social ethics. What Hegel actually deduces in the present part of his system, however, are not duties as such, but institutions. But the relations in which the individual finds himself to these institutions are his duties. Thus when once the family is deduced, it involves the relations of parents and children to each other, and the duties of each follow as a matter of course. It is not necessary on each occasion to mention that the observance of the due relation of the individual to the institution constitutes such and such a well-known duty, or that its habitual fulfilment is such and such a particular virtue. The deduction of the institution is *ipso facto* the deduction of the particular duties and virtues connected with it.

Social ethics advance through three phases (1) the family, (2) civil society, (3) the state.

SECTION I

THE FAMILY

577. The unity of moral subjectivity and objectivity at which we have arrived is called by Hegel the ethical *substance*. Such a use of the word substance is apt to be puzzling, but need not prove a stumbling-block. In the sphere of morality the good, or the unity of the will with its notion, was a mere

unattained ideal. It is now *actual*. It definitely *exists* in the form of institutions, and is therefore regarded as being now *substantial*. To call it the ethical substance is merely a way of expressing this. And in the same sense the various institutions, which are now to be deduced, are spoken of as the different phases or modes of the ethical substance.

578. The ethical substance first exists in the phase of *immediacy*.[1] This, of course, is in accordance with the general principles of the Hegelian dialectic. Now, that rationality, or universality, should exist in a phase of immediacy, can only mean that reason here exists in the guise of *feeling*. For cognition in the phase of immediacy is feeling (498). That the first existence of the ethical substance will be an *institution* follows, of course, from the fact that we are now in the sphere of social ethics, and have already deduced the idea of institutions in general. It follows indeed from the mere fact that ethical substance is ethical substance. For that means nothing except that the ethical idea has now become substantial, *i.e.* is embodied in objective institutions. Hence the first mode of existence of this substance will be (1) an institution, (2) which is based upon *feeling*. This is the **family,** the feeling upon which it is based being *love*.

579. This is the only deduction of the family which Hegel gives.[2] It cannot be regarded as satisfactory. For, apart from the considerations urged in § 239 regarding this type of deduction in general, all that is actually deduced here is the idea of an institution based upon feeling. That this feeling is love, and that this institution is the family, these further determinations of the idea are undeduced, and constitute a leap in the dark. A thousand other institutions might be conceived which are, equally with the family, based upon feeling. A murder society may be an institution based upon feeling—the feeling of hatred.

---

[1] See § 239 above.

[2] *Phil. of Right,* § 158. In the *Encyclopaedia* ("Phil. of Mind," § 518) there is also a reference to the individual finding his substantial existence in his "natural universal" or "kind." This seems to hint of a more precise deduction of the idea of family through its connection with genus, or kind. But it is too vague to be clearly understood or expounded.

The rest of the details which Hegel gives here under the head of the family seem also to be very loosely deduced, although his general views upon marriage certainly follow rigorously from his principles. The family involves three phases:

580. (1) *Marriage.* " Love is, in general, the consciousness of the unity of myself with another." [1] In marriage the two persons renounce their independent personalities to become one person. Indeed the entire family is to be regarded as one entity, the members of which, so long as they have not yet separated themselves from it, gone forth into the world, and by marrying set up new families, are not independent persons. It is for this reason that consanguineous marriages are unethical. For the essence of marriage is that two independent persons give up their independence to each other. Where this is not possible, as in the case of members of the same family who are not, as regards each other, independent persons, the idea of marriage cannot be realized.

581. Since marriage is a necessary objectification of reason and of the universal will—as is proved by its deduction in this place—it is, therefore, essentially an *ethical* bond, an absolute *end in itself.* It is not to be regarded as a mere contrivance for securing the pleasure of the individual, or for the sake of expediency, or other such ends. Its essential nature is the ethical union, and the gratification of sex is subordinate. Marriage may involve pleasure. But it is first and foremost a duty. It is an ethical end which is higher than the pleasure of the individual. Therefore, though divorce must be allowed in certain circumstances, it ought to be made as difficult as possible. It cannot be allowed merely at the pleasure of the individuals concerned. Marriage, as an ethical institution, is an embodiment of the universal, and as such has a higher right than the particular inclinations, whims, and caprices, of the individual. It is the duty of the state to uphold the right of the ethical against personal inclinations. If marriage were merely a contrivance for benefiting the individuals who marry, divorce would have to

[1] *Phil. of Right,* § 158, Addition.

be allowed whenever those individuals desired it. Or if marriage were merely a civil contract, it might be dissolved, like any other contract, by the consent of the parties. But both these views of marriage are false and ignore the ethical element.

582. For the same reasons Hegel disparages the modern romantic notion that the essential thing about marriage is "being in love." Undoubtedly personal inclination, affection between the parties, mutual sympathies, etc., are important, and cannot be ignored. But to put exclusive emphasis upon these is to base marriage entirely upon subjective feeling. No doubt marriage is based upon feeling, but only upon feeling which has reason at its core. Reason appears here in the guise of feeling. Fundamentally, therefore, marriage is, like every other ethical institution, based upon reason. Exclusively to emphasize the side of feeling, of "being in love," is to degrade marriage from the position of a rational objective institution to the position of a mere arrangement for gratifying the personal inclinations of the individual. Such a view exalts the merely subjective and particular above the objective and universal. A wisely arranged marriage, accepted by the parents and the family, based upon rational considerations, is more ethical than a marriage based purely on romantic love. Provided the husband or wife is wisely selected, mutual affection, trust, inclination, and, in general, the side of subjective feeling, will spring up in due course.

583. The public celebration of the marriage is not, as represented by some writers, an empty and meaningless formality, which might be dispensed with. It is, on the contrary, the symbol of the ethical element in marriage, of the right of society and the state to be interested therein, which right exists because marriage is not the private concern of the individuals but is an ethical and universal end.

584. (2) *The Family Means.* Just as, in the sphere of abstract right, the single person necessarily embodies his freedom in the external form of property, so the family regarded as a person must have its family property. And because the family is *one* person, and not many, this property

is the common possession of the whole family, though it may be administered by the husband as head of the family. He holds the family means in trust, and the members of the family have the *right* to be maintained, educated, etc., out of it. This is to be regarded, not as a privilege or favour, but as a right, founded upon reason. And to the rights correspond, of course, duties.

585. (3) *Dissolution of the Family*. The unity of marriage, the coalescence of two individuals into a single person, remains, in the parents, a mere subjective feeling. In the children it becomes an objective fact. In the child the parents have their love, the unity of their marriage, existing before their eyes as an independent object. Children have the right to be educated out of the family means. Education consists in instilling into them the universal mind, and thus developing into actuality the freedom which they already potentially possess. When this process is complete, the children become themselves free independent persons, with the right to possess property of their own, and the right to form new families by marriage. This process constitutes the disruption of the old family.

SECTION II

CIVIL SOCIETY

586. The notion of *civil society* follows logically from the disruption of the family. While the family still subsists as a family, its members do not bear to each other the relation of independent persons. With the disruption of the family they acquire that status. Hence arises a multiplicity of independent persons, externally related to each other as so many independent social atoms. So long as they remained within the family they were not ends in themselves, but the family was their end,—a higher end than the individual. Now, however, each independent atomic person becomes an end in himself, and admits no other end than himself. Each therefore is bent upon treating himself only as an end and treating

all other persons merely as means to his ends. In this way, however, each becomes entirely dependent upon all the others. For without them as means to his ends he cannot attain his ends. There arises, therefore, an absolute interdependence of all upon all, each using all the others as means to the satisfaction of his needs. This state of mutual dependence upon each other of independent persons is **civil society**.

587. Whether or not civil society has historically arisen in the manner described is, of course, irrelevant. As a matter of fact it may rather have arisen through the collection of scattered families by some superior force, or in any other way. But what we are here concerned with is not the question of historical origin, but that of logical origin. The rational and logical basis of civil society, its essential nature and meaning, is, in the opinion of Hegel, that described in the last paragraph. That is its *deduction*.

588. While the individual was still within the family, the family constituted his end. And this end was for him a universal end. It was not merely for his own hand that he fought and strove, not for his selfish individual interests, but essentially for the universal end, the family. Now, however, being reduced to a social atom, and treating only himself as an end, the universality of his purpose disappears and is replaced by particularity—the self-seeking pursuit of personal ends. But the universality of the family was precisely its ethical, or rational, element. Hence in civil society there appears to be a loss of the ethical. It is for this reason that society often seems in the last analysis merely to be based upon "intelligent self-seeking." And this is really true so long as we regard civil society as the final stage of development. But as we proceed we shall see that the universal is merely temporarily submerged, and again breaks through, giving rise to increasingly ethical elements which culminate in the state as the final manifestation of the ethical idea. Civil society is a mere abstraction, a one-sided moment which is superseded in the state.

589. What Hegel means by civil society as distinguished from the state, will be more fully explained shortly. Mean-

while we may note that its essential notion is that of a systematic mutual interdependence of persons, each seeking their own ends. It is essentially the moment of *particularity* that is here emphasized. Universality, which had embodied itself in the family, has disappeared. Particularity takes its place, and makes itself felt in the fact that there are now only particular persons, and that these persons are seeking, not the universal well-being, but only their own particular well-being. Thus the movement from the family to civil society corresponds with, and is in reality governed by, the movement of the Notion. The first moment of the Notion is universality,— here represented by the family. The second moment of the Notion is particularity, which involves the disappearance of the universal. This is here represented by civil society with its concomitant disappearance of the ethical. But just as, in the pure Notion, particularity is a mere moment, and, if taken by itself, an impossible abstraction, so it is here with the particularity of civil society. The particular, taken in abstraction, *purports* to be something on its own account, independent of the universal. But in fact it has proceeded out of the universal, is a manifestation of the universal, and will return to the universal. So it is here. The un-ethical self-seeking which shows itself in civil society is a mere abstract factor, which, however, is based upon the universal and the ethical, though shallow persons take it for the fundamental basis of society.

590. The beginner's natural difficulty in understanding the difference between what Hegel calls civil society, which is dealt with in the present section, and the state, which does not make its appearance till the next section, will disappear if we bear in mind that civil society is a mere abstract factor of the state which does not and cannot exist by itself without the state. Looking over the headings of the sub-sections in the present sphere of civil society, and seeing that they include such institutions as law courts, police, and corporations, we might well be inclined to ask how such institutions can possibly exist without a state, and how Hegel can be justified in supposing that they arise before the state arises,

and whether law courts and police are not essentially parts of the state, and why therefore they should be relegated to some kind of civil society which is not the state. But the answer is that Hegel does not for a moment suppose that these institutions can exist without the state. Civil society cannot exist without the state, of which it is a mere factor, and, considered apart from the state, a mere abstraction. Yet just because it is such an abstraction it necessarily arises in logical order before the more concrete institution of the state, although in point of time it may arise after the state. It is true, too, that law courts, police, etc., are essentially parts of the state, but, in the opinion of Hegel, they belong to that abstract aspect of the state which he calls civil society.

591. Civil society, therefore, may be logically distinguished from the fully developed state, though it cannot exist without it. It is simply that abstract aspect of the state in which the community is regarded as a collection of independent persons, all seeking their own ends, and attaining them, not independently of each other, but by means of each other, *i.e.* through the working of the whole social machine. The essential difference between civil society and the state is that in the former the individual is for himself the sole end, so that his end is particular, while in the latter the state is a higher end for which the individual exists, so that his end is universal.

592. Theories which regard the state as based upon intelligent self-interest; individualistic doctrines, like those of Herbert Spencer, which regard the state as a mechanical contrivance intended only to promote the greatest well-being of each individual; the theory of " laissez-faire ";—all such theories are half-truths because they have not got beyond the point of view of civil society, have not risen to the true conception of the state. What they call the state is no more than what Hegel calls civil society. These views are mere abstractions. The opinion which regards the state and the individual as opposed to each other, which sets up the antithesis between absolute individualism, or anarchism, on the one hand, and absolute socialism, on the other, and sees in actual society only a compromise between these hostile

principles, is founded on the same abstraction. It views the particular—*i.e.* the individual person—as an abstract particular, and the universal—*i.e.* the state—as an abstract universal, and believes that particular and universal are absolutely opposite and hostile principles which can only be forced together by some mechanical compromise. But the truth is that particular and universal are mere factors of the concrete Notion, and are no more opposite than they are absolutely identical. Instead of the ends and the interests of the individual being set apart on the one side, and the ends and interests of the state set apart on the other, facing each other in irreconcileable hostility, the truth rather is that the end of the individual and the end of the state are identical in their difference, as will appear when we reach the theory of the state. The false views here discussed rest upon belief in the absolute opposition of particular and universal, *i.e.* they are the views of the abstract understanding, whereas the true nature of the state is only cognizable by the speculative reason, which apprehends identity in difference.

593. The moment of particularity is essential to civil society. But the moment of universality also makes its presence felt from the very first. For the individual now seeks only his private and particular ends. But in doing so he is really serving the universal, though he neither desires nor even knows this. The fabric of society is such that each is dependent upon all. Each, therefore, in pursuing his own weal, achieves the weal of the whole community. I perform work in order to satisfy my hunger. But my work benefits the whole community. Thus in civil society the two principles of particularity and universality are both operative. But their union is not a true organic union. They have fallen asunder and appear as opposite principles between which a compromise is struck. Their genuine unity is not found until we reach the state.

594. The principle of particularity is what has been called elsewhere (560) the right of the subject. It is the individual's right to subjective personal freedom. The right of the subject is thus a necessary factor of the state. Plato in his

Republic overlooked this, and made the state, *i.e.* the universal, absolute as against the individual subject. Hence Plato's state is founded upon the abstract universal, *i.e.* the universal which excludes the particular, and not, as it should have been, upon the concrete Notion.

595. Civil society has three phases : (1) The system of wants, (2) administration of justice, (3) police and corporation.

Sub-Section I

THE SYSTEM OF WANTS

596. The independent person, regarding himself as the sole end, seeks to achieve only his private ends. Since these are merely personal, and not universal, ends, they are his *wants*,—his need of food, drink, clothing, housing, etc. They need not necessarily be material wants, but the point is that they are merely personal and selfish, and lack universality. But since the individual uses all other individuals as means to his ends, and since he is used in the same manner by them, there arises a *system* of mutual dependencies in the social fabric. I work for my own ends. But others depend on my work for the satisfaction of their wants ; and I depend on theirs. This is the **system of wants.**

597. It has three factors :

(*a*) The first factor is the *mutual dependence* just described. The essential universality of the human spirit makes its appearance here. Even when he aims at working solely for himself, man cannot help working in reality for the universal. In promoting his own ends he promotes the universal end. In this man, because he is rational, differs from the animal, whose impulses end, as they began, in particularity.

(*b*) The second factor is *labour*. Labour is the instrument whereby man moulds the crude material with which nature presents him into forms suitable for the satisfaction of his wants. The understanding analyzes and splits up each want into component parts. Each part becomes itself a want. This sub-division may proceed indefinitely in the multiplication and refinement of wants. And as labour follows these divisions which the understanding introduces, and specializes itself towards the satisfaction of these increasingly specialized needs, we get the principle of the division of labour.

(c) The third factor is *wealth*. The individual, while producing for himself, is in reality producing for all. Hence there comes into existence a general stock of wealth, which may be regarded as the property of the whole community.

598. It is in this sphere of the system of wants that there arises the division of society into classes or estates, and this division is, according to Hegel, a logical necessity, and is founded upon the Notion. The various kinds of wants group themselves into subsidiary systems of wants, and those who devote themselves to the production of the things necessary for the satisfaction of each group of wants constitute a class. There are three main classes:

(a) *The agricultural class*. This corresponds to the first phase of thought, viz. immediacy, universality in which difference and particularity are implicit, but from which they have not yet emerged. For this class lives in simple, direct, contact with nature, receiving what she gives, in a spirit of dependence and trust into which reflection—which is the moment of difference—has not yet entered.

(b) *The industrial and commercial class*. This class depends less on nature and more upon its own work. It uses the understanding to analyze wants and to mould the materials of nature to their satisfaction. It is thus the class in which the principle of understanding, of reflection, operates. It is the moment of particularity.

(c) *The universal class*. This class has for its work and purpose the universal interests of society and the state. It is the governing class. It depends upon the moment of reason.

599. It is very important to note, however, that Hegel does not make birth, pedigree, etc., the essential considerations in deciding the question to what class a man is to belong. Capacity, birth, and other accidental circumstances, he says, play their part. But the final decision rests with the free choice of the individual, and his ability to perform the functions of the class to which he aspires. He censures Plato for

making the separation of individuals into classes a function of the rulers, thus, as usual, denying the subjective rights of freedom to the individual. And he animadverts upon the caste system of India which makes birth the sole deciding factor in the matter.

Sub-Section II

ADMINISTRATION OF JUSTICE

600. Civil society is composed of persons. Because they are persons, they have rights (532). The existence of these rights does not indeed arise for the first time at this point. They were deduced at the very beginning of the sphere of objective spirit. But what happens at the present point of the dialectic is that those rights, which have existed as bare rights all through the sphere of objective spirit, are now transformed into *laws*. This happens through the mutual dependence of persons upon each other, the mutual exchange of wants and labour for their satisfaction. For there has now arisen an objective *fabric* of society. This fabric is something objective in the sense that it is established, instituted. It definitely exists, and is not a mere idea. It follows therefore that the relations between the parts of this fabric are likewise established and objective. But the parts of the social fabric are the persons, and the external relations which persons bear to each other are essentially their rights and duties towards each other. Hence what formerly existed as bare rights, existing in a subjective way only *in* the person, now proceeds forth into objectivity, becomes definitely established, instituted, and recognized as having universal validity and authority in the social fabric. When abstract right is thus established as authoritative in society, it is then no longer abstract, but is *positive* right, *i.e.* law. Hence arises the **administration of justice.**

601. (*a*) Thus the first aspect of the administration of justice is the recognition of the binding force of right, which, by means of this binding force, acquires the character of positive law. It is the *universality* of law which is its essential

feature, and this universality is ensured only by its definite establishment in objectivity. Customs, which have not yet reached the level of becoming laws, lack this universality just because they are not definitely instituted. Customs differ from laws only in this, that they are affected with accidentality and contingency. They are subjective and partial in their application. When they acquire universal application and are definitely instituted, they become laws. And hence the historical origin of early law is to be found in custom.

The subject-matter of the laws will be the relations of persons through right, wrong, crime, property, contract, marriage, etc., which have already been deduced. But it is only the *external* relations of persons to each other which can be made the subject of law, for it is only these that are objectified in the social fabric. What is internal, subjective, and private to the will, the sphere of morality proper, is not amenable to law. It is for this reason that the law does not interfere, for example, in the internal relations of the family, the private relations of husband, wife, and children. For these are not related externally to each other as independent persons. The family is rather a single person, and the relations of its members are internal and subjective.

Reason determines the laws. Their analysis, their application to special cases, the production within them of divisions and sub-divisions, distinctions, and refinements, is the work of the understanding. These sub-divisions and refinements may proceed *ad infinitum*. And in their application to the multitude of empirical particulars in the world of facts it is not to be expected that reason, or the Notion, can always be traced. For we here descend into the region of the finite, which is the region of contingency and caprice. Whether a man deserves a fine of ten dollars or ten and a half, and such questions, cannot be decided on purely rational grounds, or deduced from the Notion.

602. (*b*) The second essential in this sphere is that the laws should be promulgated and universally known. The proof or deduction of this rests, not upon expediency, but upon the Notion itself. For law is merely established right. And

right accrues to persons by virtue of the infinitude of their self-consciousness (532). The law is an embodiment of my freedom and my personality. Hence it is only binding upon me when recognized as such. It is my right to know and recognize the law as my own. Only to accept as binding what my reason recognizes as rational is part of the right of the subject. Laws made in secret, laws which are unknown to those who are expected to obey them, are enforced only as alien and external commands. And their enforcement is a violation of the rights of freedom of the subject. Therefore the laws should be made as widely known as possible. They should be embodied in codes which all may read. To bury them in inaccessible records of judicial decisions, to write them in a foreign tongue, to regard them as the esoteric knowledge of a class,—such proceedings do violence to the idea of freedom. For the same reasons the proceedings of the courts in which the law is administered should be open to the public.

Objection is often taken to the importance which the law attaches to outward forms and ceremonies. Legal formalities, however, are likewise based upon the necessity that legal acts should be established, definitely constituted, and promulgated. Thus a sale of lands without any formality remains a mere subjective act of the wills of the parties. The embodiment of the contract in a formal deed gives objectivity to the act of the will. The transfer is then something established and known. "My will is rational: it has validity; and this validity is to be recognized by others."[1] Hence the necessity of forms. We place boundary stones and keep registers of mortgages, for similar reasons.

603. (c) Right, being now established in the form of law, is an existent fact in the world. It has, therefore, to maintain itself in the world, to vindicate itself against the non-universal or capricious acts of particular wills. And it has to descend from generality to individual cases, to get itself actually carried out in the detail of life. For the performance of these offices there is necessary a constituted authority, the court of justice.

[1] *Phil. of Right*, § 217, Addition.

The punishments of wrongs by private persons acting under the sway of their private impulses and interests, *i.e.* revenge, does not vindicate right, but merely creates a new wrong (551). But the court of justice represents, not the private interests of the injured person, but rather the injured universal, the outraged law, and its judgments vindicate right.

The court need not necessarily consist of a single judge. Questions of fact are as well adjudicated upon by a jury as by a judge.

Sub-Section III

POLICE AND CORPORATION

604. (*a*) The fabric of civil society is founded upon the system of wants in which each seeks his own ends, the sum of which is his well-being. The pursuit of his well-being is not merely natural; it is his right (564). The individual's right to well-being has to be exercised in a world of empirical contingencies which tend perpetually to infringe upon it. To secure the person, property, and well-being of the individual against the inroads of the contingent, casual, and fortuitous is the function of the police. Apart from crime, arbitrary choice and capricious actions have a place in the exercise of rights of property and other lawful acts. And such acts of one individual may overlap and interfere with the well-being of other individuals. The regulation of such matters, and the protection of the individual against such injuries, is also within the sphere of the police, and is the justification for police control and supervision.

The individual's right to well-being thus involves, on the negative side, the removal of casual and fortuitous hindrances to it. This gives rise to the **police.** On its positive side it involves the right that the well-being of the individual should be actualized, instituted, and established in the world. This gives rise to

(*b*) The **corporation.** It is not the universal interests of society that are here to be considered, but rather the particular well-being of the individual which, because it is a *right*, has to be established and made objective in an institution. Hence groups of individuals, whose well-being depends upon similar interests, form associations, which are recognized and established as corporations. These occur for the most part in the commercial class.

Though a corporation pursues, in the first instance, its own special interests, its activities nevertheless promote the universal ends of society, just as the self-seeking activities of the individual do so. And since the aims of the corporation are, in any case, wider and relatively more universal than those of the single individual, their effect is to raise the individual member out of his purely self-seeking activities towards the universal. "In our modern states the citizens participate only slightly in the general business. It is, however, needful to provide the ethical man with a universal activity, one above his private ends. This universal, with which the modern state does not always supply him, is given by the corporation. We have already seen that the individual, while maintaining himself in the civic community, acts also for others. But this unconscious necessity is not enough. It is in the corporation that a conscious and reflective ethical reality is first reached."[1] This is a penetrating remark. It is a matter of experience and observation how deeply a man, once immersed in selfish ends, may become imbued with public spirit by participating in the proceedings of a chamber of commerce or other such association.

SECTION III

THE STATE

605. So far as I can see Hegel gives no genuine deduction of the state. A real transition may be said to fall into three parts. It starts (1) from the first notion,—in this case it would be the notion of civil society (or the more specialized notion of the corporation), and passes by (2) a logical movement into (3) the second or deduced notion—in this case the notion of the state—which will then be explicated (defined),

[1] *Phil. of Right*, § 255, Addition.

and its relation to the previous notions, as their unity, if it is a synthesis, or as opposite, if it is an antithesis, set out. In the present case all that Hegel does is to set forth the exposition of the notion of the state, and to show it in its relation to the previous notions, *i.e.* as the unity of the family and civil society. There is no strict logical movement from one notion to the other.

606. The transition, such as it is, is contained in the following words in the *Philosophy of Right*: "The limited and finite end of the corporation has its truth in the absolutely universal end and the absolute actuality of this end. This actualized end is also the truth of the division involved in the external system of police, which is merely a relative identity of the divided elements. Thus the sphere of civil society passes into the state."[1] After this the features of the new notion, the state, are unfolded. The *Encyclopaedia* contains no transition at all, but begins at once with the definition of the notion of the state.[2]

The passage quoted above may be expanded as follows: The family represents the first stage of the Notion, that of undifferentiated universality in which the moment of particularity is implicit, but from which it has not yet emerged. The family is one, a unity, and its members, not being independent persons, are still absorbed within it. Only with the dissolution of the family, when the members become independent persons, does the moment of particularity come to light. In civil society the moments of universality and particularity have fallen asunder and become separated (593). The particular, *i.e.* the private purposes of the individual, stands opposed to the universal, *i.e.* the universal ends of society, and this gives rise to the antagonisms between private interest and public interest, between anarchism and socialism.

As we advance from phase to phase of civil society we find the two opposed sides approaching each other, and making towards a unity. In the system of wants they are in downright opposition, but are yet mutually interdependent. In

[1] *Phil. of Right*, § 256.   [2] *Phil. of Mind*, § 535.

the administration of justice they come together to this extent, that particular and universal are brought into harmony, not throughout society, but in single special cases. The universal will, in the form of the law, gets itself definitely carried out in this or that particular instance which is the subject-matter of the suit. In the corporation a further advance is made. A relatively universal purpose now becomes identified with the private interests of a body of persons, and this unity of universal and particular covers, not yet the whole of society, but at least that considerable area of it which is included in the corporation. The completion of this process is the state. In the state universal and particular are completely reconciled. The end of the individual, and of every individual, is now identical with the universal end of the state (592). This gives the definition, or notion, of **the state**, namely, that it is the unity in difference of the universal principle of the family and the particular principle of civil society. This is what it should be as the synthesis of the triad.

607. It cannot be said that this is a genuine deduction. It is merely a comparative description of the various phases of the ethical idea. We see that, *if* we advance from the idea of civil society to that of the state, a reconciliation of the universal and particular is found. But we cannot see any logical necessity why we *must* advance. In the Logic the deduction of the category of becoming rested upon the fact that to think being *forces* us to think its passage into nothing, and *vice versa*, and that the thought of this passage *is* the thought of becoming. We then see that becoming is the unity of being and nothing. But if, instead of this, Hegel had merely pointed out that, as a matter of fact, being and nothing are opposed, and that, as a matter of fact, becoming contains both and is thus a unity of the two, so that if we choose to pass to the category of becoming we find the reconciliation we want—if Hegel had done this without proving that it is not by our mere arbitrary choice that we pass to becoming, but by a necessity of thought—then his deduction would have been inadequate. This is precisely what he has

done here. He has merely pointed out that the family as universal, and civil society as particular, stand opposed, that the state is the unity of both, so that if we choose to pass to the state we find the reconciliation we want.

608. The combination of the first two moments of the Notion, universality and particularity, produces the third moment, individuality. Hence the state is a true individual. It is a person, an organism which is self-differentiating in such a manner that the life of the whole appears in all the parts. This means that the true life of the parts, *i.e.* the individuals, is found in and is identical with the life of the whole, the state. The state is thus only the individual himself objectified and eternalized by the elimination of his merely accidental and ephemeral features and the retention of what is universal in him. The individual is *implicitly* universal. Universality is his essence. The state is the *actual* universal, and is thus simply the individual actualized and objectified. Thus the state is no alien authority which imposes itself externally upon the individual and suppresses his individuality. On the contrary the state is the individual himself. And it is only in the state that his individuality is realized. For this reason the state is the supreme embodiment of freedom, for in being determined by it the individual is now wholly determined by his essential self, by that which is true and universal in him.

609. Such is the *notion* of the state. No doubt existing states fall short of the notion, are deformed, embody untrue principles, and so on. But this is inevitable. "Although a state may be declared to violate right principles, and to be defective in various ways, it always contains the essential moments of its existence, if, that is to say, it belongs to the full-formed states of our own time ... It is in the world, in the sphere of caprice, accident, and error. Evil can doubtless disfigure it in many ways, but the ugliest man, the criminal, the invalid, the cripple, are living men." [1]

Passages like this should be remembered when such charges are brought against Hegel as that he believed that "whatever

[1] *Phil. of Right*, § 258, Addition.

is is right," that he opposed all reform, that he was a reactionary, an enemy of liberty, a supporter of the state at all hazards against the individual. A supporter of the state he most certainly was, but only because he saw in it, not the enemy of individual liberty, but the very embodiment of it. And he rightly rebuked those who in their vanity and self-conceit imagine that *their* reason, *their* particular ideas, are the universal truth which should overturn states and undo at a stroke the work of the ages. These people fail to see that existing states, with all their faults, are yet the work of the world-reason labouring through the ages towards its ends, and are the product, not of the whims of this or that individual, but of the universal human spirit. But by this it is not meant to deny that there are defects, and that these should be removed.

610. The state is rational, because it is universal, a universality which is not abstract, but concrete, inasmuch as it has absorbed its opposite, the particular into itself. It is, therefore, the absolute, final, and true embodiment and actualization of the ethical idea. The Idea here reaches the highest development which is possible for it in the sphere of objective spirit. Further development takes it outside the sphere of ethics into that of absolute spirit.

As the ethical sphere is the sphere of the objectification of the *will*, the state is the realization in actuality of the universal will. It is the identity of the will with its notion.

611. The state is not only the ethical substance in its highest phase, but it is the *self-conscious* ethical substance. The family possesses rationality, *i.e.* universality, but only in the form of *feeling*, love. The content of the family is thus universal, but its form is not. For universality is essentially thought, and that which is not thought, but only feeling, is not out and out universal. It is universal in its content, because its aims and purposes are in accord with the universal. But it is itself unaware of this. It does not know. It only feels. The absolutely universal must be universal both in content and in form; that is to say, its universal ends must not be merely groped for in vague feeling, but must be present

to consciousness in the form of thought. This absolute universality is attained in the state. It consciously seeks universal ends, and is aware of the ends which it seeks. It knows the reason of what it does, whereas the family, though it may act rationally, does so only by instinct.

612. That the state is rational means that it is no chance product of the contingent forces of nature, or of the caprice of man, but is an absolutely necessary development of the world-reason, an embodiment of the Absolute. It is not a means for securing the welfare of the individual. It is not a *means* to anything. It is an end in itself. And because it is a higher end than the individual, it may demand the sacrifice of the latter to its higher ends. But it is, of course, only for the true, universal, right, and rational, ends of the state that such a sacrifice can be demanded. Hence this doctrine must not be twisted into a justification of the arbitrary acts of rulers working for their own ends and not for the true ends of the state. Nor does it mean that the individuality and freedom of the individual, his rights and liberties, are to be denied. On the contrary, the true life of the individual, his individuality, liberty, and rights, are realized only by his being a member of the state and finding its being identical with his own.

Thus all theories which regard the state as a mere combination of individuals for mutual protection, or as existing in order to increase the wealth and strength of its members, or as a compromise or contract whereby individuals agree to restrict their liberties on condition that all other individuals do the same,—such theories are to be condemned because they make the state a mere means to carry out the ends of the individual. The state is, on the contrary, the higher end.

613. The *notion* of the state, *i.e.* what the state essentially *is* in its inherent nature, the meaning and significance of the state, these, which are here expounded, are, of course, quite independent of any question of the historical origin of states. States may have arisen by fraud, or force, or in any other way. That is irrelevant to their rational basis and nature.

614. The three phases of the state are (1) Its constitution, or internal polity, the internal relations of itself to its members,

and of its members to one another; (2) international law,—the relation of the state to other states, whereby it passes into (3) universal history.

Sub-Section I

CONSTITUTION, OR INTERNAL POLITY

615. "Everything depends on the union of universality and particularity in the state."[1] Universality is represented by the state considered in abstraction from the individual. Particularity is represented by the private ends and interests of individuals. The essence of the true state is the thorough interpenetration of these two sides, their union in a concrete identity. Both extremes, that of state right on the one hand, and that of individual freedom on the other, must be fully developed to their extreme limits and yet retained within the unity of the state. The further each is developed and the deeper the opposition between them, the more rich and concrete will be the unity to which they are brought back, the more strong and real will be the state.

The fault of the ancient states generally, a fault faithfully mirrored in Plato's *Republic*, was that they developed the side of universality exclusively, and failed to develop the principle of individual freedom and the right of the subject. Their universality, because it excluded the particular, was the abstract universal. The special feature of the modern state is that it has developed the principle of individual freedom, so that its universality contains the particular, and is a concrete universal. This error of the ancient state, the superiority of the modern state and the fundamental importance of developing the principle of individual freedom to its extreme limit, are emphatically and repeatedly asserted by Hegel in passage after passage. So that Schwegler is not justified in his remark that "Hegel has a decided leaning to the ancient political idea which completely subordinates the individual, the right of subjectivity, to the will of the state."[2]

[1] *Phil. of Right*, § 261, Addition.
[2] Schw., *Handbook of the H. of Ph.*, Stirling, 14th edition, p. 340.

616. This union of universality and particularity gives us, then, the internal relation of the state to its citizens, the main features of the **constitution** or **internal polity.** The identity of universal and particular, of state claims and individual claims, is founded upon the fact that the individual is implicitly universal, and that the state, as the actual universal, is but the objectification of the true self of the individual. And this identification is in the actual world brought about in two ways. Firstly, the actions of individuals, even when seeking solely their private ends, bring about, in spite of themselves, universal results. This we have seen in the system of wants. Secondly, the individuals in a highly civilized state tend more and more deliberately and consciously to understand the universal purposes of the state and to identify themselves therewith. The state, too, though it logically supersedes the family and civil society with its corporations, nevertheless preserves them as moments within itself, "sublates" them. For this reason the state fosters the institutions of civil society, the family and the individual. It develops their well-being and furthers their interests to the utmost. Hence the citizens come to know that the state is their best friend, that it preserves their liberties and rights, that it fosters and advances their interests, that it secures their property and persons. In this way political sentiment and patriotism spring up, and are educated. True patriotism is not the windy and bombastic sentiment so often described by that name, but is simply the deep-seated and firm conviction of the citizens that the state is their substantive basis and end, that it is the embodiment of themselves and their liberties.

617. The state is essentially an organism, which evolves its internal differences out of its own unity, gives them life as independent subsistencies, and yet retains them within its own unity (608). These differences which it develops within itself are the different functions and branches of the public affairs of the state. And because the state is the embodiment of reason, *i.e.* of the Notion, its self-differentiation proceeds in accordance with the Notion. Its aspects are the universal, the particular, and the individual. The universal aspect of the

state is its function as source of the laws, and this gives us the legislature. Its particular aspect is found in the application of the laws to special cases, and this gives us the executive (in which Hegel includes the judiciary). The moment of individuality is embodied in the person of the monarch.

If the logical order of the development of the Notion were followed, the moment of individuality would be dealt with last. Hegel, however, deals with it first, and begins the discussion of the constitution with considerations regarding the form of monarchy. No reason is given for this reversal of the logical order. Apparently it is an odd way of showing respect for the monarch!

618. But before discussing the three main branches of the state, a word must be said regarding their relations to one another. A great point is often made of the separation of the functions of legislature, executive, and judiciary. According to popular opinion each is to be regarded as a check upon the others, and this separation is looked upon as a guarantee of freedom. It is only the Notion, Hegel thinks, which can throw light upon this matter, for the state is but the Notion existent in objectivity. Now the three factors of the Notion are indeed separate and radically distinct. But they are none the less identical, and each factor contains the other two factors within itself, so that each factor is itself the totality of the Notion (318). Any talk, therefore, of an absolute separation and independence of one another on the part of the three elements of the state is quite idle. The monarch, the legislature, and the executive, must, on the one hand, be separate and clearly differentiated in function, as the factors of the Notion are. But that they should exist as independent entities, opposing and checking each other, would be an abstract state of things which could only end in the dissolution of the state. They must, on the contrary, all be taken up into the one life of the organic whole which is the state. And for this reason Hegel approves of the rule of the English constitution by which the various heads of the executive branches of the Government are at the same time members of the legislature.

We may now deal with the three functions of the state in the order in which Hegel takes them.

A. *The Monarch.*

619. The fully developed state, that is, the state which alone completely embodies the logical Notion, and which is alone completely rational, is a constitutional monarchy. In Hegel's opinion there must be a monarch, and other forms of government, as for example republics, are imperfect.

Hegel's proof of this, *i.e.* his deduction of the institution of monarchy, may be considered as resolving itself into two stages, the first of which is valid, the second invalid. Firstly, the moment of individuality in the Notion has to be represented in the state. Now individuality, as the third factor of the Notion, contains also the other two factors and is therefore the totality of the Notion. The Notion, however, is subjectivity (321). The logical Notion itself is, of course, a mere category, or abstract thought, the abstract thought of subjectivity. But the state is the logical Notion become actual and existent. Therefore the moment of individuality must give rise to an institution within the state which is essentially an actual and existent subjectivity. Subjectivity, however, is only actual and existent in a single subject, a person. The subjectivity of a mass of persons, an assembly, or a people, is a mere abstraction. The logical factor of individuality when realized in objectivity and made existent can only be *an* individual,—one person, not many.

Now individuality is the whole Notion. It is itself the totality of the three factors. This gives us the idea of the state as having a single life, as a single whole or organism. The single life governs and directs the whole organism in all its differentiated functions and activities. Hence this single life of the state, this final governing and directing centre, this ideal unity which takes up all its parts into itself, can only be actual and existent in a single existent individual. This individual embodies and represents the life of the whole.

Now this deduction gives us so far the following result, that there must be at the head of the state a single individual, who coordinates all the functions of the state, and in whom all its manifold activities meet. So far the deduction may be regarded as valid. But it does not at all follow that this single individual is to be a monarch. The president of a republic, even the dictator of a military autocracy, is equally a single individual at the head of the state. No doubt it is essential that at the summit of the state there should always be one individual, even if he is only the chairman of a committee; and, as Hegel himself points out, even in imperfect states it is invariably so. Invariably one person, a statesman, a general, a king, a chairman, stands at the apex.

By the second step in the deduction Hegel purports further to deduce that this individual must be an hereditary monarch. In the *Philosophy of Right* the deduction runs: " This ultimate self of the state's will is in this its abstraction an individuality, which is simple and direct. Hence its very conception implies that it is natural. Thus the monarch ... is appointed to the dignity of a monarch in a directly natural way, by natural birth." [1] In the *Encyclopaedia* he says: " That subjectivity ... being simple self-relation, has attached to it the characteristic of *immediacy*, and then of *nature*,—whereby the destination of individuals for the dignity of the princely power is fixed by inheritance." [2] The meaning of these passages appears to be simply this: that the ruler as an *existent* individual has been deduced: that because he is existent he is *there*, present to the senses, and in that sense *immediate*. What is thus *given* as an immediate *fact*, is not the product of spirit, but belongs to nature. The **monarch** therefore is simply presented by nature, by natural means, *i.e.* by birth. Such a deduction, with its vague associative connections between immediacy, nature, and birth, can only be regarded as utterly fanciful. One might, on identical grounds, argue that members of the legislature, the executive, even the voters, should be chosen by hereditary right,—since all these persons are equally immediately existent and *there*.

620. The fact is that Hegel has here foisted in his private

---

[1] *Phil. of Right*, § 280.   [2] *Phil. of Mind*, § 542.

opinion, his subjective preference for monarchy, into the objective movement of the dialectic. He *purports* to deduce it, and no doubt believes that he has done so. All he has actually deduced is the necessity of a single individual as head of the state; and this, of course, is as consistent with republicanism as it is with monarchism.

621. The moment of individuality contains the universal and the particular within itself. Hence the monarch, as universality, gives ultimate sanction to the laws, which are regarded as flowing from him (in the English constitution the King is, even formally, a part of the legislature). As embodying the particular, again, the monarch is the ultimate source of executive acts. In him is the final point of decision, the last " I will " which gives legality to the acts of his ministers. Thus the function of the monarch contains in itself the three elements of the totality.

622. By all this, however, Hegel does not mean it to be understood that the monarch has the absolute power of a despot. If the monarch, by himself, by his own arbitrary acts, governs, legislates, and decides,—such a state of affairs contradicts the thorough-going self-differentiation of the Notion. That differentiation involves the existence of a distinct legislature, which is independent to the extreme limit compatible with the unity of the state as an organism. It further involves the existence of a similarly independent executive. The monarch acts on the advice of his council of ministers. It is only the final act of formal sanction, the last " I will " which is the function of the prince. " For this office is needed only a man who says ' Yes,' and so puts the dot upon the i." [1] It " is not meant that the monarch can be wilful in his acts. Rather is he bound to the concrete content of the advice of his councillors, and, when the constitution is established, he has often nothing to do but sign his name. But this name is weighty. It is the summit, over which nothing can climb." [2] The completely rational state, thus, is not merely a monarchy but a constitutional monarchy.

[1] *Phil. of Right*, § 280, Addition.   [2] *Ibid.*, § 279, Addition.

B. *The Executive.*

623. To the moment of particularity in the logical Notion corresponds the function of **executive** government in the state. This function consists in the application of the universal, *i.e.* the laws and the constitution, to the individual case, and to private interests. " It is their duty," *i.e.* that of the executive officers, " to care for each particular thing in the civil society, and in these private ends make to prevail the universal interest." [1]

Hegel has some apt remarks about the selection of executive officers, their duties, the division of offices, etc. But it is doubtful how far these remarks can be regarded as flowing from the Notion.

C. *The Legislature.*

624. The laws, as such, do not regard this or that individual case, but are the general principles of the state's activity. They represent, therefore, the moment of universality, and require for their maintenance, extension, and growth a separate branch of the state, the **legislature.** No legislature, however, lays down laws for the first time, or creates the body of law *ex nihilo*. The laws already exist, and have grown up with the constitution. The function of the legislature is rather to develop and extend the already existent body of laws, and to suit it to fresh needs as they arise.

625. As regards the constitution of the legislature and the question of suffrage, Hegel is not greatly in favour of the democratic view that all individuals, as such, have the right to make their voices heard in the election of representatives. For the state is the embodiment, not of the common will, or the will of the majority, but of the universal or rational will as such (546). There is no guarantee that the majority will will the universal and rational. The principle of freedom does not consist in obeying the will of the majority, but in obeying the universal will which is the objectification of the individual's true self.

[1] *Phil. of Right*, § 287.

Hegel thinks that the right of the individual to participate in public affairs should rather take other forms. The "people," if by that phrase is meant merely the multitude of atomistic individuals, is simply an incoherent and inarticulate formless mass. The direct government by this formless mass as such is not to be desired. But this multitude becomes organized and rationalized in the shape of institutions which exist within the state, viz. the classes (598) and the corporations (604). It is rather these who should be represented in the legislature.

Secondly, the individual can make his voice heard and his opinions felt in the formation of public opinion, with which is connected the powerful weapon of the press. The state will be guided and assisted by public opinion, but not dictated to by it. Public opinion, the views of the formless mass of individuals, is not fit to take the helm of state. To the common argument that it is the people themselves who know best what their interests are, to the view that "the toad beneath the harrow knows," Hegel replies, on the contrary, that the people "does not know what it wills. To know what we will, and further what the absolute will, namely, reason, wills, is the fruit of deep knowledge and insight, and is therefore not the property of the people."[1] And further, "in public opinion all is false and true, but to find out the truth in it is the affair of the great man. He who tells the time what it wills and means, and then brings it to completion, is the great man of the time."[2]

The truth, in Hegel's opinion, is that public opinion contains *in substance* always what is right and reasonable. For the individual has his basis and foundation in the universal, which ultimately governs and controls him, even though he follows it blindly and without understanding. And for this reason public opinion is to be esteemed. But, on the other hand, the "people" has not the means of making distinctions, of raising its vague instincts to the level of definite knowledge, and hence its instincts for the universal take only incoherent and troubled shapes. And for this reason public opinion is

[1] *Phil. of Right*, § 301, note. [2] *Ibid.*, § 318, Addition.

to be despised. "Who does not learn to despise public opinion ... will never produce anything great." [1]

Thus it is not the "people," the multitudinous medley, the mere heap of individuals, who must rule, whether in the legislature or the executive. The ruling must be done by the universal class (598). But it is to be carefully remembered that membership of this class is not to be obtained through privilege, pedigree, birth, or wealth. Any individual, of whatever origin, has the right to raise himself, if he can, by his abilities, character and merits, to membership of the universal class (599).

Sub-Section II

INTERNATIONAL LAW

626. The state as an organism is a self-enclosed unity, which develops its own distinctions and its own life within itself. It is an individual. It is not a mere aggregate, or heap of parts, but a single being, an organic unity. It is therefore a "one" which, as such, excludes other ones. Thus it has its internal side, which has already been dealt with; and it has also its external side, which consists in its relations to other individuals of the same kind as itself, that is, to other states. These relations, so far as they are recognized and universalized, constitute **international law.**

627. Because each state is an individual, the fundamental character of its relation to other states is similar to the relations which subsist between the individual persons in *civil society* (586). Such persons are essentially *independent* persons. And similarly the prime feature of each state, in its relations to other states, is its independence. Consequently the fundamental *right* of the state in international law is that it should be recognized and respected as what it is, an independent sovereign state. Even when two states are at war they continue to recognize one another as independent states.

628. The relation of state to state differs from the relation of person to person in civil society in this, that persons have over them the state, whereas states have no authority above

[1] *Phil. of Right*, § 318, Addition.

them. As between states, therefore, there is no objectively existent sphere of universal right, as is the case between persons. Hence the acts of states are governed by their arbitrary will, and the highest form of right that can subsist between them must be based upon an agreement of their wills —the right of contract. This gives rise to *treaties*. The positive contents of treaties are not part of international law. International law can only enjoin in general the respect of such agreements. But because there is no authority above the states, and because the relations between them are governed, not by universality, but by contingency, these relations are continually shifting, and treaties, even if they purport to be binding in perpetuity, become in fact obsolete when the conditions which produced them change.

629. Because there is no international authority, disputes between states can, in the last resort, only be settled by war. The dream of perpetual peace is, for Hegel, only a dream. Nor is he a believer in the possibility of establishing an effective international authority.

630. It is in its aspect as an independent *individual* that the state is related to other states, whether in war or in peace. Hence the control of foreign affairs, and the decision of war and peace, are part of the function of that element of the state which embodies the moment of *individuality*, namely, the monarch.

631. The supreme necessity of the state is to maintain its sovereign independence. For without this it ceases to be a state. Hence, because the life and ends of the state are higher than the life and ends of the individual, the individual must be prepared to sacrifice his life and property for the maintenance of the state's independence.

632. Because the state, even while at war, recognizes its opponent as a sovereign state, *i.e.* as a single individual, it must make war against that individual as such, *i.e.* against the state, and not against private persons, their property, families, etc.

Sub-Section III

WORLD-HISTORY

633. States are related to each other as persons in civil society. In civil society persons represent the moment of particularity, and pursue their particular ends, needs, wants, etc. Hence states likewise, in their relations to one another, are particular, and each pursues its special interests. The particular is essentially the *differentia* between species. And hence each state has its own peculiar colour and features. Each state stands for and embodies an idea, or to be more exact, each state embodies a particular phase of the universal Idea. In history the Idea unfolds its various phases in time and the dominant phase at any epoch is embodied in a dominant people. The succession of these phases constitutes **world-history,** and this history is not governed by chance or blind fate but by the eternal reason, the Idea itself. Hence history is no blind medley of contingencies, but is a rational development. The Idea, when thus embodied in the history of the world is the world-spirit. It is spirit, because spirit means simply the concrete embodiment of the Idea.

This world-spirit is the final tribunal and judge of the nations. There is no international state or court which passes judgment upon the peoples, and none is possible. The judgment of the nations is found in the fate which awaits them in the process of world-history.

THIRD DIVISION

ABSOLUTE SPIRIT

INTRODUCTION

634. The defect of subjective spirit was that it was merely inward, and so one-sided. Objective spirit, on the other hand, exhibited the opposite one-sidedness. It was merely outward and objective, and had lost what is essential to the very notion of spirit, namely, consciousness or subjectivity. Spirit as soul, as sensation, as intellect, as appetite, as understanding, was conscious, personal, subjective. But spirit as family, as the moral law, as the state, is impersonal, unconscious, and purely objective. The state, for example, exists out there in the objective world. But it is not a conscious being, a person, an ego. It is not a subject.

Subjective spirit and objective spirit exist, consequently, as two opposite extremes, each of which limits the other. Each is, therefore, finite. But it is the very nature of spirit to be infinite. Hence arises the necessity that spirit should transcend its finite subjectivity and its finite objectivity, and should become infinite and absolute spirit. In order to be absolute, spirit must overreach the division between subjectivity and objectivity, which it has created within itself, and must embrace both sides in a concrete unity. Absolute spirit must be both subject and object at the same time.

As being subjective, absolute spirit will necessarily be a mode of human consciousness, and of individual consciousness. It cannot be a purely impersonal existence, such as the state. It must be the actual consciousness, existing in the minds of individual men, of some object. Only thus can absolute spirit satisfy the condition that it must be genuinely subjective.

It is, therefore, the consciousness of *some* object. But what object? Now since, in the absolute spirit, the gulf between subject and object is annihilated, since both are embraced in a unity, this can only mean that subject and object are, here, identical. Spirit, therefore, has for its object in this sphere, nothing else than spirit itself. Absolute spirit, therefore, is the spirit's contemplation of itself.

But there is a further condition necessary. Even the empirical psychologist has for the object of his studies spirit or mind. But psychology is not a phase of the absolute spirit. For the object which the psychologist contemplates is only the *finite* mind, that is to say, the subjective mind as opposed to, and limited by, its object. The psychologist studies sensation, intellect, emotion, and the like. And all these phases of mind have objects other than themselves; as for example, sensation has the material world for its object. But absolute spirit has for its object only itself, and is, therefore, infinite. In it accordingly the entire opposition between subject and object has been overcome. And this can only be so where the mind at length realizes that its object—any object—is only itself. The stage of absolute spirit, therefore, is only reached when the mind realizes that whatever is opposed to it as an object, the sun, moon, stars, the entire physical and non-physical universe, is nothing other than spirit itself; when it realizes that it itself is all being and all reality, that it is, in fact, the Absolute. Absolute spirit is that final phase in which the spirit knows that in contemplating itself it is contemplating the Absolute. But since such absolute spirit only exists as subjective human consciousness, it may further be said that absolute spirit is the knowledge, by human beings, of the Absolute. All the modes under which human beings can be conscious of the Absolute, whether in art, religion, or philosophy, are phases of **absolute spirit**.

Spirit and the Absolute are synonymous terms. Absolute spirit is, therefore, on the one hand, the knowledge of spirit by spirit. On the other hand it is the knowledge of the

Absolute by the Absolute. Only in absolute spirit does the Absolute come to itself, come to know itself for what it truly is. Only as such is it truly the Absolute. For only as such is it self-knowing spirit.

635. The elevation from objective spirit to absolute spirit may also be expressed in terms of the notion of *freedom*. The essential content of the human mind is freedom. This freedom is proximately realized in the state. For being governed by the state man is governed only by himself (575). Nevertheless the state, as being purely objective, is alien to his subjectivity, is something other than himself. And his freedom therein is consequently incomplete.[1] Absolutely free spirit can only be that spirit which has, finally and for ever, abolished all otherness of whatever description. Hence only the spirit which knows itself as all reality, which has no opposite, which sees in itself the whole of being, is entirely free. And since freedom, self-determination, and infinity, are but three words for the same idea, spirit as absolute spirit is, for the first time, out and out infinite. So far we have dealt only with the finite mind. But in art, religion, and philosophy, the human mind is infinite.

636. Absolute spirit has for its content the apprehension of the Absolute. And since the Absolute and God are identical terms, this sphere is in general the sphere of religion, which is none other than the knowledge of God, the apprehension of the divine and eternal. The apprehension of the Absolute takes place under three modes, which give us the three stages of absolute spirit, viz. (1) art, (2) religion (the term is used here in its more restricted sense), and (3) philosophy.

637. Since, as already pointed out, absolute spirit alone is entirely free and infinite, the above three stages are to be regarded as the grades of its progressive liberation from all finite condition. Traces of finitude still cling to the spirit in the spheres of art and religion. It is only in philosophy that it is absolutely free and infinite.

638. As to the oft-debated question of the relations which art, religion, and philosophy bear to one another, it follows

---

[1] *Osm,* i. pp. 135 *et seq.*

from what has been said that all three are identical in substance, but different in form. The substance or content of all three is the same, viz. the eternal, infinite, and divine, in a word, the Absolute. The *aim*, or end, of all three is the apprehension of the absolute truth. They differ, however, inasmuch as the *form* in which the absolute truth is presented to consciousness, is in each case different. What those forms are we shall see in the following pages. For the present we may deduce this further conclusion from what has been already said, viz. that art, as the first phase, is the least adequate form in which the eternal is apprehended, that religion comes next highest, but that philosophy is the only absolutely adequate form of its apprehension. Further, since the substance of all three is the same, it is to the form that their relative superiority or inferiority attaches. Thus religion contains the same fundamental truth as philosophy, but expressed in an inferior form. The detailed explanation of these points must be left for the succeeding chapters.

CHAPTER I

ART

SECTION I

BEAUTY IN GENERAL

639. The first mode in which the mind apprehends the Absolute is, in accordance with general principles, in *immediacy*. Since the content of all modes of apprehending the Absolute is the same, viz. the Absolute itself, this immediacy must attach to the *form* under which it is apprehended. At first, therefore, the Absolute will be manifested under the guise of immediacy, that is to say, under the guise of external sense-objects. The shining of the Absolute, or the Idea, through the veils of the sense-world—this is **beauty**.[1] It is essential to the idea of beauty that its object should be sensuous,—an actual thing present to the senses, as a statue, a building, or the beautiful sound of music, or at least that it should be the mental image of a sensuous object, as in poetry. It must be individual and concrete. It cannot be an abstraction. The beautiful object thus addresses itself to the senses. But it also addresses itself to the mind or spirit. For a mere sensuous existence, as such, is not beautiful. Only when the mind perceives the Idea shining through it is it beautiful.

640. Since the Idea is the absolute truth, it follows that truth and beauty are identical. For both are the Idea. But they are also distinct. Beauty is the Idea seen in a

[1] 239 above.

sensuous form, apprehended, in art or nature, by the senses. Truth is the Idea seen as it is in itself, *i.e.* as pure thought. It is apprehended as such not by the senses, but by pure thought, *i.e.* by philosophy.

641. Every phase of spirit, *e.g.* the family, morality, the state, is a phase of the Idea. In the present sphere the Idea is called the Ideal. The Ideal is this special form of the Idea as sensuously apprehended. It is the Idea, not in itself, but *manifest* in the sense-world.

642. Now the question arises, *how* can the Idea, or the Absolute, manifest itself in a sensuous object? One must recollect here the account of the Idea given in the Logic. The Notion, as such, is not yet the Idea. The Notion is subjectivity (321). The Idea is the concrete unity of the Notion with the object, *i.e.* it is the unity of subjectivity and objectivity (382). Now when we have an object, or collection of objects, which we perceive to be constituted as a multiplicity comprehended in a unity, in such a case the factor of unity is the side of subjectivity, or the Notion, while the factor of plurality is the side of objectivity (383). Such an object, therefore, because it manifests the Idea in objective and sensuous form, is beautiful. It is not, however, merely a mechanical unity that is here required, but an organic unity. The different parts of the object are so related that they are not a mere aggregate, like a heap of stones. In such an aggregate the parts are indifferent to one another. If they are separated from the unity, from the aggregate, they undergo thereby no loss, but remain precisely what they were before. In an organic unity, on the contrary, the parts have no meaning except as members of the whole. And the unity, on the other hand, has no meaning or even existence, apart from the members in which it is manifested. The beautiful object, *e.g.* the work of art, is essentially an organism.

643. Now the first sensuous form in which the Idea manifests itself, and therefore the first form of beauty, is *nature*. Nature is the Idea in its otherness. And since the Idea is here not the pure Idea, the Idea as it is in itself, but rather

the Idea buried in an external and sensuous medium, nature is, accordingly, beautiful. But there are degrees of beauty in nature. If we look at the lowest phase of nature, crass matter as such, we find that the Idea is so sunk and buried in externality as to be practically invisible. The parts of a lump of iron are indifferent to one another. If they are separated they remain what they are. Such an object, therefore, is scarcely to be regarded as beautiful. Rising somewhat higher we have such an object as the solar system. Here we have indeed an interdependence of the parts upon one another, and moreover a centre of unity, the sun. But the relations of the bodies of such a system are still governed only by mechanical laws. And moreover the unity, instead of being an ideal unity which pervades the members and is inseparable from them, is on the contrary itself a separate material object, the sun. The unity here is itself merely one of the parts. It is only when we reach the phenomena of organic nature, life, that we find true beauty. For in the living organism all the parts are bound in an ideal unity which is the pervading soul of the organism. The hand, when cut off, ceases to be a hand. As a hand it has no being apart from the unity of the whole. Plant and animal life, therefore, is beautiful, animal life more so than plant life because it exhibits the Idea, *i.e.* unity in difference, more completely.

644. The beauty of nature, however, exhibits grave defects. What are above all necessary for the exhibition of true beauty are *infinitude* and *freedom*. The Idea, as such, is absolutely infinite. The Idea is constituted by three factors, viz. (1) the unity of the Notion, which puts itself forth into (2) differences, plurality, objectivity, which return again into (3) the concrete unity of the above two factors. Now what is essential here is that it is the Notion *itself* which puts itself forth into differences, and then overreaches the distinctions within itself which it has thus created. Its entire development is a development out of its own resources. It is thus wholly self-determined, infinite, and free. Hence the beautiful object, if it is truly to manifest the Idea, must itself be infinite and free. It must, as an organism, evolve all its

differences out of itself. They must be seen to proceed out of the ideal unity which is its soul.

Now it is true that the living organism, regarded as a part of nature, does in a sense determine itself. Nevertheless as being a mere link in the infinite network of the necessity of nature, it is unfree. The animal, for example, is wholly determined by its environment. Even man as a part of nature is thus externally determined. To a large extent he acts under the compulsion of his various physical and material needs. He is involved in that general network of necessity which is the universe. The beauty of nature, therefore, is essentially defective on account of the finitude of natural objects. If, therefore, the human mind is adequately to apprehend the Absolute in sensuous form,—which is the demand of spirit in the present sphere—it must rise above nature. It must create objects of beauty for itself. Hence arises the necessity for **art**. Art alone is truly beautiful. The beauty of nature is inferior to the beauty of art in the same degree as nature in general is inferior to spirit. For art is the creation of spirit.

Critics of Hegel's aesthetics have generally urged that he too hastily thrusts aside the beauty of nature, and assigns it too low a place. This criticism is probably justified.

645. We come, therefore, to the proper subject of aesthetics, the beauty of art. Every work of art presents two distinct sides which are however bound together in unity. These are (1) the side of *unity*. The unity is the Notion before it has issued forth into plurality and objectivity. The Notion, however, is *subjectivity*. This side of the work of art is, therefore, essentially of a subjective nature. It is the spiritual meaning, the inner significance, the *soul* (subjectivity) of the work of art. It may be called in general the *spiritual content* or simply the *content*, of the work of art. This unity, however, does not remain an abstract unity closed up in itself. It manifests itself in (2) the plurality of differences. This is the objective, sensuous, material side of the work of art, and may be called in general the material *embodiment* or *form*. In architecture this material embodiment in which the Idea

manifests itself is composed of crass matter, of stone; in painting, colour or light; in music, sound; in poetry, mental image. These two sides do not fall apart but are bound together in perfect unity. When we have the Idea thus completely embodied in a material form, we have the perfection of the Ideal.

646. Since the work of art is to be infinite, free, and self-determined, it will exclude from its material side whatever exists in pure externality and contingency, whatever, in fact, cannot be shown as wholly issuing out of, and determined by, the inner unity or spiritual content. Thus in portrait painting, such pure externalities as warts on the skin, scars, pores, pimples, etc., will be left out. For these do not exhibit anything of the inner soul, the subjectivity, which has to appear in manifestation. Art does not slavishly imitate nature. On the contrary it is just this pure externality and meaningless contingency of nature that it has to get rid of. In so far as it takes natural objects as its subject matter at all, its function is to divest them of the unessential, soulless, crass concatenation of contingencies and externalities which surround them and obscure their meaning, and to exhibit solely those traits which manifest the inner soul or unity.

647. And if the function of art is not the imitation of nature, neither does it consist in moral instruction. To use art as a means of instruction is to do violence to the infinity which we have seen to be essential to it. For only that which is an end in itself is infinite. That which is made a means to a further end, which is outside itself, is thereby subordinated to, and determined by, that which is other than itself. And art, as self-determined, must be an end in itself.

648. It is for the same reason, viz. the freedom and infinity of art, that the artist so often takes his subject matter from a past age, and preferably from what is called the *heroic* age. A highly civilized age is not the most suitable as the subject matter of art. In epic and dramatic poetry, for example, it is necessary that the characters should appear essentially free and self-determined. They must be independent beings, whose entire activities issue out of themselves,

and are not imposed upon them from outside. But in a highly organized state human activities are determined by custom, law, and in general the pressure of organized society. Herein man appears unfree. By the heroic age is meant that age when great independent characters were still possible. What they did they did solely out of the resources of their own natures. A loosely knit state of society, where every man is his own master, and where none have yet become mere cogs in the machine of the civilized state, is best suited to exhibit such self-determined freedom and independence. The heroes of the *Iliad*, Achilles, Ajax, and the rest, are indeed subject nominally to the leadership of Agamemnon. Yet all the heroes are, in fact, absolutely their own independent masters. They come and go as they please, fight or not as they please. Achilles, conceiving himself insulted, withdraws in anger from the fray and refuses to assist the Greeks. Agamemnon never thinks of commanding Achilles to return. He can at most attempt to persuade. A similar state of society occurred in the feudal ages of modern Europe, where the knights, nominally subject to the king, were in fact entirely their own masters.

Characters drawn from the present day are, on the contrary, tied hand and foot by every sort of social customs, institutions, usages, laws. Hence, as appearing unfree, they are less suitable subjects for art. Hegel does not, of course, force this idea too far. He does not go the length of saying, what is manifestly untrue, that the artist *cannot* use modern subjects; but only that such subjects afford greater difficulties to the skill of the artist. Art also shows a manifest preference for the order of *princes*. This is not out of snobbishness, but because princes are independent and free. They are under no control save their own.

649. It is for the same reason that everything which the heroes of ancient epic use in the way of implements, weapons, tools, even food and drink, are represented in art as forged or made by themselves, as, in a sense, issuing from their own freedom and their own acts. The hero himself slays and cooks his meat. His food and drink are of those kinds in the

gathering or preparation of which he can himself do all that is necessary—honey, milk, butter, cheese. Such beverages as beer, tea, coffee, brandy, are prosaic because they remind us of the complicated chain of causes and effects necessary to bring them to our lips, because they remind us, that is, of the conditions of unfreedom.

650. Where art depicts its characters as subject to pain, suffering, and disaster, it will, nevertheless, never exhibit them as wholly overwhelmed thereby. Their essential liberty and freedom must not be crushed out of existence. Amid all suffering they will remain masters of themselves, and assert their freedom. Again and again will the spirit, torn and shattered in the conflicts of the world, restore itself out of this disunion, return upon itself, upon its own essential unity and repose. Hegel instances a picture of Murillo's. A troop of beggar boys are here depicted. One is being scolded by his mother as he munches a piece of bread. Two others, hard by, ragged and poor, are eating melons. But in this very poverty and desolation what gleams forth, as the soul of the picture, is the complete carelessness and spontaneity, the inward liberty of this beggar life. It may be that, as in tragedy, the conflict and suffering end in the destruction of the mere physical lives of the characters—but not in the destruction of their spiritual freedom. They remain true to themselves, and to their essential being. They accept their fate as itself a necessary outcome of their own actions, and therefore as issuing from their free will.

651. The soul, or spiritual content, of a work of art is everywhere the Absolute, that is to say, *thought*, or the *universal*. What is absolutely particular, contingent, or capricious, will find no place in it. Consequently where it is human life that is depicted, it will be the essential, universal, rational, interests of humanity that will form its substance—the core of human life, the moving forces of the spirit. These universal and rational interests are in fact those which have been shown to be *necessary* in the course of the dialectic, the interests, for example, of the family, love, the state, society, morality, and so on. These, however, will not appear in art

in the form of abstract universals. For art has no dealings with abstractions, but moves always in the sphere of the concrete and individual. They will appear, therefore, in the form of immediacy, as the essentially rational *emotions*, such as love of parents and children, loyalty, devotion to honour, etc. Mere individual idiosyncrasies and caprices fail to move us. Only the universal emotions of our common humanity can be the permanent subject of art. For just because they are universal they are, for that reason, manifestations of the Absolute; for the Absolute is rationality, thought, universality. Similarly *mere* wickedness and evil, as such, cannot be made the content of art. For evil is simply the irrational, the non-universal. The Satan of Milton's epic is only possible because he retains noble traits, is moved by essentially rational impulses, though these may be misdirected. It is the nobility and grandeur of this character which appeals to us, not the mere wickedness.

652. For the reason that they are rational and universal, these moving forces of humanity are essentially *justifiable*. Nevertheless they may come into collision. In tragedy we have the collision of two such eternal principles, each of which is, on its own part, right and just. Thus in the *Antigone* of Sophocles, Creon the King decrees that the body of the son of Oedipus shall remain unburied, because he had proved himself a traitor to his country. Antigone, however, cannot leave the body of her brother unburied, and so violates the decree of Creon. Out of this collision of ethical forces the tragedy arises. For the decree of Creon is right and ethical inasmuch as it embodies care for the weal of the whole city. But the impulse of Antigone, the love of her brother, is also essentially rational and right, since it issues from a rational institution, the family.

653. In such a case each of these universal forces appears embodied in one of the characters of the drama. The conflict of forces is envisaged as a conflict of persons. The characters must never, however, be mere personifications of abstract forces, lifeless abstractions, as they are, for example, in conventional allegories. In philosophy the universal appears in

its naked universality. But the demand of art is that it should be wholly clothed in concrete form, that it should appear as wholly embodied in a true and complete individual. Hence though a character in drama may have as his *predominant* trait the embodiment of such an eternal force, he will be also, at the same time, a complete living individual with all the wealth of character that such an individual presents. The main fact about Romeo and Juliet is their love. But each of them is, in addition, a concrete whole of multiple characteristics, which they exhibit in the various situations to which the drama gives rise.

SECTION II

THE TYPES OF ART

654. In accordance with the fundamental notion of beauty, every work of art has two sides which are respectively :

(1) The spiritual content.
(2) The material embodiment, or form.

Beauty is the vision of the Absolute shining through a sensuous medium. The Absolute which thus shines through is the spiritual content. The sensuous medium through which it shines is the material embodiment. Now the nature of the Absolute may be variously described, *e.g.* as subject, as spirit, as reason, as thought, as the universal. The spiritual content may, therefore, be of various kinds. It may consist in the conception, prevalent in any age or among any people, of the absolute being—the fundamental religious concepts of a race. It may be constituted by any general idea of a spiritual kind. It may be the activity of those universal forces, love, honour, duty, which sway the human heart. It may be any thought, other than a mere idiosyncrasy or caprice, anything, that is to say, which is substantive and essential and which forms a part of the inner subjectivity and soul-life of man. All that is essential is that it should be capable of acting as a focal centre of unity which displays itself in and permeates each and every part of the material embodiment. For the control of all the parts of the work of art under a single central unity, so that the whole forms an organic being, in which the unity is as the soul and the plurality of the material embodiment is as the body—this is what we saw to be necessary for the manifestation of the Idea in a sensuous medium.

655. In the ideal work of art these two sides, content and embodiment, are in perfect accord and union, so that the embodiment constitutes the full and complete expression of the content, whereas the content, on its part, could find no other than this very embodiment as adequate expression for it. But this perfect accord and union are not always attained. And the different possible *relations* which content and embodiment bear to one another give us the division of art into its fundamental types. These are three in number.

(1) Matter (embodiment) predominates over spirit (content). The spiritual content here struggles to find its adequate expression but fails to do so. It fails clearly to shine through. It has not mastered its medium. It is overwhelmed by matter. This gives us the *symbolic* type of art.

(2) The perfect balance and union of spirit and matter. This gives us the *classical* type of art.

(3) The spirit predominates over the matter. This gives us the *romantic* type of art.

656. This development of art through its three phases is fundamentally a *notional*, or logical development, which, as such, has no connection with time. Nevertheless history shows that the actual evolution of art in the world has to a large extent followed the notional development. On the whole the earliest art is symbolic, modern art is romantic, while in the intermediate ages we have classical art. But this cannot be pressed too far. All the types of art exist in all ages. Again, the different types are especially associated with different peoples. The art of the Oriental peoples, mainly the Egyptians and Hindus, is predominantly symbolic. That of the Greeks was classical. That of modern Europe is romantic. But here again, all the types exist to a greater or less degree, among all peoples. Lastly, the three types are associated with specific arts. Architecture is the symbolic art *par excellence*,

sculpture the classical, painting, music, and poetry the romantic. Yet classical and romantic architecture are wide-spread and important. There is such a thing as romantic sculpture. And traces of symbolism are to be found everywhere in painting and poetry.

Sub-Section I

THE SYMBOLIC TYPE OF ART

657. In **symbolic art** the human mind struggles to express its spiritual ideas but is unable to find an adequate embodiment. Consequently it adopts the symbol as its instrument. The essence of a symbol is that it *suggests* a meaning but does not *express* it. A lion may be taken as the symbol of strength, a triangle of the Triune God. The symbol itself is always a material thing set before us. That which it symbolizes is some thought or spiritual significance. Thus in symbolic art the symbol constitutes the material embodiment, while its significance is the content. The symbol, in order to be a symbol, must possess some trait of *affinity* with its significance, as for example the three sides of the triangle with the three persons of the Godhead. But it must also be *different* from the significance, otherwise it ceases to be a mere symbol and becomes a genuine mode of expression. Thus God has a multitude of attributes *not* possessed by the triangle. And the triangle has, or may have, attributes not possessed by God. On account of this difference the symbol is always *ambiguous*. The triangle may be taken as the symbol of God. But it might also be taken as the symbol of the delta of the Nile, and so of fertility. This ambiguity explains the sense of mystery which pervades all symbolic art, especially that of Egypt. It is a paradise of riddles and problems. And this fact renders symbolism suitable to the early ages of undeveloped humanity which have failed to solve the problems of the spirit, and to whom, in general, the world is an enigma.

658. Since the work of art involves the two sides (1) the Absolute or the content, (2) the phenomenal and material forms of the embodiment, it is obvious that there can be no

art so long as the human mind has in no way recognized the difference between the two sides, and their *separation* from one another. The demand of art is that the two sides should be brought together in a unity. Such a demand presupposes their *separation*. Hence among primitive peoples where this distinction has never yet been made, art does not exist. Thus the ancient Zend people worshipped Light as God. They did not, however, take Light merely as the symbol of God. On the contrary they regarded Light itself, in its immediate physical presence, as *being* God. God, for them, was simply the physical substance Light. But Light is itself a physical phenomenon. These people, therefore, made no distinction between the Absolute or spiritual and the phenomenal or material. They had consequently no art.

659. The realization of the separation between the Absolute and the phenomenal world, which is essential for art, may, however, be either conscious or unconscious. It may be vaguely felt but not clearly brought before consciousness. Or it may be clearly understood and deliberately expressed. In the former case, which naturally comes first, we get the unconscious symbolism of the Hindus, in the latter case the deliberate symbolism of the Egyptians and Hebrews.

660. Among the ancient Hindus the separation was vaguely felt, but the two sides were not held fast in their separation. At one moment they were kept apart, at another plunged together again. At one moment the separation is made so absolute, that God, under the name of Brahman, is conceived in utter abstraction from the world, as the formless One, empty being, of whom nothing whatever can be predicated, who is so completely severed from the world as to be entirely beyond the range either of sense or even of thought. At another moment the two sides are utterly confounded together, plunged into each other in hopeless riot and confusion. From this latter point of view any object of sense whatever is confounded with the divine. The cow, the ape, the serpent, are worshipped as being veritably God.

This plunging to and fro from one extreme to the other, this confusion of the divine and sensuous, results in that restless and fermenting phantasy, that riot of fantastic dreams and distorted shapes, which are characteristic of Hindu art.

This restlessness is evidence of the fact that the people among whom it obtains are, at least sub-consciously, aware of the contradiction which is inherent in their conceptions. This contradiction consists in the fact that while, on the one hand, the immediate sense-object, the ape, the cow, the stone, is declared to be itself divine and God, yet on the other hand the object of sense is seen to be so utterly inadequate to the divine being, that the latter is, on the contrary, projected wholly beyond the world of sense as the formless One, the complete vacuity of empty being. The Hindu imagination, therefore, is impelled to attempt in its art the reconciliation of this contradiction between the two sides, *i.e.* between the Absolute and the sense-object. It seeks to force the sensuous into congruity with the Absolute. It can only do this, however, by the measureless extension of sense-objects, which are drawn out into colossal and grotesque proportions in the vain hope that they will thus be made adequate to the divine. Hence the monstrous and distorted shapes characteristic of Hindu art. This is the cause, too, of all that extravagant exaggeration of size, not merely in regard to spatial dimensions, but also as to time-durations, the endless kalpas, the monstrous and yawning vistas of time, which we meet with everywhere in Hindu conceptions. It also explains the reduplication of the members, the many heads, arms, legs, in the statues of the Hindu Gods.

The main feature of Hindu art, then, is the total inadequacy which it reveals between content and embodiment. The spirit struggles to attain expression and cannot. And the convulsiveness of this struggle results only in distorted and fantastic shapes. Huge masses of matter here overwhelm the spirit.

661. A somewhat higher stage is exhibited by Egyptian art. Here the separation between the divine and its sensuous embodiment has been more clearly made, though not yet thoroughly grasped. Hence we get a more genuine symbolism. The world-conceptions of the Egyptian people are clearly

symbolized in the legend of the phoenix, in the pyramids, the huge Memnon statues, the obelisks, and temples. The obelisks symbolize the rays of the sun. The maze-like windings of the passages of the labyrinths symbolize the intricate movements of the heavenly bodies. We find here, too, particular *numbers* taken as symbolical, especially the numbers seven and twelve. Seven is the number of planets, twelve the number of lunar revolutions or the number of feet that the Nile must rise to fertilize the land. Thus in Egyptian temples we get twelve steps or seven pillars. The Sphinx itself is a symbol of the riddle of the universe, a symbol of mystery, a symbol of symbolism.

Here we can see more clearly the distinct severation of the two sides, and consequently the allocation of this definite symbol for that definite meaning.

662. But the completely conscious distinction of the two sides is only met with in the pantheistic art of the Hindus and Persians, and the art of the *sublime* as developed by the Hebrew poets and prophets. In both cases the Absolute is set clearly on this side, and the phenomenal world of sense on that. The Absolute is then conceived as the divine essence of the world, the *substance* of which all things are but the accidents, the sole essential *reality* of the universe, of which all else is but shadow-like appearance and manifestation. Two relations are, in that case, possible. Either the divine is conceived as the creative force of the world, immanent and *revealed* in all phenomena. In this case phenomena are exalted by art as revealing the immanent divine. This gives us the art of mystical pantheism, elaborated by the Hindus and Persians, and, in a lesser degree, by the Christian mystics of Europe. Its essential feature is that it sees, in all phenomena of nature and mind, the indwelling and habitation of the divine. Or, on the other hand, the divine may be conceived as *negating* the world, as the supreme reality before which all finite things flee away, perish, are as nothing. All phenomena are then used as testifying, by means of their own essential nothingness, to the greatness and glory of God. To this type belongs the religious poetry of the Hebrews. Of

men the Psalmist says: "Thou sufferest them to pass away like a brook; they are like as a sheep, even as the grass, which is soon withered, and in the evening is cut down and dried up. Thy scorn maketh us to pass away; Thou showest thine anger and we are gone."[1]

663. In such utterances as this we have the **sublime** as distinguished from the strictly *beautiful*. The sublime is the attempt to express the infinite, without being able to find any sensuous medium which is adequate to express it—so that it remains at last the unspeakable, the unutterable. The true sublime breaks and shatters every form in which we seek to enclose it. The strictly beautiful, on the contrary, consists precisely in this, that the Absolute finds its complete and adequate expression in a sensuous embodiment, the two sides being thus in full and harmonious accord.

664. The complete dissolution of the symbolic type of art is found by Hegel in such inferior forms of art-product as the fable, the allegory, the parable, the descriptive and the didactic poem. Hegel elaborates, with minute care, the various distinctions and affinities between these and kindred artistic types. Space forbids us to follow him into these details. What is common to all these forms is that the severation between the two necessary sides of a work of art—which *severation* is the characteristic feature of symbolic art—is carried so far that the link between them is broken, or subsists only as a relation of pure externality. In the fable, for example, we have, on the side of embodiment, a particular incident or story. The spiritual content consists in some moral or abstract truth which the fable is supposed to illustrate. Content and embodiment are here merely tacked onto each other in a purely external way. There is no natural affinity between them. They are mechanically forced together. But the very notion of a work of art necessitates the organic unity of the two sides. Hence such forms as these are not genuine art at all. And in them the symbolic type of art perishes. Its essential defect throughout all its phases is the incongruity between content and embodiment, whereby

[1] 90th Psalm.

the content never truly gets itself *expressed*, but is only hinted at and suggested by means of symbols. It is this defect which forces art onwards to another type, the classical type of art.

Sub-Section II

THE CLASSICAL TYPE OF ART

665. In symbolic art the spiritual content does not reside immanent *in* the embodiment. It remains external to it. This defect, however, is itself due to a profounder cause, namely, that the content in symbolic art is *abstract* instead of being concrete. We have seen that art is the apprehension of the Absolute, and that the Absolute is spirit. Consequently in art the spirit apprehends itself. But spirit is essentially concrete. Mere consciousness is not, as such, true spirit. True spirit is *self*-consciousness. Only when spirit as subject has put itself forth from itself, has made itself an object to itself, and has thereafter again annulled this division, over-reached the distinction, and comprehended both sides in a unity—only then is it the *concrete* unity of self-knowing spirit. Or to put the same thing in another way, spirit is the universal, but not the abstract universal. As *universal* it must sunder itself into the *particular*, and again comprehend its universality and particularity in concrete *individuality*. If then art is to enable the human spirit to grasp the essential nature of spirit—and this is precisely the function of art—this can only be completely possible where it conceives spirit as concrete. But spirit in symbolic art, as seen in the side of content, is revealed only as abstract. The spiritual content of symbolic art consists solely in mere abstraction. This is most clearly visible in the case of Hindu art, where the Absolute is envisaged merely as the formless One. This One is the barest and emptiest of all possible abstractions. It is no more than pure being. In its utter abstraction from the world of sense, in its infinite exaltation above all the particularity of nature, it shows itself as the empty universal, in which neither particularity nor individuality have any part.

The failure of symbolic art to combine content and form in real unity arises from this abstractness of the content. The very meaning of the abstract universal is that it is a universal which does *not* pass over into the particular and individual, which does not, in fact, embody itself in individual forms. Hence the attempt made by symbolic art to exhibit its abstract conceptions in those individual embodiments which are necessary to the very notion of art, is doomed to failure. An abstraction is precisely that which *cannot* combine with a sensuous individual embodiment. The formless One of the Hindus, for example, is such that its very nature is to reject the sensuous, to refuse all combination with it.

If, therefore, art is to attain the Ideal, that is, the harmonious balance and accord of content and form, this can only be possible where the content is concrete. The concrete universal, just because it is concrete, goes forth of its own accord into the particular, and constitutes itself an individual. Such a content has therefore an inherent suitability for sensuous embodiment. It combines readily with its external form But in order that art may rise to this level it is necessary that the people who create it should have ceased to view the Absolute as a bare abstraction and should have learned to grasp it as concrete.

This step was taken by the Greeks. For them the divine is no longer empty being, empty universality, but spiritual individuality. The Greek gods are personal and individual beings like ourselves. The task which art sets itself is to know the Absolute in its truth, and this can only mean to know it as spirit. Now when spirit comes to know the Absolute, not as empty being, but as spirit, what it learns is that the Absolute is *itself*. Hence anthropomorphism becomes the dominant note, and the Absolute is conceived under the mode of human individuality. Anthropomorphism is the leading feature of classical art.

Because the spiritual content is no longer a formless abstraction, but a formed individuality, it readily combines with its sensuous embodiment. Hence the essential notion of the **classical type of art** is that in it content and form are in perfect agreement and balance. The content no longer remains external to the form, as in symbolic art, but enters into it, is immanent in it as its soul. The outward form perfectly expresses the inner content. Nothing is left over unexpressed. And since the perfect embodiment of the Idea in sensuous form is the Ideal of art in general, it follows that art reaches its perfection here in the classical type. Romantic art, as we shall see, is indeed a higher stage of spirit than classical art, but just for that very reason it tends to transcend art altogether and pass into a higher sphere.

666. The Greek mind pictures the divine as a Pantheon of human-like gods. Since the principle of formed individuality is essential to art, these gods are no mere abstract personifications but genuine individuals depicted with a wealth of intimate characterization. Nevertheless because it is the *universal* in them which, as divine, must be emphasized, their universality must not descend too far into the *particularity* of the finite world. Though in the world, they are not of it. Into the infinite welter of empirical particulars they do not enter. They remain aloof in their blessed repose, their eternal calm, exalted above all mere transitoriness and contingency. This atmosphere of calm and immortal blessedness is the outstanding feature of the gods as depicted in Greek sculpture. In it is emphasized the *universality* of the divine. For the universal, as such, is that unity into which division, difference and strife, have not yet entered.

667. Since classical art is essentially anthropomorphic, the sensuous form which it selects as that most suitable to embody its content is the *human form*. Because the Absolute is now conceived as concrete spirit, man sees the Absolute primarily in *himself*. And the human form is alone, of all the forms of the world of sense, entirely suited to be the dwelling place and embodiment of spirit. The human body is, in fact, spirit in its material shape. Hence *sculpture* is *par excellence* the classical art, the art which most perfectly sets forth the classical ideal. For sculpture, although not entirely restricted to the human form, yet takes it as its most essential subject-matter. Sculpture, too, is, among all the arts, the most

suited to express that infinite and blessed repose which is characteristic of the classic type of art. It is specially fitted to express rest rather than action.

668. The classical type is especially associated with the Greeks, just as symbolic art was with Egyptians and Hindus. But this association is no rigid restriction. Any art, wherever found, in which content and form are in perfect balance, belongs to the classic type. Nor were the other types of art entirely foreign to the Greeks. Traces of symbolism are found everywhere in their art. Moreover in their poetry, and especially their drama, they possessed an art essentially romantic. Poetry is a romantic art. Yet even their poetry is stamped with the characteristics which have here been described as classical.

669. The dissolution of the classical type takes place through the gradual realization of the fact that the conception of the divine which it embodies is defective. The divine ought to be free and infinite spirit. But the Greek gods are neither free nor infinite. As a plurality they are limited by each other. They are not the supreme masters of the world, nor even of their own destinies. Above them stands an inscrutable and mysterious Fate. They are, after all, merely finite beings, not free, but subject, as men are, to the necessary course of events.

Sub-Section III

THE ROMANTIC TYPE OF ART

670. What really happens, when it is realized that the classical divine is finite and unfree, is that spirit finds that no individual and sensuous form is genuinely adequate to express its nature. For the individual, as being merely one among others, is finite and unfree. And since no sensuous shape is adequate to spirit, spirit now retires out of its sensuous embodiment, retires into itself and its own subjectivity. This gives rise to a new type of art, a type in which spirit tends more and more to expatiate within its own realm, to drop the veils of sense altogether, to withdraw into itself, to divest itself of its material embodiment. The side of material

embodiment thus gets whittled away; spirit predominates over matter. This is **romantic art**.

671. The fundamental character of romantic art is thus laid down for it. In symbolic art content remained external to form because it had not yet entered into it. Matter there overwhelmed spirit. In classical art content has genuinely entered into, and become immanent in, form. Expression is perfect. Spirit and matter are completely fused in an harmonious unity. In romantic art spirit has not merely entered into, but has passed out beyond, material form. Spirituality predominates, enters on an independent existence, leaves its sensuous embodiment behind. Here again, therefore, content and form have become, as in symbolic art, but in a converse way, external to each other, the perfect union of the two being left behind.

672. In one sense romantic art is the highest type of art, and in another sense classical art is the highest. Since what is involved in the very notion of art is the complete unity of content and embodiment, classical art, because it alone attains that end, is the sole perfect type of art. But, on the other hand, since in romantic art spirit more clearly grasps its own true nature, romantic art is, for that reason, a higher mode of spiritual development than classical art. But in so far as romantic art departs from and transcends the perfect type of art it to that extent transcends the limits of art altogether. It is, in fact, a transitional stage, in which spirit is already beginning to leave the sphere of art behind and pass into the higher sphere of religion.

673. Spirit, then, now finds that no sensuous embodiment is truly adequate to it. What alone rises to the dignity of spirit is its own inward spiritual life, untrammelled by any material forms. The inward life of the soul, its absolute subjectivity—this is the essential subject-matter of romantic art. Romantic art is, for all intents and purposes, the art of modern Europe, the art of Christendom.

674. We saw that if spirit is to grasp the nature of itself, the nature of spirit, truly, it must conceive it essentially as *concrete* spirit, as the spirit which does not remain in the

blissful repose of its universality, but sunders itself in division and conflict with itself, and again reconciles itself to itself, heals the division, and returns to a repose and bliss which is not that of inaction, but is won out of the heart of conflict. To exhibit this process of spirit is an essential function of romantic art. Spirit has to overcome its other. In classical art this other was nature, or in general the world of sense. The spiritual content there reconciled itself to its other, *i.e.* the sensuous medium, with which it found perfect accord. But because in romantic art spirit has now withdrawn from the sense-world into its own realm, the division which it has to reconcile must now be *within itself*. Its other is not the sensuous, but rather a spiritual other. The inner conflict of spirit with itself, its alienation from itself and its ultimate self-reconciliation, become the content of romantic art.

It is for this reason that, whereas the classical work of art bore always upon it the stamp of an eternal, blissful, undisturbed, immortal, repose and calm, romantic art, on the contrary, tends to depict conflict, action, movement. And whereas pain, suffering, and evil were, in classical art, either excluded altogether as unbeautiful, or at least relegated to the background, they now enter into the essential fabric of romantic art. The classical artist did not depict these things. But suffering and evil, even the *ugly*, find their place in romantic art. For it is the *torn* soul, the soul in conflict with itself, that is here the subject of art. Spirit only becomes truly spirit when it has rent itself in twain, and has again healed and reconciled this division, when it has gone forth into the particularity of the world—and evil and ugliness are simply the moment of *particularity* in the spheres of morality and art respectively—has overcome them, and has returned, triumphant over them, into itself. Only then is it a *concrete* unity.

This conflict and triumph of the spirit are envisaged especially in Christian consciousness as the life, death, and resurrection of Christ, and the same is again reflected in a lesser degree in the similar experiences of the apostles, saints, and martyrs. Hence these subjects are especially suitable to romantic art, and the great era of mediaeval painting is almost wholly concerned with them. The story of Christ sets visibly before the imagination the profound truth of the new conception of the Absolute as concrete spirit. The divine is no longer mere universality, subsisting above all mundane affairs in blissful repose. The divine, as universal, sunders itself into particularity, enters the actual world, becomes flesh. God is this individual actual man, Christ. The divine, in Christ, in his life, death, pain, suffering, Calvary, enters into all the conflict of the finite world. This is the universal sundering itself into the particular. But in the resurrection and ascension we have the *third* moment of the Notion, the return of the spirit into itself, into concrete unity, the overcoming and reconcilement of the division which it has made within itself.

675. Since the spirit has, in romantic art, withdrawn into itself, what it now regards as alone of infinite worth is itself. The external and material world is degraded to the significance of a cipher. The *infinite worth of personality* becomes, therefore, a leading feature of this type of art. This is emphasized especially in the literature and art of *chivalry*. Chivalry has three essential features—honour, love, and loyalty. The principle of each of these is the infinitude of personality, of the ego. The principle of honour is that I, this bare ego, am a *person* who, as such, am of infinite value (532). Honour contends, not for the common weal, nor for any ethical or substantive end, but simply for the recognition of my inviolability as a *person*. Romantic love involves the same principle, the recognition, in this case, of the infinite worth of *another* person, and the finding of my own true self in that other. Loyalty, or fidelity in the service of a master, lastly, does not attach itself to the objects of ethical value which that master may subserve, but to the *person* of the master in whatever enterprises, good or bad, he may undertake. The recognition of the ego as an end in itself, and therefore as infinite, constitutes the essential principle of honour, love, and fidelity. None of these ideals are found in Greek art. The wrath of Achilles is aroused, not by any insult to him as a *person*, but, on the contrary, by the loss of what he regards

as his share of the booty. Only what is actual and outward, the booty as an external thing, is here regarded as of value. If that is restored all is well. Personal honour does not enter into the matter. So too romantic love, which is the characteristic note of modern art, has no place in classical art at all. Not spiritual, but purely physical love, is there understood as the sole intelligible relation between the sexes.

676. A further consequence of the emphasis which romantic art lays upon the side of subjectivity—*i.e.* the side of spiritual content—and its neglect of the objective side—*i.e.* the side of material embodiment—is this. Whereas the characters in ancient literary art tended each to embody some universal ethical principle, such as the love of family or the care of the state, the characters in modern literature represent chiefly themselves. The source from which their activities derive is no ethical principle but purely the individual peculiarities of their personal characters. They pursue, not universal ends, but their own private ends. These may be good or they may be bad. But if they are good, *i.e.* if they are *intrinsically* universal, they are still pursued not for that reason, or on principle, but merely because the individual chooses to make them *his* personal ends. Thus the source of the action in ancient drama was essentially the conflict of universal ethical forces. In modern drama the source of action is simply the conflict of individual characters as such, each of whom stands not on any ethical basis, but simply on the basis of his own personality. This is pre-eminently true of the characters of Shakespeare. Each acts entirely from the internal resources of his own character, sticks to his personal aims through thick and thin, remaining self-consistent till the end. Not the *objective* life of the state, of the family, of civil society, but the inward soul-life and *subjectivity* of the individual, is here depicted.

677. Painting, music and poetry are the three pre-eminently romantic arts (though Gothic architecture is essentially romantic). This is so for two reasons. Firstly, romantic art is concerned with action and conflict, not repose. Architecture cannot represent action at all, sculpture very little. Painting,

music, and above all poetry are, by their very natures, fitted to represent action and movement. Moreover sculpture depicts outward spatial *form*, but not inward soul-life. Thus the eye, which is the window through which we look into the depths of soul-life, is, in the best sculpture, usually *blind*. The eye is not represented except as a cavity, or blind ball. Painting, however, can give the gleam and expression of the eye. And since it is the subjective soul-life which romantic art undertakes to express, sculpture is not suitable to its purpose. Sculpture, as emphasizing the material *form*, in which spirit resides, and as representing spirit as in blessed repose, is essentially the classical art. Secondly, the material media of painting, music, and poetry, are more ideal, more removed from the purely material plane than those of architecture and sculpture. The latter have as their media solid matter and spatiality in its three dimensions. Painting uses only two dimensions and presents merely the *appearance* of matter without its reality. Music abstracts from space altogether, and subsists in time only, and its medium is *tone*. Poetry, lastly, has for medium the wholly subjective and inward forms of the sensuous *image*.

678. Romantic art has the germ of its dissolution within itself. Art is, according to its very notion, the union of spiritual content and outward form. Romantic art has, to some extent, already ceased to be art by virtue of the fact that it breaks up the harmonious accord of the two sides which was present in classical art. Romantic art implies that the two sides are, in reality, incompatible, since spirit now finds that no sensuous embodiment is sufficient for it. The logical development of this principle can only result in the two sides falling asunder altogether, and when that happens we have the complete dissolution of art. Spirit finds then that art is not its true and perfect medium. A new sphere is required for the self-realization of spirit, and this new sphere is religion.

SECTION III

THE PARTICULAR ARTS

679. For the reason that the side of sensuous embodiment is an essential moment in the notion of art, art cannot remain merely an idea, but must come into actual sensuous existence, as an object for the senses. And since the content of art is in all cases the same, viz. the Idea, the difference between the arts must reside in the sensuous medium employed. The arts will, therefore, be classified according to the different material media through which the Idea makes itself visible.

680. Just as art, in its general types, showed a logical *progress* from lower to higher, from symbolic to romantic, so the particular arts arrange themselves in a similar necessary order, and exhibit an advance from lower to higher forms. What constituted the advance in the general types of art was an increasing *spirituality*. In symbolic art the spirit was overwhelmed by matter. In classical art matter and spirit stood on a level. In romantic art spirit has emerged predominant. Exactly the same principle governs the development of the particular arts. The first and lowest, architecture, is predominantly material. It takes as its medium solid matter in its three dimensions. At the other extreme we have poetry, as the last and highest art. The material side is here whittled away to almost nothing, consisting in words, *i.e.* sounds used as signs, and sensuous *images* which are purely subjective and inward. The progress consists, to put the same thing in another way, in the increasing *subjectivity* of the arts.

For this reason, too, the advance of the particular arts coalesces with the advance of the general types. The lowest art, architecture, is fundamentally symbolical, though it has its classical and romantic phases. Sculpture is the classical art. Painting, music, and poetry, are the romantic, *i.e.* the subjective arts of soul-life.

Sub-Section I

THE SYMBOLIC ART OF ARCHITECTURE

681. In **architecture** the Idea takes, as the medium of its appearance, huge masses of crass matter, matter in all its solidity and three dimensions. The forms used are primarily those of inorganic nature. It does not yet, as sculpture does, take the organic human form as its basis. Matter as governed, not by the laws of life, but by the mechanical laws of gravity, is its medium. For this reason it is the straight line, the rectangle, and other abstract figures, which constitute the main shapes into which it disposes matter. The vision of the Idea, *i.e.* of unity amid difference, is mostly exhibited in the abstract forms of symmetry, equality, conformity to rule, etc.

Architecture passes through three stages (1) symbolical, or Oriental, (2) classical, or Greek, (3) romantic, or Christian.

682. (1) *Symbolic Architecture.* The predominant feature of the symbolic building is that it exists as an independent end for itself. It subserves no purpose save to symbolize some abstract conception. Classical temples, on the contrary, exist, not for themselves, but in order to form the sanctuary of the statue of the god. Hence, since art is essentially an end in itself, architecture has, in the classical period, ceased to be a pure independent art. It has become subservient to sculpture. It is, therefore, the independent or symbolic type which is the fundamental type of architecture as a fine art.

The content which the independent architectural work of art symbolizes is invariably some abstract general idea, or else some phase of nature generalized and regarded as sacred and divine. The earliest mythical example is the Tower of Babel. This tower subserved no purpose, and was therefore entirely an independent work of art. It symbolized the idea of the unity of the peoples who built it. The city of Ecbatana, again, was enclosed within seven concentric walls, and in the centre was the royal stronghold and its treasure, symbolizing the spheres of heaven which enclose the stronghold of the sun.

The obelisks of Egypt serve no purpose save to represent the rays of the sun. And in Egypt, too, we find vast areas covered by forests of pillars, memnons, sphinxes, walls, and passages. These are neither temples nor dwelling places, but were built solely to symbolize various abstract conceptions. The tortuous windings of the passages of the labyrinths were not made for the puerile purpose of creating for the wanderer the problem how to find an exit, but represented the courses of the heavenly bodies. The passages within the pyramids— which are tombs—stand for the various wanderings and migrations of the soul after death.

683. (2) *Classical Architecture.* Classical architecture is not independent, but dependent. For it serves the purposes of providing a sanctuary for the statue of the god, and a place of assemblage for the worshipping community. This feature of dependence shows itself, further, in all the details of the buildings. The columns do not stand up for their own sakes, as the obelisks did, but serve the useful purpose of being *supports* for the roof. This is their essential function. A column which supports nothing is a sham and a falsehood. As the Greek temple advances through the Doric, Ionic, and Corinthian styles, we have exhibited an increasing spirituality. For the Doric building is the most massive and material, the Corinthian the slenderest.

These temples are not, primarily, symbolical of anything. They are wholly determined by their central idea, which is to provide an enclosure and suitable environment for the statue of the god. Yet they are not merely useful, but are also, in themselves, beautiful. Symbolical architecture could not properly be described as beautiful. In its colossal proportions and overwhelming masses it was, at the most, sublime. But the Greek temple is relatively small and fair. The Idea is not here found vainly struggling with unwieldy masses of matter, but has entered harmoniously into the external form.

684. (3) *Romantic Architecture.* The chief examples of this are found in the Gothic churches of modern Europe. Because we are still in the sphere of architecture, and because architecture is especially the symbolic art, for these reasons

symbolism prevails here too. The cruciform shape, the spires, the general trend of the buildings upwards into vast and aspiring heights,—all is symbolical. Yet the spirit of this symbolism is throughout romantic. These forests of spires and points rising one above the other, the upward-pointed arches and windows, the vast height of the buildings, represent the upward aspirations of the soul which has withdrawn from the outward world into its own self-seclusion. The essential feature of romantic art is, as we have seen, precisely this withdrawal of the soul from the external and sensuous world into the subjectivity of its own inner soul-life. And this in general is what the Christian Church represents. The Greek temple with its walks and colonnades is open to the world. It invites ingress and egress. It is gay and pleasant. It is flat, low, and wide, not, like the Christian Church, narrow and high. This flatness and horizontal extension represents extension outwards into the external world. All these features are reversed in the Gothic Church. The pillars are not outside but inside. The whole is entirely enclosed, forming an abode of the soul shut off in self-seclusion from the outside world. The sun only enters in a glimmer through the stained-glass windows. Everyone comes and goes, prays upon his knees and moves away. All kinds of religious acts are going on at the same time. But all this variety of changing life cannot fill it, cannot disturb the vast peace of the huge empty spaces and shadowy vistas of the soaring vaults overhead. The absorption of all this life as in these infinite silent spaces, represents, in sensuous fashion, the infinity of the spirit and its aspirations. What is emphasized here, then, is the inner soul-life, cut off from the world, the subjectivity which is the essential principle of romantic art.

Sub-Section II

THE CLASSICAL ART OF SCULPTURE

685. The medium of **sculpture** is still, no doubt, solid matter. But whereas in architecture it was simply *crass* matter, that is, inorganic and therefore unspiritualized matter

controlled by the mechanical and physical laws of gravity, the medium of sculpture is now matter that has been infused with the breath of spirit, *organic* matter controlled by the laws of life and by its own inward subjectivity, and especially organic matter in the shape of the *human* form. Moreover, sculpture abstracts from, and whittles away, at least one aspect of matter, namely colour. It is true that many statues have been painted, and this too among the Greeks. But the typical statue is without colour; or at least—since some colour it must have to be visible—its colour is indifferent and undifferentiated. It has the uniform colour of bronze or marble. And since colour is thus obliterated, all that is essential is the shape, the abstract spatial *form*.

The human form constitutes the centre of sculpture—animal and other forms being merely subsidiary—because the human body is the soul material embodiment adequate to be the expression of spirit. In the last resort, as we have seen, spirit finds that *no* sensuous form is adequate to it. In saying, then, that the human body is its adequate mode of presentment, we mean only that it is adequate to the highest extent that the purely sensuous can be adequate. And since the spirit is here immanent in the form, since content and embodiment are found in perfect equipoise and unity, it is for these reasons that sculpture is pre-eminently the classical art.

686. The medium of sculpture is not matter in all its qualitative crassness. The qualitativeness of matter, that is to say, chiefly, its colour, is abstracted from, and we are left mainly with its quantitative aspect, its aspect, that is, as pure extension, as spatial form, mere *outline*. To this abstract and therefore universal character of the sensuous medium what pre-eminently corresponds, on the side of the spirit, is the universal and substantive traits of spirit. These are, accordingly, the fitting subject matter of sculpture. This means that sculpture will depict spirit in its undisturbed universality and repose, and will exclude the violent agitation of the spirit which has descended into the vortex of the particular activities of the world. The statues of the Greek gods all bear the stamp of this lofty and other-worldly calm,

this immortal serenity. Yet this does not mean that sculpture should depict empty abstractions and personifications, such as Fortune, Love, Justice, and so on. On the contrary, its creations will be essentially concrete individual living characters. But what *should* be delineated are the permanent and substantial features of the character, its general qualities, such as goodness, honest dealing, courage, exceptional intelligence, and so forth. Mere passing phases of mood and emotion, such as anger, surprise, etc., should be excluded. Painting can delineate these, but not sculpture. Neither does the requirement of universality and calm mean that all motion of any kind is excluded. Many famous statues, such as those of the disc-throwers, exhibit motion. But it must represent action of a simple type. It must not disturb or distort the essential features of the character. In violent anger a man's whole personality is absorbed in that one emotion, and his substantive traits disappear in it. Such states of the soul are unsuitable for the art of sculpture. The figure must remain poised on the basis of its substantive universality. Mere idiosyncrasies of expression, mere caprices of action, all the more subjective and purely personal states of the soul, must be excluded. It is for this reason that the *glance* of the eye is absent in statuary of the best type, although it is present in painting. For it is only in romantic art that the subjective depths of soul life can be delineated.

Symbolical and romantic sculpture, though briefly touched upon by Hegel, are of insufficient importance to be dealt with here. Sculpture is overwhelmingly classical in its best creations.

Sub-Section III

THE ROMANTIC ARTS OF PAINTING, MUSIC AND POETRY

687. Romantic art possesses for its principle the withdrawal of spirit from the external and sensuous world. For that very reason, however, the external world now for the first time in art gains an independent right to exist on its own account. In classical art the sensuous only appeared as

bound up with, and therefore dependent upon, spirit. Now, however, each side breaks loose from the other—though the bond is not wholly severed, since that would mean the dissolution of art altogether—each stands facing the other independently existing in its own right. Subjectivity and objectivity become severed; art definitely takes subjectivity for its principle and increasingly rejects the objective. The term subjectivity, however, has a twofold meaning. On the one hand, it means the conscious life of ego as opposed to the material world. On the other hand, it means what appertains to *this* particular ego, as opposed to that, *i.e.* the individual idiosyncrasies, caprices, and peculiarities of this or that person as opposed to the universal, substantive, and permanent features of human life, which are from this point of view, the objective.

Romantic art becomes subjective in *both* these senses. On the one hand it concentrates itself on the inward life of the soul and progressively dissipates the side of sensuous embodiment. On the other hand it tends to depict more freely the peculiarities and capricious characteristics of particular persons.

A. *Painting.*

688. The dissipation of the sensuous embodiment in romantic art takes, in the first instance, the form of the negation of space. This is not accomplished, however, all at once. **Painting,** the first romantic art, abstracts from only one dimension of space, and is left with the other two, *i.e.* with plane surface, as its medium. Thus it has no longer as its basis heavy solid matter actually existing, but only the *appearance* of such. This illusion, this appearance of solidity, is created by the artist. Thus whereas the sensuous existence of the work of architecture or sculpture was an actual material *thing*, the sensuous side of the painting is only partly material. The remaining part is *mental*. In this way the side of subjectivity now makes its appearance even in the very heart of the sensuous embodiment. That the painting is merely an illusion is not, as some have supposed, a defect, but is the

very mark of its advance beyond sculpture. For the rest, the material medium of painting is light and colour. It is through the differentiation of colour that the illusion is created.

689. The increase of subjectivity also means, as already explained, that painting, as a romantic art, is not confined, as sculpture is, to the universal and permanent traits of human character. Individual peculiarity, caprice, and idiosyncrasy, and in fact the entire wealth of soul-life, are open to its delineation. Surprise, anger, a passing smile, and all similar momentary moods of the soul, can be its subject-matter. It is for this reason that the glance of the eye now becomes important. And it is for the same reason that the characters need no longer be depicted in serene repose, but may be exhibited in all the animation of movement and activity. Yet painting is in this respect limited because it can only exhibit a single moment of time. It is not in itself, as both music and poetry are, a process in time which can develop the various stages of an action.

690. Since the characters in a painting need not remain fixed in their universality and repose, but can descend into particularity, therefore pain and suffering can enter into it. These must not, however, be carried too far. The fundamental condition of art is that it should manifest spirit in its reconciliation with itself. And this fact forms the motive of the great era of mediaeval Christian painting. Even the anguish of the Madonna at the loss of her Son is an anguish through which can be perceived the triumph of spirit, its reconcilement with itself.

691. The severation which romantic art affects between spirit and the external world has for one of its results the independent subsistence of the latter in its own right (687). The external world merely as such can become, therefore, the subject of painting, and this gives rise to *landscape*-painting. This style of painting portrays what at first appears to be the simply soulless and non-divine,—nature. It is, however, still essentially subjective soul-life which forms the subject of such pictures. The artist discovers in the varying moods of nature a kinship with his own moods. Nature is calm and

peaceful, or angry and fierce, or sombre and melancholy. It is really these moods of his own soul that the artist paints, not the mere external objects of nature.

B. Music.

692. **Music** negates space altogether and exists only in *time*. Hence, since whatever is seen by the eye must exist in space, this art ceases to address the sense of sight and makes its appeal to the sense of hearing. Its material medium is, therefore, the succession of sounds or tones in time.

693. This complete negation of space makes music a purely subjective art. The statue has an independent existence of its own in space. It is an independent *thing*. This objectivity is in painting partially annulled. The picture is only an appearance. Nevertheless, even the picture has an external existence as a thing. Musical tone, however, has no such permanence or subsistence. In the very moment of its utterance it vanishes and ceases to exist. It has thus no genuine objectivity. Hence in the case of music the separation of object and subject, present in the other arts, does not arise. The spectator contemplates the statue or the picture as something outside himself. The ego in such case is separate from its object. But since this external objectivity disappears in music, the separation of the work of art from its beholder disappears also. The musical work penetrates, therefore, into the very core of the soul and is one with its subjectivity.

694. It is for the same reason that music is the most *emotional* of the arts. In sensation, thought, and conception, the subject stands over against the object, contemplating it. In emotion this separation is absent. The soul is absorbed in its object, is interwoven with the object in a thorough-going identity—identity in the sense that the soul is not in such a case aware of the distinction between itself and the object, since awareness is not an emotional but a cognitive state. Hence music appeals immediately to the emotions.

695. Even in nature cries are recognized as the direct expression of the inner emotional life. But a mere medley of sounds or cries is not in itself art. It only becomes art when the soul

has introduced into it an architectonic fabric of *ordered relations*. Such ordered relations introduce unity into the differences of sound. A crass plurality is not beautiful. But a plurality which is throughout governed and controlled by a unifying principle discloses the Idea, and is therefore beautiful. Symmetry and conformity to rule, the equality of time-beats amid the inequality of tone-lengths, are here of importance. Both harmony and melody are modes of introducing unity into the quantitative and qualitative differences of tones.

696. Rhythm and time-beat perform a special function in music, as also in poetry. The philosophical basis of time-beat, and the explanation of the extraordinary grip which it has on the soul, consists in the fact that the ego finds in it the absolute counterpart of itself. Time in itself is an even, undifferentiated, continuous flow. This abstract continuity corresponds to the bare universality of the ego which is empty of content. But the true nature of the ego is not this abstract universality. Only when the ego has sundered itself in twain, made itself an object to itself, and again annulled this division and returned into itself, is its real nature disclosed. Now time-beat introduces into the abstract continuity of time a division into equal intervals. But every moment of time, though thus distinguished from the next moment, is nevertheless *identical* with it. For one moment of time is indistinguishable from another. Each is a *now*. Time-beat, therefore, introduces division into the bare continuity of time, but this sundering is again annulled in the absolute identity of the intervals. The ego finds *itself* in this process; for it finds there a bare unity, sundering itself, and again returning into unity and identity with itself. Hence the profound satisfaction which the time-beat in music produces in us.

C. *Poetry.*

697. The withdrawal of spirit from its sensuous envelope is, in **poetry,** complete. For the medium of poetry is the wholly internal and subjective mental *image* or representation. It retains, however, in common with music, *sound,* not as its

actual embodiment, but as the means of communication from mind to mind. But the sound is not now, as in music, itself as mere sound the essential end. The sound now becomes a *word*, which has in itself no significance, but is merely the arbitrary *sign* for an idea or representation. The true form or *embodiment* in poetry is thus the idea or representation itself. This mental imagery and ideation is, however, at the same time the *content*. It possesses in itself the features both of content and form. Because it belongs to the side of spirit and inward subjectivity it is content. But because it is never merely an abstract universal, but is always steeped in individuality and clothed in sensuous imagery, it belongs from that point of view to the side of sensuous embodiment.

698. Stone, colour, and tone, the media of the other arts, are, as we have seen, restricted in various ways as regards the content which they can embody. Language, however, is capable of expressing anything whatever which can form the content of human consciousness. Poetry, therefore, is not restricted, as the other arts are, to the expression of some particular phase of spirit. The entire wealth of spirit is its domain. It is for this reason the universal art, the synthesis of all the others. It can be symbolic and sublime like architecture. Like sculpture it can express the universal and substantive, the calm repose of the divine. Like painting it can articulate the idiosyncrasies of the individual and the most fleeting phases of mood. Like music it can give utterance to the profoundest emotion. And it is not confined, as painting is, to a single moment of time. It can depict action and movement in every successive phase of their development. As being thus universal it is neither solely symbolic, classical, nor romantic. It is all these. It exists in all periods and in all countries.

699. Any content whatever may be the content of poetry. Whatever the human mind is capable of thinking—that can be the subject of a poem. The distinction between the prosaic and the poetical does not consist, therefore, in the nature of the content. For any content can be made poetical. The distinction arises from the peculiar mode under which the

poet works up his material. In poetry the universal is not sundered from the particular, but the two coalesce in vital unity. Poetry does not, as prose does, contrast law and phenomena, end and means, or relate one in subordination to the other. Science is essentially prosaic, because it separates the universal in abstraction from its embodiment; it abstracts the law from the phenomena in which it is manifested. Poetry, however, holds the abstract and the sensuous in vital unity. Hence what really distinguishes the poetical from the prosaic is—what is the universal condition of all art—that the poem is an organic unity, an infinite organism, wholly free and self-determined. It is pervaded and controlled by a single idea. The particular parts, images, ideas, etc., derive their life entirely from this focal centre and exist solely as its manifestation. Poetry, therefore, conceives its subject matter under the infinite categories of the Notion, the categories of life, organism, etc. Prose, on the other hand, conceives its object under the finite categories of the understanding, *i.e.* the categories which import dependence and unfreedom, such as cause and effect. History, though it may be presented under the light of a single unifying conception, is not poetry, because it depicts things in this unfree concatenation of dependent conditions, causes, effects, and so on. Oratory, though suffused with emotion, is not poetry, because the oration is never an end in itself, but subserves some ulterior end, such as persuasion, policy, edification, or instruction.

700. An example may make clear the manner in which poetry clothes the abstract in sensuous form and thus holds the two sides, universal and particular, in unbroken unity. Such words as " the sun," " the morning," etc., convey a meaning to the mind. But when such words and phrases occur in ordinary speech what is present before the mind is not an image, but merely a concept, possibly faintly tinged with colour, yet pale and barely visible. Such a mental content is a thought, a universal, an *abstraction*. But if the poet says, " When now the dawning Eos soared heavenwards with rosy fingers," here without question the previous abstraction is made sensuous and concrete as a clear image which rises up

before the *vision* of the mind. The former content in its abstraction is prosaic; the latter in its sensuous concretion is poetic.

701. Versification is important to poetry for much the same reasons that time-beat and rhythm are important to music. An unregulated and orderless stream of words, such as we have in prose, is, by means of metre, reduced to definite laws which introduce unity and cohesion into the undefined plurality. The philosophical basis of metre is the same as that of the time-beat in music (696). Rhyme and alliteration satisfy us because, in the regular recurrence of the same sound amid different sounds, the ego discovers the analogue of its own essential nature as unity in difference.

Though there are numerous subsidiary and intermediate types, poetry falls into three main divisions, namely, epic, lyric, and dramatic.

702. 1. *Epic Poetry.* The principle of the epic is *objectivity*. The poet retires into the background and sets before us the presentment of an objective world of persons, things, and events. He is merely the narrator. Comments of his own, the interposition of his own point of view or personality, are here unsuitable. No doubt he is the creator of the poem. But what has to appear is the creation, not the poet. In this respect epic poetry is the opposite of lyrical poetry. For in the latter it is essentially the *personality* of the poet which is important.

703. The epic poem must describe particular actions performed by particular persons. But this action should appear on a background which gives us the entire life of a people or age. In the *Iliad* and the *Odyssey* the whole life of the Greek people is mirrored. Hence the characters, though they must be genuine living individuals with all the wealth of their individual traits, should, nevertheless, be to some extent universal characters. The entire spirit of the nation should be concentrated in the hero of an epic. He should be typical of his age and country. A primitive state of society, neither merely barbarous on the one hand, nor yet on the other overcivilized and fettered by the prosaic conditions of developed

family and state life—in a word, the heroic age—is the best suited to be the background of an epic. For in such conditions the characters are free and independent.

704. Owing to the prevailing objectivity of the epic, the development of the action is as much conditioned by external circumstances as by the characters of the persons depicted. In drama whatever happens should have its source solely in the characters of the play. Merely external events and adventitious accidents should not be made the instruments by which the action works itself out. But because the epic is not only a picture of character but also of the objective world in which the character operates, therefore the events may have their source as legitimately in that external world as in the soul of the hero. Thus in the *Odyssey* the hero in his wanderings happens upon a host of adventures which arise purely from external circumstances and in nowise from his peculiar character.

705. The parts of an epic may be loosely connected, and there is room for purely episodical actions. But the whole must be fused together by some unifying idea, *e.g.* the single spirit of the hero, or the unity of the purpose towards which the entire action cooperates. In the *Iliad* it is the wrath of Achilles which forms the focal unity of the whole.

706. (2) *Lyrical Poetry*. The principle of lyrical poetry is *subjectivity*. Not the outward form of events, but the inward soul-life of the individual poet here finds expression. The lyric is essentially the utterance of his special and peculiar personality; his private feelings, moods, joys, sorrows, hopes or fears. There is, therefore, no possibility of the lyric poem extending the borders of its subject-matter to depict an entire national life. It is always some *particular* phase of feeling or idea that is expressed. The slenderest thought, the most passing mood, is sufficient. Yet, although it is the special personality of the poet that is embodied in the lyric, the feelings or moods upon which it is founded should for all that be universal in their substance so as to appeal generally to the human heart as such. It is the personality of the poet, his peculiar vision of the world, his individual

outlook, which fuses the parts of the poem into a unified whole.

707. (3) *Dramatic Poetry* is the unity of the lyric and the epic to the extent that it combines in itself their separate principles of subjectivity and objectivity. It is objective because it places before us a definite series of events which take place in the outward world. It is subjective because the outward action is developed through the inward soul-life, uttered in speech, of the characters. It is, moreover, the inward soul-life of the persons of the play that is the cause of all that happens. The events are merely the realization of their wills in objectivity. The whole action must develop out of character. That it should be determined merely by external accidents and events is, therefore, a condition which, though suitable to the epic, contradicts the notion of drama.

708. The action in every drama is necessarily a *collision*. It may be a collision of universal ethical forces embodied in the contending characters of the play. Or it may be more particularly simply a collision of different individual wills. But in either case what we have here, in more or less degree, is essentially the divine, *i.e.* spirit, which has passed out of the repose of its universality into the sphere of particularity and division, and therefore comes into contradiction with *itself*. But the manifestation of the Idea, which is the *raison d'être* of art, is not complete until the Idea has returned into itself out of division. In the *dénouement* of the drama, therefore, the contradiction exemplified by the collision of forces must necessarily be resolved. Reconciliation must be reached. The drama cannot end with an unreconciled contradiction. The catastrophe must therefore show the divine as *justifying* itself. In some way, whether in tragedy or comedy, we have the vision of the eternal justice which governs the world finally composing its conflict with itself and returning out of division and strife into the eternal repose of its own substance.

The following types of drama make their appearance :—

709. (a) *Tragedy*. The essence of tragedy is that it involves a conflict between forces which are each, in themselves, ethically *justifiable*. The content of tragedy is therefore

those universal, essentially right and rational impulses, which constitute the substantive core of human life. Such are the love of husband and wife, of parents, children, and kinsfolk, the life of communities, the patriotism of citizens, the will of those in supreme power. The truly *tragic* character is one who, albeit he is a genuine individual with a wealth of subordinate traits, essentially embodies some such ethical force, commits himself wholly to it, and carries it through with uncompromising self-consistency to the end. He therefore comes into collision with other particular ethical forces. Each side of the contradiction is, by itself, valid and right. Yet each, because it is *one-sided*, because it negates and denies the other equally legitimate power, to that extent comes under *condemnation*. That which is abrogated in the tragic issue is not the ethical principle itself, but merely its false and one-sided particularity. The absolute truth, the Idea, the eternal justice, restores itself, restores its ethical substance and unity by means of the downfall of the individuality which has disturbed its repose.

Modern tragedy differs from ancient in its increased subjectivity. The conflict of eternal forces is still visible. But the strife of the individual wills and characters is more emphasized. The ancient tragic hero rested entirely on the foundation of some substantive power, such as the interest of the state or the care of the family. The modern tragic hero rests more upon his own individuality, his personal aims, ambitions, and desires. Yet, though he may be wicked, as Macbeth was, he must be a character of essential and genuine worth and ethical force, and to that extent an embodiment of the rational and universal. He cannot be a *worthless* person, a poltroon. This increase of subjectivity is in accord with the advance from classical to romantic art, of which latter subjectivity is the essential principle.

710. (*b*) *Comedy*. In comedy the universal and substantive is again justified, but in a different manner. Comedy justifies ethical worth by exposing the hollowness and emptiness of whatever is worthless. We have, as a rule, one of two cases. Either the comic character aims at some end

which is without real content, empty and vain, and which, by its own essential hollowness, collapses and comes to naught. Or he aims at some genuinely substantive end, but his own individuality is too small and mean to be used as an instrument for the attainment of such an end, so that his pretensions come to nothing. In either case the comic character *fails*, in the first instance because his aim is worthless, in the second because his means are insufficient. But the genuine comic character must not be overwhelmed in this failure. He must be capable of rising above it with an infinite geniality which experiences no taint of bitterness or sense of misfortune. He is conscious that what he strove after is really of no great importance, or else that his own pretensions to attain it were not to be taken seriously, so that he can rise with spontaneous amusement above his own failure.

711. (c) Of less importance is a third type of play, the "modern drama" or "social play" which attempts a coalescence of the principles of tragedy and comedy. The antithesis of the two sides in the tragic collision is so far weakened that it becomes compatible with a reconciliation of interests and a harmonious union of ends and individuals.

712. In drama the entire development of art comes to a close. Poetry is the highest of the arts, and drama is the highest form of poetry. But just for this very reason poetry is at the same time the dissolution of all art and the transition to a higher phase of spirit,—religion. For in poetry the side of spirit has withdrawn itself entirely from the side of the sensuous embodiment. The two sides are thus severed. But the essential notion of art is the organic unity and coalescence of spiritual content and sensuous form. And when, in poetry, this union is completely severed, the whole of art thereby annuls itself and collapses. Spirit passes on to a higher sphere.

CHAPTER II

RELIGION

SECTION I

RELIGION IN GENERAL

713. The reader may have observed that the logical rigour of the dialectic deductions, which was maintained in previous parts of the system, has, within the sphere of art, been considerably relaxed. In his *Lectures on the Philosophy of Fine Art* Hegel frequently reiterates the assertion that the development of art through its three main types, and again its development through the five specific arts, are necessitated by the Notion, or are, in other words, logically deduced. We cannot feel, however, that these assertions are justified. A genuine deduction involves two things. Firstly it involves that the particular notion before us, say that of symbolic art, should develop contradictions within itself. Secondly, it involves that these contradictions should be annulled in a new notion. But in regard to this latter point it is an essential condition that the contradictions should not *be* merely annulled but that they should annul themselves. It must not be merely that *we*, either as individuals or as humanity in general, finding a contradiction within the notion, hunt about to find a new notion which will resolve the contradiction. This new notion must not be *found* by us, but the old notion must itself *produce* it out of itself. In other words the transition must be objective, and not merely *our* subjective act. Now it is true that such a notion as that of symbolic art develops a contradiction within itself. The contradiction in that particular

case is that such art, because it is art, is for that reason the unity of content and form, yet on the other hand, because it is merely symbolic, is at the same time *not* the unity of content and form, but is on the contrary, an external relation of content to form in which they are seen to lie apart from each other, essentially separate and not one. Thus far the deduction is good. But next we are told that the human spirit overcomes this contradiction by a new type of art. We see how the new notion, that of classical art, does resolve the contradiction of the old notion. But there is a hiatus in the deduction. We are not shown how the old notion itself produces the new notion. It is not the notion itself which develops itself. It is we, it is the Greeks even, who do this. The transition is thus not shown to be an objective necessity. It is only a subjective necessity which the human spirit experiences as a need, and which it satisfies by itself creating a new type of art.

This same laxity of deduction appears, not only in the department of art, but throughout the whole sphere of absolute spirit. Thus we see that each religion, as it comes before us, develops contradictions, which are resolved in higher religions. But the transitions are subjective, not objective. And there is, in just the same way, no genuine transition from the sphere of art to that of religion. Neither in the *Encyclopaedia*, nor at the end of the *Lectures on the Philosophy of Fine Art*, nor at the beginning of the *Lectures on the Philosophy of Religion*, will a genuine deduction be found.

714. The deduction, such as it is, of religion from art, may be stated as follows.

Absolute spirit is, in general, the apprehension of the Absolute by the human mind (634). Its *content* is, in every case, the Absolute. Its different phases are constituted by the differences of *form* under which this absolute content may be cognized. In the first form, that of art, the Absolute appears in the form of sense-objects. But art has been seen to develop within itself a contradiction. This contradiction, implicit in art from the beginning, only becomes plain and explicit in romantic art. The principle of romantic art is that, because the Absolute is spirit, it can only be known as spirit, and no sensuous form is adequate to it; but, on the other hand, the very notion of art involves the apprehension of the Absolute, not as spirit, but essentially as sense-object.

Art being thus inadequate and self-contradictory, a new form is required for the apprehension of the Absolute. It must no longer be apprehended as sense-object but as what it is, spirit. Now the essence of spirit is not feeling, or emotion, or sense-consciousness, or even understanding, but reason, or in other words, the Notion or the Idea. Its essence is thought as thought, the universal. Consequently any genuine apprehension of the Absolute will cognize it, not as sense-object, but as pure thought, as reason, as the universal. Such a knowledge of the Absolute, however, is only found in philosophy. But the mind does not rise at once from the apprehension of the Absolute as sense-object (art) to the apprehension of it as pure thought (philosophy). There is an intermediate stage in which the Absolute is cognized neither in a purely sensuous way nor in a purely rational way. This intermediate stage is **religion.**

The *content* of absolute spirit is the Absolute, which is thought. In art this absolute thought, the Idea, takes the *form* of sense-object. In philosophy it takes the form of thought, so that in philosophy content and form are identical. Both are thought. In religion the content is the same, viz. absolute thought, but the form is intermediate. It is partly sensuous and partly rational. It is what Hegel calls *Vorstellung*, which we may translate picture-thinking, pictorial or figurative thought.

715. A *Vorstellung* is to be distinguished from a mere mental picture or image (*Bild*). I may conjure up a mental picture of my mother's face. Such an image is purely sensuous; it is an image of this single particular sense-object. It has no element of universality, no element of thought, about it. It is entirely individual. But a *Vorstellung*, though it is certainly pictorial, always has a universal significance. It is a pure thought or universal, clothed however in sensuous imagery. It is the figurative bodying forth of some rational

truth. Thus the popular idea of the creation of the world is a *Vorstellung*. The philosophical truth for which it stands is that the Idea puts itself forth into externality and otherness and becomes the world. Truly understood, this is not an act or event in time, but an eternal or timeless process of the Idea. It appears in philosophy as the transition from Logic to nature. But popular thought conceives this truth as an event which *happened*. The Idea is here called God. And God, at some unascertainable date in the past, " created " the world. This is a *Vorstellung* because it represents a universal thought but represents it in a sensuous form. To " create " is an image borrowed from the technical and mechanical operations of man, and it represents the origin of the world as happening *in time*, *i.e.* in one of the forms of externality in which the sensuous appears.

Again, the persons of the Godhead are represented as Father and Son. Obviously the relationship of father and son is a purely sensuous relationship which cannot possibly be taken in strict literalness here. It is, however, the finite relationship which most nearly corresponds to the truth. The truth for which it stands is the differentiation of the moments of the Notion within itself. The Universal, *i.e.* the Father, puts forth the Particular, *i.e.* the Son, from itself. The Incarnation, *i.e.* the idea of the God-man, is a *Vorstellung* which stands for the central truth of all religion, namely, the unity of God and man, the fact that, as we have seen (634) it is spirit which is the Absolute. The popular idea of God as a person is itself a *Vorstellung* which stands for the truth that the Absolute is spirit, that the highest category is, as shewn in the Logic, not cause or mechanism, or even life, but personality, self-consciousness, or, as Hegel calls it, the Absolute Idea.

716. The defect of art was that it represented the Absolute simply as *this* sense-object. In romantic art this was partly corrected inasmuch as that type of art involved a complete retirement of spirit into its own sphere. But the form adopted in the highest romantic art, poetry, namely the mental image, though it was inward and subjective and no longer an actual outward sense-object, was still lacking in the essence of spirit,

universality. It was still this single mental picture. The *Vorstellung* is, like the mental image, purely inward, but is in addition a definite step towards the universality of thought. It is in this respect that religion constitutes an advance upon art, and solves, at least proximately, the contradiction immanent in art.

717. Figurative thought of the kind which is contained in the various religions of the world is the highest kind of thinking of which the masses of men are capable. Pure abstract thought is beyond them. The truth, therefore, has to appear to the masses in the popular form of religion instead of in the pure form of philosophy. The question of the truth of any religion, therefore, is to be determined by whether or not its inner thought-content is found to be true, after its figurative and sensuous form has been stripped off. It is in this sense, for example, that Hegel calls Christianity the one absolutely true religion,—not because its figurative expressions, as of Father and Son, Creation, Heaven, the Fall, etc., can be taken literally, but because the inner meaning and thought-content of these will be found to be identical with the principles of the true philosophy, *i.e.* Hegel's own philosophy.

718. The general definition or notion of religion, then, is that religion is the manifestation of the Absolute in the form of picture-thought. Every religion, however, possesses essentially three moments which correspond respectively to the moments of the Notion. These are:

(*a*) *The moment of universality*.
This is God, the universal mind.

(*b*) *The moment of particularity*.

The universal mind of God sunders itself into particularity. Thought in this phase is the finite minds of individual men. The universal mind and the particular mind are, at this point, in a state of separation. God and the human mind stand over against each other as opposites. The human mind is therefore aware of God as its object, and is also aware of its separation and alienation from God. This alienation, this falling away, from God, appears as sin and misery.

(c) The moment of individuality.

This gives rise to the element of *worship*, an essential phase of every religion. For individuality is the return of the particular into the universal, the healing of the division which has made its appearance. This means, in the sphere of religion, that the human mind seeks to annihilate its separation and alienation from God, and strives to unite itself to Him, to become identical with Him, to be reconciled to Him. This effort is worship.

Thus the essential burthen of all religion is the unity of God and man. It presupposes a sense of separation from God, which renders a reconciliation necessary. This reconciliation consists in the return of the isolated finite mind into identity with God.

It will be seen that this content of religion, the unity of God and man, is precisely what we have seen to be the content of absolute spirit as such. Spirit becomes absolute when it knows that its object is itself. In the sphere of art, religion and philosophy, the human mind knows that it is itself all reality, that it is itself the Absolute. This is nothing else than the unity of God and man.

719. Hegel here enters a strong protest against the identification of his philosophy with pantheism. Pantheism asserts that every individual object, this stone, this tree, this animal, this man, is God. And its meaning is that these objects are already, as they stand in all their immediacy and particularity, identical with God. But the Hegelian position is the very opposite of this. This individual human mind, in its immediacy, its particularity, its finiteness, is *not* God. It is precisely because of its immediacy, particularity, and finiteness, that it feels and knows itself as separate from God, as alienated from Him. It is only by renouncing and giving up its particularity that it can enter into union with God. I, as this particular ego, with all my selfish impulses, my foolish whims and caprices, am essentially *not* the universal mind, but only a particular mind. Nevertheless the universal mind is in me, and is my essential core and substance. We have already seen, in the spheres of morality and the state, how the

individual mind has to forego its personal ends, adopt universal ends, and thereby develop the universal mind within itself. And the universal mind is none other than the mind of God, who is, therefore, my inner core and essence in so far as I can give up my particularity and rise to the height of the universal. It is not held to be either pantheism or blasphemy to say that God is in the hearts of good men; and this is the Hegelian position.

SECTION II

DEFINITE RELIGION

720. In the last section we dealt with the *subjective* notion of religion. Religion, however, cannot remain thus a mere idea. It must put itself forth into *objectivity*, and when it does so it comes to *exist* in the form of the many **definite religions** of the world. The only religion which completely accords with the notion of religion, as outlined in the last section, is Christianity. For in that the reconciliation of God and man is completely realized. Christianity combines in a fully developed totality all the essential moments of the notion of religion. Nevertheless these moments are found existing in a state of separation in the other religions of the world. Isolated moments make their appearance in these different religions, which are, consequently, essential phases of the religious Idea. These phases are not chance products, but the Idea develops itself through them dialectically, in advancing stages, until it is finally fully realized in Christianity. These other religions are, therefore, isolated aspects of the truth, which are gathered up into a concrete totality in the Christian religion. They are true, because they are aspects of the truth. They are false because they are fragmentary, abstract, and one-sided. Whatever truth they possess is summed up and included within the Christian religion.

721. The evolution of the different religions is, of course, a logical and timeless development. Nevertheless, as in the case of art, an element of time-development may also be

found here. The lowest phases of religion are on the whole the earliest.

722. Since religion in general is a necessary phase in the dialectic development of spirit, it follows, of course, that it is no mere chance that it exists. It is no mere human contrivance. It is a necessary work of reason in the world. It is a genuine, true, and necessary manifestation of the Absolute. At an earlier stage (525) we saw that the state is not a mere human invention to meet ends of utility, but is a logically necessary phase of the self-realization of the Absolute, and has its roots in the fundamental nature of things. What was said there of the state applies with equal force here, not only to religion in general, but to the different phases of religion, that is, to all the religions of the world. All alike are the work of the one reason, the one spirit, whose achievements constitute the "divine governance of the world." It is the Notion itself, one and the same Notion, which produces itself in these religions, however widely separated they may be in place and time.

723. The three great phases of religion are (1) natural religion, (2) the religion of spiritual individuality, (3) the absolute religion, *i.e.* Christianity.

724. It is a very curious omission on Hegel's part that although he has numerous scattered references to the religion of Islam, he assigns it no place in his scheme of religions.

Sub-Section I

THE RELIGION OF NATURE

725. The phrase "natural religion" is commonly used to characterize that religion to which, it is assumed, reason alone would lead man, without the aid of revelation. Hegel's use of the phrase, however, has nothing at all to do with this. He includes under the head of natural religion all those religions in which spirit has not yet gained the mastery over nature, in which spirit is not yet recognized as supreme and absolute. As soon as the Absolute is conceived as spirit we have passed beyond the religion of nature. But wherever God, or the

Absolute, is conceived as anything less than spirit, for example as substance or power, in all such cases the spiritual principle in general is not recognized as the creator, ruler, and master of nature, so that such religions regard the human spirit, too, as still within the power of nature. These are **natural religions**. Natural religion exists first as

A. *Immediate Religion, or Magic.*

726. The developed notion of religion necessarily presupposes that the separation between the universal mind, which is God, and the particular mind, which is man, has already made itself felt in consciousness. The aim of all religion is precisely the bridging of this gulf of separation, the reconciliation of God and man. Where this separation has not yet made itself felt religion proper cannot exist, or can only exist in the crude form of magic, which, because it is based upon the immediate unity of universal and particular, *i.e.* the unity which precedes the differentiation or mediation of the two sides, is here called *immediate* religion.[1] The distinction between God and man is the same as the distinction between the universal and the particular. Hence where the aforesaid separation does not yet exist, the universal is not yet recognized. Everything is particular. There is nothing but this tree, this river, this animal, this man. Hence man does not distinguish himself from nature. He is merely a unit, like any other unit, amid a chaos of particular objects. Nevertheless since the supremacy of spirit must, because it is the moving force at the back of all spiritual development, force itself in some dim way into consciousness, it appears here as the idea that I, this particular ego, am superior to stones, and rocks, and clouds, and have power over them. By the exertion of my mere will I can command the clouds, the storms, the waters, and they will obey. This is **magic**.

What it is essential to notice at this stage is the following. Since there is as yet no distinction drawn between the universal mind and the particular mind, it follows that it is not I, as a rational and universal being, who have power over natural

[1] See 239 above.

objects. Much less is it I as a moral being. It is this ego in all its particularity and immediateness which can exert power. Power is exerted, therefore, not for any universal end, but purely on behalf of my particular passions, desires, needs, or caprices. The force of my passion itself, my quite selfish will, can control nature for my own purposes. Thus although it is true, in a sense, that even here the mastery of spirit over nature is recognized, yet this spirit which controls objects is not conceived *as* spirit, that is to say as rational and universal, but only as a mass of particular impulses and passions. These impulses and passions, because they are immediate and particular, not universal, belong to the natural, not to the spiritual side of man. They belong to man, not as a spirit, but as a part of nature. Hence spirit is, after all, not conceived as supreme over nature, but as still part of, and in bondage to, nature.

B. *The Division of Consciousness within Itself. The Religion of Substance.*

727. When the distinction between universal and particular comes to be made, we have the first possibility of genuine religion. Man feels himself to be only this particular empirical consciousness, and over against himself he sets the universal, which thereby becomes objective to him. This is the separation and division which is presupposed in all religion. But this universal which man now conceives as an objective reality is, in the first instance, the purely abstract universal. It is simple universality, destitute of any particularity, void of all content. In other words, it is pure being. But to this there is added the feeling that all particularity is swallowed up in this pure being, that the particular empirical consciousness, together with all the particulars of nature and the finite world, are as a nullity before this universal. This universal is thus the absolute being. All other being is dependent upon it, arises out of it, and again disappears into it. Such an essential being, which produces all finite existences as transitory and unessential modifications of itself, and then again causes them to vanish in itself, is *substance* (300) ; and these modifications

are its *accidents*. At this stage, therefore, the essential characteristic of religion is that God is conceived as substance. Such religion is pantheism.[1] There are three stages of the **religion of substance,** namely, the Chinese religion, Hinduism and Buddhism.

728. Certain fundamental characteristics of these religions flow from their determination of God as substance. In the first place, since the activity of substance is *power* (303), God is the absolute power. But the power of substance is not yet determined by ends. The teleological conception of ends belongs to the doctrine of the Notion, whereas substance arises at the stage of essence. Hence in these religions God is not a wise God, but is blind power, and the spiritual conception of God as wisdom directing its activities towards the good, is wholly lacking. Secondly, since here the finite mind, as being merely accidental, is wholly swallowed up in substance, is a nullity, has no reality, no right of independent existence as against substance, it is for that reason not free. The human spirit is here still in bondage, and the notion of freedom is lacking. Thirdly, for the same reason, these religions go hand in hand with despotic government in the political sphere. The political institutions of a people always correspond to their religious conceptions. Only with an exalted and spiritual conception of God can there be good laws and good government. Free governments are only for those peoples who possess the religion of freedom, who are free in their innermost consciousness, who know God as free spirit.

The distinct grades of the religion of substance are the following :

729. (a) *The Chinese Religion.* Here God is primarily the wholly undifferentiated universal, contentless and empty being. What corresponds in the material universe to pure being is

[1] Hegel uses the term pantheism in two distinct senses, (1) as meaning the doctrine that all particular objects are, as they stand in their crude particularity and immediateness, God. This is the sense in which it is used in the first section of this Chapter (719). (2) Pantheism, in the second sense, means the view that God is substance in which all finite particularity is swallowed up. This is Spinozistic pantheism, as also the pantheism of the oriental religions here dealt with. Hegel's own doctrine is, of course, distinguished from this latter pantheism by the determination that God, the Absolute, is not merely substance, but is spirit.

Heaven, the sky, emptiness. Heaven, therefore, is here conceived as the absolute power,—Heaven under the name of T'ien. But, as in the religion of magic, so here too the idea of the supremacy of spirit must needs force its way, however crudely, into human consciousness. But the spirit conceived as supreme is still a particular empirical consciousness, not universal spirit. It is this particular spirit, the Emperor. The Emperor represents Heaven, is Heaven. Religion consists in obeying the edicts of the Emperor. The Emperor is divine and has absolute power on earth. Not only his subjects, but the elements of nature and the spirits of the dead are subject to his power.

730. *(b) Hinduism.* In Hinduism the conception of substance is more explicitly developed. Since substance is wholly abstract, it is for that reason undetermined, without any differentiation within itself. There is, therefore, only one substance, for a multiplicity of substances would involve differentiation. For the same reason this one substance is formless, for to be undetermined is to be without form. God, therefore, is now the formless One, Brahman. Brahman is abstract unity. As against this One all other existence is unreal, merely accidental. Nothing has any right of independent existence in itself. It arises out of the One and again vanishes in the One. This is the fully developed conception of substance and accident (300). Though the One may frequently be spoken of in terms which seem to imply personality, yet it is not spirit that is the real content, but only substance. Such phrases merely imply superficial personification. The One is essentially neuter.

731. Out of this one substance, and as its accidents, proceed all beings, all worlds, all men, all gods. But since the One is not concrete in itself, but is completely empty and abstract, all particular things, including the gods, fall outside it. It does not genuinely produce them out of itself and then again restore its own unity by taking them back into itself. It does not produce them, and therefore they simply *are*, that is to say, although it is *asserted* that they have proceeded out of the One, and are therefore dependent beings, yet since the

One is abstract and has *not* itself produced them, they are for that reason in reality independent beings. Hence since the unity, the One, does not here retain the multiplicity within its grasp, but rather stands on the one side entirely excluding the multiplicity on the other, therefore this multiplicity of independent beings is a crass multiplicity without unity, a chaos of disconnected forms. For the element of connection, the unity, the One, abandons these independent beings to their own devices. They are then an uncontrolled, ungoverned, multitude, without order, connection or reason. They are abandoned to the caprice of imagination. This it is which explains the fantastic chaotic world with which Hindu imagination presents us. And it also explains the fact that while Hinduism is a pure monotheism, it is yet at the same time the wildest and maddest of polytheisms. For the One, just because it is entirely contentless and abstract, because it has not its particularizations in itself, lets them fall outside it, lets them escape in uncontrolled confusion. Because it does not retain them within its grasp, they are therefore outside it, independent of it, and riot in this independence.

732. It is only a superficial philosophy which sees in the Trimurti a genuine prefiguration of the Christian Trinity. No doubt it is true that the Notion, the essential reason at work in the world, is dimly seen in this Indian threefold Godhead. But the conception is, in the Trimurti, entirely undeveloped. If it were to be identified with the Christian Trinity, which is the perfect realization of the Notion in the religious sphere, then the third god, Siva, ought to be the unity of the other two. The three gods, corresponding to the three moments of the Notion, should be Brahma, the universal, Vishnu, the particular, and Siva, the individual. Siva as the individual should be the unity of the universal and particular, should be the return of the particular into the universal, the reconciliation of the division which the universal had created within itself. But Siva is nothing of the sort. He represents the category of *becoming*, mere change. The two sub-categories of becoming are *origination* and *decease* (179), and therefore Siva has the twofold aspect of being at once the

creator and the destroyer. But the third moment of the Notion, individuality, though it is certainly change, is not *mere* change,—not the infinite progress, the meaningless change of one indifferent thing into another. It is rather the change involved in the passage back from the particular into the universal. Moreover, the three-foldness of the Trimurti does not, as it should, enter into substance at all. Substance is not, in its own self, three-fold. It is only One. The three Gods are merely three forms, three manifestations of substance. They lie outside substance and do not affect its inner nature. This is the same as saying that the Trimurti is not a concrete unity, as the Notion is. The three gods are not concretely one. They are merely different forms in which the Godhead appears.

733. The element of worship in Hinduism corresponds to its conception of God. God is here substance, the undetermined, abstract, contentless, emptiness and vacancy. Now worship means essentially the annulling of the separation between God and man, the reconciliation, the restoring of the unity and identity of God and man. Hence in Hinduism what man has to do in order to become identical with God is to empty himself of all content, to become that very vacancy which God is. Thus the state aimed at is an emotionless, will-less, deedless, pure abstraction of mind, in which all positive content of consciousness is superseded. God is here a pure abstraction, and man, in becoming the same abstraction, becomes identical with God, attains " union with Brahma." Thus worship aims at the complete submergence of consciousness.

In regard to this, two points require notice. Firstly, God, truly conceived, is spirit; and spirit is not abstract, but concrete. The essential character of the worship in any religion corresponds everywhere with its conception of God. Hence in the free religions of the world salvation is not attained through this process of mental abstraction, but, on the contrary, through the concrete work of the spirit, through its striving after universal ends, in morality, in the state, and in religion.

Secondly, when the Hindu renounces this world, renounces all finite and worldly aims, sacrifices all personal ends, in order to attain union with the One, it is not to be supposed that we have here the Christian idea of self-sacrifice, or that this renunciation imports any sense of sin, any atonement for guilt. Such ideas are totally foreign to this sphere, because, again, the Hindu God is abstract. It is only the concrete Idea which produces concrete morality and law out of itself. The One abandons the multiplicity of the world to itself, and the element of unity, reason, order, is therefore not found in this world. And since morality is essentially the product of reason and unity, it is lacking here. No doubt Hindus have their moral codes. But morality and righteousness are no essential part of worship in this sphere.

734. (c) *Buddhism.* In Hegel's time Hinduism was arousing deep interest in Europe, was being widely studied. Many of its sacred books had been translated.[1] Very little, on the other hand, was then known of Buddhism. Consequently, while Hegel's knowledge of Hinduism is on the whole surprisingly good, is at any rate quite sufficient for his purpose, his information on the subject of Buddhism was obviously very deficient. He appears to have been ignorant of Hiniyana Buddhism, and to have received only a somewhat distorted account of Mahayana Buddhism. His section on Buddhism is, therefore, not very satisfactory. Its main points are the following.

Buddhism is the last phase of the religion of substance. But this substance is now recognized as what it is, vacancy, emptiness, nothing, not-being. God is Nothing, Not-being. As we saw earlier (727), the Absolute is, in these religions, only pure being. Or it is raised from the category of being to that of substance only by virtue of the fact that it contains *power*, which is a determination of substance. The position of Buddhism may therefore be represented by saying that it has reached the stage where pure *being* is seen to be identical with *nothing*. The Absolute is this nothing, this

---

[1] A fact which explains Schopenhauer's obsession with oriental modes of thought.

emptiness. Out of nothing all things arise. To nothing they all return.

Worship here, accordingly, aims at the attainment of nothingness, annihilation, by the suppression of all desire, the withdrawal from everything particular, from every activity of life. This is Nirvana, the attaining of which puts an end to rebirth.

In Buddhism, as in the religion of China, substance becomes embodied in a particular empirical consciousness, Buddha, or the Dalailama, who are accordingly worshipped as the absolute power.[1]

C. *Religion in transition to the Religion of Spiritual Individuality.*

735. From the point at which we have arrived right up to the absolute culmination of religion in Christianity, the advance which we have to register consists essentially in the ever-increasing spirituality of the idea of God. We are now at the point where God is no more than substance. In the religions of spiritual individuality, to be dealt with in the next subsection, God has unquestionably become spirit, but not yet fully developed, completely concrete spirit. Only in Christianity is God concrete spirit out and out. At the present stage we have to deal with certain religions which exhibit the transition from substance to spirit. What is common to these religions is this, that though God is not yet definitely spirit, increasing traces of the idea of spirituality begin to make their appearance. They appear here in a fragmentary way as isolated moments of spirit. And in order that, as they arise before us, we may be able to recognize them for what they are, it may be well to remind ourselves at this point what the essential distinction between substance and spirit is. Spirit is the universal, and substance likewise is the universal. But substance is an empty and abstract universal, which does not differentiate itself, which is destitute of any determination

---

[1] In Hiniyana Buddhism, which is apparently the pure original doctrine of the founder, Buddha is *not* worshipped. Nor has the Dalai, or any other lama, a place in it.

within itself, so that all determination, all particularity falls outside it. Spirit, on the contrary, is the concrete universal. That is to say, it is no longer the undetermined, but is both determined and, what is more, determined by itself. It is the universal which by its own act puts forth the particular (which is the element of determinateness) out of itself, and then gathers the particular back into itself so that it attains individuality. It first creates a division within itself by sundering itself into universal and particular, and then, in the moment of individuality, heals the division and restores itself to unity. The particularity which spirit produces out of itself is its opposite, its other. Individuality, the restoring of unity, consists in this, that spirit resumes the other into itself, finds that the other is not an other, but is only itself.

Fragmentary elements of this idea now begin to appear in the following religions:

736. (a) *Zoroastrianism.* Here God is no longer the wholly undetermined. He has a determination. He is the Good. Brahman, being entirely empty, being wholly indeterminate, was neither good nor evil. What is formless and without any features at all cannot have the feature of being good. And it was for this reason that morality constituted no essential part of Hinduism. But God is now the Good. Yet because we are still nearer to the conception of substance than that of spirit, and since power is a moment of substance, this Good is power. The Good as absolute power,—this is Ormazd. And that God is not wholly undetermined, but is determined as the Good,— this is the first trace of the advance from substance to spirit.

This Good, however, is still completely abstract and one-sided. And for that reason the opposite one-sidedness, the opposite abstraction, stands over against it. This is evil, Ahriman. Evil is the other of Ormazd. But the fact that the Good is abstract means that it does not produce its other out of itself. Hence the other, evil, because it does not arise out of Ormazd, is itself an absolute being, independent of Ormazd, —an absolute opposite. This is dualism. Between these opposites, good and evil, there is waged an everlasting strife. Here we have the second trace of spirit. The universal, the

God, now has an other. There is division, opposition, strife. But what is essential to the idea of spirit, namely, that this division, this strife, should be *within itself*, is lacking. The Good here wages war with a wholly external principle.

737. Although Ormazd and Ahriman are, in a sense, personal beings, it must not be supposed that they are genuine spiritual individuals. What we have here is merely superficial personification of the abstract principles of good and evil. These are not persons, with definite characters, as the Greek gods are. They are not, if one may use such an expression in connection with divine persons, real flesh and blood. They are bloodless abstractions. The fact that they are not genuinely spiritual, but that we are still within the religion of nature, comes out most emphatically in the identification of Ormazd with light, and of Ahriman with darkness. These are not mere symbols. Light is not a symbol of the Good any more than the Good is a symbol of light. Light *is* the Good. The two are simply identical.

738. (b) *The Syrian Religion.* In Zoroastrianism religion has advanced to this extent, that the universal has an other, with which it is at strife. This represents the division of the universal and the particular. But in Zoroastrianism this other is an external principle, and the strife and division fall outside the universal. The advance registered by the Syrian religion consists in the remedying of this defect. Its essential principle is that the God has his other within himself, and is divided within himself, so that the strife is internal and proceeds within the substance of the god himself. This, as we have seen, is an essential element in the idea of spirit.

This conception of inner division appears here, however, in symbolical fashion. The Syrian religion has at its centre two myths—that of the phoenix and that of the god Adonis. The phoenix is a bird which burns itself, but ever rises rejuvenated from its own ashes. The god Adonis dies, but rises again on the third day. The festival of Adonis consisted in a three days lamentation for the death of the god, followed by joyous celebrations for his resurrection on the third day. Here we have for the first time the profound conception of the death of the god. Death is a natural event. It is the negation of spirit so far as spirit is a part of nature. These legends mean then that the element of negation does not lie outside the god, as a mere external opposite, but enters into the very substance of god-head. Negation is the same as otherness. The god has his own other in himself. He negates himself. The strife, the division, is within the god. This, then, is the advance made here. The Zorastrian god has his other outside him. Here the other, the opposite, the negative, is within the universal itself.

739. (c) *The Egyptian Religion.* The characteristics of the Syrian religion are retained and further developed in the religion of Egypt. Amidst the masses of confusing myths here, philosophy has to pick out what is essential, what most clearly exhibits the central core of thought which the religion contains. The chief god in this sphere is Osiris. Osiris, like Adonis, has the element of negation within himself. He dies. It is true that, in the first instance, the negation, the other, is a being external to Osiris, just as Ahriman is external to Ormazd. This other of Osiris is Typhon, the evil principle. But in spite of this, negation enters into the substance of the god, for Osiris suffers death, is slain by Typhon. But Osiris rises again, and becomes, after this resurrection, not only lord of the living but also ruler over the spirits of the dead. In this latter capacity Osiris is the judge, awards punishment for evil, finally triumphs over Typhon.

The most important point here is the emphasis which is laid on the idea of resurrection. If death is the negation of spirit, resurrection is the negation of this negation. Death is slain. Here we have the *third* moment of the Notion. First, we have the death of the god, that is, the universal negates itself, suffers division into particularity. Next, death is itself overcome, that is, the particular is itself negated and returns into the universal. The division is healed, the contradiction which has appeared within the godhead is reconciled. Spirit is the universal which, firstly, particularises itself, negates itself, produces its opposite out of itself, and then, secondly, negates this negation, resumes its opposite into identity with itself. The death of the god is the first of these movements; his resurrection is the second.

740. These are the essential points in the Egyptian religion. Hegel discusses various other characteristics at length. We have room here for only one point. Although, by means of the determinations just discussed, the conception of spirit has now been definitely reached, so that we can pass over to the religions of spirituality, yet it must be remembered that we are still here within the sphere of the religion of nature. Consequently the purely natural, or sensuous side, is emphasized. It is for this reason that the Egyptian religion is throughout symbolical in character. Its effort is everywhere to find a sensuous symbol for the spiritual content. Its worship consists chiefly in those vast works of architecture which symbolize its mysteries. And connected with this same fact, namely, the entanglement of spirit in the sensuous, is the prevalence of zoolatry among the Egyptians. The ape, the monkey, the cat are worshipped. For the animal is on the one hand a living being, and has that in common with spirit. But, on the other hand, it is wholly a part of sensuous nature. Zoolatry appears here because this religion is midway between nature and spirit, and contains the principles of both.

Sub-Section II

THE RELIGION OF SPIRITUAL INDIVIDUALITY

741. In the foregoing three transitional religions we have seen the moments of the idea of spirit appearing in a fragmentary and scattered way. There, however, they were still conceived in a sensuous symbolical manner, and were thus still entangled in nature. The next step in advance will consist in the gathering up of these fragmentary moments into the single definite idea of spirit, and the exaltation of spirit above all sensuous entanglement. Hence in the religions with which we are now about to deal, God or the gods are no longer merely substance, but have become subject or spirit. Or, as we should say in present-day phraseology, we have reached the stage of the idea of a *personal* God. The divinities of

preceding stages, Siva, Ormazd, Osiris, Adonis, no doubt have the superficial appearance of being persons. But they are not so in reality. They are only superficial personifications of abstract principles. Thus Ormazd is the Good. Siva is change, creation and destruction. The essential being of Ormazd is not personality. At bottom he is simply the abstract idea of the Good. The Good is what he essentially is. The personification of this principle is merely, so to speak, poetical embroidery, a superfluous addition of the imagination. Now, however, in the religions which follow, the very essence of the godhead is personality. Thus we have advanced from substance to spirit. God is now definitely spirit. Nevertheless all that this means is not unfolded here. Not until we reach Christianity is the nature of spirit completely understood.

742. Substance, because it is empty and abstract, because it excludes all finitude and particularity from itself, is therefore cut off from the world, does not enter into the world. The infinite substance stands on one side, the finite world on the other. A gulf divides them. But since spirit is essentially the concrete universal which goes forth into the particularity, the gods of the stage which we are now about to study, enter into the world and take part in its operations. We now come to gods who are the founders of states, the conservators of morality, of marriage, of agriculture, and so forth. And whereas substance is merely power, does not work in accordance with ends, and is destitute of wisdom, spirit, on the other hand, sets ends before itself. God is now wisdom.

743. Lastly, in spite of the fact that in the Jewish religion a certain element of servitude appears, these religions are, on the whole, the religions of freedom. So long as God is conceived as substance, the human spirit is mere accident, which has no right of independent existence as against substance. Now, however, God is spirit. But spirit is precisely that universal which allows the particular to go forth out of itself in free independent existence. The particular does not merely vanish in the universal, as the accident does in substance. The Notion, which is what spirit is, does indeed

produce the particular and then again annul it, taking it back into itself. But in this annulling it also preserves (*aufgehen*) the independence of the particular. Hence the finite and particular mind has, in these religions, a definite right to exist on its own account, and is free. And it is in accordance with this that the religious life is no longer conceived as withdrawal from the world, asceticism, absorption in the One, but rather as the active life of morality, life in the state, etc. For morality and the laws of the state are the laws of freedom, and the product of the free spirit.

744. (*a*) *The Jewish Religion, or the Religion of Sublimity.* It is difficult to apply some of the above observations to the prevailing features of the Jewish religion, which would appear, in many respects, to have strong affinities with the religions of substance. And it is noticeable that although, in the philosophy of religion, Hegel introduces Judaism here, yet in the philosophy of art he places Jewish conceptions, along with Hindu and Egyptian art, in the sphere of oriental symbolism (662). Symbolic art corresponds roughly to the religion of nature, while the religions of spiritual individuality correspond in the same way to classical art. There is thus a certain inconsistency here, due possibly to the somewhat hybrid character of Judaism. No doubt, however, Hegel classed the Jewish religion as a religion of spiritual individuality because of its fundamental determination that God is a person.[1]

God is personal; but personality, spirit, is not yet understood as the concrete spirit which differentiates itself within itself and has the particular in it. And this abstractness, this absence of differentiation, implies that this personality is an undivided One. God, therefore, is now One, not the impersonal One of the Hindus, but One Person—Jehovah. Jehovah alone is independent reality. And since the particular is not part of Him, it is unreal, has no independent existence

---

[1] There is a similar inconsistency with regard to the culture of the Zend people. In the philosophy of art it appears in the pre-artistic sphere, that is to say, as inferior even to symbolic art (658). In the philosophy of religion Zoroastrianism appears in the phase of transition from substance to spirit.

(the affinity with the religions of substance lies here). The finite world, all particular things, are nullities, and flee away from before His face. Nevertheless, since the universal must, in some shape or other, produce the particular out of itself, this production of the particular is conceived here as the creation of the world by Jehovah. But the world thus created is a nullity, has no right to exist. That it does exist is an act of grace on the part of God. This is the goodness and mercy of God. And that all finite things are negated by the One, that they perish, thereby exhibiting their finiteness and the nothingness which they essentially are,—this is the justice, the righteousness of God. God is awful and holy.

745. God, as spirit, must act in accordance with ends. This is the wisdom of God. But Jehovah is Himself the sole reality, and therefore finite ends receive no recognition. God's end is Himself. There is only this one end. All things are for the glory of God. Worship too consists in this, that man should recognize the glory of God, and should know his own worthlessness and nothingness. And since the finite consciousness has no standing before God, exists not of right but merely by grace, and is one with all other finite things which are negated by the One, for these reasons the attitude of man towards God is essentially one of fear. God is the Lord, and the Lord is to be feared. Man, as having no right of existence, is the bond-servant of the Lord. He is not free. The people of God is a people adopted by covenant and contract on the conditions of fear and service.

746. Lastly, since God as spirit has transcended all entanglement with the sensuous, he exists accordingly in no sensuous shape, but solely as spirit, solely for thought. There is no image of God, no statue. The sensuous representation of God in natural forms, the making of images and idols, is an abomination.

747. (*b*) *The Greek Religion, or the Religion of Beauty.* The finite world is the other of God. In Judaism God negates this other. As soon as it is seen, however, that it is God Himself who puts forth this other out of Himself, it follows that the other is itself part of God, is divine. God is in nature.

Nature, the sensuous, is not, according to this view, the opposite of God, godless, worthless. It is precisely in the sensuous that God manifests himself. He appears in sensuous forms, in works of beautiful art. This is the point of view of the Greek religion. And since the sensuous is fundamentally not unity but multiplicity, the divine must appear here as a multiplicity of divine plastic figures. The one God of the Hebrews splits into the many gods of the Greeks. These gods are spiritual; they are genuine persons, not mere personifications of abstract principles. It is true that Zeus is the atmosphere, Apollo the sun, Poseidon the sea. But they are not *mere* personifications of these elements. The are infinitely more than the atmosphere, the sun, and the sea. Each is a living individuality with a wealth of character, a multiplicity of traits,—not personifications of a single attribute. They are human, and this religion is the religion of humanness.

Man, as no longer merely negated by God, as an essential manifestation of God, has the right of independent existence. Hence he is self-determined and free. This is a religion of free men. And the divine, as no longer merely negating the finite sensuous world, dwells in it, is on friendly terms with it. In Judaism the finite flees away before the face of God. But the Greek gods are friendly beings. The finite has no need to fly from their wrath. Theirs is rather an infinite geniality and tolerance of all things. Man is no longer afraid. He is free. He is a spirit. And the gods, too, are spirits. They are like him. They are human and gracious. All is well. Man can rejoice. This is the religion of joyousness. Worship consists in games, festivals, processions, songs, plays, works of art. The gods are the founders of states, the guardians of the law. Zeus is a political god, the god of laws, of sovereignty.

748. But behind this multiplicity of gods there must needs be an underlying unity. The many gods have arisen by the differentiation of unity. The unity behind is dimly felt, vaguely seen. But since all content is in the gods, none is left over for the unity. Hence it is empty, abstract, the dark womb out of which the gods proceed, and which finally governs and controls them. This one power which rules over even the

gods is a mere emptiness, a darkness; it is incomprehensible, blind, irrational. For what is completely empty cannot be known. There is nothing on which knowledge can fasten. What is utterly abstract is incomprehensible, and what is incomprehensible is irrational. This power which remains in the background, which rules in a blind irrational way, is necessity, Fate.

749. (c) *The Roman Religion, or the Religion of Utility.* The religion of the Romans is often superficially identified with that of the Greeks. But despite the fact that many of its divinities are identifiable with Greek gods, its fundamental character is totally different. We have seen that, in the present sphere, God is necessarily conceived as acting in accordance with ends. Now the Hebrew God had but one end, infinite and universal in character, namely, Himself. The Greek gods, on the other hand, identify themselves with a multitude of particular and finite ends. This is necessitated by their multiplicity and their human character. They are, in fact, finite beings with finite ends. Thus Athene identifies herself with the life and prosperity of Athens, Bacchus with Thebes, and the other gods with various particular localities and purposes. The Roman religion arises from combining the characters of the Jewish and the Greek religions. It is, in this respect, their unity and synthesis. In common with Jehovah, the Roman Divinity serves a single universal end. But in common with the Greek conception, this end is a finite particular end, a human end, an end belonging to this world. This single end, finite and earthly, yet broadened out till it is universal in its scope, can only be the state; not the state however as a rationally articulated organization, but the state as a universal power bringing all peoples within the scope of its sovereignty. Jupiter Capitolinus is the embodiment of this idea. He has for his end the universal sovereignty and dominion of the Roman people.

Yet there are a multiplicity of gods serving particular ends. To reconcile this with the single end of sovereignty can only mean that these many ends are made subservient to the one end, the many gods to Jupiter Capitolinus. The Greek gods were free, independent, and joyous. But now the gods are degraded to the rank of means. They are not beautiful. They are useful. They subserve innumerable ends all of which culminate in the one end of the state. Thus utility is the prevailing note here. The Greek religion was poetical. The Roman religion is prosaic. The Greek gods were genial and joyous. The Roman gods, chained to the ends they serve, are earnest, pale and anxious. They lose spirituality and life, become grey and lifeless beings even in the hands of such a poet as Virgil.

Since this is a religion of utility, everything useful is revered as divine. The art of baking ranks as divine. Fornax, the oven in which the corn is dried, is a goddess. Vesta is the fire used for baking bread.

But the universal end is that of the state, power, dominion. It was nothing wonderful, then, when the actual present power who was the embodiment of that end, the Emperor, namely, came to be worshipped as a god.

SECTION III

THE ABSOLUTE RELIGION: CHRISTIANITY

750. Christianity is the absolute religion because it has for its content the absolute truth. Its content is, according to Hegel, identical with the Hegelian philosophy. Hegelianism is esoteric Christianity. For though the content is the same, the form is different. Philosophy presents the absolute content in the absolute form, the form of pure thought. Christianity presents this identical content in the form of sensuous and pictorial thought, *Vorstellung*. The fact that Christianity contains the absolute truth also necessarily involves that it is the *revealed* religion. It is the religion in which God completely and finally reveals Himself as what He is, as concrete spirit, the full nature of which is now made manifest. And since Hegel finds the truth revealed, in the form of *Vorstellung*, in the dogmas of the Christian Church,

the Trinity, the Creation, the Fall, the Incarnation, the Redemption, the Resurrection, and the Ascension, he has consequently no patience with that type of "rationalizing" theologian who attempts to dilute and explain away these dogmas to meet the demands of the understanding and to satisfy the shallow enlightenment of the age. These dogmas contain the essence of Christianity. They are true, because they contain the substance of the truth, albeit in the form of *Vorstellung*.

751. As to the proof of the truth of Christianity, this should not be rested on miracles or other external evidences. A miracle is something that is perceived by the senses to have happened. It is an external event. Spiritual truth is eternal and rests on its own foundation, nor is it dependent upon the sensuous and external, upon whether this or that event has happened. To make the spiritual truth dependent upon miracles and other sensuous evidences is to degrade the spiritual. It is a matter of absolutely no importance or interest whether water was turned into wine at Cana, or whether this or that person was healed. The truths of the spirit are absolute and eternal and independent of the sensuous. If proof there is to be, it must be spiritual proof. The only proof of the spiritual is the witness of the spirit itself. As to what this witness of the spirit is, it may appear in many forms. In the masses of men it can only make itself known in the form of feeling, in the instinctive response of the spirit to what is noble and true. In the completely cultivated consciousness, on the other hand, the witness of the spirit will be thought, philosophy itself. The entire Hegelian system is nothing but the proof of the truth here. The whole controversy about miracles is a shallow one. And equally shallow are the attempts made in some quarters to belittle Christian doctrine by showing that it has borrowed from external sources, that it has adopted pagan rites, that the Incarnation and the Trinity are heard of in earlier and alien religions, that Adonis, like Christ, rose again in three days, and so on. For in the first place the question of the origin of a thought has absolutely no bearing on the question of its essential value and truth. And

in the second place, since it is the one Notion which everywhere seeks to produce itself in the world, it is absolutely essential that the truth should have made its appearance, in fragmentary, one-sided, and abstract forms, in earlier religions.

752. The fundamental determination of Christianity is that God is concrete spirit. We have seen this foreshadowed in earlier religions. Now it is completely unfolded. Concrete spirit is that which, in accordance with the moments of the Notion, is (1) the *universal* which suffers diremption into (2) the *particular*, which returns to identity with the universal in (3) the *individual*. Now, in the most general sense, the universal is the logical Idea. In Christian *Vorstellung* this appears in the form of God as He is in His own self, before the creation of the world. The second movement is that the universal becomes the particular, *i.e.* God creates the world, nature, including man so far as man is finite and a part of nature. Lastly, the particular returns into the universal. This is, according to Hegel, the Church. And with these three spheres, God as He is in Himself, the world, and the Church, he deals under the titles of the Kingdoms of the Father, the Son, and the Spirit.

753. (*a*) *The Kindgom of the Father.* This is the doctrine of the nature of God as He is in Himself before the creation of the world. God, as such, is the Idea, the Notion. The Notion is threefold; and God is therefore threefold in Himself. As universal He is God the Father. The universal produces the particular out of itself, *i.e.* God the Father begets God the Son. The particular returning into the universal, is the individual, *i.e.* God the Holy Spirit. The three factors of the Notion are not three *parts* of it. Each factor is itself the entire Notion. Thus the universal is not merely the universal; it is also the particular and the individual. And the particular likewise is the universal and the individual. How this is has already been proved in the Logic (318). The Notion, although it contains three moments, is yet one undivided Notion, for each moment is the entire Notion. This appears in Christianity as the doctrine of the Trinity. God is undividedly one. Yet God is three Persons. But the Son and the Spirit are not

different from the Father. For each is, not a part of God, but the entire Godhead. Thus that God is the Triune God is necessarily involved in the assertion that God is spirit. For this concrete unity and identity of the three moments of the Notion is precisely what spirit is.

Whoever has understood the Doctrine of the Notion as expounded in the Logic has understood the Trinity. Hence the assertions of "rationalists" that the Trinity is contrary to reason, and the assertions of some religious persons that it is a mystery which transcends reason, are alike wide of the mark. It is certainly incomprehensible and self-contradictory to the finite understanding which proceeds upon the principle of identity. It is, however, not only comprehensible to reason, whose principle is the identity of opposites, but it is the very essence of rationality itself.

754. (b) *The Kingdom of the Son.* The logical Idea passes over into nature. This is, of course, not an event in time, but an eternal and logical development. But Christianity represents it in pictorial fashion as something that happened, as the creation of the world by God. This would make it appear as if it were an accidental and arbitrary act of God, as if God either might or might not have created a world. In reality, of course, it is a logical necessity that the Idea must come out of itself into otherness. It lies in the very nature of God to create a world. And that this world should exhibit estrangement from God and should finally be reconciled to him, also lies in the nature of the Notion, but is here presented as a divine history, a divine plan of events which have happened in the world. The world is the other of God. Or, to express it otherwise, the universal allows the particular to go forth from it in free independence. Thus there arises that division and separation between the universal and the particular, which appears as the estrangement between God and the world. This estrangement, in its special reference to man as a part of nature, is presented in the doctrine of the Fall. Man, as particular spirit, is in his essential nature distinguished from, estranged from, the universal spirit, which is God. My particularity and finitude are precisely the factors which constitute

my lack of identity with God. This is the meaning of the doctrine that man is by nature evil, a far profounder truth than the modern shallow view that man is by nature good. For evil is simply particularity. I do evil when I persist in my particularity, when I follow my particular ends instead of identifying myself with universal and rational ends. Man is evil, is estranged from God, just because he is particular and finite spirit. This estrangement, therefore, is in reality inherent in the very notion of man. It is an eternal truth. But the story of the Fall, of course, represents it, like the Creation, as an event which happened.

This estrangement necessitates reconciliation. Man must return to God. In terms of the Notion, this reconciliation occurs by the return of the particular into the universal in the moment of individuality. This, likewise, is not an event, but an eternal truth. Or to put it otherwise, the human mind, in its very separation from God, is at the same time identical with Him. For I am not merely the particular finite mind. I am also the universal mind, the infinite mind. The universal is in me as my core and essence. This reconciliation, this essential unity of God and man, appears in religion in the doctrines of the Incarnation, the death of Christ, His resurrection and ascension. God is not the abstract universal. He particularizes Himself, enters into the finite world, becomes flesh. In the person of Christ the popular consciousness finds the unity of God and man placed before it as an absolutely immediate sensuous fact. God not only becomes finite, but proceeds to the extreme of finitude; he suffers death. Negation, otherness, finitude, are part of the very substance of God, and this is a necessary element in the idea of God as spirit. But He rises again from the dead and ascends to the Father, that is, the universal which became particular now returns into itself. In this act the particular, which was sundered from the universal, becomes identical with it. Reconciliation is complete. The estrangement between God and man is overcome.

755. (*c*) *The Kingdom of the Spirit.* God and man are one. Their unity is now represented in this fashion, that the spirit

of God is in man, not however in man as particular man, but in a community of men, the Church. The Holy Spirit is actually present in His Church. If the Kingdom of the Father was the Logical Idea, God before the creation of the world; and if the Kingdom of the Son was that Idea in its Otherness, nature; the Kingdom of the Spirit, as the third moment, the moment of individuality, is the unity of two foregoing. For the Church is, on the one hand, the pure spirit of God, but it is also, secondly, *in* the world, actually present. It is the Kingdom of God upon earth.

Note on the Doctrine of the Immortality of the Soul. I have not been able to fit into this chapter any consideration of this doctrine, though it would naturally come here. Hegel nowhere deals exhaustively or clearly with it. The clearest and fullest passage will be found in the *Lectures on the Philosophy of Religion*, transl., London, 1895, vol. iii. p. 57. It is a matter of dispute whether Hegel believed in immortality in its *literal* sense. I have only space here to indicate, without reasons, my own opinion, which is that he did not take it literally, but regarded it as a *Vorstellung* for the infinitude of spirit and the absolute value of spiritual individuality. Immortality is a present quality of the spirit, not a future fact or event. The poet Blake expresses a similar idea:

> To hold infinity in the palm of your hand
> And eternity in an hour.

CHAPTER III

PHILOSOPHY

756. The absolute religion has for its content the absolute truth. But its defect is that it presents this truth in the form of contingency. For example, the creation of the world is represented by it as a chance event which happened. God might or not have created the world. Again, it represents the alienation of God and man, which is in reality an essential necessity in the nature of things, as an accidental fact which might have been otherwise. The reconciliation of God and man it likewise presents in the form of the story of an event. This defect is removed by substituting the form of necessity for the form of contingency. To show that anything is necessary means to show that it is logical and rational, *i.e.* to give it the form of pure rational thought. In this process it is the element of *Vorstellung* which disappears, for it is just this *Vorstellung* which pictures logical relations as outward events and so invests them with the form of contingency. When this *Vorstellung* is stripped off and nothing but the pure thought is left we have **philosophy,** which gives the absolute content in the absolute form.

757. But this absolute philosophy does not appear in the world fully complete in the first instance. Its complete form, Hegel believes, is the Notion as it appears in the system of Hegel. It does not attain this at once. As in art and religion, isolated moments of it appear first. Completed philosophy sees the Absolute as Idea. The first and most abstract moment of the supreme category of the Idea is the

category of pure being. The earliest genuine philosophy, that of the Eleatics, regards the Absolute as being. After that we have Heraclitus with his higher category of becoming, and so on. It is evident that by "the absolute truth in the absolute form" Hegel means his own philosophy, in which the truth of all previous philosophies is gathered up and absorbed, just as the truth of all lower religions is comprised in Christianity.

758. This absolute philosophy thus constitutes the final phase of absolute spirit. Philosophy, so conceived, is the knowledge of the Absolute, not as the sense-object of art, not as the *Vorstellung* of religion, but as what it essentially is, as thought, or more precisely, as the Idea. It is the knowledge of the Idea by itself. For what is known is the Idea, and what knows, the philosophic mind, is itself now disentangled from sense, is pure thought, is Idea. The Idea is thus both subject and object here. The whole development of spirit from its earliest stages has been motivated by this one impulse,—to bridge the gulf between subject and object, and this is now complete, and with this the development of spirit is complete. Subject and object are now identical. Absolute reconciliation is reached.

And since the Idea now has itself for object, it is seen as what it is, self-consciousness, the Absolute Idea. This is the same result as we reached at the end of the Logic. But the Absolute Idea as found at the end of the Logic was still abstract to this extent that it was merely a category. Absolute spirit is the same thing which has now given itself actuality, has passed from the sphere of pure thought, of categories, into actual existence. Philosophy is the existence of the Idea. And since in this, that the Idea should realize itself completely in existence, it attains its end, the philosophic spirit is accordingly to be regarded as the attainment of the end and purpose of the world-process.

759. This conclusion has subjected Hegel to a good deal of ridicule, since what it implies is that the sole purpose of the entire universe, with all its immense stellar systems, was to arrive at the Hegelian philosophy. But if, instead of the

Hegelian philosophy, we substitute the final and absolutely true philosophy (which would be omniscience, and which is no doubt an impossible ideal), the conclusion appears less ridiculous. The philosophic mind which should have attained omniscience would be nothing less than the mind of God. And it does not appear ridiculous to say that the purpose of the universe is the complete realization of the mind of God in actuality. The fact that Hegel should have regarded his own system as this final and absolute knowledge has no doubt an element of absurdity in it. But on the other hand every creator of a system must surely needs regard his system as the truth. No doubt even with a profound conviction of the truth there must go, in any sensible man's mind, a deep sense of the illimitable darkness which envelops our tiny light of knowledge. And I cannot but believe that Hegel too felt this, and that his failure to give it any weight in his writings is more connected with his peculiar mannerism than with any essential defect in his vision. At any rate it is not incumbent on us to take Hegel's conclusion in its precisely literal meaning. And if we take it as meaning that the perfect philosophic mind would be the completion of the plan of the universe, I believe that this is no unreasonable conclusion. It was, at any rate, also the view of Aristotle.

760. The sphere of absolute spirit ends the Hegelian system. It appears as the final result of all development. In accordance, however, with Hegelian principles, it is also the absolute foundation, the beginning. Thus the end of philosophy is also the beginning. This is what Hegel means when he says that philosophy is a circle which returns into itself. Here at the end of the system of philosophy we reach philosophy. If we ask what is this philosophy which we have reached the only answer possible is to begin again at the beginning of the Logic. Thus having reached the end, we must, to explain it, begin again at the beginning. This is the circle of philosophy. The Logic, with which we began, treated of the Idea. Here at the end of the philosophy of spirit we again reach the Idea, the Idea now as actual, existent in the philosophic mind. It

is here that the world-process is consummated. "The eternal Idea, in full fruition of its essence, eternally sets itself to work, engenders and enjoys itself as absolute mind (spirit)." [1]

[1] *Phil. of Mind*, § 577.

INDEX

The numbers refer to the numbered paragraphs of the text.

A.

Absolute, The, 30-32, 101, 116, 162, 167, 168, 170, 174, 181, 207, 214, 236, 248, 302, 349, 367, 405, 418, 439, 442, 525, 612, 634, 636, 638, 639, 642, 644, 651, 654, 658, 660, 662, 663, 665, 667, 714, 715, 716, 718, 722, 725, 734, 757, 758; as the universal, 13, 77; as thought, 32, 37; as mind, 32, 38; as substance, 302; as personality, 161; as spirit, 160, 634; as subject, 325, 385, 386; as self-consciousness, 404; as a system of categories, 89, 102, 103; knowableness of, 69.

Absolute Idea, The, 148, 149, 150, 151, 160, 167, 170, 174, **404-408**.

Absolute Mechanism, **374**, 375, 376.

Absolute Negativity, 204, 303.

Abstract and Concrete, meaning of; 142.

Abstract Right, 531 *et seq.*

Abstract Universal, 113, 144, 319.

Accident, 300, 303.

Achilles, 648, 675, 705.

Action and Reaction, 304-306.

Actuality, 27, 28, 153, **291-306**, 466; as equivalent to rationality, 295-299.

Actual Soul, The, 465-467.

Administration of Justice, 600-603.

Adonis, 738, 739, 741, 751.

Agamemnon, 648.

Agricultural Class, The, 598.

Ahriman, 736, 737.

Ajax, 648.

Allegory, 664.

Alliteration, 701.

Alteration, 193-196; as distinguished from becoming, 196.

Analogy, 359.

Analytic Method, The, 401.

Anarchism, 560, 592, 606.

Anaximander, 270.

Anthropomorphism, 665, 667.

Antigone, 652.

Antigone, The, 652.

Antithesis, 126, 166.

Apollo, 747.

Appearance, 3, 5, 9, 12, 13, 15, 17, 56, 59, **271-290**; the world of, 274-275.

Apperception, transcendental unity of, 366 (footnote).

Appetite, 484.

Architecture, 681-684; symbolic, 682; classical, 683; romantic, 684; Gothic, 684.

Arithmetic, 50.

Aristotle, 1, 2, 7, 19, **20-38**, 41, 45, 75, 98, 136, 141, 149, 153, 270, 297 (footnote), 325, 355, 377, 389, 404, 418, 427, 474 (footnote).

Art, 639-712: Symbolic, 655, 657-664; Classical, 655, 665-669; Romantic, 655, 670-678; Hindu, 660, 662, 665; Egyptian, 661; Persian, 662; Hebrew, 662; Greek, 665, 666, 668, 669; Christian, 673, 674, 690.

Ascension, The, 750, 754.

Athene, 749.

Athens, 749.

Atomism, 100.

Atomists, The, 174, 207, 370.

Atoms, 100, 207, 370.

Attention, 500.

Attraction and repulsion, **209**, 282.

Aveling, 92 (footnote).

INDEX

B.

Babel, The Tower of, 682.
Bacchus, 749.
Baillie, J. B., 268.
Beauty, the nature of, 639, 642; identified with truth, 640; of Nature, 643, 644.
Beccaria, 552, 553.
Becoming, in Eleaticism, 2, 125, 153; in Heraclitus, 174, 306; Aristotle on, 153; Hegel's category of, 125, 126, 142, 145, 146, 148, **179, 180**, 183, 196.
Being, in Eleaticism, 2, 11, 294; Hegel's category of, 93, 123-125, 142, 145, 146, 148, 149, 150, 151, **177**; why being is the first category, 114-120; distinguished from existence, 184, 263; general character of categories of, 163, 171.
Being-for-other, 189.
Being-for-self, 203 *et seq.*
Being-in-self, 189.
Berkeley, 3, 9 (footnote), 47.
Blake, 755 (footnote).
Bradley, 103.
Brahma, 732, 733.
Brahman, 273, 288, 294, 660, 730, 736.
Bruce, Addington, 460 (footnote).
Bhudda, The, 734.
Buddhism, 734.
Burke, 545 (footnote).
Burnet, 2 (footnote).

C.

Calvary, 674.
Cana, the miracle at, 751.
Caste system, 599.
Capital punishment, 553.
Categorical Imperative, The, 515.
Categories, 57-58, 84-88, 102, 110, 308.
Causality, 46, 71-72, 248, **303**, 304, 306, 307.
Cause and effect, 303.
Chastity, 558.
Chemism, **375**, 377, 383.
Chinese Religion, The, 729.
Chivalry, 675.
Choice, 516.
Christ, 674, 751, 754.
Christian Art, 673, 674, 690.
Christianity, 17, 367, 717, 720, 735, **750-755**.

Church, The, 752, 755.
Civil Society, 586-604.
Classical Art, 655, **665-669**.
Cognition, **395** *et seq.*, 496.
Cognition proper, 399-401.
Comedy, 710.
Commercial Class, The, 598.
Communism, 535.
Concepts, 6, 7, 8, 33, 34, 91.
Concrete and Abstract, meaning of, 142.
Concrete universals, 319.
Conscience, 560, 569, 570, 571.
Consciousness, 468 *et seq.*
Consciousness proper, 471-479.
Constitution, of the State, 615 *et seq.*
Content and form, **276-277**, 278.
Contingency, 297, 298, 414, 425-428.
Continuous magnitude, 217-220.
Contract, 540-545; theory of the social, 545, 612.
Contradiction, Law of, 128, 136, 138, 254.
Contrariety, 256, **258-259**.
Corporations, 604.
Correlation, categories of, 278-290.
Courts of justice, 603.
Creation, the doctrine of, 715, 717, 744, 750, 754.
Creon, 652.
Crime, 331, 548, 552, 556.
Croce, 131 (footnote), 435 (footnote).
Custom, 601.

D.

Dalai Lama, The, 734.
Darwin, 131, 434.
Death, 331.
Decease, 179.
Deduction, 122, 150, 151, 153.
Degree, 224 *et seq.*
Democracy, 560, 625.
Democritus, 100, 207, 370.
Descartes, 41, 101, 133, 134, 147.
Design, 377.
Desire, 484.
Determinate Being, 185 *et seq.*
Development, 28, 434.
Dialectic Method, **121-153**, 401.
Difference, **255-259**, 261, 264.
Discrete magnitude, 217-220.
Disease, 331.
Diversity, 256.
Divorce, 581.
Drama, 707-712.
Dualism, 128, 418, 427, 736.

INDEX

E.

Ecbatana, 682.
Edification, 198.
Education, 585.
Effect, 303.
Ego, the Notion as, 321.
Egyptian Art, 661.
Egyptian religion, 739-740.
Eleatics, The, **2-3**, 5, 10, 11, 106, 128, 174, 219, 294, 757.
Emotion, in art generally, 651 ; in music, 694.
Empedocles, 370.
Ends, 377, 379, 380, 381, 383 ; persons as, 532, 534, 536.
Epic poetry, 702-705.
Epicureans, The, 41.
Epistemology, preface, 162.
Equality, political, 536.
Error, 381.
Esdaile, Dr., 460 (footnote).
Essence, **242** *et seq*., 387 ; general character of, 164, 171, 172, 243-249.
Euclid, 133.
Evil, 73, 295, 381 (footnote).
Evolution, 131, **434**, 442 ; of philosophy, 174.
Excluded Middle, Law of, 136.
Executive, The, 623.
Existence, as distinguished from reality, 3, 12, 14, 15, 19 ; as distinguished from pure being, 184, 263 ; Hegel's category of, **262-263**, 271.
Explanation, 70-75.
Explicit, meaning of, 27-29.
Externality, in mechanism, 370, 376 ; of space, 433.
Eye, The, in sculpture, 677, 686 ; in painting, 689.

F.

Fable, 664.
Faculties, in psychology, 262, 371, 448, 512, 515, 516.
Fall, The theological doctrine of the, 717, 750, 754.
Family, The, 577-585.
Family Means, The, 584.
Fate, 669, 748.
Father, Kingdom of the, 753.
Feeling, 511-513 ; subjective character of, 512-513.
Feeling Soul, The, 459-464.
Fichte, 62.
Finite, The, **192**, 195, 200.

Force, and its Manifestation, **281-285**, 286.
Form, in Aristotle, 20, 27, 28, 325, 377, 418 ; and matter, **269-270**, 271, 274, 277, 278 ; and content, 276, 277 ; in art, 645.
Formal Logic, 57, 78, 85, 153, 313, 322.
Formal Mechanism, **372**, 373, 375, 376.
Fornax, 749.
Fraud, 548.
Freedom, Free Will, 311, 518, 523, 527, 575, 635.
Free Mind, 518.

G.

Geometry, 50, 54, 133, 134, 135, 401, 454.
God, 30-32, 161, 236, 246, 248, 367, 715, 718, 719 *et seq*.
Good, The, 381, **402**, 404.
Goodness and Wickedness, 566-570.
Gorgias, 3 (footnote).
Gravitation, 374, 436.
Great Men, 289.
Greek Art, 665, 666, 668, 669.
Greek Religion, 747-748.
Ground, The, **260-261**, 262-264.

H.

Habit, 463-464.
Happiness, **517**, 518.
Harmony, in music, 695.
Harris, W. T., 197 (footnote), 419 (footnote).
Heaven, 717, 729.
Hebrew Art, 662.
Heraclitus, 174, 181, 306, 757.
Heroic Age, 648, 703.
Hindu Art, 660, 662, 665.
Hinduism, 273, 288, 294, **730-733**.
History, 174, 289, **633**, 699.
Holy Spirit, The, 752, 755.
Hume, David, **45-48**, 306, 402 (footnote).
Hypnosis, 460, 460 (footnote).

I.

Idea, The, 167, 168, 170, 173, 174, 202, 205, 248, 302, 306, 365, 368, 381, **382-408**, 418, 419, 421, 423, 430, 431, 432, 438, 525, 610, 633, 639, 640, 641, 642, 643, 644, 645, 654, 665, 679, 681, 695, 708, 709, 714, 715, 733, 752, 753, 754, 757, 758, 760.

INDEX

Ideal, The, 641, 645, 665.
Ideal Theory of Plato, The, 6, 11, 13, 18, 19, 83, 107-110, 113, 122, 556 (footnote).
Identity, **253-254**, 261, 264, 314, 315; of subject and object, 383, 385, 386, 404, 491, 493, 758.
Identity, Law of, 134, 135, 136, 138, 254.
Idolatry, 746.
Iliad, The, 648, 703, 705.
Imagery, 93, 502, 503, 506; in poetry, 697.
Immediacy, 143, 163, 165, 239, 244, 308, 366, 475.
Immortality, 755 (footnote).
Implicit, meaning of, 27-29.
Impotence, of Nature, 428.
Impulses, The, **514-516**, 517.
Incarnation, The, 715, 750, 754.
Inclinations, The, 514, 515, 517, 526.
Individual, The, as a factor of the Notion, 317; the State and, 573, 574, 592, 608, 612, 615.
Induction, 153, 358, 401.
Industrial Class, The, 598.
Infinite, The, 44, 385, 406; the spurious infinite of quality, 197-198; of quantity, 229-231; of measure, 241; the true infinite, **199-202**; the Notion as, 312; the Absolute Idea as, 406.
Infinite of Measure, The, 241.
Infinite Progress, The: the qualitative, 197, 198; the quantitative, 229-231.
Inner and Outer, 286-290.
Insanity, 462.
Inspiration, 512.
Instinct, 511, 513.
Institutions, 440, 444, 519, 521, 523, 525, 571, 573.
Intellect, 476-479.
Intention, 563-565.
Interests, 546, 547.
Internality, of thought, 433.
Internal Polity, of the State, 615-625.
International Law, 626-632.
Intuition, **498-500**, 512.
Ionics, The, 174.
Irrational, The, 427.
Irritability, 391 (footnote).
Islam, 724.

J.

Jehovah, 744, 745, 749.
Jewish Religion, The, 743, **744-746**.
Johnson, Doctor, 3.
Judaism, 744-746.
Judgment, 245, 313, **322-346**, 508; the qualitative, 327 *et seq.*; the affirmative, 328; the negative, 329; the infinite, 330-331; of reflection, 332 *et seq.*; the singular, 333; the particular, 334-337; the universal, 338; of necessity, 339 *et seq.*; the categorical, 340; the hypothetical, 341; the disjunctive, 342; of the Notion, 343 *et seq.*; the assertoric, 344; the problematic, 345; the apodeictic, 346.
Judiciary, The, 617, 618.
Jupiter, 749.
Jury system, 603.
Justice, 550-552; administration of, 600-603.

K.

Kant, 1, 41, 45, **48-62**, 63, 83, 84, 86, 88, 89, 94, 101, 102, 110, 111, 112, 117, 162, 169, 272, 306, 308, 321, 322, 355, 366, 366 (footnote), 367, 401, 402 (footnote), 426, 515, 526, 565 (footnote), 567.
Kind, The, 394, 579 (footnote).
Knowledge, relation of, to objectivity, 2, 94-103, 382-387.
Krug, 425, 427.

L.

Labour, 597.
Laissez-faire, 592.
Landscape painting, 691.
Language, 504.
Law, 530, 600, 601, 602; international, 626-632; laws of nature, 477, 478.
Law Courts, 603.
Legislature, The, 624-625.
Leibniz, 41.
Life, Aristotle's conception of, 377; Hegel's category of, 389 *et seq.*
Life-Process, The, 393.
Light, worshipped as God, 658, 736.
Likeness and Unlikeness, **257**, 261, 264.
Limit, 190-198.
Limitation of quantity, 220.
Living Individual, The, 392.
Locke, John, 46, 401.
Love, 578, 580, 582, 675.
Lyrical Poetry, 706.

INDEX

M.

Macbeth, 709.
Mackintosh, R., 213 (footnote).
Macran, H. S., Preface, 74 (footnote), 319 (footnote), 423 (footnote).
Madonna, The, 690.
Magic, 726.
Magnitude, continuous and discrete, 217-220; extensive and intensive, 224-226.
Manifestation, 17, 294.
Many, The, 208.
Marriage, 544, 545, 575, **580-583**.
Materialism, 100, 214, 294, 365.
Mathematics, 50, 54, 133, 134, 135.
Matter, in Plato, 6, 18; in Aristotle, 20, 27, 28, 149, 325, 377, 474 (footnote); Hegel's category of matter and form, **269-270**, 271, 274, 277, 278; physical, 214, 436.
Matters, The Thing and, **267-268**, 269.
Maya, 3, 17, 139, 273, 294.
McTaggart, 183 (footnote), 237 (footnote), 282, 298, 301, 337, 357 (footnote), 365, 366 (footnote), 380 (footnote), 398, 406 (footnote).
Means, The, 377, **379**, 383.
Measure, 233 et seq.
Measureless, The, 240.
Mechanics, 436.
Mechanism, **369** et seq., 383, 432; externality of, 370, 376.
Mechanism with Affinity, 373.
Mediation, 143, 164, 165, 244, 308, 366, 475.
Melody, in music, 695.
Memnon statues, 661, 682.
Memory, 505.
Meteorological Process, The, 375.
Method, the dialectic, 121-153, 401; the analytic, 401; the synthetic, 401; the geometrical, 134, 135, 401.
Mill, J. S., 153, 475.
Milton, 651.
Mind, the Absolute as, 32, 38; theoretical, 497 et seq.; practical, 509 et seq.
Miracles, 751.
Moment, meaning of, 146.
Monarch, Monarchy, 619-622.
Monism, **104** et seq., 418, 427.
Morality, 555-570; utilitarian view of, 525.
Murillo, 650.

Music, 692-696; as a romantic art, 677; emotion in, 694.

N.

Nature, the philosophy of, 409-436.
Natural Soul, The, 450 et seq.
Negation, sub-category of, 187.
Negative, power of the, 43.
Negative relation, meaning of, 208.
Nemesis, 236.
Neo-Platonism, 41, 106.
Neutral Product, The, 375, 376.
New Realism, 7, 33-34.
Nirvana, 734.
Noel, 298.
Nothing, not-being, 123, 142, 145, 149, **178**.
Notion, The, 145, 305, **307**, et seq.; general characteristics of, 165, 171, 173, 307-312; as Notion, 314-321; as infinite, 312; as subjectivity, 321; as ego, 321; applications of the word notion, 556 (footnote).
Number, 223.

O.

Obelisks, 661, 682.
Object, The, 364-381.
Objectivity, 365, 366, 376; relation of, to knowledge, 94-103, 382-387; how related to universality, 365, 520; as principle of epic poetry, 702, 704.
Odyssey, The, 703, 704.
One, The, Hegel's category of, 206, 207; in Hinduism, 660, 665, 730 et seq.; in Plotinus, 201.
Ontology, Preface, 162.
Opposites, identity of, 99, 126, 128, 136, 138, 139, 310.
Oratory, 699.
Organics, 436.
Organism, 377, 383, 389-391, 392, 393, 394, 395; the geological, 436; the vegetable, 436; the animal, 436; the state as an, 608, 617; the work of art as an, 642.
Origination, 179.
Ormazd, 736, 737, 741.
Osiris, 739, 741.
Outer, and inner, 286-290.

P.

Painting, 688-691; landscape, 691; as a romantic art, 677; the eye in, 689.

Pantheism, 719, 727, 727 (footnote).
Parable, 664.
Parmenides, **2-3**, 93, 101, 125, 153, 170, 174, 181, 306.
Particular, The, **316**, 318.
Parts and Whole, **279-280**, 281.
Passion, 515.
Patriotism, 616.
Perception, 474-475.
Performance, in contract, 543.
Persian Art, 662.
Personality, nature of, 531-533; infinitude of, 532; infinite value of, 675; God as, 161, 715. See also under Persons.
Persons, independence of, 580, 585; as ends in themselves, 532, 534, 536.
Phenomenality, 275.
Phœnix, The, 661, 738.
Physical Alterations, 456-457.
Physical Qualities, 451-455.
Physics, 436.
Plato, 1, 2, **4-19**, 45, 49, 77, 83, 84, 93, 95, 98, 107-110, 113, 122, 141, 144, 185, 270, 418, 427, 556 (footnote), 594, 599, 615.
Pleasant, The, 511.
Plotinus, 128, 201.
Poetry, 697-712; distinguished from prose, 699; as a romantic art, 677; as the universal art, 698; epic, 702-705; lyrical, 706; dramatic, 707-712.
Police, 604.
Poseidon, 747.
Positive and Negative, **258-259**, 260, 264.
Possession, 537.
Possibility, 297.
Potentiality, 27, 28, 153, 297 (footnote).
Practical Feeling, 511.
Practical Reason, 515.
Prescription, Law of, 538.
Pringle-Pattison, Preface.
Properties, of the Thing, **265-266**, 267, 476; as distinguished from qualities, 266.
Property, 534-539.
Propositions, 245.
Prose, 699.
Protagoras, 5.
Protestantism, 560.
Psychology, empirical, 91, 92, 444, 446, 447; Hegelian, 492 *et seq.*
Punishment, nature of, 525, 549-552, 556; capital, 553.

Pure Principles or Categories of Reflection, 252-261.
Pure Quantity, 216.
Purpose, **562**, 563.
Pyramids, The Egyptian, 661, 682.
Pythagoras, 270.

Q.

Quality, 176 *et seq.*, **186**, 266; mechanical theory of, 370.
Quantitative Infinite Progress, The, 229-231.
Quantitative Ratio, The, 232.
Quantity, 186, **210** *et seq.*
Quantum, 216, **221-223**.

R.

Raisonnement, 132-133.
Ratio, **232**, 233.
Reaction, Action and, 304-306.
Realism, The New, 7, 33-34.
Reality, 3, 5, 9, 10, 12, 13, 17, 39; Hegel's sub-category of, 187.
Realized End, 380-381.
Reason, as a stage of spirit, 491, 508; distinguished from understanding, 127, 136-140, 166, 349; as opposed to sensation, 2, 5, 8, 9; as universal, **76-78**, 512; as self-determined, **79-82**, 152.
Reciprocity, 57, **304-306**, 307.
Recollection, 502-503.
Redemption, 750.
Reflection, 249, 252.
Reflection-into-another, 264, 267, 271, 273, 274, 281, 285, 286, 287.
Reflection-into-self, 207, 264, 267, 271, 273, 274, 281, 285, 286, 287.
Relation, categories of, 278-290.
Religion, 713 *et seq.*; the Chinese, 729; the Hindu, 730-733; the Buddhist, 734; the Zoroastrian, 736-737, 744; the Syrian, 738; the Egyptian, 739-740; the Jewish, 743, 744-746; the Greek, 747-748; the Roman, 749; the Christian, 750-755. See also under Christianity.
Relinquishment, The right of, 537, 541.
Representation, 501-505.
Reproduction, 391 (footnote).
Republic, The, of Plato, 615.
Republicanism, 620.
Repulsion and Attraction, **209**, 282.
Responsibility, in morals, 562, 563.
Resurrection, The, 750, 754.

INDEX

Revenge, 551.
Rhyme, 701.
Rhythm, 696.
Right, 531-554; of the subject, 560, 562, 569, 594, 615; of the object, 560.
Roman Religion, The, 749.
Romantic Art, 655, 670-678.
Romeo and Juliet, 653.
Rousseau, 546 (footnote).
Russell, Bertrand, 33 (footnote).

S.

Satan, 651.
Sceptics, The, 41.
Schelling, 62, 385, 385 (footnote), 421.
Schiller, 565 (footnote).
Scholasticism, 41.
Schopenhauer, 62, 734 (footnote).
Schwegler, 615.
Science, 172, 173, 245-246, 325.
Sculpture, 666, 667, **685-686**.
Self-consciousness, 404, 480 *et seq.*; universal self-consciousness, 490; recognitive, 485-489.
Self-determination, 44, 104, 199, 311; of reason, 79-82, 152.
Self-feeling, 461-462.
Self-mediation, 308, 309.
Sensation, Kant on, 49-56.
Sense-perception, 5, 6, **474-475**.
Sensibility, 391 (footnote), **458**.
Sensuous consciousness, 472-473.
Sensuous universals, 95, 416-417.
Sex, 375, 457, 558, 581.
Shakespeare, 676.
Sin, 718.
Singular, The, **317**, 318.
Siva, 732, 741.
Slavery, 488, 489, 490.
Sleep, 457.
Social Contract, theory of the, 545, 612.
Socialism, 535, 592, 606.
Socrates, 4, 520.
Son, Kingdom of the, 754.
Sophists, The, 520.
Sophocles, 652.
Soul, 448, **449** *et seq.*; the natural soul, 450 *et seq.*; the feeling soul, 459 *et seq.*; the actual soul, 465 *et seq.*; mechanical conception of relation of soul to body, 371, 372.
Sovereignty, 627, 631, 632.
Space, Kant on, 53-55; infinity of, 197 (footnote), 198, 200, 230; discretion and continuity of, 218; infinite divisibility of, 218; Hegel on, 431-433; externality of, 433.
Specific Quantum, The, 238-239.
Spencer, Herbert, 64, 65, 434, 592.
Sphinx, The, 661.
Spinoza, **42-44**, 80, 101, 102, 104, 106, 127, 128, 129, 132, 133, 134, 135, 170, 174, 201, 248, 302, 306, 385, 401, 727 (footnote).
Spirit, Kingdom of the, 755.
Spiritual Individuality, Religion of, 741-749.
Spurious Infinite, The, 197-198.
State, The, 377, 440, 525, **605-633**; Plato's state, 594; the state as an organism, 608, 617; the state and the individual, 573, 574, 592, 608, 612, 615.
Stirling, J. H., 306, 434 (footnote).
Stoics, The, 41.
Subject, The, the right of, 560, 562, 569, 594, 615; identity of subject and object, 383, 385, 386, 404, 491, 493, 758.
Subjective End, The, 378.
Subjectivity, 365, 366, 376; the Notion as, 321; in art, 645, 676, 680, 684, 687, 689, 709; as principle of lyric poetry, 706.
Sublation, meaning of, 144.
Sublime, The, 662, 663.
Subsistence, of universals, 7, 33, 95.
Substance, in Spinoza, 44, 80, 101, 102, 106, 170, 174, 248-302, 306, 385; Hegel's category of, **300-302**; the religion of, 727-734; the ethical substance, 577, 611.
Suffering, in art, 650, 674, 690.
Suicide, 539.
Sum and Unity, 222.
Syllogism, The, 313, 322, 325, **347-363**; the qualitative, 351 *et seq.*; the mathematical, 355; the syllogism of reflection, 356 *et seq.*; the syllogism of allness, 356, 357; the syllogism of induction, 358; the syllogism of analogy, 359; the syllogism of necessity, 360 *et seq.*; the categorical, 361; the hypothetical, 362; the disjunctive, 363.
Symbolic Art, 655, 657-664.
Symbols, nature of, 657.
Symmetry, in art, 681, 695.
Synthesis, meaning of, 126, 166.
Synthetic Method, The, 401.

INDEX

Syrian Religion, The, 738.
System of Wants, The, 596-599.

T.

Teleology, **376** *et seq.*, 383, 432, 434.
Thales, 100 (footnote).
Thebes, 749.
Thesis, 126, 166.
Thing, **264-270**, 476; the thing and its properties, **265-266**, 271, 272, 274; the thing and matters, 267-268; things as subject to persons, 534; thing as distinguished from object, 365.
Thing-in-itself, The, 56, 58, 59, 61, 62, 97, 98, 306, 367, 424, 426.
Thinking, 506-508.
T'ien, 729.
Time, Kant on, 53-55; in Hegel, 436.
Tragedy, 650, **709**.
Treaties, 628.
Triads, 126, 144, 155, 166, 320.
Trimurti, The, 732.
Trinity, The, 732, 750, 751, 753.
True, The, **399** *et seq.*
True Infinite, The, 199-202.
Typhon, 739.

U.

Ugly, The, in art, 674.
Understanding, The, 127, 136-140, 166, 245, 252, 306, 349, 400, 479, 508.
Unessential, The, 249, 253.
Universal, The, as the real, 9, 10, 12, 13; as a factor of the Notion, **314-315**, 318.
Universals, 6, 7, 33; sensuous universals, 95, 416-417.
Universal Class, The, 598, 625.
Universal self-consciousness, 490.
Unknowable, The, 63-69.
Unlikeness, **257**, 261, 264.

Unpleasant, The, 511.
Unpremeditated wrong, 548.
Urtheil, 323.
Utility, the religion of, 749.

V.

Variety, 256.
Vedantism, 128, 139.
Vendetta, The, 551.
Versification, 701.
Vesta, 749.
Virgil, 749.
Virtues, The, 576.
Vishnu, 732.
Volition, 397, **402-403**, 404.
Vorstellung, 715 *et seq.*, 750, 756, 758.

W.

Wallace, William, 1.
Wants, 596.
War, 629, 630, 632.
Wealth, 597.
Well-being, 563-565.
Whole and Parts, The, **279-280**, 281.
Wickedness, 566-570.
Will, The, 397, 402 *et seq.*, 509 *et seq.*, 520, 521, 522, 523, 527, 531, 534, 537, 538, 539, 543, 546, 547, 549, 551, 552, 556, 557, 560, 562, 563, 564, 566, 570, 573.
World of Appearance, The, 274-275.
World-History, 633.
Worship, 718, 733, 734, 745, 747.
Wrong, 546-554, 556.

Z.

Zend people, Art among the, 658, 744 (footnote).
Zeno, the Eleatic, 2, 219, 272.
Zeus, 747.
Zoolatry, 740.
Zoroastrianism, **736-737**, 744 (footnote).

193
H462s   66965

Stace, Walter Terence
The philosophy of Hegel, a systematic
  exposition.

SINCLAIR COMMUNITY COLLEGE LIBRARY
444 WEST THIRD STREET
DAYTON, OHIO 45402

DISCARDED